The Workers of African Trade

Volume 11
SAGE SERIES ON AFRICAN MODERNIZATION AND DEVELOPMENT

Catherine Coquery-Vidrovitch
Paul E. Lovejoy
Editors

The Workers of African Trade

SAGE PUBLICATIONS   Beverly Hills   London   New Delhi

For information address:

SAGE Publications, Inc.
275 South Beverly Drive
Beverly Hills, California 90212

SAGE Publications India Pvt. Ltd.
M-32 Market
Greater Kailash I
New Delhi 110 048 India

SAGE Publications Ltd
28 Banner Street
London EC1Y 8QE
England

Printed in the United States of America

Library of Congress Cataloging in Publication Data

Main entry under title:

The workers of African trade.

(Sage series on African modernization and development ; v. 11)
"The chapters in this volume were originally presented at a conference held at York University, Toronto, in September 1983"—Acknowledgments.
Includes bibliographies and index.
1. Transport workers—Africa, Sub-Saharan—History—Congresses. 2. Africa, Sub-Saharan—Commerce—History—Congresses. I. Coquery-Vidrovitch, Catherine II. Lovejoy, Paul E. III. Series.
HD8039.T72A3575 1985 380.1'0967 85-2259
ISBN 0-8039-2472-0

FIRST PRINTING

Contents

Acknowledgments

The chapters in this volume were originally presented at a conference held at York University, Toronto, in September 1983. The editors wish to thank the Social Science and Humanities Research Council of Canada, York University, the Université de Paris, and Laboratoire Tiers-Monde, Afrique (L.A. 363) for their financial assistance. Various participants at the York conference also contributed valuable comments; special thanks to Myron Echenberg, Martin Klein, Sydney Kanya-Forstner, David Newbury, David Northrup, Joel Gregory, and Gerry McSheffrey. The papers were typed by Secretarial Services, York University, under the direction of Ms. Doris Rippington.

1

THE WORKERS OF TRADE
IN PRECOLONIAL AFRICA

CATHERINE COQUERY-VIDROVITCH
PAUL E. LOVEJOY

The idea of this work arises from the fact that our theoretical understanding of the mechanisms of long-distance trade in Africa have advanced considerably over the past thirty years (Bohannan and Dalton, 1962; Gray and Birmingham, 1970; Meillassoux, 1971; Hopkins, 1973; Isaacman, 1972; Curtin, 1975; 1983; Amselle, 1977; Lovejoy, 1980a). Until now, however, there has been little attention to the question of the work involved in this commerce (but see Cummings, 1973; Northrup, 1982; Alpers, 1975; Kea, 1982).

And the work of African trade was considerable. In societies that were restrained by a low level of technology, necessary work depended to a very great extent on human energy, even though sometimes animals could lessen this burden. The transport of commodities over long distances, therefore, was a tremendous consumer of manpower. The caravans of the sahel and Sahara could exceed 20,000 camels (Lovejoy, 1985); movements of 3,000 or more were very common, although individual units of these caravans, which could break away to travel on their own, often numbered 300 camels (McDougall, chapter 5, this volume). Such a scale of operation necessarily required services of a large number of teamsters who had to load and unload the animals, bring them to pasture and water, tether or otherwise enclose them, prepare camps, gather firewood or other fuel, and otherwise conduct

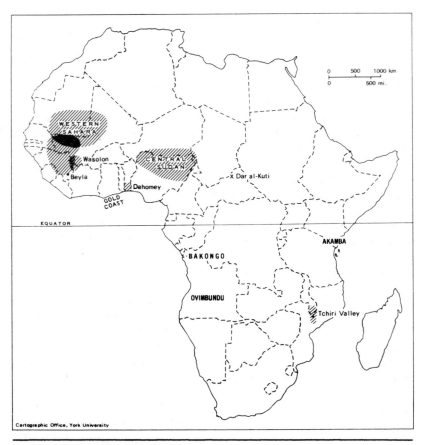

Map 1.1:   Location of Case Studies

the endless tasks required on long journeys. The donkey caravans of the savanna never attained the same scale as the largest desert caravans, but savanna merchants still traveled in groups of many hundreds, even several thousand members (cf. Amselle, chapter 6; Duffill and Lovejoy, chapter 7). Donkeys carried less than camels, and consequently the input of labor was greater per unit of weight. Often there were as many people as animals. In the forest and southern savannas, the manpower requirements were even greater, since very few—and often no—animals were used. Porters traveled in caravans of 500 to 1000 in many places (Heywood, chapter 11; Samarin, chapter 12; Cummings, chapter 9; Isaacman and Mandala, chapter 10), but even where it was safe to operate on a smaller scale—3 to 10 people—as many as 3000 porters and merchants often passed along a route in the course of a single month (Goerg, chapter 4; Samarin).

These workers—porters and teamsters—constituted the most ancient and one of the most massive forms of labor migration in African history. How was this migration organized? What were the institutions used to mobilize this work force? What was the role of the family, wage employment, slavery, and the entrepreneur? There was certainly remuneration for the workers and the accumulation of surplus, but by whom and how much? What—if any—correspondence existed between the penetration of Western commercial capitalism and the appearance of a "proto-proletariat" characterized by a sharp cleavage between the worker and the means of production? To what extent did the development of trade promote individualism that derived from a new sense of professionalism, and did this social change result in the emergence of "class consciousness" that was revealed through struggle over the terms of employment? And if such developments took place, then what were the origins of this class-in-the-making? Such are the questions with which we are concerned; in the chapters that follow, we will see that some interesting answers are provided, despite the caution and qualifications that are usually attached to them.

All parts of sub-Saharan Africa are represented in this volume, including East Africa (Cummings); southeastern Africa (Isaacman and Mandala); north-central Africa (Cordell, chapter 8); west-central Africa (Samarin, Heywood); the central Sudan (Duffill and Lovejoy); the West African coast (Manning, chapter 3, Gutkind, chapter 2); the western savanna (Amselle, Goerg); and the Sahara and sahel (McDougall).

The political systems of the regions under study were of considerable variety: the "neo-feudalism" of the Mozambique *prazos* (Isaacman and Mandala); the centralized slave societies of Dar al-Kuti (Cordell), Samori (Goerg, Amselle), and the Guinea coastal states (Manning); the federated structure of the vast Sokoto caliphate (Duffill and Lovejoy); the shifting alliances of Saharan nomads (McDougall); and the small-scale and decentralized societies elsewhere that were more or less governed by principles of kinship (Samarin, Heywood, Cummings). In general the basic organization of work for long-distance trade was unaffected by these different political structures, except in those extreme cases where slavery and slave-raiding were dominant and militarism was therefore most pronounced (Cordell). Otherwise political authorities were largely content with extracting some surplus from commerce. The organization of the labor of trade was left to the merchants.

Almost all of the studies are concerned with the second half of the nineteenth century, just before and/or at the time of colonial occupation. Only Gutkind examines the history of labor over a long period (late fifteenth to eighteenth centuries). Because of this temporal bias, it is not possible to reach any conclusions about the work of African trade before the time of capitalist penetration. Gutkind's study, despite its uniqueness and great value, is similar to the rest of the cases in that he examines labor in the context of capitalist penetration; European merchant capitalism had an earlier impact on the Gold Coast than almost everywhere else. All the studies, therefore, examine the labor of trade in the context of capitalist penetration, no matter how tentative and hesitant that penetration was.

The concentration on the nineteenth century highlights the spread of capitalism, but it is still possible to examine the indigenous structures of society as they affected the organization of work before external markets had much influence. The various studies demonstrate that existing mechanisms of labor mobilization were manipulated to accommodate the penetration of capitalism but that the autonomy of local societies was still largely guaranteed until the colonial conquest. Whether in the desert (McDougall), the savanna (Duffill and Lovejoy), or East Africa (Cummings), existing institutions could accommodate the need for labor; initially the pull of world markets only affected these institutions indirectly and indecisively. Despite the temporal limitations of the following studies, we are relatively confident that our conclusions are very revealing about earlier periods for which source material is poor or unavailable. The combination of written documents and oral data enables us to uncover much about the daily life of the mass of the poor, silent, and forgotten people of history. The nature of the sources—shallow in their time depth in the case of oral data, foreign and unsympathetic in much of the written material— does not allow us to uncover the history of these people very far into the past, and even the contribution that this volume makes to this important area of social history is only confined to the most visible of the poor—the workers whose specialized activities were indispensable to the foreigners with whom they were always in direct contact (cf. the Gold Coast canoemen in Gutkind).

THE WORK OF PRECOLONIAL TRADE

Common sense dictates that long-distance trade always involved a lot of work, and it is well documented that commerce is very old indeed. The trade of iron for salt, slaves for textiles, and the export of gold, copper, and slaves to the Mediterranean and Indian Ocean demonstrate the significance of this labor far into the distant past, well before the rise of the Atlantic trade in slaves. The Atlantic trade increased the volume of commerce and thereby correspondingly required the services of more workers. This commerce created numerous petty producers—free and slave—who made salt, mined iron, hunted ivory or men, sold agricultural surplus, or engaged in crafts. Their production only resulted in a surplus on the condition that goods were moved long distances, whether or not the producers themselves or professional merchants actually traded these goods. The accumulation of surplus and the creation of value only occurred along the trade routes. The monopoly of these routes was the basis of wealth and power of precolonial states, and consequently the labor of this trade was fundamental to the process of accumulation.

The aim of long-distance trade was profits; the major part of these profits enriched the privileged few, including state officials, principal chiefs, traditional notables, large merchants, and heads of caravans. These privileged few recruited workers, sometimes through kinship, other times through slavery, and other times still by attracting individuals who would work for wages. With all these people (except, without doubt, trade slaves), the notion of profit was clear. Despite restraints on the form of remuneration, people engaged in trade—as workers as well as merchants—in order to profit. The returns were often in usable goods or luxuries rather than in money. Household members received a share of the profits, directly or indirectly; herders who lacked animals might benefit from a pledge of unborn livestock; most often workers simply were given trade goods. Certainly these profits remained risky. The route was long—distances of 1000 kilometers were not uncommon—and the work was dangerous and hard. Nonetheless, profits could be considerable, as much as seven times the initial investment (Goerg). Merchants distinguished between "good" porters and inexperienced ones (Heywood), and the law of supply and demand very much affected the labor supply (Duffill and Lovejoy). Profits ultimately depended upon the mobilization of an enormous work force.

In order to understand the mobilization of this labor force, it is not necessary to distinguish between domestic work that was the source of social production of the group, in which the profit motive is supposed to be absent, and the work whose goal was surplus and hence a possible source of accumulation. The isolation of domestic labor from work in general arises out of a model of social organization that is mythical in origin. In fact household labor was needed for both the reproduction of the household itself and for surplus. For ecological reasons, this surplus was often nonexistent or marginal in the agricultural sector and hence was all the more likely to be drained off through local or regional trade (Hymer, 1970; Coquery-Vidrovitch, 1978; Meillassoux, 1960). But in certain cases regional trade in provisions or in the output of craftsmen could develop to the point where there was some surplus (Amselle; Cordell; Gnobo, 1985; Lovejoy and Baier, 1975; Kea, 1982: 43-48, 173-179). Practically all our authors insist on the interconnection between long-distance trade and the production network for local trade. Finally, the domestic economy was rarely the sole source of survival for the family but was part of a political system that included the production and extraction of surplus through war and/or slavery (Lovejoy, 1983). What characterized the domestic or lineage mode of production was less the absence of surplus than the use to which it was put. Surplus was almost exclusively channeled into reproduction (as expressed through the accumulation of women), conspicuous consumption, redistribution as gifts, and other forms of social insurance that in effect constituted the destruction of surplus (Meillassoux, 1968).

Nonetheless, at a certain moment, the surplus value that arose from the labor of long-distance trade was no longer retained in its entirity by the domestic economy but rather become a source of accumulation of capital. The question then becomes: When did the producers of this surplus begin to recognize their exploitation? In other words, when did the concentration on domestic accumulation become ensnared in the web of capitalist accumulation? When did a proto-class begin to emerge that gradually became conscious of itself—a class being not an object in itself but a series of relationships (Thompson, 1968: 83).

THE MOBILIZATION OF WORK

In many of our studies, almost all the adults and a significant number of children were employed on the trade routes at one time or another during the year (Goerg, Heywood, Samarin). All the studies included here except three (Cordell, Gutkind, McDougall) examine the work of porters. Four examine the role of caravans and teamsters in the region of the sahel, desert, and savanna (Duffill and Lovejoy, Goerg, Amselle, McDougall). Two are devoted in whole or in part to canoemen (Gutkind, Manning). The use of soldiers—protectors or raiders depending on the case—comes up several times (Samarin, Cordell, Isaacman and Mandala). The role of artisans is examined at least twice (Amselle, Cordell). Even hunters were important in trade (Cummings, Isaacman and Mandala). Finally, recourse to the work of women and children is often mentioned (Heywood, Manning, Samarin), while the position of women is inadequately documented in some cases (Goerg).

Recruitment based on kinship was common, although reliance on kinship did not conflict with the use of slaves, who were rarely used to the exclusion of other forms of labor (Cordell). Finally the emergence of a category limited to individuals who were paid for their work—in kind and later in money—on the basis of individual contracts was sometimes long established (Gutkind), but paid labor became more common in the nineteenth century.

The primary means of controlling labor was based on the domestic mode of production. Until the early colonial period the traditional social structure based on kinship remained capable of offering manpower and necessary animals, varying with the type of commerce and the region, from the desert (McDougall) to the forest (Gnobo, 1985), and for all stages of production (gathering salt, picking kola nuts, hunting ivory) and of transport. The sons, nephews, and other dependents recruited for commercial journeys on a regular basis by their elders, lineage heads, and chief merchants were certainly exploited. That is to say, only a part of the surplus as well as the product went to these dependents. They were not only conscious of this situation, but the work they provided was not free and voluntary. In exchange for their labor and often under the guise of apprenticeship, youths were only fed and not paid. Social constraints and the obligation of submission counted for a lot (Heywood, Duffill and Lovejoy), and even if the youths found, after leaving on the trip, a way of freeing themselves from the domination of their elders who remained at home (Amselle). The objective was for the merchant to increase his profits—or those of his house—through cheap labor, and everyone knew it.

The trade slave was sometimes employed in transport, but much less than one might have thought. The reason is clear. The labor of the slave could not be exploited without endangering the market value of the slave. The trade slave who was poorly treated, without motivation, and inferior in quality was twice as bad a worker as the free porter or domestic slave. This situation was similar to that of the forced labor of the colonial era.

Only in the raiding states at the end of the nineteenth century did slaves become a source of labor almost exclusively. Slave society had a formidable simplicity (Cordell, Isaacman and Mandala). The principal workers included the warriors (who were often slaves themselves) who produced slaves and the slave producers who did virtually everything else; they were porters, cultivators of vast plantations, and artisans. The use of slaves on this scale resulted in greater extraction of surplus than had been possible from traditional peasants who had supplied provisions and the primary products necessary for inter-regional and international trade (Lovejoy, 1983; Cordell; Isaacman and Mandala).

Occasionally, the labor of trade relied almost entirely on the work of women, as among the Bete, where women dominated every stage for kola production and marketing (Gnobo, 1985). Women were certainly used as much as they were in Bete society elsewhere in the Guinea forest, if one can judge by the extent to which women continue to be important in commerce in this region. Despite this role, however, it is necessary to emphasize the way in which female labor strengthened the recuperative power of the lineage system. The preeminence of the great Bete merchant women and their troops of dependents, apprentices, female porters, and hired porters aside, it was definitely males who emerged and stayed on top. It was the husband of a prosperous woman who rose to the position of village head, not the woman herself. The lineage system exploited the work of women more than other systems, often as porters, but in many other ways including managing the home, cooking, caring for children, fetching water, cultivating provisions, and supervising young people (aged 8 to 12), who in their turn were porters or were assigned odd jobs.

THE CONFUSION BETWEEN
CLASS AND SOCIAL PROMOTION

It is difficult to establish a typology that defines the social relations between the exploited and the exploiter. The porter or teamster did not simply carry goods for others, any more than canoemen, hunters, and artisans performed functions that clearly separated them from an exploiting class. The porter and teamster were commercial producers—transporters produced surplus value by carrying commodities over great distances and hence enabled the owner of those goods to realize a profit. In this capacity the porter or teamster carried for his parents, his master, and his employer—the nature of the relationship varied considerably depending upon these conditions. But the porter or teamster also carried for himself and as such he was also a small merchant, an individual entrepreneur, or a partner in a family business. Such a confusion in roles was common in the very long distances involved in the sahel and Sahara (McDougall) and was sometimes the only situation found in the forest (Goerg). For this reason, it was sometimes difficult to recruit wage labor (Heywood). Moreover, individuals joined large caravans for security, so that differences between types of porters or teamsters was often blurred even more. All employees and dependents carried personal items as well as trade goods (Cummings, Samarin, and so on).

One manifestation of this confusion between class relationships on the one hand and the individualism of workers trying to improve their social position on the other hand was the emergence of a group of petty entrepreneurs. They represented one of the crucial contradictions in the social formation. The worker was not separated from the means of production in that the porter or teamster was often a petty producer at the same time that he worked for others. All porters and teamsters (dare we state the anachronism) shared a petty bourgeois mentality. The ideal in the end was not to extract better working conditions or terms of remuneration from the merchant but to amass enough capital through commerce to climb the social ladder and become a merchant entirely.

The confusion is all the greater if the porter was paid in kind and wanted to be (Amselle, Cummings). The trade goods that he received served to encourage local trade in provisions—in order to secure his rations—the rest he exchanged himself along the way, accumulating a bit of salt or a couple hundred kola nuts. After this first hurdle, the hope was that he would end up with enough to buy ivory or acquire a slave and therefore place himself on the road to accumulation and social advancement. It is understood that the successful cases in this "penny capitalism" were rare. But the hope remained and a few big names were there to maintain this illusion.

Most porters (male and female) came from the lower rungs of the population, slaves and the poor (Cummings, Duffill and Lovejoy; Isaacman and Mandala; cf. Kea, 1982: 105-107), but it was far from always the case. In the context of a low level of technology portering and teamstering were the normal means of circulation for goods and the advancement of individuals. In the context of the lineage, employment in trade provided the occasion for the youngest and the most adventuresome to acquire the means to liberate themselves from the control of the group and launch themselves into individual enterprise (Meillassoux, 1971). In the Islamic context, it was the occasion for the student to perfect his knowledge of Islam by studying with the Muslim scholars along the routes; this procedure of recruitment was used extensively in the nineteenth century by Muslim scholars and merchants (McDougall) and even as late as the twentieth century by the Mourides of Senegal who mobilized their students as a work force.

The same contradiction also applied to slaves (but not trade slaves). The slave porter or teamster freed himself from the hold of his master through trade. His chances of success were probably better than those who only engaged in agricultural work (Cummings, Isaacman and Mandala; Duffill and Lovejoy). He could acquire a little and eventually become an experienced caravan leader in the same way that a free porter could. A slave cannot be viewed simply as an employed worker; a slave also must be seen as an entrepreneur. The difference between free and slave was defined by their social status more than by the nature of their work or even the means of payment.

The hope of social advancement depended upon payment in kind; we understand why the Kooroko porters refused cowries, which were not current among the Moors with whom they did business (Amselle) or why at the very end of the nineteenth century the Akamba porters resisted the introduction of ruppees, which could only be used in foreign markets (Cummings). A money payment would have encouraged the proletarization of the workers and hence it was refused.

The canoemen of the Gold Coast consistently wanted to be paid in gold, not in cloth (Gutkind). Gold was recognized, through a complex system of exchange, as a monetary equivalent by Europeans (Kea, 1982: 186-191), but while gold was the basis of the international Western monetary system, the weights and gold dust of the Gold Coast (as well as the copper manillas elsewhere) remained a local commodity currency—the merchandise most secure, most valued, most noble. The canoemen had not really entered the era of monetarization. The emergence of real money—as distinct from a currency of equivalencies—required the financial calculations and therefore the payment of fixed wages in reference to the market in its entirety.

But porters, teamsters, and canoemen remained attached to the working value of their remuneration—so attached that they were even able to strike *not* to sell their work. They did not want to *sell* their work; they wanted to *exchange* it. This fact is characteristic of societies in transition, where the method of exploitation was rooted both in the domestic and capitalist spheres and depended upon the interaction between those spheres. African societies were not exceptional in this sense. Hobsbawm (1964) has observed how long it took before the English worker calculated his wages on the basis of market demand rather than on use-value. At the beginning of the industrial era, workers still did not understand the rules of the economic game; they had to learn to sell their work like merchandise. They still wanted a wage barely equivalent to the level of subsistence, if not the equivalent in subsistence, by protecting their rural ties to agricultural fields, or after finishing the day in the factory, they worked in their gardens. They were content as long as their industrial wages were roughly twice that of their agricultural work.

In Africa social development was not as advanced. Retraction always took place, because it was always possible for profits to be transferred into the circuit of the lineage (Heywood). Each time that the method of precapitalist exploitation became strong enough, the lineage recovered, at least temporarily, control over the organization of work. The most apparent example is the Kololo porters who had lived many years as wage laborers in the service of Livingstone and who voluntarily withdrew to develop their own system of exploitation based on slavery. Instead of being exploited directly under capitalism, they found themselves exploiters of a precapitalist system tied to Western capitalism (Isaacman and Mandala).

SOCIAL ASSERTION AND
THE DEVELOPMENT OF CONSCIOUSNESS

The slowness of the process of monetarization hobbled the development of consciousness. The failure of proletarianization did not mean that the workers were not conscious of the fact that they were providing work or that this work deserved to be paid for. Expressions of discontent were frequent, as the strike of the canoemen in 1753 demonstrates (Gutkind). Boycotts of recruitment are mentioned to varying degrees by all the authors in this volume. Such actions must have been more numerous still. They are at least a sign that a group, if not a conscious class, was aware of being exploited. Such knowledge arose out of a common experience that society was hierarchical and had been for a long time. This perceived hierarchy had not only religious, political, or institutional dimensions, but was also founded on the basis of the economic relations between rich and poor. The "strikes" were professional strikes that were caused by bad treatment (excesses of portering that were the basis of the revolts against Samori [Amselle], as later they were the basis of the violent reaction against colonialism), or by wage disputes.

The canoemen reacted in 1753 because the increased work load resulting from the transport of the materials for the construction of the fort at Anomabu was not accompanied by a parallel increase in their remuneration. But neither this nor other disputes were capable of transcending the professional level to become political acts of a revolutionary nature that might have affected the structure of society (except perhaps the revolts against Samori, which expressed a general discontent of this order). The canoemen who navigated the surf were specialized technicians conscious of being indispensable to the Europeans and were not prepared to be mistreated, even though they often were. They were the closest to being a class because of their social and professional homogeneity, their group spirit, their collective interests, and especially their direct contact with Western employers. Still, kinship reinforced ethnicity, thereby guaranteeing the transmission of occupational specialization within the group. The men (generally free) who were paid regularly for work that was indispensable to commerce inadvertently acquired the knowledge of the value of their work and the legitimacy of their disputes, but expression of this knowledge was rare because workers were exposed to dangerous reprisals, the most serious of which was to be sold as slaves (Gutkind).

The case of the Gold Coast canoemen is relatively exceptional; most often the social cohesion of the group was much less developed. The caravan was a disparate group of large merchants, petty entrepreneurs, clients, dependents, paid workers, domestic slaves, and trade slaves. Still the members of a single caravan had a definite sense of collective consciousness. The vertical solidarity based on kinship, clientage, common residence, language and/or culture counteracted the potential for conflict generated by horizontal interests (Duffill and Lovejoy). The work was specific and highly organized; the members even adhered to an oath of collective security (Duffill and Lovejoy). It was in the interests of merchants to promote this identity. They needed relatively qualified workers because certain jobs required an undeniable specialization. The inspection and handling of kola nuts, fragile and perishable, was no simple task (Goerg; Gnobo, 1985). Teamsters had to load and unload animals each day without damaging products that were often fragile (for instance, salt bars). The work required patience, competence, and careful attention (McDougall).

Because all the social layers of society were gathered together, strategies of disputes were therefore necessarily more individual than collective. Pilfering could constitute one sign of dispute (Isaacman and Mandala). Bargaining was the prototype of this behavior; it played a role of socioeconomic regulation by forcing people to find the best possible price to avoid a direct conflict over wages (Duffill and Lovejoy). On the Ghana coast the collective action periodically took the form of ritualized rebellion, somewhat resembling the ancient Bacchanal and was as much a means of compensation as social appeasement (Kea, 1982: 291).

Finally, there were other obstacles to the development of class consciousness. Even professional workers were rarely full-time specialists. Seasonal changes required the periodic return of workers to agriculture during the rainy season, even if trade continued year round (Goerg). Family attachments permitted the maintenance of links between brothers and between cousins; individuals rotated their activities from the village to the trade route—they were part peasant, part entrepreneur, part wage-earner, and consequently the porter or teamster was only partially conscious of his social condition. Occupational ambiguity blurred the movement between two worlds—capitalist and domestic. Circulating from the one to the other literally and figuratively, they were not inclined to oppose one or the other, except haphazardly and irregularly.

Specialization became more pronounced the more one climbed the social ladder. The small porter was also a peasant; the teamster was also a herder; the domestic slave was also a man who had to be trusted. The caravan leaders (the most successful merchants) and other merchants were the principal employers on the road, while the landlords—acting as intermediaries and wholesalers—had enough goods and the social contacts to shelter and feed the caravan members, to tend livestock, and to protect the merchandise. At the top of the ladder, landlords and other great merchants supplied the capital, the stock of goods, and the network of dependents. At this level, the merchants were sometimes sedentary, content to control caravans through intermediaries—men in whom they had confidence (kin and slaves). They were definitely specialists rooted in the local system, but they also profited from their position on the margins of the international market.

If the workers of long-distance trade had difficulty in becoming conscious of their exploited condition, by contrast the great merchants increasingly developed an attitude that was more and more entrepreneurial. They were aware of their preeminence and tried to increase their profits. The merchants promoted their interests through corporate structures based on a shared ethnicity (Hausa, Juula, Kooroko). There existed a hierarchy based on wealth, from the petty merchant who carried his own loads to the very large merchants as powerful as they were few in number, such as those who received from Samori the privilege of provisioning his army (Amselle). They organized the market and constituted the indispensable partners of state power to the point where they even seized power itself (Cordell, Isaacman and Mandala). More often they became allies—the instruments, bankers, and creditors—of political authorities (Meillassoux, 1969).

Class consciousness undoubtedly filtered down from the top of the ladder. Those who found themselves well placed at the pinacles of trade networks weighed the advantages of playing the two systems (domestic and capitalist) against each other. They used the forces of social custom (dependents, clients, slaves) for the ends of commercial capitalism. The merchant/clerics of the sahel and large caboceers of the Gold Coast undoubtedly abandoned the sphere of use-value to petty producers and small-scale porters and teamsters and placed themselves in direct relation to the external market and the sphere of market-exchange. They based the accumulation of their wealth on the profits of their operations and the interest from their loans, and they were themselves conditioned by the continuous expansion of the sphere of commodity circulation (Kea, 1982: 177).

That done, they contributed to the isolation and retardation of the social structure. It was in their interest to exploit the domestic system; therefore they used their profits to enlarge their affairs and to reinforce the weight of the traditional structure, which thereby restricted the development of consciousness among the exploited.

Wherever there was direct contact between African workers and merchant capital class relations were beginning to emerge. Whether one talks of the canoemen of the sixteenth century or the porters who were crushed under the weight of colonial coercion at the end of the nineteenth century (Samarin), the benefits of capital passed to the privileged through their control over the environment and their manipulation of the social relations of precapitalist society (domestic or slave). Because the existing social contradictions were maintained, the evolution towards a full-scale class struggle was halted. Only the presence of exploiters related to the development of capitalism could generate in time the emergence of class consciousness among the exploited. But an examination of that process is beyond the scope of this volume.

REFERENCES

ALPERS, E. A. (1975) Ivory and Slaves in East Central Africa. Changing Patterns of International Trade to the Later Nineteenth Century. Berkeley: University of California Press.

AMSELLE, J. L. (1977) Les négociants de la savane. Paris: Anthropos.

AUSTIN, R. (1979) "The trans-Saharan slave trade: a tentative census," pp. 23-76 in H. A. Gemery and J. S. Hogendorn (eds.) The Uncommon Market. Essays in the Economic History of the Atlantic Slave Trade. New York: Academic Press.

BOHANNAN, P. and G. DALTON [eds.] (1962) Markets in Africa. Evanston, IL: Northwestern University Press.

COOPER, F. (1980) From Slaves to Squatters. Plantation Labor and Agriculture in Zanzibar and Coastal Kenya, 1890-1925. New Haven, CT: Yale University Press.

COQUERY-VIDROVITCH, C. (1978) "Research on an African mode of production," pp. 261-288 in J. D. Seddon (ed.) Relations of Production: Marxist Approaches to Economic Anthropology. London: Cass.

CUMMINGS, R. (1973) "Notes on the history of caravan porters in East Africa." Kenya Historical Review 1, 2: 109-138.

CURTIN, P. D. (1984) Cross-Cultural Trade in World History. Cambridge: Cambridge University Press.

——(1975) Economic Change in Pre-Colonial Africa: Senegambia in the Era of the Slave Trade. Madison: University of Wisconsin Press.

GNOBO, J. Z. (1985) "The pre-colonial kola trade of Daloa (Ivory Coast)." African Economic History 10.

GRAY, R. and D. BIRMINGHAM [eds.] (1970) Pre-Colonial African Trade. Essays on Trade in Central and Eastern Africa Before 1900. London: Oxford University Press.

HOBSBAWM, E. J. (1964) "Customs, wages and work-load," pp. 344-370 in Labouring Men: Studies in the History of Labour. London: Weidenfeld and Nicolson.

HOPKINS, A. G. (1973) An Economic History of West Africa. London: Longman.

HYMER, S. (1970) "Economic forms in pre-colonial Ghana." Journal of Economic History 30, 1: 33-50.

ISAACMAN, A. (1972) Mozambique. The Africanization of a European Institution. The Zambezi Prazos, 1750-1902. Madison: University of Wisconsin Press.

KEA, R. (1982) Settlements, Trade and Politics in the Seventeenth Century Gold Coast. Baltimore: Johns Hopkins University Press.

LOVEJOY, P. E. (1985) Salt of the Desert Sun. A History of Salt Production and Trade in the Central Sudan. Cambridge: Cambridge University Press.

———(1983) Transformations in Slavery. A History of Slavery in Africa. Cambridge: Cambridge University Press.

———(1980a) Caravans of Kola: The Hausa Kola Trade, 1700-1900. Zaria and Ibadan: Ahmadu Bello University Press and University Press.

———(1980b) "Kola in the history of West Africa." Cahiers d'études africaines 20, 1-2: 97-134.

———(1978) "Plantations in the economy of the nineteenth-century Sokoto caliphate." Journal of African History 19, 3: 341-368.

———and STEVEN BAIER (1975) "The desert-side economy of the Central Sudan." International Journal of African Historical Studies 7, 4: 551-581.

MEILLASSOUX, C. [ed.] (1971) The Development of Indigenous Trade and Markets in West Africa. London: Oxford University Press.

———(1968) "Ostentation, destruction, reproduction." Cahiers de l'I.S.E.A., Économies et Sociétés 2, 4: 759-772.

———(1960) "Essai d'interprétation du phénomène économique dans les sociétés traditionnelles d'auto subsistence." Cahiers d'études africaines 1, 4: 38-67.

NORTHRUP, D. (1982) "Porterage in Eastern Zaire, 1885-1930: labor use and abuse in war and peace." Presented at the annual meeting of the African Studies Association, Washington, D.C.

ROBERTS, R. (1980) "Linkages and multiplier effects in the ecologically specialized trade of precolonial West Africa." Cahiers d'études africaines 20, 1-2: 135-148.

THOMPSON, E. P. (1968) The Making of the English Working Class. Harmondsworth, Middlesex: Penguin.

2

TRADE AND LABOR IN
EARLY PRECOLONIAL AFRICAN HISTORY
The Canoemen of Southern Ghana

PETER C.W. GUTKIND

        As the Portuguese captains hugged the West African coast in the late fifteenth century, they discovered that the powerful surf (initially referred to as "the burnings") pounding the beaches made it virtually impossible for even their shallow-draught sailing vessels to cast anchor close to shore. They also noted the almost total absence of natural harbors. It is these physiographic features that gave rise to an initially small labor force of canoemen whose skills, obtained as fishermen, turned out to be indispensable. Thus began the long history of the canoemen of Southern Ghana as workers in the transatlantic trade.

Author's Note: Research on the history of the canoemen of Ghana has received generous support from the Wenner-Gren Foundation for Anthropological Research, the Social Sciences and Humanities Research Council of Canada, the Africa Committee of the Social Science Research Council (U.S.A.), the Social Science Committee, Graduate Faculty, McGill University, and, in the early stages of research, from the Centre for Developing-Area Studies, McGill University. Among the many individuals who have assisted in my research, I would like to thank D. K. Fiawoo, John Hobbins, Myron Echenberg, Richard Price, Robin Cohen, Jeff Crisp, Lyn Garrett, Greg Teal, Paul-Arden Clark, and the retired surfboatmen at Cape Coast, Elmina, and Accra who had the patience to answer my questions.

In December 1481 a large armada left Portugal under the command of Diego d'Azambuja, comprising 500 soldiers, numerous craftsmen such as masons, coopers, and carpenters, and some prefabricated building materials.[1] On arrival, the sailing ships were met by small canoes. The paddlers, the canoemen, offered assistance and eventually began to ferry passengers and cargo to the beach at the small village of Adina. Diego d'Azambuja was greeted by the local potentate and negotiated with him the right to establish a permanent settlement that came to be known as Sao Jorge da Mina (henceforth Elmina—the mine). The visitors knew what they wanted. "Mina," M. N. Dias (1960: 383) wrote, "arouses appetites—a land where gold could be traded for trinkets."

Unfortunately, the Portuguese archives reveal little about this early history and even less about the use of canoemen in the period between 1482 and approximately 1502. Unlike the English and Dutch, who settled on the coast some hundred years later, the Portuguese did not keep very good records. Those that were kept either never made it back to Portugal or were damaged by salt water, burned when pirates captured and destroyed outward or homeward vessels, or were destroyed by officials who had much to hide due to widespread corruption and privateering. J. A. Faro (1957, 1958) is one of the few Portuguese writers who has given us some idea of the administration of Elmina during the first quarter of the sixteenth century. Yet, like others with an interest in this early period, he makes only limited references to the canoemen although he recognizes their importance. We are left to guess how the canoemen were recruited, whether they were slaves or "free labor," or how they were remunerated, although it is likely that "trade goods"—cloth and ironware as well as liquor—were given. As Elmina, which was given the status of a city in 1486 at which time also King John II took the title of Lord of Guinea, was for some time the only settlement (until 1503 when the Portuguese constructed another but significantly smaller fort at Axim), the need for canoemen was limited; this, however, in no way reduced Portuguese dependency on these workers. Storeships from Portugal were few, averaging about six per year in the early years and gradually increasing to twelve per annum.

The administration of Elmina, which had grown to imposing dimensions by the early sixteenth century, was authoritarian and hierarchical. Europeans and castle slaves rarely ventured beyond the surrounding area. Initially small but rapidly expanding African settlements grew up under the massive castle walls. Economically, the gold, ivory, and, later, slaves were the dominant objectives. The Portuguese crown was quick to institute complete control over the gold and ivory trade. Violations of a vast range of regulations designed to control every aspect of trade were punished with great severity. Yet corruption and privateering were, by all accounts, widespread and many a private fortune was made.

During the reign of Manuel II (1495-1521) new and very severe regulations were passed which came to be known as "Manuelinas" (Blake, 1977: 203-204; Birmingham, 1970; Brasio, 1958-1964; Sanceau, 1969: 77-78; Teixeira da Mota, 1978; Vogt, 1974: 103, 107; 1979: 34-35, 115). A cascade of ordinances and minute regulations literally poured from the court codifying a system of "monarchical monopolistic capitalism." Numerous regulations applied to all those connected with loading and unloading the ships and hence were applied to the canoemen, captains, crew, factors, writers, and warehousemen. They regulated the remuneration of canoemen, African "bomboys" (supervisors), and those Africans taken on for training as craftsmen and artisans. One is tempted to characterize certain aspects of these ordinances as labor legislation. Particularly severe measures were imposed on the canoemen, captains, and sailors to prevent theft of gold, ivory, and trade goods. Canoemen in particular were constantly suspected of theft, while the Europeans invariably suspected each other, no doubt to protect their own guilt, a condition that contributed to racial and interpersonal conflict. Every item landed or shipped was recorded in huge ledgers (only a few of which remain in the Portuguese archives) and canoemen were always carefully supervised. But the regulations were broken with impunity; the records indicate that violators frequently ended up in jail, where they were placed in irons, or were returned to Portugal where they were brought before the king and, occasionally, put to death. Canoemen who violated the regulations were lucky if they were only placed in irons as some of them were sold into slavery and taken to the West Indies.

RESPONSE OF CANOEMEN
TO PORTUGUESE RULE

Already in the period 1482 to approximately 1530, canoemen responded to the conditions of their employment (although the archival record is scanty) when, as in 1499, Governor Fernao Lopes Correia

claimed that the canoemen "have once again refused to work and all
our efforts to punish them have made them more objectionable." He
concluded that greater supervision was needed adding that the "worst
among them must be placed in irons." In 1513 a Portuguese factor,
Paulo da Mota, had, it appears, a physical confrontation with a group
of canoemen on the beach just below the castle walls. He noted that
some canoemen attempted to beat him with "billets of wood and large
stones." The cause of this disturbance appears to have been the demand by the canoemen to be paid with gold rather than cloth. On yet
another occasion in 1521, Governor Duarte Pacheco Pereira noted that
some canoemen had used their *almadias,* canoes, to "attack a [Por-
tuguese] storeship and set it on fire" because a canoeman had been
flogged for stealing and had died of his injuries. The governor concluded that he had simply enforced the existing regulations, which,
he added, "are always opposed by these thieves." Yet two years later
in 1523, Governor D. Afonso de Albuquerque sent a message to Lisbon
lauding the canoemen for their faithful service and expressed the view
that when they are treated "correctly" they will "work long hours and
carry out the work with skill and care."[2]

In the mid-1550s, specifically during the governorship of Rui de
Melo (1552-1556), when the Portuguese had to battle against attempts
by the English to destroy their trading monopoly followed by the Dutch
somewhat later in the sixteenth century, hostile attitudes toward and
repression against the canoemen appears to have increased.[3] Thus
the governor complained in 1555 that canoemen were no longer "loyal"
to the Portuguese (which is hardly surprising as their repression had
always been very severe), that they assisted not only the ships of other
nations but they were tempted by better trade goods offered by
privateers who, of course, needed the canoemen as badly as everyone
else. He also noted that African merchants began to employ canoemen
thus draining labor away from the Portuguese. As in subsequent years,
when the Royal African Company and the First and Second Dutch
West India Company dominated the trade on the Ghana coast, Governor Melo proposed the more extensive use of slave canoemen as more
secure and cheaper (generally slaves received some remuneration) than
"free" labor (Gutkind, in press).

With the expansion of trade in the seventeenth century, the need
for canoemen also increased. English, French, and Dutch ships
journeyed to the Gold Coast in a successful bid to break the Portuguese
monopoly on West African external trade; by the end of the century

they were joined by Danes, Swedes, and Brandenburgers. Quite apart from the increase in licensed trade, the number of interlopers also increased significantly and became a permanent feature of coastal trade. Because the interlopers had to conduct their trade in secret, the canoemen took considerable risks to service the ships, to supply them with water and wood and transport African traders to the ships. By 1650, the number of free canoemen was about 350, and the number rose to 800-1000 by 1790, making these workers a significant labor force whose presence was felt in many areas of political and economic life, particularly as active participants, and often as rioters *(agyesemfo)* in the frequent civic disturbances in the African towns. As such they also became night workers hoping via the cover of darkness to escape retribution from the companies. Governors, commandants, and factors did their best to prevent this illegal trade, and many a canoeman was placed in irons in the late seventeenth and eighteenth centuries. In order to rid the coast of these unwanted interlopers, ships were put to the torch, always with the help of canoemen. During the prolonged Anglo-Dutch wars between 1652 and 1667, for example, the canoemen became seriously embroiled in international conflicts that spilled over to the various settlements on the coast.

Apart from these more dramatic involvements of the canoemen, their true importance rests on their employment as passenger and cargo transporters. As such the canoemen were the predecessors of the dockworkers, whose work began in 1926 when the first artificial harbor was opened at Takoradi. While the transport of passengers was clearly of vital importance, so was the canoemen's participation in the slave trade, an activity that is occasionally cited in the records, and is portrayed in an excellent woodcut in Barbot (1746, v. 5: 99). Equally vital was the unloading of the storeships and the constant need to supply the smaller settlements with trade goods and a great variety of provisions. The essential supplies ranged from massive quantities of construction materials, huge amounts of brandy and tobacco, thousands of yards of cloth, and tons of food and medicines. Over time the canoemen carried a vast number of letters (thousands of which are in various national archives), a service that alone made them indispensable. The canoemen were remunerated for all these activities with trade goods such as cloth, or rum, brandy, tobacco, and, occasionally, gold. All the companies kept very careful records of these disbursements, usually recorded under the heading "Canoemen Hire." The registers enumerate "Slave Canoemen" and "Free Canoemen," the latter outnumbering the former by a very considerable ratio. Some of the larger settlements such as Elmina, Cape Coast, and Accra employed, but not on a permanent basis, from 75 to 85 free canoemen, while the number at the smaller places varied from 18 to 35, and trading posts and lodges might use the services of between 9 and 16. When storeships arrived, the number of canoemen working per day sometimes rose to 150. Despite this, complaints about undue delays in unloading were common. The number of slave canoemen appearing on the annual establishment lists varied from 16 at Cape Coast Castle in 1721 to a low of 8 in 1752 rising again to 21 in 1777. Some chartered companies used slave canoemen more frequently than others and all of them fell back on slaves when the free canoemen refused to work or when the metropolitan-based headquarters of the companies considered the expenditure on this ''free'' labor to be excessive. But, generally, the number of canoemen varied with the conditions of trade, the international political climate, and African-European relations. Interethnic conflict was also a factor in the availability of free canoemen. When civil disturbances took place in the African towns, not infrequently engineered by Europeans pitting one ethnic group against another, canoemen generally became involved.

A shortage of canoemen also occurred when they came out in support of caboceers, elders, and headmen who had not received gifts, or when rents were not paid to local chiefs. On the whole free canoemen were available, yet they also knew the appropriate occasions when to withdraw their labor. They readily did so when Europeans abused them, or when they objected to a cruel African bomboy or a rapacious merchant. Occasionally they would refuse to work in support of a fellow worker who had been mistreated, or because they believed that they had been cheated on their remuneration. There are no indications that the canoemen refused to take part in the slave trade, although a factor at Winnebah recorded in 1753, ''unless we can secure more canoemen this part of our trade will occasion difficulties for us.''[4] No reason is offered why these difficulties arose, but we can speculate to what degree this traffic in human cargo depended on the willingness of the canoemen to be engaged. It was not uncommon for the London office of the Royal African Company to question whether the various settlements made the best use of canoemen and other labor. Thus the Court of Assistant in London wrote to the factor at Cape Coast on 18 July, 1728:

We cannot but think that a much smaller number than sixty-one canoemen may answer all your occasion, and in that case we recommend it to you always to employ as many of them only as can be spared in fishing.[5]

In the same account some figures are given about the number of slaves, pawns, canoemen, and other workers on the coast.

We observe the contents [of your letter] in relation to the numbers of castle working slaves and canoemen employed on the Gold Coast and at Wydah which by the lists you have sent us we find amount to no less than six hundred and seventy-seven in all a very considerable number and in our opinion more than sufficient to do all the necessary business of the company [even if it] had the whole trade of the coast to themselves.[6]

There are no indications in the records how canoemen reacted to being declared redundant. But on the whole labor protest, and the many forms it took, was a reaction to unacceptable treatment and the low remuneration received. Canoemen expressed their discontent in a classic manner in 1753 when they went on strike during the construction of the English fort at Anamabu. Like strikers today, they simply stopped work and demanded better terms. Unfortunately for them they did not succeed (Priestley, 1965: 25).

EMPLOYMENT AND ACTIVITIES
OF THE CANOEMEN

As an increasing number of ships came to the Ghana coast, the canoemen found themselves occupied almost daily, particularly during the months of October to May when the storeships arrived from Europe. The records of the Royal African Company and those of the Dutch West India Company record arrivals and departures of the canoemen on a daily basis as they moved newly arrived cargo and passengers to the various settlements or loaded ships with cargo and slaves. Thus the records mention that a thirteen-hand canoe arrived at Cape Coast from Winnebah, or a seven-hand canoe from Accra. Such entries are followed by the remuneration given. There are literally thousands of such entries that convey a picture of constant communication from one settlement to another whatever the season. Some records even give the time of day when canoes arrived or departed and, if passengers are carried, the names are given.

The quantities carried by the canoemen from ship to shore and back to ship, or from settlement to settlement, are truly astounding and could be treated as a separate discussion. During the construction of Anamabu Fort in the 1750s we can get an idea of the loads the canoemen handled, although "long boats," which were carried by the sailing ships, but were quite unsuitable to cut through the heavy surf, were also used to speed up the unloading. John Apperly, chief engineer at Anabu, requested 1 million bricks and 400 tons of lime in 1753, and another 267,600 bricks and 280 tons of lime soon thereafter. In 1756 a further 1.8 million bricks were required and another 600 tons of lime so that the walls of the new fort might reach "14 feet high . . . and 5 feet 4 inches thick."[7] Year by year thousands of gallons of brandy and rum were unloaded as well as thousands of fathoms of tobacco. Brandy arrived in large casks often too bulky for the narrow canoes. The following is typical of hundreds of similar entries.

> By the 7 hand canoe you will receive 35 cases of Brandy. . . . There seems to have been some Rogery committed indeed in the canoe on the Beach [probably a reference to theft].[8]

The canoemen also transported large quantities of firearms and thousands of barrels of powder (and "letting sparks from their pipes fall upon [the barrels] without concern, which created a terror in us to see and by which means they are frequently blown up"; Churchill, 1732: 223), and livestock such as sheep and, in the nineteenth century when larger surfboats replaced the canoes, we are told about the transport of a polo pony (Moore and Guggisberg, 1909). Loads were often so heavy and so bulky that the canoes capsized, spoiling the cargo and drowning the passengers, most of whom, unlike the canoemen, could not swim. When the surf was too rough, canoe activity oftentimes ceased for days. Such unavoidable circumstances, and the refusal of canoemen to work for other reasons, frequently resulted in severe shortages of provisions at the smaller settlements. Thus in December 1757 the factor at Komenda wrote to the governor at Cape Coast:

> Our supplies are very short, we lack in everything. If the canoemen refuse to work this factory will cease. The canoemen are making fools

of their masters; they must be forced to work as informed by the [London] Committee. We have no supplies.[9]

Life was lonely, often desperate, and generally confining for the European residents on the coast. Canoemen were the link to friends and officials stationed elsewhere—and they brought letters and parcels from home. Often, the canoemen were dispatched to ships lying in the roads to meet captains and crew or, as in the following case, to obtain a little liquid cheer. The factor at Tantumquerry dispatched a canoe on 5 February, 1775, with the following request. He had learned "that you have a quantity of Rasberry Brandy by you [and wonder whether] you could spare some. On this presumption I have sent this canoe and will be very obliged to you for 3 or 4 bottles of it."[10] The records are replete with desperate requests like this.

Perhaps this little episode highlights one aspect of the indispensability of these workers. Everyone, from governor to laborer, as well as important African merchants such as John Kabes, who owned a fleet of canoes and employed many canoemen, recognized the importance of these workers. The officials in the settlements often recorded that this was so, however ambivalent their attitudes toward the canoemen. Despite their indispensability, or perhaps because of this recognition, these workers were often described as "rascally," "impudent," "ruffians," "outcasts," "vagabonds," "wretched," and "criminal." Others were satisfied with less evocative language saying that the canoemen were "lacking in obedience," that it was "so difficult to get them to work." But there were also those Europeans who recorded that "the canoemen for the past two months have behaved exceedingly well. . . . I do not know that I have had occasion to be angry with them."[11] John Roberts, president of Cape Coast Council, writing to the factor at Sekondi in February 1750, urged him to reprimand a Captain Bignal for mistreating the canoemen, for "refusing them the common allowance," and wounding one of them in "the shoulder with his sword," adding that such an act may be considered mere

play to [Captain Bignal] but it is earnest to them that they feel his blows. . . . They are free people and work only for their hire and not to be abused, beaten or starved by those who have no right to exercise such cruelty upon them especially as they are very willing and desirous to do any work . . . for pay and good wages.[12]

Some sixty years later Meredith (1967: 23) made much the same observation.

> When these men are employed by us, as canoe-men, they perform their duty with cheerfulness; and if encouraged, will go through a vast deal of labour: but they must be treated with exactness and punctuality.
>
> When they call for any customary allowance, or for payment, they do not like to be put off; they expect that their labour should be met with instant reward. If they be not punctually attended to, they become neglectful and unattentive to the interest of their employers.

But Meredith (1967: 23) could not avoid a final and negative observation, for he concluded that the canoemen

> are much addicted to that vice [theft] which prevails in almost every part of the world, and, indeed, are very expert in the practice of it, particularly as to small articles, which they can easily conceal.

LABOR PROTEST

Much of the labor protest that took place might be set in a discussion of "free" versus "unfree" labor, a rather hoary issue that is, however, central to labor history and the understanding of the labor process (Corrigan, 1977; O'Connor, 1975). The slave labor that kept the settlements operating is no doubt a classic example of unfree labor. But, one might well ask, how free is free labor under even incipient forms of capitalist intrusion into the coastal societies of Ghana? Much of the treatment meted out to the free canoemen was harsh, contemptuous, and totally unequal compared to the conditions under which non-Africans were employed. True enough, canoemen could and did protest, could and did withdraw their labor, could and did engage in direct responses that at times took a violent form, physically or verbally. But the fact remains that the canoemen lived under a dispensation and control not of their own making and contrary to their own desires, their hopes, and, perhaps, aspirations. The canoemen were the direct producers of services, services that were critical to accumulation of wealth that was not redistributed. They fell in a category, as workers under capitalism do today, of being unfree free labor (Corrigan, 1977; Klein, 1969). Thus, in 1855, a later period really outside the primary interest of this chapter, Campbell makes this interesting observation about the canoemen of Ghana.

In the strict sense of the term, there is no such thing as free labour in Lagos, except what is imported; and, even that of the Gold Coast canoe men, is, in reality, Slavery; for very few of them, excepting the head men, are really free.[13]

If one were to accept the view that explicit free labor does not, and cannot, exist among workers used for the production of surplus value, then free labor can never be totally free in the wider and more significant meaning of this concept and the actuality of freeness. Again, if this formulation has meaning in both structural and experiental terms, then the canoemen were merely fractionally freer than genuinely unfree labor. This then would account both for their class and political consciousness as well as their labor protest.

As was indicated above, the most common form of protest was the refusal of the canoemen to work, desertion, theft, and what might be viewed as a local version of Luddism, that is, damage to canoes, canoesheds, and cargo deliberately allowed to be spoilt by salt water. Labor protest can be, as we know, informal or formal (Cohen, 1976, 1980) although the former is often difficult to distinguish from the latter, and the emphasis on informality gives the impression that workers only react rather than take a reasoned and formal political (class) position. The labor protest by the canoemen should be viewed in light of the fact that the Europeans were aware of their dependence on this labor while the former were equally aware of their indispensability. This certainly, to a degree, gave the canoemen the upper hand and made the Europeans conscious of the negative consequences of repressive measures that could and did lead to the withdrawal of labor. As early as 1647, the Dutch at the newly captured castle of Elmina reported that "the rimadores [paddlers] give us constant trouble. They demand goods in excess of the work they perform. Today 9 of them refused to unload a ship and I [Director-General I. van der Well] ordered two of them confined in irons."[14] In 1652 Chief Factor George Middleton at Kormantin referred to the canoemen as "ignorant and arrogant thieves and labourers who want more than their due, and if we do not give this they refuse to work."[15] In 1664 Captain William Short refused to provide advance subsistence to some canoemen whom he had hired to take him to (Dutch) Sekondi from (Dutch) Boutri. The canoemen, he recorded, had been "impertinent and left me on the shore." He had drawn his "sword because I fear'd stones and their rais'd hands and Fear'd for my life."[16]

It was also common for canoemen to refuse work for which they were not engaged and which they considered, so it appears, beneath their station, such as work normally done by common carriers. Edward Barter (Henige, 1972) recorded the following event in 1695:

> [I] paid some canoemen 3 taccoes to take some of the corn in. The canoe overturns. The reason my beating one of them [a canoeman] was because he would not help to carry the corn to the croome [town-village] that was wet with water, [but] he told me he came to paddle not to carry corn at all.

Desertion, theft, and refusal to work were not infrequently punished by selling canoemen into slavery, as occurred in a case in 1704 when a local caboceer at Cape Coast brought a case against a Captain Hamilin, who had attempted to sell a canoeman into slavery to be taken to the West Indies simply because he had deserted and, so claimed the captain, had also damaged a canoe. Canoemen also feared being taken prisoner during periods of international conflict (such as the Anglo-Dutch wars), which may account for their frequent refusal to transport troops and military equipment. All canoemen, slave or free, were always known as either English, Dutch, or Portuguese canoemen. As such English canoemen feared crossing the sea in front of a Dutch settlement, while Dutch canoemen expressed similar fears crossing the English roads. It was also common practice to *panyar* (kidnap) canoemen (Kea, 1982: 243) or any African, to be held as a pawn for another person's debt. Canoemen were particularly vulnerable to this practice because they moved about among the coastal settlements. When canoemen deserted they generally took refuge in another settlement or were protected by their fellow citizens in African towns. Recovery of deserters, the demands by English officials to return canoemen who had taken refuge in a Dutch settlement, frequently resulted in minor international conflict, very prolonged negotiations stretching over many weeks, or the arbitrary capture of persons who came from the same settlement where the deserters lived. Such events and a significant increase in refusals to work, as well as the maltreatment of canoemen, are very marked during the busy eighteenth century. Between 1730 and 1750 English and Dutch records are peppered with brief, yet significant, references to "undue delays" unloading the ships; that "we must wait for eternal time" because canoemen refused to work; of shortages of trade goods and all manner of provisions (par-been very obnoxious and have refused to do their common duty, we give them their due but they refuse to work. I told them if they still refuse we can do without them and take them as slaves."[20]

The eighteenth century was one during which their consciousness as workers increased, as did their courage to give it expression. We do not know what lessons, if any, the Europeans drew from these manifestations, nor how other canoemen along the coast perceived the actions of their fellow workers. As news traveled fast, it is rather unlikely that workers elsewhere were not aware of these protests. The documentation rarely reveals the public voice of the canoemen in their own terms. This is a serious limitation, but I do not think that it destroys the basic argument made. Although the historical record is one of European attitudes, responses, and analyses of events, it gives us an insight into the conditions for labor at the time.

That the canoemen were conscious of the value of the remuneration they received in relation to their perception of the value of the work they did is clear from their frequent objections to be paid in worthless trinkets. They demanded gold when they were offered tobacco or liquor (both of which they treated more as subsistence than wages). The haggling that ensued often resulted in prolonged disputes, as in 1778 between Mr. John Clemson, a free trader at Cape Coast, and some canoemen (Gutkind, in press). The canoemen were offered liquor, which they refused, and asked for gold instead "upon which Mr. Clemson took a cane and flogged one of them," the appointed spokesman of the canoemen.[21]

The canoemen, like other skilled African workers such as artisans, were subject to supervision by African bomboys, a small group whose involvement in labor disputes is frequently recorded. No information has so far come to light how these African supervisors were recruited or remunerated, but there are many indications that they were disliked and seen as extensions of their European and African masters. In 1718 a small group of canoemen attacked a bomboy who had been sent by his master to collect some cargo from the beach. The canoemen beat him as they suspected him of being a thief and they would be blamed. On yet another occasion a bomboy was verbally abused by the canoemen because his master had told him that the canoemen would not be paid for several days, a message that the poor fellow had to convey to them. Yet in 1788 some bomboys refused to work, to "get the canoemen to unload the Storeship" that had arrived at Cape Coast. Hence Governor Thomas Norris ordered that the pay of the bomboys

ticularly medicines) leading to expressions of desperation such as "our supplies are run out we are in a sick state"; of factors complaining that they "do their best to offer due speed to the captain but the canoemen impede our trade."

Finally, in the mid-1750s during the construction of Anamabu Fort, a formal strike took place. Thomas Melvil writing from Cape Coast to the London Committee on January 25, 1753, recorded the event as follows:

Gentlemen,

My last letter by the [ship] Tubah of Bristol is inclosed. Since that time we have been busy landing the stores at Annamaboe where we meet with many Rubs. The Canoemen raised their wages upon us, and left off work. I sent all those belonging to myself and Partners to assist the Company and with these we wrought several days. This has brought the Fantees to reason and they now assist for the Old Wages. Every day produces fresh Demands, from the Cabboceers who say now is their time to eat when we are going to Build our Fort. . . .

The Canoemen would not work, I have sent down my own Canoemen with yours to show them once more that we can do without them.[17]

While the strike failed, as "wages" were not raised, the fact that it took place was as significant as the outcome. Yet this was not the first time that canoemen had shown their collective strength.

In March 1685 canoemen refused to unload the *Mavis*, which had arrived from London with provisions, a few soldiers, and some building materials to establish a settlement at Succondee (Sekondi). The chief factor, Captain Henry Nurse, reported on 17 March that "despite our effort the rascally canoemen have refused to unload the 'Mavis,' their caboceer has told me that the canoemen were beaten [hit] by some Dutch at Mina and now do not wish to work for us."[18] In December 1717 Agent-General William Johnson also complained that the canoemen had set fire to some canoesheds because "they were angry with us and said that they had been suffered [hurt] by Mister James because he refused to give them their due Brandy and had voiced to beat them";[19] and in May 1739 Chief Factor William Tymewell reported "with regret" to the London office that "all the canoemen have run away and some of them attempted to set fire to our stores on the beach." He noted that "in the last months the canoemen have "be discontinued from 23 December 1788, being the Time they refused to get the Canoemen to unload the Storeship. This to be understood to hold good unless the [London] Committee should order to the contrary."[22] We are not told why the bomboys refused to carry out their supervisory duties.

As indicated earlier, the canoemen often refused to transport troops and military supplies, which, during the last part of eighteenth and much of the nineteenth century, arrived in considerable quantities. In 1794 Commander Dod had to use his own long boats, particularly unsuitable for passenger transport through the surf, and expressed his anger at the canoemen. "The most disagreeable part," he wrote, "is the refusal of the canoemen to land the Troops at Amoko. . . . However disagreeable it is to me to be obliged to submit to the Caprice of the rascally Canoemen, I propose to land the Troops tomorrow morning."[23]

By the nineteenth century labor unrest was common and by no means restricted to the canoemen. Workers in many trades demanded better pay and better conditions of employment including the hammockmen, another group of direct service producers well worth closer attention. We are also given some indication that navigational improvements might have been rejected by the canoemen who sensed that these might lead to redundancy. In 1818 plans were made to construct a breakwater at Cape Coast to assist larger vessels to discharge bulk cargo more safely and quickly. Sir George Collier investigated the possibility of such a plan but wondered how the canoemen might respond, "I am not prepared to say," he noted,

> how far the natives of Cape Coast Town would estimate such work as a large part of their means is derived from Canoe labour for which they are highly paid . . . It would perhaps be satisfactory to their Lordships if the African Company were directed to state the general daily expenses of Canoe hire, during the time their Store Ship is in the Roads.[24]

But such issues bring us into the contemporary period, which is not the primary concern of this chapter.

Many of the actions by the canoemen might be interpreted as mere antisocial activity (such as theft, smuggling, willful damage, and freebooting), rather than true labor protest and that what there was of the latter was haphazard and unorganized. This may well be so if we were to take no account of the rapidly evolving class structure within and beyond the settlements, the rise of important African merchants, traders, and middlemen, the progressive specialization of skills and division of labor, and, above all, the commoditization of labor that radically altered an older labor process. Kea (1982) has exposed the extent and kind of poverty in the coastal settlements and has, I think, shown clearly the emerging lines of stratification particularly in the seventeenth century.[25] The language alone adopted by the Europeans vis-à-vis the canoemen is ample evidence of the class position occupied by these workers. Canoemen were perceived by some as outcasts, as villainous, and always as lazy, but also cunning, ambitious, and determined to set themselves up as traders in their own right. The following comment is not unusual:

> Canoemen in this country [Ghana] are such Thieves, such Lazy and runaway rogues, and so protected by their Relations, Countrymen and Acquaintance, and so Countenanced even by all the Blacks of this Towne [Cape Coast] that it takes a considerable time, when on the run, to get them again.[26]

Because canoemen did attempt to trade on their own account, particularly with the help of the interlopers, they were accused of undermining the monopoly of trade that each nation reserved for itself and the appointed officials. Kea (n.d.c: 18) has pointed out that canoemen, although treated as commoners, were not prevented from engaging in trade and that

> It was from among the ranks of the canoemen that the brokers and merchants of the past emerged. . . . Canoemen with mercantile aspirations began their careers as traders by borrowing gold or trade goods from those who possessed them. Usually this meant that they were obliged to place themselves in pawn.

This is not an unusual move for workers who facilitate the entrepreneurship of others and see the opportunity for the acquisition of property that might pave the way for their *costumier* aspirations (Hobsbawm, 1964). That some of the canoemen were successful and rose in rank and status is supported by one Quaquo who became a trader and eventually managed to pay off a substantial debt in 1669 to a Dutch commandant. Others who attempted to trade on their own account came to a grievous end as in English Komenda when, in 1715, a canoeman was placed in irons for "taking trade from the Company." He had had the help of a local caboceer and his son who "shot himself" rather than, one is led to believe, being put in irons as well. His father being a caboceer evidently did not expect similar punishment. In the years following abolition the canoemen were enticed by all manner of rewards to facilitate the illicit slave trade. Because their activity involved them in great risk, they were paid large quantities of trade goods, which they then attempted to use to set themselves up as traders—albeit on a relatively small scale.

The evidence does suggest that the canoemen revealed a class consciousness, and a political force, that transcended mere antisocial behavior and aspirations of entrepreneurship. Their consciousness rested on the foundation that they were the direct producers of services that created a considerable wealth for others both locally and in the distant metropolitan centers. Like workers everywhere, past and present, they protested when they felt entitled to a larger share of this wealth.

Central to this consciousness, fed by an economistic rather than a reformist or apocalyptic vision of the future, is the question of their own internal organization. Despite extensive and prolonged searching of the records, no information has come to light on this important issue. Some eighteenth century records occasionally suggest that the canoemen might have been organized in an *asafo,* but the references are too brief and unclear to draw any firm conclusions. Muller (1968) noted such an organization in 1676, but, again, the reference is too inconclusive. It is vital for us to know how the canoemen were recruited, what comprised a "crew," and whether they had their own headmen. Very occasionally there are references to the "Headman of the canoemen," but beyond this nothing further is recorded. The absence of such information does leave a rather large gap, which, one hopes, can be filled in the future. By the middle of the nineteenth century, when the documentation greatly improves and oral history can also be taken into account, surfboatmen, the successors to the canoemen, had their own asafo. Indeed, to this day retired surfboatmen will gladly take the visitor to Elmina to a house, magnificently decorated, which is their asafo meeting place. At a meeting held in their hall they claimed that they and their predecessors, the canoemen, had always had their own asafo, which regulated who could be surfboatmen, how they were recruited, the authority they obeyed, and how conditions of work were negotiated. But more needs to be done to determine the accuracy of these statements.

THE CLASS SYSTEM IN SOUTHERN GHANA

The canoemen, without whose labor coastal and inland trade in Ghana would have been severely restricted, comprised a distinct laboring class that fitted into an established class system that residents of and visitors to the settlements from the sixteenth century on have described (Villault, 1669: 296; Fage, 1980a: 289, 293, 295). The free canoemen were "waged" employees. But, despite this, were the social relations of production ultimately embedded in kinship (even though their labor was primarily for Europeans) and juridicial determinants, and as such not dominated by imported economic conditions and structures? Most students of precolonial societies view them as precapitalist and, indeed, perhaps anticapitalist; that the domestic economy was small; that markets and exchanges met only basic needs for social reproduction; and that social rather than economic values were maximized.[27] Precapitalist societies, it is argued, do not pay "wages" to producers whose labor is rewarded and contained in networks of kin and the larger ethnic group. But such an orientation places exclusive emphasis on the structure of an economy and not complementary emphasis on the consequences of that structure; on formal political structure rather than on its operation and, again, its consequences; on the social organization as ideal rather than as praxis. Where there was hierarchy there was class, and there is no doubt that the Ghanaian coastal societies were hierarchical to various degrees. Kea (1980: 373) suggests as much in describing the various means of surplus extraction that coexisted in Akwamu from 1681 to 1730.

The southern Ghanaian social formations were complex and rested on unequal distribution of wealth and authority, characteristic of capitalist modes of organization. Kea (1982) has produced the most detailed and analytically strong documentation of class formation for this coastal region, applying a three-stage periodization, and has suggested that the roots of class structure can be traced back to the thirteenth or fourteenth century. The evidence suggests that the first clear signs of considerable class-based unrest became evident with the arrival of the Portuguese. The class of indigent increased sharply in the period of mercantilism (fifteenth to early eighteenth centuries), which also saw the rise of banditry when trade assumed great importance and agricultural production declined. Cordeiro (1881: 24) has noted that

> Because of the many commodities the Dutch have brought and are bringing, all have abandoned farming and have become and are still becoming merchants. Those who cannot pay become robbers of other merchants. There are no farms and no agriculture, and all of the neighbouring coastal Kings are in despair and lament that they are lost and ruined, and that they will lose everything, and that they will die of hunger.

De Marees (1912: 112-113) also reported that in the early seventeenth century many families were in debt to rich, *abirempon,* urban townspeople. In particular, a number of writers have noted that the port settlements became progressively the residences of the poor; that theft, robbery and crime were common, resulting in considerable disorder. Ratelband notes (1953: 183-192) that Elmina in particular harbored a "delinquent rogue" who, after being caught and put in prison, eventually hanged himself. Kea (n.d.b) suggests that some of the (class-based) crime was associated with organized gangs of young men known as *sika den,* black gold, who were without regular employment and engaged in the kidnapping of peasants on behalf of African and European traders.

Craft production, concentrated in the coastal towns, rose rapidly; guilds developed and military leadership assumed considerable importance in the eighteenth century. As southern Ghana became firmly incorporated into an evolving international system of trade and commerce (the *zona comercio* as the Portuguese named the Costa de Mina), primitive accumulation received a major boost (a process that likely commenced considerably prior to the arrival of the Portuguese during the period of the land-holding captaincy system). Production for export of gold and ivory expanded and the resources of the country came under pressure. An export-oriented capitalist mode of production took root and consolidated itself into the present. One is reminded of the view offered by Marx (1977: 874-875) who suggested that

> The process of primitive accumulation can be nothing other than the process which divorces the worker from the ownership of the conditions of his own labour; it is a process which operates two transformations, whereby the social means of subsistence and production are turned

into capital, and the immediate producers are turned into wage-labourers. So-called primitive accumulation, therefore, is nothing else than the historical process of divorcing the producers from the means of production.

The dynamic of this process, Marx (1961: 331) suggested, is revealed in

the operation of merchant capital in pre-capitalist modes of production with limited surplus products generally concentrated in the hands of the ruling classes lends itself to manifestations of violence. Violence arises from conflict between merchant capital and ruling classes over distribution of the surplus product between them.

Kwame Arhin (1983: 18) has documented this process of surplus extraction in his description of the class system on the Mina coast, while Daaku (1971: 169) specifies those residents in the coastal towns who had come to "sell their services [such] as the canoemen" as a new phenomenon:

In the coastal towns like Elmina, Cape Coast, Annamabo, Axim and Accra, there emerged a group of people who owed their new positions to trade. Some of them had come down to the coast specifically to sell their commodities but there were many who came to these towns to sell their services as canoemen, masons, soldiers, bricklayers, interpreters, etc. The fact that these people received regular monthly wages for their services gave them a completely new status in the traditional set up. . . . [What had emerged was a] new wage-earning group.

European contact did not create new structures but advanced those already in place, as Arhin (1983: 15) has also observed. The canoemen provided the direct services so essential to the development of internal and external trade and to enrichment of European and African merchants whose fortunes rose but could also decline. The canoemen and other labor created for some a capitalistic paradise. One unnamed writer (Sarbah, 1904: 196) of the period (probably the seventeenth or eighteenth century) had considerable insight.

For the Golden Coast, [as one quaintly wrote] where man may gain an estate by a handful of beads, and his pocket full of gold for an old hat; where a cat is a tenement, and a few fox-tails a manor; where gold is sold for iron, and silver given for brass and pewter.[28]

Those who received the beads and the old hat were, of course, those who labored to create the gold and silver. This leads me to conclude that the history of people and their labor is always one of struggle. James Connolly, the great Irish republican socialist, put it simply in 1916: "The cause of labour is the cause of Ireland, and the cause of Ireland is the cause of labour." Of course, we must be mindful that polemicism and rhetoric do not run away with our hopes. We must not be father to a wish that might remain unfulfilled. I have deliberately not suggested that the canoemen were a proletarianized working class (although I was sometimes tempted to say this [Sandbrook, 1981]); nor have I said that the canoemen were the true Ghana. What I have tried to suggest is that early precolonial African labor history can become an interesting field of study. I have also said that we might try to experiment with new models, which I think are best taken from that large range that Marx bequeathed to us. My own interests are both theoretical, which means different things to every social scientist, and ideological. We ought to try to set the record straight, if I may use a now rather dated expression. I would like to suggest that we should look toward a "History of the Conditions of the African Working Class." Somewhere there must be an Engels among Africanists. Lots of distinguished colleagues have contributed to the history of the western working class. It seems equally appropriate to devote energy to workers who were such a distinctive and indispensable part of the history of precolonial Africa. Such workers cut out for themselves an important and permanent place in the history of labor. The successors to the canoemen of Ghana are the dockworkers who inherited their skills and activism. But that is another but equally exciting story.

NOTES

1. A number of writers have accepted the view that large quantities of prefabricated building materials were carried by the ships leaving Portugal in December 1481. Van Dantzig and Priddy (1971: 7) and Lawrence (1963: 91-94, 104) have disputed this. See also Sanceau (1959: 211-222), Major (1967: 322), and Claridge (1964: 43) for the more conventional view, that is also supported by a number of Portuguese writers.

2. Archivo National de Torre do Tombo, Lisboa, 85m. doc. 75, 1499-1560.

3. Even before this date the Company of Merchant Adventurers for Guinea or the Merchant Adventurers to the Coast of Africa and Ethiopia was launched in 1553 but ceased in 1567. Even earlier, in 1540, some Southampton merchants formed a trading company engaged in the African trade at Senegal.

4. To Thomas Melvil, 7 October 1753, Public Record Office, London (henceforth PRO), T70/30.

5. Court of Assistants, Royal African Company to Philip Franklin, 18 July 1728, PRO, T70/53.

6. Ibid.

7. PRO, T70/30; T70/1518; CO. 388/46 (1753, 1754, and 1756).

8. PRO, T70/1470, 28 May 1780.

9. To Nassau Senior, 11 December 1757, PRO, T70/1527.

10. PRO, T70/1479, 1775.

11. PRO, T70/1515, 1750

12. Ibid.

13. PRO, F.O. 84/1002, Campbell to Clarendon, 18 February 1855. (Supplied by A. G. Hopkins.)

14. Archief van de Nederlandse Bezittigen ter Kuste van Guinea, 194, 1647.

15. PRO, T70/1515.

16. PRO, T70/75, 1664.

17. PRO, T70/29. See also T70/1520, both for 1753.

18. PRO, T70/81.

19. PRO, T70/1464.

20. PRO, T70/94.

21. Recorded by Richard Miles, Cape Coast Castle, 19 November 1778. PRO, T70/1468.

22. PRO, T70/153, 1789.

23. PRO, T70 1569.

24. National Maritime Museum, Greenwich, WEL/10, 1818.

25. The vocabulary reflected this stratification. The *abirempon* were the rich and the *anihumanifo* the poor; others were described as *konkonsafa* or *mantemantanni* who were the dispossessed, those who were degraded and of inferior status.

26. PRO, C.113/273, part 1, 1709.

27. This, of course, opens up the substantivist-formalist debate and a large literature supportive of one side or the other. (Leons and Rothstein, 1979). Marxist models differ fundamentally from both "mainstream" approaches.

28. PRO, C.113/36, part 2, no. 1010, 1709.

REFERENCES

ALPERS, E.A. (1973) "Re-thinking African economic history: a contribution to the discussion of the roots of underdevelopment." Ufahamu 19: 97-129.

ANDERSON, P. (1980) Arguments Within English Marxism. London: New Left Books.

ARHIN, K. (1983) "Rank and class in Asante and Fante in the nineteenth century." Africa 53: 2-22.

BARBOT, J. (1746) Description of the Coasts of North and South Guinea. London: Lintot and Osborn.

BIRMINGHAM, D. (1970) "The Regimento da Mina." Transactions of the Historical Society of Ghana 2: 1-7.

BLAKE, J. W. (1977) Europeans in West Africa, 1454-1578. London: Curzon.

BOSMAN, W. (1705) A New and Accurate Description of the Coast of Guinea Divided into the Gold, the Slave, and the Ivory Coasts. London: Knapton.

BOWDICH, T. E. (1966) Mission from Cape Coast Castle to Ashantee. London: F. Cass.

BRADBY, B. (1975) "The destruction of natural economy." Economy and Society 4: 127-161.

BRASIO, P. A. [ed.] (1958-1964) Monumento Missionari Africana. Africa Ocidental. Lisboa: Agencia Geral do Ultramar.

CHURCHILL, J. A. [comp.] (1732) Collection of Voyages and Travels, vol. 5. London: Walthoe.

CLARIDGE, W. W. (1964) A History of the Gold Coast and Ashanti from the Earliest Time to the Commencement of the 20th Century, vol. 1. London: F. Cass.

COHEN, R. (1980) "Resistance and hidden forms of consciousness among African workers." Review of African Political Economy 19: 8-22.

———(1976) "Hidden forms of labour protest in Africa." Birmingham: University of Birmingham, Faculty of Commerce and Social Science.

CORDEIRO, L. [ed.] (1881) "1516-1619. Escravos e Minas de Africa." Viagens exploracoes e conquistas dos Portuguezes, vol. 6. Lisboa: Impresna National.

CORRIGAN, P. (1977) "Feudal relics or capitalist monuments? Notes on the sociology of unfree labour." Sociology 11: 435-463.

DAAKU, K. Y. (1971) "Trade and trading patterns of the Akan in the seventeenth and eighteenth centuries," pp. 168-181 in C. Meillassoux (ed.) The Development of Indigenous Trade and Markets in West Africa. London: Oxford University Press.

DeMAREES, P. (1912) Beschryvinghe ende Historische Verhael van het Gout Konincrijck van Gunea anders de Gout-Custe de Mina genaemt liggende in het Deel van Africa, (S.P. L'Honore Naber, ed.). The Hague: Linschoten Society.

DIAS, M. N. (1960) "A organizacao da rota Atlantica do Ouro da Mina e os mecanismos dos resgates." Revista de Historia 44: 369-398.

DONELHA, A. (1977) An Account of Sierra Leone and the Rivers of Guinea and Cape Verde (1625). Lisbon: Junta de Investigacoes Cientificao do Ultramar, Centro de Estudos de Cartografia Artiga, no. 19.

FAGE, J. D. (1980a) "Slaves and society in western Africa, c. 1445-c. 1700." Journal of African History 21: 289-310.

———(1980b) "A commentary on Duarte Pacheco Pereira's account of the lower Guinea coastlands in his Esmeraldo de Situ Orbis and on some other early accounts." History in Africa 7.

FARO, J. A. (1958) "A organizacao fiscal de S. Jorge da Mina em 1529 e as suas relacoes com a ilha de S. Tome." Boletim Cultural da Guine 13: 305-365.

———(1957) "Estevao de Gama capitao de S. Jorge de Mina e a sua organizacao administrativa em 1529." Bolatim Cultural da Guine Portuguesa 12: 385-442.

FEINBERG, H. M. (1979) "An eighteenth-century case of plagiarism: William Smith's A New Voyage to Guinea." History in Africa, 6.

GUTKIND, P.C.W. (1983) "Workers are workers and Marxist intellectuals are mere intellectuals (said Alice)." Contemporary Marxism 7: 184-193.

———(1974) The Emergent African Proletariat. Montreal: McGill University, Centre for Developing Area Studies.

————(in press) "The canoemen of the Gold Coast (Ghana), 1481-1930; an exploration in pre-colonial African labour history," in Proceedings, Congresso International os Descrobrimentos Portuguese E A do Europa Renascimento, June 1983. Lisbon.

HAIR, P.E.H. (1974) "Barbot, Dapper, Dairty: a critique of sources on Sierra Leone and Cape Mount." History in Africa 1.

HENIGE, D. P. [ed.] (1972) A Guide to Rawlinson. (unpublished)

HOBSBAWM, E. J. (1964) Labouring Men. Studies in the History of Labour. London: Weidenfeld and Nicolson.

HOPKINS, A. G. (1967) "The western Sudan in the middle ages: underdevelopment in the empires of the Western Sudan." Past and Present 37 (July).

JENKINS, R. (1977-1978) "Impeachable source? On the use of the second edition of Reindorf's history as a primary source for the study of Ghanaian history, I." History in Africa 4.

JONES, G. S. (1973) "History: the poverty of empiricism," in R. Blackburn (ed.) Ideology in Social Science. New York: Random House.

————(1971) Outcast London: A Study in the Relationship Between Classes in Victorian Society. Oxford: Clarendon.

KAPLOW, S. B. (1978) "Primitive accumulation and traditional social relations on the nineteenth century Gold Coast." Canadian Journal of African Studies 12: 14-36.

KEA, R. A. (1982) Settlements, Trade, and Polities in the Seventeenth-Century Gold Coast. Baltimore: Johns Hopkins University Press.

————(1980) "Administration and trade in the Akwamu Empire, 1681-1730," pp. 371-392 in B. K. Swartz and R. E. Dumett (eds.) West African Cultural Dynamics: Archeological and Historical Perspectives. The Hague: Mouton.

————(n.d.a.) "Primitive accumulation and regional systems in Ghana: fifteenth-twentieth centuries." (unpublished)

————(n.d.b.) "I am here to plunder on the general road: bandits and banditry in the pre-nineteenth century Gold Coast." (unpublished)

————(n.d.c.) "Settlements, polities, and trade in the seventeenth century Gold Coast." (unpublished)

KLEIN, N. A. (1969) "West African unfree labour before and after the rise of the Atlantic slave trade," pp. 87-95 in L. Foner and E. D. Genovese (eds.) Slavery in the New World. Englewood-Cliffs, NJ: Prentice-Hall.

LAW, R. (1982) "Jean Barbot as a source for the Slave Coast of West Africa." History in Africa 9.

LAWRENCE, A. W. (1963) Trade Castles and Forts of West Africa. London: Cape.

LEE, R. B. (1979) The !Kung San: Men, Women and Work in a Foraging Society. New York: Cambridge University Press.

LEONS, M. B. and F. ROTHSTEIN [eds.] (1979) New Directions in Political Economy: An Approach from Anthropology. Westport, CT: Greenwood.

LUBECK, P. M. (1981) "Class formation on the periphery: class consciousness and Islamic nationalism among Nigerian workers," pp. 37-70 in R. L. Simpson and I. H. Simpson (eds.) Research in the Sociology of Work, vol. 1. Greenwich, CT: JAI.

MAJOR, R. H. (1967) The Life of Prince Henry of Portugal Surnamed the Navigator and Its Results from Authentic Contemporary Documents. London: F. Cass.

MALOWIST, M. (1967) "Rejoinder." Past and Present 37 (July).

————(1966) "The social and economic stability of the Western Sudan in the Middle Ages." Past and Present 33 (April).

MARX, K. (1977) Capital, vol. 1. New York: International Publishers.

————(1961) Capital, vol. 3 (F. Engels, ed.; S. Moore and E. Aveling, trans.) Moscow: Progress Publishers.

MAYHEW, H. (1968) London Labour and the London Poor. New York: Dover.

McLENNAN, G. (1981) Marxism and the Methodologies of History. London: New Left Books.

MEREDITH, H. (1967) An Account of the Gold Coast of Africa, with a Brief History of the African Company. London: F. Cass.

MOORE, D. and F. G. GUGGISBERG (1909) We Two in West Africa. New York: Scribner.

MULLER, W. J. (1968) Die Africanische auf der Guineische Gold-Cust Gelegene Landschaft Fetu. Hamburg: Graz Akademische Druck. (Originally published in 1676.)

O'CONNOR, J. (1975) "Productive and unproductive labor." Politics and Society 5: 297-336.

PRIESTLEY, M. (1965) "An early strike in Ghana." Ghana Notes and Queries 7: 25.

RATELBAND, K. [ed.] (1953) Vijf Dagregisters van het Kasteel São Jorge da Mina (Elmina) aan de Gout Kust, 1645-1647. The Hague: M. Nijhoff.

SANCEAU, E. (1969) The Reign of the Fortunate King 1495-1521. New York: Archon Books.

————(1959) The Perfect Prince: A Biography of the King Dom Joao II Who Continued the Work of Henry the Navigator. Porto: Livraria Civilizacao.

SANDBROOK, R. (1981) "Worker consciousness and populist protest in tropical Africa," pp. 1-36 in R. L. Simpson and I. H. Simpson (eds.) Research in the Sociology of Work, vol. 1. Greenwich, CT: JAI.

————and R. COHEN [eds.] (1975) The Development of an African Working Class: Studies in Class Formation and Action. London: Longman.

SARBAH, J. M. (1904) "The Gold Coast when Edward IV was king (1461-1483)." Journal of the African Society 3: 194-197.

TEIXEIRA da MOTA, A. (1978) "Some aspects of Portuguese colonization and sea trade in West Africa in the 15th and 16th centuries." Bloomington: University of Indiana, African Studies Program, Hans Wolff Memorial Lecture.

THOMPSON, E. P. (1978) The Poverty of Theory. London: Merlin.

VAN DANTZIG, A. (1976) "English Bosman and Dutch Bosman: a comparison of text." History in Africa 3-7, 9.

————(1974) "William Bosman's New and Accurate Description of the Coast of Guinea: How accurate is it?" History in Africa 1.

————and Priddy, B. (1971) A Short History of the Forts and Castles of Ghana. Accra: Ghana Museums and Monuments Board.

VILLAULT, N. (1669) Rélation des côtes d' Afrique appellées Guinée. Paris: Denys Thierry.

VOGT, J. L. (1979) Portuguese Rule on the Gold Coast, 1469-1682, Athens: Georgia University Press.

————(1974) "Private trade and slave sales at Sao Jorge da Mina: a fifteenth-century document." Transactions of the Historical Society of Ghana 15: 103-110.

3

MERCHANTS, PORTERS, AND CANOEMEN IN THE BIGHT OF BENIN
Links in the West African Trade Network

PATRICK MANNING

        The initial objective of this essay is to document the importance of two major trade routes that are left off virtually all maps of West African commerce (e.g., Hopkins, 1973: 59; Adamu, 1978: 65). These are the north–south porterage route from Grand Popo to Djougou, dominated by trade in salt, and the east-west canoe route from Lagos to Keta, dominated by food–stuffs trade. Their importance stems not only from the large volume of goods they carried, but from their strategic placement: The east-west route linked all the major coastal population centers between Accra and the Niger, while the north-south route provided the major link from the coast to the great interior route between Kano and Salaga. My second objective is to analyze the labor conditions along these long-distance routes: The analysis contrasts the porters, unspecialized, part-time workers who acted as petty trader-transporters, with the specialized canoemen, who worked in corporate groups and often received wages. The study begins with an analysis of the commerce and the work process along each route, and along various spurs and corollary routes of the Bight of Benin, at the opening of the twentieth century, when they are best documented. The third aspect of the essay, a longitudinal study of the nineteenth and early twentieth centuries, is intended to reaffirm the

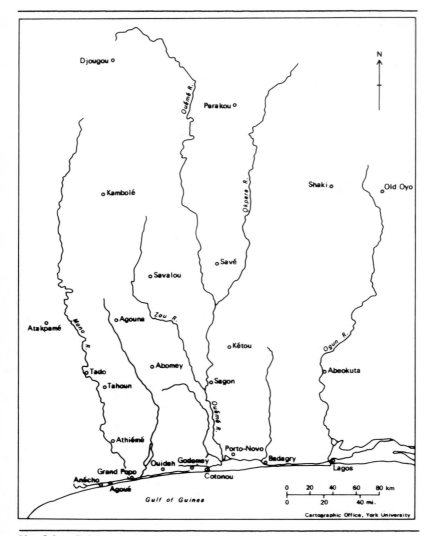

Map 3.1:   Dahomey, Late Nineteenth Century

significance of the routes, to further elucidate the nature of the work performed along them, and to show the impact of politics and changing technology on commerce.

THE WORK OF THE PORTERS

Most of the long-distance overland trade of nineteenth-century Bight of Benin was carried by unspecialized porters working on their own or in small groups. Overall, that is, the Bight of Benin head transport system contrasted sharply with the greater specialization and division of labor in the Hausa-dominated interior commerce, even though the two systems met at such junctures as Sansanné-Mango, Djougou, Parakou, Shaki, and Ilorin.

The patterns of such porters' work emerge most clearly from the documents on the north-south route from Agoué and Grand Popo to Djougou. This route, in common with other north-south routes from the Volta to the Niger, was focused on the movement of salt northward to the Niger valley, in return for the southward movement of foodstuffs. According to the observations of French administrators at Kambolé and Savalou in the early twentieth century, some 90 percent of the tonnage of northward-moving goods consisted of salt. The salt commerce recorded at the interior points of the trade route was a significant proportion of salt imports to colonial Dahomey: Total salt imports to Dahomey ranged from 1000 to 3000 tons per year, and roughly two-thirds of that amount went to Grand Popo. The salt observed passing Savalou and Kambolé ranged from 250 to 350 tons per year and, accepting the assessment of administrators there that they saw only 40% of the commerce, we would conclude that some 600 to 900 tons of salt per year passed northward along that route (Tables 3.1 and 3.5; Manning, 1982: 356-363, 378).

Of the other northward-moving goods, textiles were most important in volume and value, followed by dyes, beads, alcoholic beverages, gunpowder, guns, mats, and baskets. Small amounts of such goods as tobacco, matches, and copper bars were noted (Table 3.2). Cowries had ceased to be carried north by the time of this survey, but they had been important in earlier days.

Salt commerce in particular seems to have lent itself to pursuit by individuals and small groups, as is clear in a description of the activities of such individuals during February 1906:

Les négociants de Djougou se sont approvissionés et les grosses caravanes ne se reformeront que plus tard; pour le moment, ce sont des groupes

Table 3.1   Northward-bound Commerce Recorded at Kambolé, March 1905-February 1906[a]

Month	Persons	Salt (kg)	Textiles (pieces)	Dyes (pkgs)	Gunpowder (kg)	Guns (pcs)	Alcoholic Beverages (barrels)	Beads (pkgs)	Tobacco (kg)	Matches (pkgs)	Estimated kg/porter
March 1905	338	11,000	438	110	70	19	6	120			35
April	190	4,000	56	30	25	3	12	44			22
May	473	13,000	307	241	171	8	29	127			29
June											
July	567	19,000	197	242	366	13	11	11			35
August	597	20,000	332	524	199	15	22				35
September	497	18,000	390	100	198	5	20	54	9	121	38
October	682	24,000	246	42	50	20	10	38	17		36
November	731	18,000	173	297		5	12	40	5	19	25
December	1283	44,000	540	74	43	10	18		1	5	35
January 1906	730	35,000	243		17	24	3	1212		1	48
February	477	12,000	295	436	40	18	8	193	72	53	28
Total	6565	218,000	3217	2096	1179	140	151	1839	104	199	35 (median)

SOURCE: Archives Nationales du Dénin (ANB), 2-D-82, Savalou, March 1905-February 1906
a. Salt volumes converted from bags or loads to kilograms at the rate of 25 kilograms per bag.

Table 3.2 Southward-bound Commerce Recorded at Kambolé, March 1905-February 1906[a]

Month	Persons	Makari (kg)	Beans (kg)	Shea Butter (kg)	Pepper (kg)	Kola (kg)	Potash (kg)	Sopa (kg)	Turkeys (head)	Sheep (head)	Cattle (head)	Horses (head)	Estimated kg/porter
March 1905	280		2,600	150	b				b	13	36	22	10
April	243		2,200		b	75			20	5	7	3	9
May	245		1,100		b	200				10	12	3	5
June													
July	593	6,500	1,800			50				12	21	1	14
August	629	8,600	1,900	450		25				17	17	3	17
September	594	4,100	3,800	1,800		75	375			7	10		17
October	494	3,300	1,800	4,450		75	b		39	6	6	3	20
November	1547	12,300	7,100	8,400	50	50		675		15	15	3	19
December	1187	7,500	4,100	7,400	125	275	125	325		10	23	1	17
January 1906	1172	12,600	3,800	6,400	75		550	125	74		20	6	20
February	437	3,800	900	1,600	50		500			7	26	9	16
Total	7421	58,700	31,100	30,650	250	825	1000	1125	133	202	193	51	17 (median)

SOURCE: ANB, 2-D-82, Savalou, March 1905-February 1906.
a. Weight figures given in kilograms in source. Other products listed, without volume, included calabashes and mats.
b. Listed but no quantity given.

de 3 à 4 Gambaris au plus, faisant du cabotage, le sel étant monté par tous les indigènes de Savalou, Banté, Cabolé, Bassila qu'ils soient ou non commerçants.

Des qu'ils ont un pécule suffisant, ils se rendent à Abomey, Toffo, Paouignan et même Savalou, achètent un sac de sel qu'ils vont vendre a Bassila, Aledjo, Léméré ou Djougou. Les autres articles sont l'apanage des négociants Gambaris ou nagots.[1]

That is, during the dry season, the roads were dominated not by the caravans of large Gambari (that is, Hausa and other northern) merchants, but by traders and cultivators from the region north of Djalloukou and south of Djougou who took their savings and a load of agricultural produce south to exchange for salt, which they then carried north. The commodities of a less prosaic and elementary nature remained in the hands of the Gambari and of certain Yoruba merchants.

Human porters, rather than donkeys, carried the salt and other goods along this route. Donkeys are scarcely mentioned in the records of this trade (except for the occasional driving of a lone animal to the south for sale), a pattern that reaffirms the contrast of transport on this route with that of the further interior. The porters carried heavy loads of up to 40 to 50 kilograms of salt, and moved their loads by carrying them a distance of some 800 to 1000 meters, after which they rested their burdens against the fork of a tree, assisted in this by a pole that they carried for that purpose. The size of the burdens is borne out by administrative statistics: the median burden, as measured both at Kambolé and Savalou, was 35 kilograms per person[2] (Table 3.1). The median figure is brought down because not all caravan members carried full burdens—some drove animals, and the children in the caravans carried smaller loads. An estimate of some 700 persons in caravans passing Abomey on their way from Savalou to Cotonou indicates that one-third of them were women and 5 percent were children, but it gives no indication as to the size of the burdens women carried (Table 3.4).

The standard day's journey was roughly 25 kilometers, perhaps slightly less for those carrying salt. The 400-kilometer journey from the coast to Djougou thus required some sixteen days plus rest stops. Assuming a layover of two weeks at the terminus, a full-time porter would make a one-way journey from Djougou to Grand Popo in a month and a round-trip journey in two months; such a porter would

Table 3.3   Persons Moving in Caravans through Kambolé, 1905-1907

| | 1905 | | 1906 | | 1907 | |
Month	Northward	Southward	Northward	Southward	Northward	Southward
January			730	1172	1482	1155
February			477	437	1199	1237
March	338	280	348	511	1470	1274
April	190	243	817	516		
May	473	245	524	493		
June			549	558		
July	567	593	470	467		
August	597	629	120	117		
September	497	594	204	408		
October	682	494	830	937		
November	731	1547	739	602		
December	1283	1187	1054	925		

SOURCE: ANB, 2-D-82, Savalou, March 1905-March 1907.

Table 3.4   Southward Commercial Movement at Abomey, 1910

Month	Men	Women	Children	Burdens	Cattle	Sheep and Goats
Jan.-Feb.	117	45	17	239	236	120
March	38	28	16		142	21
April	141	52	4	133	89	145
May	128	94		115	231	256

SOURCE: ANB, 2-D-2, Abomey, March-May 1910.

be able to make six trips in a year. If one thousand tons of goods moved north each year in burdens of 35 kilograms on the heads of porters who made six trips a year, it would take roughly 5000 full-time porters to carry the commerce along this route. In fact, since many of the porters were not full-time specialists, the total number of people involved in porterage along this route was much larger than 5000 (Table 3.3). Further, since the total male and female adult population in the region through which this commerce passed was within the range of from 40,000 to 80,000, it may be seen that transport along the route was indeed a major activity for this region (Afrique Occidentale Français [AOF], 1911).

The southward-bound trade, dominated by commerce in the agricultural produce of the inland areas, further clarifies the character of this route as one carried by small-scale rather than large-scale commerce. The main product, both in volume and in value, was *makari,* a green paste made from the fruit of the nété or African locust bean tree. Shea butter was next in importance: It was used for cooking in

Table 3.5   Salt Moving Northward, Kambolé and Savalou, 1905-1914, in Kilograms

Month	1905 (Kambolé)	1906 (Kambolé)	1912 (Savalou)	1913 (Savalou)	1914 (Savalou)
January		35,000	35,500		48,000
February		12,000			
March	11,000				
April	4,000		53,470		
May	13,000				
June				24,750	32,990
July	19,000		12,870		
August	20,000				21,400
September	18,000				10,775
October	24,000				36,675
November	18,000		53,235		46,695
December	44,000				12,040

SOURCE: ANB, 2-D-82, Savalou, March 1905-February 1906; 2-D-83, Savalou, January 1912-December 1914.

areas north of the oil palm forest, and soap made from shea butter was also carried southward. Beans followed shea butter closely in volume and value. Small numbers of cattle, sheep, and horses were driven southward. Mats, calabashes, and pepper were other goods of northern provenance that flowed southward: These goods, rarely reported by European observers, seem sometimes to have dominated southward-bound caravans[3] (Table 3.2).

Certain of the southward-moving goods, however, were surely linked to the efforts of large-scale merchants whose geographical range and financial power exceeded those of the small-scale porters who were most numerous on this route. Kola, for instance, was diverted in small quantities from its primary destination of the Sokoto Caliphate, and flowed into the kingdom of Danhomè and neighboring areas. In addition natron, mined near Lake Chad, was exported in all directions, and some of it came south along this route (Table 3.2; Lovejoy, 1985).

An east-west porterage route, linking such towns of the coastal plateau as Abeokuta, Abomey, and Atakpamé, intersected the Grand Popo-Djougou route at Tahoun in the middle Mono valley: This route focused on the exchange of local manufactures and foodstuffs but also carried goods from Europe and from the far interior. At the Dahomey-Nigeria border between Kétou and Meko, the main products moving west in 1912 were natron, originating in northern Nigeria, dyes, Yoruba textiles, jars, calabashes, gunpowder, and beads. Goods moving eastward were dominated by guns, gunpowder, pepper, kola, textiles, and sheep.[4] Some of the livestock came from the region of Abomey. West of Abomey, as registered in December 1905, the westward trade included ceramic jars, cowries, oranges, natron, and calabashes, while the eastward trade was led by maize, but also included beans, indigo, and textiles. During that month, just after harvest, 4800 loads (some 120 tons) were carried eastward, and 2700 loads (65 tons) were carried westward.[5] This trade carried on, step by step, to Tahoun, Atakpamé, and other points west. By a calculation similar to that carried out above for the north-south route, one may estimate that this level of transport required, for the Abomey plateau, a full-time equivalent labor force of some 2000 porters, which may be set against an adult male population of roughly 30,000 for the region (AOF, 1911).

THE WORK OF THE CANOEMEN

European writers on the Bight of Benin, while recognizing the great importance of canoe transport along the lagoons and rivers, rarely sought out details on the volume of commerce, on the organization of transportation, or on the financing of the water-borne commerce. Instead they contented themselves with capsule portraits of lagoon transport, of which the best was given by the agronomist Norbert Savariau (1906: 27):

> Il existe dans tous les centres importants riverains des lagunes ou des cours d'eau de véritables corporations de piroguiers ayant chacune un chef auquel les intèressés s'adressent pour se procurer les pirogues dont ils ont besoin. Les prix de transport sont toujours établis à forfait, c'est-à-dire à l'avantage du plus rusé des deux traitants. On peut les évaluer en moyenne à 0 fr. 02 par tonne kilométrique. Nous deduisons ce chiffre des tarifs usités entre Porto-Novo et Cotonou.

Two-person canoes, usually of four to five meters in length and fifty to sixty centimeters in breadth, carried a sizable amount of such short-distance commerce as could be accommodated to the trade of fish. Among the Tofin of Lake Nokoué the women's trade canoes, known as "mosquito canoes," were often somewhat smaller than the men's fishing canoes. Larger dugout canoes, up to some 12 meters in length and 140 centimeters in width, could transport twenty to thirty persons or a cargo of two to three tons; these traveled longer distances and

carried a wider range of goods. Crews of four to six men propelled
such canoes by poles or paddles; they also employed a mast and sail
that could be hoisted in a favorable wind. The largest lagoon boats
were flat-bottomed, up to twenty meters in length and four or five
meters in width. Crews of four to six "taximen" transported cargoes
of five tons or up to seventy persons between main towns and ports,
also relying on paddles, poles, or sail (Bourgoignie, 1972: 194-196;
Gruvel, 1913: 83; Foà, 1895: 142). The ethnic specialization of
canoemen reflected this technical and occupational differentiation:
Fishing specialists of the coast, including the Tofin of Lake Nokoué
and the Hueda of Lake Ahémè, relied primarily on small canoes; the
specialized canoemen who hired themselves out came dominantly from
the Gen of the Togo lagoons, the Hula of Grand Popo and Kéténou,
the Tori of the Porto-Novo lagoon, and such riverain Yoruba peoples
as the Ijebu.

A break in the coastal lagoon system—necessitating a porterage between two parallel lagoons at some point between Ouidah and
Godomey—divided the canoe transport system in two. To the east,
large canoes linked Godomey and Abomey-Calavi with Porto-Novo,
Badagri and Lagos; in addition, canoes went up the Ouémé River as
far as Sagon, and in the 1880s they began to go in growing numbers
to the port of Cotonou. In the west, large canoes went along the lagoon
from Avrékété and Ouidah to Grand Popo, Agoué, and on to Keta;
canoes went up the Mono to Tokpli and, in smaller numbers, up the
Couffo to Long Agomey. Several observers attested to the importance
of the nineteenth-century water-borne trade in foodstuffs—for
example, from the hinterland of Agoué, a rich agricultural area with
a major regional market, to Ouidah with its concentration of population (Lambinet, 1893: 15, 22; d'Albéca, 1889: 61; Fonssagrives, 1900:
382; Bouche, 1885: 305). Lagos, as it grew, exerted a similar attraction on the areas west and north of it.

The 30-kilometer journey from Porto-Novo to Cotonou took six
hours by canoe, and the 35 kilometers between Ouidah and Grand
Popo took six to eight hours, the latter journey requiring that the
canoemen negotiate their way through numerous barrages maintained by fishermen. Officials at strategically placed toll gates collected
fees on passengers and merchandise. At the mouth of the Aro, the
effluent of Lake Ahémè, which formed the south-western frontier of
Danhomè, the fee for passing Europeans in the 1880s was one head
of cowries plus a bottle of tafia (rum); local merchants paid as much

as one-tenth of their cargo plus some tafia (d'Albéca, 1895: 152). The trade canoes moved at a speed of some five kilometers per hour, roughly twice the speed of porters. Freight rates of 0.2 francs per ton-kilometer were about one-fifth the rate for head porterage. At the same time, this work appears to have provided revenues that reached three francs per day per worker, and that therefore permitted both a profit for the canoe owner and a canoeman's wage, which exceeded the porter's daily wage of roughly one franc (Savariau, 1906: 27; d'Albéca, 1889: 57; 1895: 151; Bouche, 1885: 300).

Another group of boatmen transported goods across the hazardous surf to and from European ships that anchored from one to three kilometers offshore. The work of the surf boatmen was, if anything, more strenuous and certainly more dangerous than that of the lagoon canoemen. Along the coast of Togo and at Grand Popo this work was done by Gen and Hula boatmen, while at Ouidah and Godomey beach the boatmen were Ga from Accra; east of Cotonou, most goods crossed the surf via Lagos harbor, with incoming and outgoing goods moving between Lagos and other points through the lagoon network. Many of the surf boats were owned by European merchant firms. At Cotonou—before construction of the pier in 1893, after which lighters no longer had to pass through the surf—these firms hired boatmen at a salary of thirty francs per month plus a ration of rice, as well as a bottle of tafia each day, and a bottle of tafia to be divided among the crew with each trip; the boats made a maximum of sixteen trips each day (d'Albéca, 1895: 10).

Boatmen working both in the surf and in the lagoons were widely reputed to have added to their wages by stealing from the cargoes they were handling. At times, as we will see below, such theft took on the character of group rather than individual activity.

Boats were hired, as Savariau (1906: 27) implied, individually or in groups; fees went, therefore, to individual boat owners, or to owners of fleets of boats, or to corporations of boat owners. The evidence thus makes it appear that the roles of merchant and transporter were distinct, though it remains possible that large merchants may have owned fleets of canoes. The chief of the town of Sagon, situated at a strategic head of navigation on the Ouémé River, had control over a fleet of canoes and large numbers of porters.[6] This may, however, have simply been political control rather than actual ownership or employment of the canoes, porters, and boatmen. Thus, while it is

clear that the large canoes were owned by firms, the internal organization of the firms remains hazy. Many canoemen, however, were clearly
wage workers, employed by canoe owners (Fonssagrives, 1900: 384-386;
Couchard, 1911: 56).[7] Lineages and slavery, on the other hand, provided alternative forms for labor organization. Many slaves passed
through the hands of boat owners, making it likely that many
canoemen were recruited via enslavement. Further, the corporate
lineage structure among the Gen, Hula, and other lagoon peoples was
such that young men were not simply free agents to be employed at
the going rate, but men who could be pressed into work through the
manipulation of family ties, and who could also be given the hope
of rising to a position of influence in the family and in the canoe
corporation.

If the precise organization of the canoe work force remains
speculative, its numbers may be surmised through estimates of the
volume of merchandise transported. For the transport of goods across
the surf, some 40,000 tons of goods were carried each way annually
in colonial Dahomey at the end of the nineteenth century; slightly
smaller amounts were moved in Togo, and larger quantities were moved
in Lagos. These estimates are consistent with a full-time equivalent
work force of perhaps 400 boatmen with some seventy boats for the
coast of colonial Dahomey, or 1000 canoemen for the entire Bight of
Benin, based on assumptions of six men per crew, ten trips per day,
150 days per year, with cargoes of one ton each. A much larger work
force was required for lagoon transport because of the longer distances
involved: assuming a minimal volume of 40,000 tons carried each way
annually, one may guess that some 1000 full-time equivalent canoemen,
with 180 boats, were required for each thirty-kilometer segment of the
coast, which corresponds to 5000 for the area of colonial Dahomey
and perhaps 10,000 for the entire Bight of Benin. This estimate is based
on assumptions of a two-ton cargo being moved thirty kilometers per
day by a crew of six working 200 days per year. Some confirmation
of these estimates is provided by the fact that the French Army, in
its invasion of Danhomè in 1892, requisitioned a reported twenty of
the flat-bottomed, twenty-meter boats and 100 of the twelve-meter
boats: This imposition required crews totaling some seven hundred
men, probably a majority of those available in the region (d'Albéca,
1895: 70; Ross, 1971: 144-169). Additional confirmation comes from
the volume of palm products moved each year via lagoon from Porto-
Novo to Lagos (Manning, 1982: 347, 352-354).

Something of the outlook of the canoemen, and of their ability to defend their interests through group action, may be gleaned from the conflicts surrounding the construction of a road inland from Grand Popo in 1910 and 1911. The conflicts centered about the region's commandant de cercle, Antoine Rouhaud, who became widely known as "l'homme de la route de Grand Popo à Lokossa." The idea of a road crossing the marshes that surrounded the lower Mono was a threat to the livelihood of canoemen in any case: It would divert the southernmost leg of the Grand Popo-Djougou route from the river to land. Rouhaud, however, compounded the conflict by diverting funds that should have gone to canoe transport, cutting boatmen's wages in half, and by relying heavily on forced labor.

Construction began in May 1910, and immediately various groups of boatmen began selective slowdowns of transport. Canoemen in Athiémé, near the head of navigation on the Mono, opposed construction of the road, and European merchants there reported numerous thefts. The merchants had to call on canoes from Grand Popo to get goods moved down the river. The German merchants in Grand Popo were able to find boatmen, but the French had to come to the administration for help. Canoe transportation of goods from Grand Popo to Ouidah, which normally took six or seven hours, was taking up to six days for French houses (Manning, 1982: 207-209).

After the suspension of road construction and the transfer of Rouhaud, the conflict continued, though in a different vein. The focus of the slowdown now shifted to the surf boats and to the German houses. When the firm of Althof reported a theft of goods, the administration found some of the goods among some boatmen, and sentenced fifty of them to penalties of up to two years in prison. The other boatmen refused to land goods for Althof at any price for several months, and some ships were forced to leave port without loading or unloading their cargoes. The administrator attempted to mediate between the boatmen and the commercial houses but had to be satisfied with handing an ultimatum to the canoe chiefs that they would have to end their boycott or they would be arrested and forced to work on the roads, from which they had previously been exempt. To punctuate his threat, he arrested ten boatmen. A subsequent dispute flared up in December 1911, as canoemen refused to take loads to Ouidah for the firm of Cyprien Fabre because it was too late in the day. The administrator rejected Fabre's complaint, but warned the boatmen that they should obey their chiefs and employers.[8] Both the unity and the divisions among canoemen are revealed in their conflicts with employers and government.

CHANGING PATTERNS OF COMMERCE AND TRANSPORT WORK

From the eighteenth century into the twentieth century, the needs in the Bight of Benin for foodstuffs, salt, and local manufactures provided stability in the commerce along the main routes of the region. In contrast, the old trade in slaves and the new trade in palm products overlaid the underlying stability of this commerce with disturbances and successive transformations. Before 1770 the slave trade of the Bight of Benin, the most active of any African region but Angola, had drawn overwhelmingly on captives from the Aja peoples of the coastal band—that is, from Danhomè and the areas immediately surrounding that kingdom. The slaves from the interior of the Bight of Benin were taken among the Bariba and the peoples of the Atakora mountains, and they were evacuated along the western route, through Grand Popo, to avoid the high duties of Danhomè and its port of Ouidah (Manning, 1982: 35-36). Then the Oyo empire deepened its involvement in slave exports, particularly in the reign of the *alafin* Abiodun (1774-1789), and promoted the route from Oyo south and west to Porto-Novo, along which many Yoruba slaves were sold; the Shabe kingdom was allied to Oyo and the town of Savè was thus linked to this commerce. Further north, the wars of the Sokoto Caliphate resulted in the capture and export of many slaves after 1804; Hausa and Nupe slaves were, for a brief time, exported in large numbers in the late eighteenth and early nineteenth century (Law, 1977: 176-180; Marty, 1926: 142-144; Manning, 1982: 335).

The breakup of the Oyo empire during the 1820s led to the export of a much larger number of Yoruba slaves and to an eastward deflection of their routes of evacuation: In a major political realignment, Danhomè, now freed from a century of subservience to Oyo, expanded its influence eastward, while Ibadan and Abeokuta rose as new centers of Yoruba political influence. Danhomè greatly weakened the Shabe and Ketu kingdoms and entered into a half-century of confrontation with Abeokuta. Porto-Novo, now brought under the influence of Danhomè rather than Oyo, lost its position as terminus of the main eastern route first to Badagri and then to Lagos, although Porto-Novo remained the staging point for the route running up the Ouémé River and to Parakou (Law, 1977: 278-302; Biobaku, 1957).

In the second half of the nineteenth century the export of slaves declined to a virtual halt. Lagos had become, during the 1840s, the regional slave exporting center, but the British occupation in 1851 ended that. Slave exporting had become a clandestine business: In hurried transactions, slaves came to be traded against silver coin— Maria Theresa dollars— rather than against bulky goods and cowries. In Danhomè all available surf boats, including those of European palm oil merchants, were occasionally requisitioned to load slaves who had been force-marched to a point of embarcation (Laffitte, 1873: 124-125). The domestic trade in slaves continued, however, now oriented around the needs of palm oil producers.

Palm oil, for which serious exports from Ouidah began in the 1830s, had by the 1850s become the main export from the Bight of Benin, and palm kernels provided a significant addition to export revenue beginning in the 1860s. The Atlantic commerce of the region became, more than ever before, focused on its coastal fringe. This new commerce relied heavily on water transport, but it also required the development of paths on which to roll 300-gallon puncheons and a new work force of puncheon-rollers, as well as a network for bulking oil and kernels.

This rising coastal commerce in palm products reinforced certain aspects of commerce with the interior. The Brazilian repatriates who settled in Agoué and other points between Keta and Lagos, particularly from the 1840s to the 1860s, illustrate the links of coastal and interior trade. The d'Almeida family, for instance, claimed origins among the Mahi of Savalou and the Yoruba north of Savalou. While the d'Almeidas were active in commerce all along the coast, they were also well placed to participate in ventures along the route to Djougou (Turner, 1975: 102-114). Salt, cowries, foodstuffs, and slaves provided the links between the rising palm oil trade and the interior commerce.

Palm oil exports generated continuing demand for slaves, as labor was required for palm oil production, porterage, and canoeing. The royal and private oil palm plantations of Danhomè depended upon this slave labor. Outside that kingdom the major slave markets at Tahoun on the western route and at Okeodan to the east supplied planters in those areas (Newbury, 1961: 36; d'Albéca, 1895: 168; Coquery-Vidrovitch, 1972: 107-123; Manning, 1982: 50-56). These markets thrived almost until the end of the century. Most of the slaves sold there came from the Yoruba and Aja peoples within the Bight of Benin, but Gambari merchants brought in some slaves from more northerly regions.

Demand for palm oil caused European merchants to resume delivery of Indian Ocean cowrie shells to the Bight of Benin, now to be exchanged for palm oil. The supply of cowries—the money of the Bight of Benin for the previous two centuries at least, imported in exchange for slaves—may have been cut back sharply in the early nineteenth century, limiting money supplies for both coast and interior. The resumption of cowrie imports with the rise of palm oil trade meant that sacks of calciferous currency flowed not only into the hands of coastal planters, but also moved into the interior in exchange for slaves, agricultural commodities, and manufactures. But as German merchants in the 1850s and 1860s introduced East African cowries, the volume of cowrie imports grew to the point where prices inflated rapidly, and transport of burdens of inflated currency ultimately became impractical (Hogendorn and Johnson, in press).

In addition to cowries, merchants began importing European salt to exchange for palm oil and kernels; this salt competed with the domestic salt-purifying industry centered in the lagoons adjoining Grand Popo and Kéténou. The lagoon industry had supplied consumers both on the coast and, via the Grand Popo-Djougou route, in the interior, and it survived, despite foreign competition, well into the twentieth century. Hula and Hueda villagers in the vicinity of Grand Popo still produced an estimated one hundred tons of salt in 1940 (Grivot, 1944: 23-24; Officiers, 1895: 54; Foà, 1895: 134; d'Albéca, 1895: 57). To the east, the Hula of Kéténou also purified salt and in the nineteenth century sent salt northward via Porto-Novo, Savè, and Shaki. One may speculate that, with the rise of salt imports, the people of the areas of Grand Popo and Kéténou cut back their activities as saltmakers and diverted their energies to expanded involvement in production and transport of palm products. Salt dominated merchandise moving inland, with imported salt progressively displacing domestic salt. Cowries and slaves declined in importance on the Grand Popo-Djougou route after the mid-nineteenth century; after that, neither of these commodities ever threatened the position of salt.

The merchant population and its activities changed along with the trade. Slave merchants redirected their efforts toward the provision of a work force for oil palm plantations; merchants on the Atlantic littoral began exporting palm oil as well as slaves. During this mid-century transition two Brazilian merchants—Francisco Felix de Souza and Domingo Martins—dominated the export trade of Danhomè in slaves and palm oil; their commercial leadership serves also to emphasize that, at this time, the Atlantic import and export trades of

the Bight of Benin remained oriented toward Brazil and the Carib-
bean (Turner, 1975: 88-102; Ross, 1965: 79-90; Manning, 1982: 46-56).
European merchants settled on the coast beginning in 1841, after an
absence of several decades, but not until the end of the century had
the Europeans, exporting palm products and importing cowries, textiles, alcoholic beverages, and salt, fully displaced the Brazilians and
reoriented Bight of Benin commerce toward Europe.

Much of the east-west commerce along the coastal route in the late
nineteenth century was handled by immigrant groups, particularly
Brazilians and Saros (Sierra Leonians). Brazilian families, dominant
in the trade of Anecho and Agoué, were also significant in the trade
of Grand Popo, Ouidah, Porto-Novo and Lagos (Kopytoff, 1965;
Turner, 1975). The Saros, though less numerous than the Brazilians,
came to dominate the trade of Lagos. These networks stretched into
the interior, as with the Saro connection to Abeokuta and the Brazilian
ties to the interior from Porto-Novo and Agoué. Merchants based in
coastal and interior towns were also significant: Leading Ijebu and
Abeokuta merchants may be noted (Biobaku, 1957). In Danhomè the
equivalent merchants, known as *ahisinon,* were chartered by the
monarchy and were led by such Ouidah families as Adjovi, Houenou
(Quénum), and Dagba (Quénum, 1938: 134-135; Forbes, 1851: II,
112-113; Marty, 1926: 105-107). Further west, Gen merchant families,
bearing such names as Lawson and Johnson, competed with the
Brazilian merchants (Newbury, 1961: 38, 113; Manning, 1982: 263).
Gambari merchants established *zongos* (caravansarai) in each of the
main towns of the Bight of Benin. Paul Marty toured these zongos
in colonial Dahomey early in the twentieth century, and reported
groups of 1000 Gambari in Ouidah, several hundred in Porto-Novo
and in Grand Popo, and smaller numbers in other centers (Marty, 1926:
94-95, 112-113, 116-117, 122, 131, 135). Further inland, beyond the
oil palm belt, the roles of merchant and king seem to have overlapped
more thoroughly. Kpohizon, who was king of Tado, the ancestral
center of Aja-Ewe kingship, acted as a merchant as well as a king:
In fact a commercial dispute with Gbaguidi, king of Savalou, ultimately
led Kpohizon into conflict with the French and to his deposition and
exile in 1900.[9] The king of Danhomè also participated in commerce,
though indirectly through agents (Bay, 1979: 1-15).

The merchants recruited transport labor by relying on their wealth
in association with a variety of mechanisms. The ahisinon of Danhomè
and the great merchants of Ijebu were heads of large lineages and sus-

tained large followings by maintaining their family structures. The Brazilian families grew in size because of the accretion of relatives through marriage, the attraction of clients and the incorporation of slaves. Gambari merchants, in order to build retinues, drew on family structures and on the need of young men to gain commercial experience. In addition to utilizing these institutions, merchants could recruit labor through wage employment and by appealing to states for support in recruitment. The majority of transport workers were apparently of free rather than slave status, although little information on the relative number of each is yet available (Oroge, 1971: 146-211).

Porters and canoemen worked in the manners described above well into the twentieth century. But the scope of their activity underwent progressive restriction and its nature was ultimately transformed by economic and political constraints. In the end, the most powerful forces of restriction and transformation were those of technological innovation and capitalist investment. But just as precolonial border changes had displaced trade routes, so too did the drawing and redrawing of colonial frontiers bring new limits to commerce.

With the mid-nineteenth-century expansion of the influence of Danhomè, regional trade routes became increasingly oriented toward Abomey. At the same time, Porto-Novo provided a second focus of trade because of its alliance with France (tentatively in the 1860s and then decisively in 1882). The drawing of colonial frontiers, in turn, led to more dramatic changes in routes. The French, with a foothold in Porto-Novo, sought to end the commercial dependence of that town on Lagos and worked energetically to build up the new port of Cotonou. This policy, in turn, led to confrontation with Danhomè and to the eventual French conquest; France also succeeded, after 1895, in reducing Porto-Novo's ties to Lagos. Virtually all of Porto-Novo's Atlantic trade prior to 1895 was transshipped at Lagos: some 20 percent of both imports and exports recorded at Lagos was in fact transit trade to Porto-Novo (Manning, 1982: 344). Nonetheless, the importance of Lagos as a regional metropolis was now such that the ties could not be wholly interrupted. Even before the twentieth century, a substantial smuggling industry grew up along the lagoon linking Porto-Novo and Lagos, which spread to the adjoining land routes, and which grew in importance with the passage of the colonial era (Mondjannagni, 1963: 17-57).

Political changes along the western frontier of colonial Dahomey, however, had a more severe effect on trade. Anecho in German Togo was cut off from Agoué in 1887, and in 1897 the French ceded to Togo the entire right bank of the Mono River, with the result that Agoué was severed from its hinterland: Across the lagoon lay the village of Agouégan (site of a major regional market for provisions), the fields of the farmers of Agoué, and the trade route to the north. German taxes and customs regulations cut off most contact across the lagoon, and within months Agoué declined from a flourishing port to a village dominated by old people. In 1914 the French ceded to Togo the canton of Tado, in the lower Mono valley, and the canton of Kambolé, two hundred kilometers inland: The towns promptly declined, and the western trade route underwent another contraction (Garcia, 1969: 36-44).[10]

More important in redirecting trade were the railroads. As the railroads in Dahomey, Lagos Colony, and Togo reached inland to the coastal plateaus, they almost immediately captured the carrying trade in salt. The old routes from Grand Popo, Porto-Novo, and Badagri were truncated, and certain rail stations replaced them as the key points in transshipping salt "to the caravans" (Officiers, 1894: 42). While the northern portion of the salt trade continued much as before, the old coastal segments of that trade died out at the turn of the twentieth century, and those who lived by that commerce were powerless to prevent its diversion. This collapse brought unmistakable reverberations along the southern segment of the western route. Chiefs in dry areas along the route—in Aplahoué, Adjaha, and Agouna, for instance—applied to the French administration to dig wells to give the caravans easier access to water, and a flurry of well-digging ensued, but to no avail. Disputes among merchants and canoemen broke out on the southern, water-borne portion of the route as business contracted. The efforts of Antoine Rouhaud, the overachieving administrator, to build a great road from Grand Popo to Lokossa may be seen as an attempt to regain the region's lost commerce, but Rouhaud succeeded only in bringing the area to the verge of rebellion (Manning, 1982: 181).

The more easterly route, running north from Porto-Novo, had already been a casualty of the fall of Oyo in the early nineteenth century, and the railroad reduced its importance even further. A long-distance trade in salt, textiles, staple foods, and local manufactures continued to be based in Porto-Novo, but it was much diminished by the decline of the towns of Kétou, Savè, Shaki, and Old Oyo. The Ouémé River, long a part of this route to the interior, was later reduced to the status of a local artery as rail lines were built on either side of it. Indeed, the story of Aholoupé, confirmed by the French as chief of the canton centered on Sagon, at the head of navigation on the Ouémé, reveals something of the organization of this trade route, even though the story depicts its disassemblage:

> Autrefois le Chef du canton de Sagon était le plus riche de tous. Tout le mouvement de voyageurs et de marchandises du Sud au Nord et vice-verse, se faisait par l'Ouémé jusqu'a Sagon ; le chef fournissait journelle-ment des piroguiers, des porteurs et des hamacaires en grand nombre. Il touchait des primes importantes. Cette source de bénéfices est pres-que complètement tarie, depuis la création du chemin de fer et le Chef de Sagon n'avait pas la chance de trouver une compensation dans les remises provenant des travaux de la voie ferrée, parce que ses administrés, mal conseillés par les féticheurs, refusaient de se rendre sur les chan-tiers. Aholoupé et son sous-chef Ahijadé étaient donc devenus pauvres. Ils s'étaient laissés aller, pour se procurer des ressources, a des exac-tions qui ont soulevé contre eux non seulement les chefs de village, mais aussi la population toute entière du canton. Ce mouvement populaire a abouti à des plaintes portées devant moi, au remplacement des deux chefs et à leur comparution au justice.
>
> J'espère que cette petite révolution aura de salutaires effets.[12]

The laborers could respond to the loss of their livelihood only by disappearing, and the big men could respond only by pressing additional exactions on their laborers: It was left to the colonial administration to organize the "revolution" and to reestablish peace and quiet.

As the colonial era proceeded, railroads and particularly trucks replaced porterage. The canoe transport system, however, remained remarkably resilient in the face of the threats of rail and motor transport. The lagoon route was affected by modern technology over one short stretch, where the railroad from Cotonou to Ouidah and Segbohoué (completed in 1906) could compete effectively because of the need for a portage in the lagoon route between Godomey and Grand Popo. It took the colonial government until 1930 to link the towns of Cotonou and Porto-Novo—thirty kilometers apart—by road and rail; in the interim, the fleet of lagoon canoes maintained contact between the port and the capital. Surf boats, too, survived into the 1930s, as some small freighters still called at Grand Popo (Desanti, 1945: 209; Manning, 1982: 147).

THE SOCIAL RELATIONS OF TRANSPORTATION

Transportation in the Bight of Benin was more than just a technical function that needed to be performed; it was a major economic activity that both reflected and influenced the overall social order. The work of transportation, both for local and long-distance commerce, required a level of labor input that may be estimated at from 5 percent to 15 percent of the total labor output of the region (Manning, 1982: 82-84). The large role of transportation in the total regional output of labor was required for two reasons: the devotion of the region's people to commerce, both local and long-distance, and the relative inefficiency of the transport system, especially that of head porterage. In the twentieth century, rail and motor transport would enable the region to rely even more heavily on commerce but with a much smaller labor input.

The transportation system was linked to other elements of the economy not only because of the commodities that were passed among merchants and from producer to consumer, but because the labor force also did work in other and competing areas. In good agricultural years, more labor was required to tend and harvest the bumper crops; yet more labor was also required to carry the produce to market. Such strains of competitive labor demand were less serious in canoe transport, where laborers were specialized to that task, than in porterage. In poor years, labor released from the fields tended to seek out porterage work. Salt production, of course, did not depend on the level of local agricultural output, but demand for imported salt did. Thus the demand for labor in transportation was regulated, in the short run, by the annual agricultural cycle and the vagaries of the harvest; in the long run, demand for labor was regulated by the level of commercial activity and the backward technology of porterage (Manning, 1982: 83-84, 112-113).

As noted above, the internal organization of this work force is more difficult to analyze than are its activities and even its size. The social order of nineteenth-century Bight of Benin, as it underwent repeated transformations, appears in one sense to have been fluid and in another sense to have been complex and contradictory. Competing organizational systems for labor coexisted, and individuals moved back and forth among them.

Among the boatmen, three labor systems coexisted. In the lineage system, boats owned by a family were manned by lineage members who received remuneration from the boat chief or family chief, and who remained members of the family firm with opportunity for rising within it. In the slave system, boatmen were the property of the boat chief or boat owner: They received subsistence for their work, but otherwise had little right to participate in the affairs of the firm. In the wage system, boatmen received daily or monthly wages, and their connections with the boat owner or firm owner did not extend beyond that wage contract.

While elements of each of these labor systems are clearly visible in the documents on Bight of Benin canoe transport, the boundaries between the systems remained hazy. Certainly it was possible to pay a wage to a lineage member, or to allow a slave to rise in the firm, or to link a wage earner to the family. Even the limits of the firm are hard to define—the firm might have been as small as the operation of an individual boat, or as large as a great agricultural and commercial complex which owned a fleet.

For the porters, the activity of individual porters working on their own account can be treated as a commodity exchange (or simple commodity production) system (Manning, 1982: 7). Viewed in this way, the porters acted as atomistic participants in the transportation system. With a slightly different emphasis, however, these same porters could be seen as having participated in a tributary system. That is, while they did not generally pay direct tribute to rulers in the regions through which they carried goods, aside from tolls at gates and markets, they can be seen as having subsidized rulers and monarchical trading operations indirectly by doing work to maintain roads and by accepting prices for their goods that were lower than those received by the kings. The kings, in turn, provided protection for the commerce which the porters carried. In addition to these structures, porterage included the familiar institutions of landlord and broker (Meillassoux, 1971), and porters included lineage members and slaves of caravan leaders.

The social relations of transportation in the Bight of Benin were based on a clear and basic distinction between porterage work and boatmen's work. On the one hand, boatmen worked collectively in crews and they were specialized laborers: They developed an artisanal mentality. They supported each other when facing accusations of theft, and they acted collectively in responding to threats to their wage levels or to the volume of their cargoes. Porters, on the other hand, worked as individuals or in ad hoc groups on a given trip. They were part-time workers and usually agriculturists too, who developed the mentality of a casual labor force. When conditions of work were unsatisfactory, they simply escaped back to their peasant existence.

NOTES

1. Archives Nationales du Bénin (ANB), Porto-Novo, 2-D-82, Savalou, February 1907.
2. ANB, 2-D-82, Savalou, January 1907.
3. ANB, 2-D-1, Abomey, December 1905.
4. ANB, 2-D-94, Zagnando, January-July 1912.
5. ANB, 2-D-94, Zagnando, January-July 1912.
6. ANB, 2-D-92, Zagnando, Rapport annuel, 1905.
7. ANB, 2-D-11, Grand Popo, July 1910.
8. ANB, 2-D-41, Grand Popo, May 1910-December 1911.
9. ANB, 1-E-42, Dossier Pohizoun, 1912.
10. ANB, 5-E, Mono (frontières), 1885-1907; ANB, 2-D-83, Savalou, February 1913.
11. ANB, 1-Q, Mouvement caravanier, 1909; 1-E-42, Dossier Pohizoun, 1912.
12. ANB, 2-D-92, Zagnando, Rapport annuel, 1905.

REFERENCES

ADAMU, M. (1978) The Hausa Factor in West African History. Zaria: Ahmadu Bello University Press.

Afrique Occidentale Française (AOF) (1911) Annuaire du Gouvernement Général de l'Afrique Occidentale Française, 1910. Paris: Author.

AGIRI, B. A. (1972) "Kola in western Nigeria, 1850-1950." Ph.D. thesis, University of Wisconsin, Madison.

ALBÉCA, A. (1895) La France au Dahomey. Paris: Hachette.

———(1889) Les Etablissements français du Golfe de Bénin. Paris: L. Baudoin.

BAY, E. (1979) "On the trail of the Bush King: a Dahomean lesson in the use of evidence." History in Africa 6: 1-15.

BIOBAKU, S. O. (1957) The Egba and their Neighbours, 1842-1872. Oxford: Clarendon.

BOUCHE, P. (1885) Sept ans en Afrique occidentale : la Côte des Esclaves et le Dahomey. Paris: Plon.

BOURGOIGNIE, G. E. (1972) Les Hommes de l'eau : Ethno-écologie du Dahomey lacustre. Paris: Presses Universitaires de France.

COQUERY-VIDROVITCH, C. (1972) "De la traite des esclaves a l'exportation de l'huile de palme et des palmistes au Dahomey au XIXe siecle," pp. 107-123 in C. Meillassoux (ed.) The Development of Indigenous Trade and Markets in West Africa. London: Oxford University Press.

COUCHARD, A. (1911) Au Moyen-Dahomey : notes sur le cercle de Savé. Bordeaux: Imprimerie commerciale et industrielle.

DESANTI, H. (1945) Du Danhomé au Bénin-Niger. Paris: Larose.

FOA, E. (1895) Le Dahomey. Paris: H. Hennuyer.

FONSSAGRIVES, J. B. (1900) Notice sur le Dahomey. Paris: Alcan-Lévey.

FORBES, F. E. (1851) Dahomey and the Dahomans, 2 vols. London: Longman.

GARCIA, L. (1969) "La Genèse de l'administration française au Dahomey, 1894-1920." Thèse de 3ᵉ cycle, Université de Paris.

GRIVOT, R. (1944) "L'Industrie du sel dans la subdivision de Grand-Popo." Notes africaines 21: 23-24.

GRUVEL, R. (1913) L'Industrie des pêches sur la côte occidentale de l'Afrique. Paris: Larose.

HOGENDORN, J. and M. JOHNSON (in press) Shell Money of the Slave Trade. Cambridge: Cambridge University Press.

HOPKINS, A. G. (1973) An Economic History of West Africa. London: Longman.

KEA, R. A. (1982) Settlements, Trade and Politics in the Seventeenth-Century Gold Coast. Baltimore: Johns Hopkins University Press.

KOPYTOFF, J. H. (1965) A Preface to Modern Nigeria: The "Sierra Leonians" in Yoruba, 1830-1890. Madison: University of Wisconsin Press.

LAFFITTE, J. (1873) Le Dahomé : souvenirs de voyage et de mission. Tours: Mame.

LAMBINET, E. (1893) Notice géographique, topographique et statistique sur le Dahomey. Paris: L. Baudoin.

LAW, R. (1977) The Oyo Empire, c. 1600. – c. 1836. Oxford: Oxford University Press.

LOVEJOY, Paul E. (1985) Salt of the Desert Sun. A History of Salt Production and Trade in the Central Sudan. Cambridge: Cambridge University Press.

MANNING, P. (1982) Slavery, Colonialism and Economic Growth in Dahomey, 1640-1960. Cambridge: Cambridge University Press.

MARTY, P. (1926) Etudes sur l'Islam au Dahomey. Paris: E. Leroux.

MEILLASSOUX, C. [ed.] (1972) The Development of Indigenous Trade and Markets in West Africa. London: Oxford University Press.

MONDJANNAGNI, A. (1963) "Quelques aspects historiques, économiques et politiques de la frontière Dahomey-Nigeria." Etudes dahoméennes 1: 17-57.

NEWBURY, C. W. (1961) The Western Slave Coast and its Rulers. Oxford: Clarendon.

Officiers de l'Etat-Major du Corps expéditionnaire du Bénin (1894) Notice géographique, topographique et historique sur le Dahomey. Paris: L. Baudoin.

OROGE, J. A. (1971) "The institution of slavery in Yorubaland with particular reference to the nineteenth century." Ph.D. thesis, University of Birmingham.

QUENUM, M. (1938) Au Pays des Fons. Paris: Larose.

ROSS, D. A. (1971) "Dahomey," pp. 144-169 in M. Crowder (ed.) West African Resistance. London: Africana.

———1965) "The career of Domingo Martinez in the Bight of Benin, 1833-1864." Journal of African History 6, 1: 79-90.

SAVARIAU, N. (1906) L'Agriculture au Dahomey. Paris: A. Challomel.

TURNER, J. M. (1975) "Les Bresiliens—The impact of former Brazilian slaves upon Dahomey." Ph.D. thesis, Boston University.

4

SUR LA ROUTE DES NOIX DE COLA EN 1897
Du moyen-Niger à Boola, marché kpelle[1]

ODILE GOERG

De mars à septembre 1897, une moyenne mensuelle de 126 chefs de caravane accompagnés de plus de 400 porteurs et 90 ânes fut enregistrée à Beyla, chef-lieu de cercle du Sud du Soudan mais surtout ancien marché à la frontière de la zone forestière. C'est ce que nous indiquent d'intéressantes statistiques commerciales,[2] source quantitative peu fréquente sur le commerce à longue distance; ces listes de colporteurs présentent l'image de pistes caravanières grouillant de monde: plus de 3500 personnes, porteurs et commerçants, transportèrent du Nord vers le Sud environ 60 tonnes de sel et des tissus et remontèrent avec 8 263 000 noix de cola. Cette étonnante activité—alors qu'il s'agit en grande partie de la saison des pluies peu favorable aux déplacements—met en valeur le travail engagé dans l'activité commerciale: celui des commerçants eux-mêmes mais surtout l'immense travail de portage en l'absence d'autre moyen de transport.

Les échanges envisagés ici concernent la région allant du Moyen-Niger à la Haute-Guinée, zone souvent négligée car les flux commerciaux y étaient moins denses que le long du Niger:

Une partie des dioulas se rend de Médine et Kayes vers le sud. Nous ne les suivrons pas dans cette voie, car leur commerce n'offre rien de particulier. . . . Ils sont du reste de beaucoup les moins nombreux [Baillaud, 1902: 41].

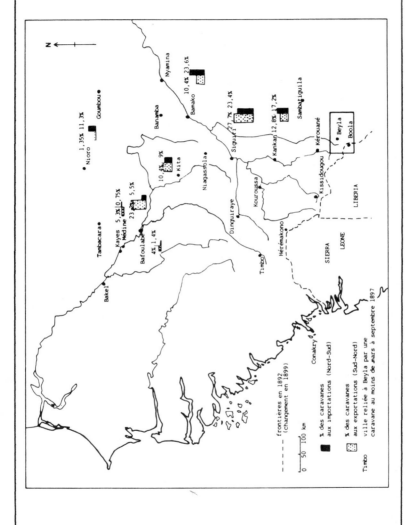

Map 4.1: Less echanges entre le Nord du Soudan et Beyla

L'échange de base se faisait entre le sel du Sahara et les noix de cola de la forêt, produit redistribué dans tous les centres commerciaux du Sahel. Les réseaux et marchés témoignent de l'ancienneté et de l'importance de ces échanges reposant essentiellement sur des produits autochtones mais en liaison avec le commerce atlantique par l'intégration de certains produits européens comme les tissus, la coutellerie. Alors que diverses études ont déjà analysé ces réseaux (produits, communautés marchandes), peu les ont abordés sous l'angle du travail. L'absence de sources écrites ou leur silence fréquent sur ce thème permet d'expliquer en partie cette lacune en ce qui concerne la région forestière, un des pôles de ce commerce. C'est dans ce contexte que la source disponible s'avère particulièrement intéressante, bien qu'elle ne permette d'aborder que quelques aspects du facteur "travail" dans l'organisation commerciale. Les récits de voyageurs, tardifs dans cette région, ou les rapports des premiers administrateurs négligent généralement cette question: ils s'intéressent surtout aux capacités de production des cercles occupés, aux produits que l'on peut réquisitionner pour le ravitaillement. Le recours à la coercition comme principal moyen de recrutement de main d'oeuvre évite aussi de poser réellement le problème de la mobilisation, dans une société rurale, de travailleurs pour des buts commerciaux.

Il ne s'agit pas ici de redécrire les mécanismes fondamentaux des échanges entre le Sahel et la forêt (Meillassoux, 1971; Curtin, 1975; Hopkins, 1973; Perinbam, 1977; Person, 1968) mais d'évoquer les éléments utiles à la compréhension de cette source et d'approfondir—en les quantifiant—certains aspects du travail engagé dans cette activité: l'organisation des caravanes, le portage, le statut des porteurs, les réseaux. L'exemple du commerce des noix de cola (Lovejoy, 1980a: 97-134) est particulièrement intéressant car il s'agit d'une denrée périssable supposant une très bonne organisation des échanges—par réseaux ou relais sur plus de 750 km—une rotation rapide des marchandises; d'autre part son aspect encombrant implique le participation d'un nombre élevé de commerçants et porteurs, tous soustraits au travail agricole. Il s'agit bien d'une spécialisation professionnelle dont les listes de colporteurs permettent de saisir quelques principes d'organisation.

Rescapés des archives car celles de Beyla furent détruites par un incendie en 1900,[3] les bulletins commeciaux conservés au poste voisin de Nionsomoridougou présentent des listes très précieuses et complètes des commerçants passant officiellement par le poste de Beyla et ceci de mars à septembre 1897.

CONTEXTE HISTORIQUE ET SPATIAL

La localisation de ces listes dans le cercle de Beyla en augmente l'intérêt du fait de sa situation de cercle-frontière et de l'ancienneté de l'implantation commerciale dans un milieu animiste. La convention du 8/12/1892 attribuait l'essentiel de la région productrice de noix de cola au Libéria.[4] Ainsi les différents marchés forestiers où s'échangeaient les colas se trouvèrent coupés—administrativement—du gros centre qu'étaient Beyla et son faubourg Diakolidougou. La création de Beyla remonterait au 16/17°s. selon Person (1974, 170-271; 1968) lorsqu'un important groupe de Maninka se fixa dans la région (le Konian); on les désigna par le suite sous le terme de Konianke. Ils détenaient un quasi–monopole sur les rapports avec les producteurs et généralement chaque communauté de commerçants avaient des relations privilégiées avec un groupe de forestiers. La volonté de contrôler le commerce des colas avait certainement été l'une des motivations principales de ces migrations, repoussant les population Kpelle et Loma plus au Sud.

Quatre types de listes commerciales récapitulent les échanges: d'une part le commerce extérieur ("exportations hors du Soudan" et "importations directes de la frontière"), d'autre part le commerce intérieur ("importations" et "exportations de cercle à cercle") précisant le marché d'origine ou de destination des caravanes. Ce système comptable existe depuis 1897; il présente l'inconvénient de compter deux fois la même produit (par exemple le sel provenant du Nord et réexporté en partie vers Boola) ou les mêmes commerçants, mais l'intéret de le faire ouvertement; en effet auparavant, depuis 1895, tout était cumulé sans distinction. De plus l'analyse comparée du commerce intérieur/commerce extérieur est instructive en elle-même: comment expliquer la différence de tonnage? où part le reste du sel?

En fait le commerce avec le Libéria ne concerne que les échanges entre Beyla et Boola, un des premiers marchés forestiers situé en zone kpelle à quelque 50 km de Beyla.[5] Il s'agit d'un important centre de concentration des noix drainant les producteurs dans un rayon de plus de 100 km; le marché s'y tenait tous les jeudis en dehors du village.[6] De nombreux jula y étaient installés pour servir d'intermédiaires dans les échanges et des commerçants venus de tout le Moyen-Niger le fréquentaient. Ainsi les commerçants Soninke s'approvisionnaient-ils surtout sur ce marché en échangeant des bandes de coton—tissées par leurs esclaves et teintes à l'indigo—contre les noix (Pollet et Winter, 1971: 117).

La date pour laquelle nous disposons de ces listes appelle quelques commentaires. L'année 1897 est en effet antérieure aux mesures de contrôle et de taxation des jula et suffisament de temps s'est écoulé depuis la période des conquêtes pour que le commerce, désorganisé par les guerres, ait repris activement. La région de Beyla fut occupée en 1893, année de création du poste, et le cercle de Beyla créé en 1894. Le contrôle des jula commença réellement en 1897 lorsque l'administration chercha à les connaître (sic), les immatriculer et à leur imposer une patente de colportage;[7] ceci resta dérisoire par manque de moyens, à cause de la mauvaise connaissance de la région (localisation des marchés, itinéraires) et du peu d'intérêt que semblaient présenter ces colporteurs peu intégrés au commerce européen. Les mécanismes commerciaux n'étaient donc pas encore bouleversés bien que certains événements fondamentaux aient eu lieu comme l'exode de Samori vers l'Est en 1893[8] ou la prise de contrôle du Fouta-Djalon par les Français en 1896.[9] Les choses allaient changer peu apres car les colonisateurs français, conscients du potentiel économique de la région, inposèrent peu à peu leur présence plus au Sud aux dépens du Libéria (Peyrissac, 1912); ils créèrent en 1899 les postes militaires de Sampouraya et Diorodougou ainsi que des postes douaniers comme à Boola-même; la taxe était de 0,10 fr. par kg de noix auquel s'ajoutait 0,10 fr. de droit de circulation (le prix du kg était évalué par Chevalier à 0,37/0,45 fr. et très exceptionnellement 0,90 fr., soit le plus souvent 50% du prix d'achat, Chevalier et Perrot, 1911: 375)! Ceci entraîna des heurts avec le libéria mais surtout une résistance locale acharnée jusqu'en 1911.[10] En 1903 la taxe sur les colas (supprimée le 1/1/1900 lors du rattachement du district de Boola à la Guinée) fut rétablie et perçue, entre autres, à Boola c'est-à-dire loin de la frontière théorique:

Cette taxe extraordinairement prohibitive puisqu'elle s'élevait sur les lieux de production à plus de 200%, eut pour résultat de favoriser la fraude dans des proportions inattendues. Les postes douaniers . . . sont demeurés impuissants à assurer la surveillance des routes et, en définitive, une quantité énorme de Kolas de l'hinterland de Libéria pénètre dans la Guinée sans acquitter de droits mais ces noix ne passent plus par les grands marchés de notre territoire: ceux-ci sont en partie anéantis [Chevalier et Perrot, 1911: 378].

Le marché de Boola fut par conséquent déserté.

Quelques réflexions sur les mois concernés: comme le montre très nettement le graphique 4.2, plus la saison des pluies est avancée, plus la nombre de caravanes est limité, ceci pour des raisons évidentes de facilité de déplacement, de difficulté à protéger les marchandises . . . Cependant les listes mettent en valeur la continuité des échanges pendant l'hivernage et leur importance:

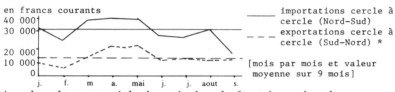

en francs courants
40 000
30 000
20 000
10 000
0

    j.   f.   m   a. mai   j.   j. aout s.

_____ importations cercle à cercle (Nord–Sud)

_ _ _ exportations cercle à cercle (Sud–Nord) *

[mois par mois et valeur moyenne sur 9 mois]

*   la valeur mercuriale des noix de cola étant basse dans la zone productrice (12 frs les 1000), le montant total des exportations est toujours inférieur à celui des importations.

Graphique 4.1: Valeur mensuelle des échanges

Ceci contredit les affirmations fréquentes selon lesquelles il y aurait quasi-interruption du trafic, le sel ne circulant pas lors des pluies (Meillassoux, 1963: 208). Des statistiques trimestrielles pour l'année 1897[11]—ne correspondant pas exactement avec les données mensuelles— confirment l'importance des échanges durant les mois étudiés. De même la présence d'ânes—souvent niée en hivernage—est attestée, même si leur nombre diminue avec les pluies.

RICHESSE DES INFORMATIONS

Les informations portent sur la composition des caravanes, le détail des marchandises et leur valeur mercuriale. Ainsi chaque caravane est décrite avec son "dioula chef de caravane"—identifié par son prénom, son patronyme et le numéro de sa patente (ceci permet de débusquer les nombreux homonymes et de reconstituer plus facilement des itinéraires)—le nombre de bêtes de somme—en l'occurrence uniquement des ânes—et le nombre de porteurs désignés sous le terme d' "hommes libres"; en effet une colonne "captifs" est prévue mais elle reste vide. De même toutes les marchandises (à l'importation et à l'exportation) sont détaillées; bien que l'échange fondamental soit sel contre cola, d'autres produits interviennent dans les transactions et nous renseignent sur les liaisons commerciales (produits européens par exemple), sur les liens entre commerce et production (des tissus dans le Sahel) et sur les produits que les administrateurs prévoyaient ou auraient aimé voir échangés. Dans le sens Sud-Nord ne remontent que des noix de cola et un peu d'argent. La variété est plus grande en ce qui concerne les importations de la zone courtiere et productrice de noix; sont distinguées "marchandises indigènes" et "marchandises françaises/anglaises." Les premières sont les plus nombreuses (14 catégories) et dominent dans les échanges.

Les produits européens occupent une place limitée dans les échanges. Il est intéressant de signaler l'absence de sel marin ou sel gemme européen; celui-ci en effet n'est pas compétitif avant l'achèvement du chemin de fer Conakry-Kankan en 1914. L'étude des différentes marchandises, de leur provenance, des quantités échangées—qui dépasse notre propos—mériterait elle-aussi d'être approndie.

LIMITES ET FAIBLESSES
DE CETTE SOURCE

Bien entendu se pose le problème de la crédibilité de cette source. Ainsi il faut compter non seulement avec la sincérité des commerçants interrogés mais aussi avec les erreurs de compréhension ou de transcription de la part d'administrateurs peu au fait des sociétés concernées. Le fait que certaines marchandises ne soient jamais mentionnées—comme l'ivoire—peut également étonner et déboucher sur des hypothèses comme celle de leur exportation vers le Sud. Autre restriction, et de taille, en 1897: ces listes ne témoignent que d'une partie des échanges effectués dans et à travers le cercle de Beyla à cause de l'importance de la fraude (volontaire ou non car les colporteurs ignoraient en fait la nouvelle réglementation), du manque de moyens des administrateurs et de leur mauvaise connaissance des pistes de commerce; en effet ni frontière matérialisée ou même reconnue de tous, ni poste douanier n'existaient à cette date. Le fait que le commerce ne concerne que les relations avec Boola montre aussi le caractère partiel du contrôle: le total des noix exportées vers le Nord est bien supérieur à celui venant de Boola (le double ou le triple souvent) alors que le cercle de Beyla lui-mème n'est pas producteur; ceci met en valeur le rôle de marché-relais de Beyla. Autre limite de la source: l'indication de la valeur mercuriale et non de la valeur d'échange des marchandises; l'on ne peut pas saisir la réalité des transactions et les fluctuations de prix selon les mois. L'appel à d'autres sources (rapports administratifs, enquêtes contemporaines . . .) permet cependant de pallier cette lacune. L'analyse des patronymes en relation avec la provenance des commerçants serait également intéressante; les listes seules ne suffisent pas pour le faire car un même patronyme peut être porté par différents peuples ou groupes sociaux; ainsi les nombreux Kone ou Taraore peuvent être soit Soninke, soit Bambara, soit Maninka. L'importance des références islamiques est évidente soit par les prénoms comme Karamoko, soit par les patronymes comme les Kaba, Maninka-Mori de Kankan généralement ou les Aidara, marabouts. L'analyse permettrait certainement d'affiner l'étude des réseaux; ainsi Dioumé Diawara pourrait être un commerçant Kooroko (voir la liste des ''importations directes de la frontière'' du 19/7/97).

Malgré leurs limites, ces listes de colporteurs permettent d'aborder certains aspects de l'organisation du travail tout en restant sans réponse sur de nombreuses questions: elles nous donnent un tableau instantané de nombreuses caravanes mais demeurent muettes sur le pourquoi, le comment ainsi que sur le vécu des travailleurs eux-mêmes.

OU IL EST QUESTION DE CARAVANES, D'ANES ET DE PORTEURS

Le lien le plus direct entre le travail et le commerce à longue distance est manifestement le mode de transport des marchandises. Selon Person dans l'étude du ''monde du kola'' (Person, 1968:101sq), trois moyens de transport sont envisageables: navigation fluviale, animaux de bât, porteurs. Le premier ne concerne pas la région au sud de Kouroussa. Les renseignements concernant le portage et le transport par ânes sont par contre nombreux et intéressants car ils contredisent diverses études sur la question.

On voit la continuité des échanges même pendant la saison des pluies (114 caravanes en moyenne par mois dans le sens Nord-Sud et 138 du Sud au Nord), leur importance mais aussi le décalage considérable en-

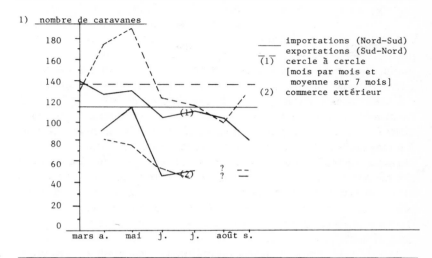

1) nombre de caravanes

importations (Nord–Sud)
exportations (Sud–Nord)
(1) cercle à cercle
[mois par mois et
moyenne sur 7 mois]
(2) commerce extérieur

Graphique 4.2: Nombre de caravenes mensuelles

tre le commerce intérieur et extérieur: ceci souligne le rôle fondamental de Beyla et de sa communauté marchande dans la redistribution
des produits venant du Nord ainsi que dans la concentration des noix
de cola; ainsi sur 41,6 t. de sel entrées dans le cercle en 5 mois (c'est-à-
dire sans mars et août incomplets pour le commerce extérieur), seules
12,69 t. sont enregistrées à la sortie du cercle vers Boola: 28,91 t. sont
soit sorties vers Boola en fraude, soit acheminées vers d'autres marchés.
De la même façon sur 6 367 400 colas transportées vers le Nord en
5 mois 2 527 700 sont entrées officiellement par la frontière de Boola.
Amselle (1977: 103-104, 137) souligne d'ailleurs le rôle des Konianke
dans ce commerce: ils approvisionnaient le marché de Kurukoro
fréquenté par les Kooroko; de mars à septembre une seule caravane
vint directement de cette région, de Sambatiguila en mai 1897, con-
duite par un Kamara. Il indique également qu'après l'occupation
française—et surtout l'arrestation de Samori en 1898—les "négociants
de la savane" se rendirent eux-mêmes dans les marchés forestiers de
la 2ème zone et notamment celui de Boola.

LA TAILLE DES CARAVANES

L'essentiel des caravanes—soit 60% en moyenne—ont de 0 à 3 porteurs alors que 4% seulement en comporte 10 et plus.[12] Le nombre maximum de porteurs est aussi significatif: une caravanes de 19 porteurs venant de Bamako en août. En ce qui concerne le commerce entre Beyla et Boola, les chiffres sont encore plus bas: 2,15% des caravanes ont 10 porteurs et plus; ceci peut s'expliquer par les conditions écologiques et géographiques différentes (plus grande difficulté à se déplacer dans des régions montagneuses et à végétation dense) mais aussi par le mode de relations propre à cette zone courtière. Se dégage ainsi une majorité de commerçants-transporteurs travaillant avec un capital limité (le minimum se situe entre 10 et 20 frs) et effectuant toutes les opérations: il s'agit de la forme la plus simple d'organisation commerciale. Lorsqu'est fait appel à de la main d'oeuvre complémentaire, l'on peut supposer qu'il s'agit de dépendants (cadets, esclaves) car le commerce pratiqué sur une échelle aussi modeste permet rarement d'accumuler suffisamment de capital pour recourir à des travailleurs salariés.

Ces indications vont à l'encontre de l'idée généralement répandue de vastes caravanes, même s'il est signalé par ailleurs que celles-ci peuvent être divisées en sous-unités pour faciliter le déplacement.[13] Ainsi Pollet et Winter (1971:113) évoquent pour la période pré-coloniale des caravanes de 20 à 60 personnes accompagnées de nombreux ânes (jusqu'à 100) et Amselle (1977: 135), dans son étude sur les Kooroko circulant dans des régions comparables, mentionne des caravanes allant jusqu'à 100 personnes au début de la colonisation. De même Lovejoy (1971: 537) parle de caravanes de 100 à 200 personnes (dont hommes, femmes et enfants) et autant d'ânes pour le commerce Hausa des colas au XIX°s. Parlant des Maraka, Roberts (1980: 176) indique une dimension plus restreinte des caravanes devant permettre une rotation rapide des marchandises: de 30 à 40 porteurs.

Les caravanes beaucoup plus réduites attestées en 1897 sont-elles le résultat de contraintes spécifiques, de bouleversements récents ou bien faut-il remettre en cause cette image de vastes caravanes décrites par Caillié, Mollien . . . ? Bien sûr on ne peut exclure le fait que des caravanes—présentées comme autonomes à leur arrivée ou formation à Beyla—voyagent ensemble. On ne peut pas tirer argument du déplacement en hivernage car les mois n'offrent pas entre eux de divergences significatives (par exemple entre mars sec et août pluvieux). Les chiffres moins complets portant sur 1894[14] confirment une moyenne de 2 à 4 porteurs. Peut jouer par contre la moindre densité des flux commerciaux. De même aucune mention n'est faite dans les listes, ni dans les rapports commerciaux, ni dans les nombreuses enquêtes de la fin du XIX°s (d'Ollone, 1901: 313; Blondiaux, 1895-1896) de la présence de femmes accompagnant les caravanes. S'agit-il là aussi d'une caractéristique spécifique, d'une évolution récente ou de l'extrapolation répandue à partir de certains témoignages?

LE STATUT DES PORTEURS

La question du statut des porteurs pose le problème de leur rémunération, du profit commercial et des possibilités ou non de "formation de classe" ou tout au moins de création d'un groupe professionel spécialisé aux intérêts similaires, plus mobile et par conséquent plus susceptible de répondre aux nouvelles formes de travail proposées/imposées par la colonisation. Différents statuts sont généralement envisagés: esclaves volontaires engagés, porteurs recrutés dans le cadre de relations de clientèle ou de parenté; dans ce dernier cas il s'agit souvent d'une étape dans la formation d'un futur colporteur.[15]

Avant d'apporter quelques éléments de reponse, abordons un problème préliminaire: s'agit-il de porteurs (esclaves ou non) ou de captifs vendus comme tels, de marchandises? Est-ce que, comme Person (1966: 113) le suggère, "les deux produits du Sud, l'un portant l'autre, remontaient vers le Niger où tous deux étaient vendus?" Est-ce que, comme l'avance Curtin (1975: 286), les porteurs libres prédominaient dans les relations Nord-Sud?[16] Comme cela a été mentionné, les listes de 1897 maintiennent une colonne "non libres" bien que la traite des esclaves ait été interdite en octobre 1894 dans le Soudan. En application de cette règlementation, les "captifs" disparurent dès novembre 1894 des statistiques commerciales: il n'y eut plus que des porteurs alors que de juin à octobre 1894 110 esclaves en moyenne étaient exportés mensuellement du cercle de Beyla, procurant plus de 50% en valeur des sorties. A partir de ce moment il n'est plus question de "captifs" mais le nombre de porteurs gonflant soudainement ne peut tromper personne. Qu'en-est-il en 1897 alors que la pratique interdite est loin d'avoir disparu?[17]

Ceci entraîne plusieurs réflexions sur la nature-même du portage aussi bien avant qu'après octobre 1894. En effet lorsque la traite des esclaves était officielle, les listes distinguaient des "hommes libres" porteurs et des "captifs" porteurs tout en indiquant par ailleurs la valeur marchande de ces derniers (170 à 196 frs) et donc le fait qu'ils étaient avant tout destinés à être vendus dans le Nord. Ne faut-il pas y voir plutôt d'un côté des porteurs et de l'autre des marchandises et donc s'interroger sur le statut d'hommes libres des premiers? Faut-il prendre cette affirmation au pied de la lettre? De même lorsqu'en 1897 la colonne "captifs" reste vide, peut-on en déduire qu'aucun porteur n'est dépendant, que tous sont des salariés embauchés ou des colporteurs-transporteurs et qu'aucun porteur n'est un captif de traite camouflé? Le problème reste ouvert; d'autres sources confirment l'existence aussi bien de porteurs engagés que de porteurs captifs comme le suggèrent d'ailleurs la plupart des auteurs (Curtin, 1975; Pollet et Winter, 1971: 113-115; Person, 1968: 113sq). Ainsi les enquêtes faites en 1904[18] en prévision de l'abolition—prudente—de l'esclavage opportent certains éléments.[19] Dans le cercle de Beyla par exemple, où les esclaves sont estimés à 1/3 de la population, il est dit:

> Les captifs des Dioulas ont une existence plus pénible (que d'autres captifs); ils portent de fortes charges et sont obligés d'aller à l'eau, au bois ou de cuisiner à l'arrivée au gîte d'étape pendant que le chef dioula se repose. En revanche ils ne font presque rien quand les dioulas ne voyagent pas.

Pour le cercle de Kankan, la présence d'esclaves est liée à celle des Maninka-Mori, commerçants musulmans. Ainsi Kankan et ses environs comprendraient 6000 esclaves sur 10 500 habitants soit 57% alors que les cantons "fétichistes" (sic) n'en auraient que 5,4%. Les esclaves étaient essentiellement employés au travail agricole dans des villages de culture (rente en produits)—autre forme de liaison entre travail et commerce—mais: "chez les musulmans ce sont eux aussi qui sont à peu près exclusivement chargés de tous les gros travaux (portage, débroussaillement)".

Autre remarque concernant le cercle de Dinguiraye, ancien centre de l'empire toucouleur d'Aguibou, fils d'El Hadj Omar, puis de Maki Tall (exilé en 1899 à Bamako) précisant le rôle tenu par des esclaves: "Souvent si le maître a reconnu de l'intelligence chez l'un d'eux, il

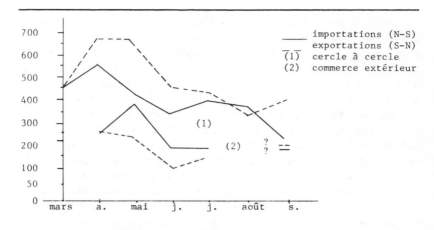

Graphique 4.3: Nombre mensuel de porteurs

lui confie des marchandises pour faire le métier de traitant." Cette utilisation des esclaves, dotés de la même fonction qu'un homme libre, est confimée par d'autres sources.

Les listes permettent d'étayer l'hypothèse d'une traite des esclaves camouflée sous du portage car de nombreuses caravanes remontent vers le Nord avec une disproportion flagrante entre le nombre de porteurs et le volume de colas transportées. Etait-il "rentable" d'employer des porteurs dans ces conditions alors que la valeur d'échange des marchandises acheminées était bien supérieur au coût local des noix de cola: une charge de sel équivalait à 60 frs (une barre de 25 kg) contre 24 à 30 frs pour une charge de colas. Que penser d'une caravane dont les porteurs transportent chacun 360 colas—et les exemples sont nombreux—alors qu'une charge de noix en compreend généralement 2500 à 3000, ce que de nombreuses caravanes emportent? Que penser du fait que plus de porteurs remontent vers le Nord, soit 3415 "porteurs" (exportations cercle à cercle) contre 2739 dans le sens Nord-Sud (importations cercle à cercle)? Le calcul sur 7 mois permet d'éliminer les chevauchements des caravanes de mois en mois—selon le temps passé aux échanges—et l'on retrouve ainsi une différence moyenne de 96 personnes, similaire à celle des captifs exportés officiellement en 1894: coïncidence?

Ainsi une partie seulement des "hommes libres" serait réellement des porteurs (esclaves ou non). Les autres seraient des esclaves de traite et l'on peut douter de leur utilisation effective comme transporteurs de colas vu le volume souvent limité de noix; en effet la fragilité des noix, le savoir-faire que nécessite leur manutention (ouvrir les paniers fréquemment, humecter les noix, les trier pour enlever celles attaquées par les charançons (Chevalier et Perrot, 1911: 351) laissent à penser que cette tâche ne pouvait être confiée au hasard et supposait un certain apprentissage. Ceci est confirmé par d'autres sources: ainsi dans une interview recueillie par Curtin, Tierno Hamady Madi SY indiquait que le portage était délicat, qu'il était fait par le commerçant lui-même et des porteurs salariés dans le cadre de petites caravanes (jusqu'à 10 porteurs).[20] Nous tenons certainement là une des raisons structurelles de la taille limitéee des caravanes décrites ici. Cela rejoint l'analyse de Roberts car le commerce des noix de cola nécessitait effectivement une parfaite organisation des transports pour limiter au maximum les pertes; cela se combine mal avec le déplacement de larges caravanes qu'il faut loger, protéger.

Cependant, bien que les esclaves de traite ne semblent pas avoir joué un rôle déterminant dans le travail de portage (il fallait préserver leur valeur marchande), leur participation à cette activité met en valeur une des modalités de recrutement de la main d'oeuvre commerciale: par ponction d'un systéme économique sur un autre, en l'occurrence de communautés marchandes islamisées—renforcées par l'organisation politique de l'almami Samori—au détriment des sociétés forestières non centralisées. C'est en réaction contre cet état de fait et pour s'organiser contre les razzias que des tentatives hégémoniques visèrent à regrouper différentes chefferies dans la région forestière: ainsi dans le zone kpelle sous la direction de Gbankundo Saxajigi, vaincu par Samori en 1883. Acheminés vers le Nord, ces esclaves pouvaient être peu à peu intégrés à une unité familiale puis participer directement aux activitiés commerciales, assurant ainsi la reproduction du cycle d'échanges.

LE ROLE DES ANES
COMME TRANSPORTEURS

Contrairement aux affirmations fréquentes excluant l'utilisation d'ânes au Sud de Kankan (Curtin, 1975: 22,286; Meillassoux, 1963: 208; Pollet et Winter, 1971: 113) du fait de la trypanosomiase ou tout au moins évoquant leur remontée vers le Nord lors de la saison des pluies,[21] les listes témoignent de leur présence tout au long de l'année.

La pourcentage de caravanes avec ânes(s) ainsi que le nombre total d'ânes diminue très nettement avec l'avancée de la saison des pluies: 40 à 60% d'avril à juillet avec plus de 100 ânes par mois contre 20% environ en septembre. Le rôle des ânes est beaucoup moins important entre Beyla et Boola que dans le reste du Soudan, phénomène que les conditions sanitaires et géographiques expliquent aisément: le nombre d'ânes par mois est généralement inférieur à 40. Ailleurs il est loin d'être négligeable. Ceci est un moyen d'accroître considérablement le volume du commerce puisqu'un âne porte en général 3 charges (70 à 80 kg) et se contente de peu, l'inconvénient étant sa lenteur (16 km par jour en terrain accidenté). Pour un jula cela représente donc une possibilité de gain considérable mais aussi un investissement important.[22] On ne peut pas associer l'utilisation d'ânes à un type précis de caravane; toutes les combinaisons sont possibles: peu de porteurs et plusieurs ânes ou même un jula seul et 8 ânes (en mai, importations cercle à cercle), nombreux porteurs et nombreux ânes (en août aux exportations cercle à cercle l caravane comprend 7 ânes et 9 porteurs), grande caravane sans âne (en avril aux importations cercle à cercle, l jula accompagné de 10 porteurs); de façon générale le nombre le plus élevé d'ânes correspond à des caravanes importantes. Le nombre maximum reste très modeste (8 ânes), ce qui est à mettre en relation avec les conditions somme toute peu favorables des zones traversées.

QUELQUE DONNEES SUR LES RESEAUX

Ces données ne concernent que le commerce intérieur au Soudan puisque le commerce extérieur n'est enregistré qu'entre Beyla et Boola. L'analyse des marchés d'origine et de destination des commerçants met en valeur les grands centres commerciaux—concentration du sel ou redistribution des noix de cola—les axes d'échange, les lieux de rupture de charge mais aussi, indirectement, les réseaux et transactions se greffant sur l'échange fondamental sel/cola. Le périple de la cola se fait à travers quatre zones différentes: la région productrice (ici zone kissi-loma-kpelle), le secteur des marchés courtiers, les savanes du Sud et la zone consommatrice. Le contrôle du commerce pouvait être effectif d'un marché sahélien à Beyla, zone courtière, ou Boola, marché forestier; un même colporteur pouvait ainsi relier directement les régions productrices et consommatrices en utilisant les services d'un réseau commercial. L'échange sur d'aussi longues distances pouvait aussi être réalisé par relais, rupture de charge dans certains marchés, plaques tournantes des transactions. La carte témoigne bien de l'orientation Nord-Sud, caractéristique des échanges et de l'existence de ces deux pratiques commerciales. Huit lieux d'échange monopolisent pratiquement les relations commerciales avec Beyla en totalisant 94,25% des caravanes aux importations (Nord-Sud) et 96,75% aux exportations (Sud-Nord). L'on peut opposer les centres des régions septentrionales parmi lesquels dominent Nioro, Médine et Bamako aux deux marchés-relais dans les savanes du Sud (Siguiri, Kankan).

Siguiri, à proximité des placers aurifères du Bouré/Séké, joue un grand rôle dans les échanges. Les marchandises venant du Nord sont acheminées par voie fluviale de Bamako ou viennent du Haut-Sénégal. Les noix de cola sont ensuite redistribuées dans des marchés locaux comme Didi, Dentinian ou transportées plus loin vers l'Ouest (Fouta-Djalon, Dinguiraye . . .). Gallieni (1891: 232) perçut tout de suite le rôle important de ce lieu d'échange: "Siguiri est le lieu de passage de toutes les caravanes venant des Etats de Samory (en 1888) et se rendant à nos comptoirs du Sénégal et des Rivières du Sud." Certains commerçants limitent par conséquent leur rayon d'action à une zone restreinte, centrée sur un de ces marchés-relais. Ainsi Keleeba Konde, interrogé vers 1897,[23] dit avoir "fait le dioula" entre Moriguédougou au Sud-Ouest de Kankan, Bamako et le Bouré.

Kankan, sur le Milo, tient le même rôle de marché-relais au carrefour de nombreuses routes vers le Nord et les marchés sahéliens, vers l'Est et le Wasulu, vers l'Ouest et le Fouta-Djalon et bien sûr vers les marchés courtiers du Sud. De nombreux Konianke, intermédiaires et entrepositaires à Beyla, préfèrent ne pas trop s'éloigner de leur base de départ alors qu'à Kankan-même les Maninka-Mori prennent le relais.

Sur les marchés septentrionaux, les spécialisations se situent soit dans la concentration du sel, soit dans la redistribution des noix de cola. Ainsi Nioro et Bamako (dont partent respectivement 11,3 et 23,6% des caravanes chargées essentiellement de sel) sont d'importants points d'arrivée des Maures apportant le sel du Sahara. Ces derniers s'aventurent rarement plus au Sud du Niger et remontent avec des tissus, des esclaves . . . Baillaud (1903: 40,62) en 1898/99, s'est beaucoup intéressé à ces transactions: "A côté de la gomme et de la guinée, il arrive à

Nioro un troisième produit: le sel. Ce sel provient des carrières de Tichit et est apporté au Soudan par les Maures.'' ''Bamako est également un des points importants du passage du sel.''

Le rôle de Bamako est confirmé par l'étude de Meillassoux (1963: 208): ''Bamako, donc, était moins une étape pour les caravanes qu'un point de rupture, un marché où les produits passaient des mains d'un intermédiaire à celles d'un autre.'' Un sondage sur le mois d'avril montre que les caravanes partant de Nioro sont plus importantes—22 caravanes avec 120 porteurs (soit 5,45 en moyenne) et 30 ânes-, et uniquement chargées de sel et que celles venant de Bamako comportent des marchandises plus variées (tissus, colliers) bien que le sel reste le produit dominant.

Dans le sens Sud-Nord ces marchés n'attirent respectivement que 1,35 et 10,4% des caravanes; ceci se comprend aisément, surtout pour Nioro qui joue un faible rôle dans la redistribution des noix de cola. Celles-ci sont dirigées de préférence vers Médine (23,2% des caravanes contre seulement 5.5 partant de là), Kita . . . L'on peut ainsi reconstituer des trajets supposés puisque les caravanes, partant chargées de sel de certains marchés, retournent dans d'autres pour échanger leurs noix de cola contre des tissus ou de l'argent avec lesquels elles acquièrent à nouveau du sel; le cycle commercial est bouclé: il aura duré plusieurs mois et occasionné un long périple pour des profits certains mais parfois aléatoires (problème de la conservation des noix).

Ils confirment le rôle spécifique de Bamako/Nioro (achat de sel) et de Médine (vente des colas) ainsi que l'existence de colporteurs au rayon d'action plus limité (liaison entre Kankan et Siguiri par exemple). L'on peut aussi déduire de ces ''trajets'' le temps passé aux transactions dans la région de Beyla (2 à 4 semaines) et le profit théorique réalisé par le commerçants. Sur l'exemple de Diané Soumsana on arrive à la multiplication de la mise de départ par 7 entre Nioro et Médine.[24] Ceci doit être confronté bien sûr au travail pénible de 7 à 8 personnes et 3 ânes sur plus de 1000 km, soit un cycle total de 1 à 2 mois minimum. La mise est multipliée par 5 environ pour un jula seul achetant 1000 colas—le minimum pour une charge—pour 12 frs et pouvant espérer les revendre 100 frs et plus dans le Nord (60 frs en comptant les pertes inévitables, les cadeaux). L'éloignement entre producteurs et consommateurs est à la base de ce profit; joue en effet ce qu'Amselle (1977: 210) nomme l'opacité du marché c'est-à-dire "la méconnaissance par l'acheteur et le vendeur des prix d'achat et de vente des marchandises par le commerçant".

Derniere remarque concernant les réseaux: la très faible intégration de ces circuits avec le commerce atlantique de la côte de Guinée ou de Sierra Leone; en tout et pour tout 4 caravanes vinrent de la côte à Beyla, 1 de Conakry et 3 de Sierra Leone. Ceci découlait déjà de l'analyse des marchandises, puisque très peu nombreuses étaient celles d'origine européenne; le commerce des noix de cola et du sel conservait ses réseaux et ses commerçants spécialisés. Notons aussi l'absence du caoutchouc, non mentionné dans ces listes commerciales alors qu'il est demandé en paiement de l'impôt dans le Sud du Soudan depuis 1896; en 1897 12% de la capitation du cercle de BEYLA et 15% de celui de Kankan était payé en caoutchouc tandis que celui-ci n'était pas intégré aux circuits commerciaux de ces régions. L'administration dut se charger de son transport vers le Nord; c'est en 1904 seulement qu'une maison de commerce européenne s'installa à Beyla (Gobinet frères).

Cette étude a permis d'éclairer sous un jour nouveau les échanges à longue distance, de donner une vision quantifiée de leur organisation et notamment de préciser l'importance du travail mis en jeu dans ces transactions. Quelques caracteristiques peuvent être dégagées: *la participation de nombreux commerç*ants-transporteurs, intégrés éventuellement à des caravanes plus importantes. Ceci ressort de la taille limitée des caravanes. La pratique du commerce semble donc avoir joué un rôle moteur—dans les sociétés qui en prennent l'initiative comme les communautés jula ou les Maninka-Mori de Kankan— puisqu'elle attirait de nombreux individus dont le capital de départ pouvait être très limité. De là découle le mode de mobilisation de la main d'oeuvre commerciale: l'essentiel du travail de portage devait être le fait de dépendants—esclaves ou non—recrutés dans la cadre des obligations familiales. Il n'est pas fait mention dans cette région de porteurs volontaires salariés, plus ou moins dégagés de l'organisation lignagère.[25] Les plaintes des premiers administrateurs ou voyageurs, les difficultés ultérieures de recrutement et le silence des sources permettent d'aboutir à cette conclusion. A cela s'ajoute la ponction en captifs sur les sociétés forestières, les esclaves de traite ne semblent pas, en tant que tels, avoir joué un rôle vital dans le travail de portage, mais leur intégration partielle dans la société prédatrice contribue par la suite à renforcer la puissance du groupe et sa disponibilité en main d'oeuvre. Seules se détachent quelques caravanes plus fournies: le succès commercial n'est pas à la portée de tous; l'échange des noix de cola suppose en effet une bonne connaissance du marché permettant de profiter des prix les plus avantageux et comporte de nombreux aléas.

Le recours aux ânes même pendant la saison des pluies, et leur rôle appréciable dans les transports; en comptant une moyenne de 3 charges par âne, l'utilisation de ces bêtes de somme permet d'accroître le volume transporté de façon considérable puisque leur part constitue 30% du total des charges. L'importance du travail fourni par les ânes explique pourquoi les commerçants n'hésitent pas à entrainer ces animaux loin dans le Sud malgré les risques de mortalité accrue que cela comporte.

La continuité des échanges tout au long de l'année, malgré un net ralentissement des transactions au moment des pluies. Ceci pourrait également être une donnée structurelle liée aux noix de cola: la demande dans les zones consommatrices est à peu près constante alors que la production est saisonnière; or le stockage ne peut être réalisé sur place car le climat sec du Nord du Soudan ne convient pas aux noix (Cohen 1966: 21). Le stockage se fait dans les régions productrices d'où les noix sont écoulées au fur et à mesure de la demande. Les producteurs ont ainsi un rôle fondamental puiqu'ils contrôlent les greniers de réserve. Leur travail de récolte est également considérable et intervient donc indirectement dans ce processus d'échange. La continuité des échanges renforce l'idée de l'existence d'un commerce professionnel, organisé 12 mois sur 12 de façon efficace et ayant recours à de nombreux porteurs; ceux-ci sont recrutés même pendant l'hivernage, saison où le travail des champs retient les commerçants occasionels. Cette spécialisation professionnelle—temporaire ou non—s'intégrait à l'organisation globale de la société qui pouvait prendre en charge un certain pourcentage de non-paysans.

Il serait intéressant de confronter ces résultats à ceux tirés d'autres listes portant sur des régions différentes du Soudan; il faudrait aussi pousser plus loin l'analyse en cherchant des corrélations entre, par exemple, la taille des caravanes et leur provenance ou la composition des marchandises et le lieu d'approvisionnement; l'étude des patronymes, en relation avec les marchés d'origine, pourrait également préciser nos connaissances des réseaux. Des zones d'ombre subsistent cependant. Ainsi qu'en est-il du mode de rémunération, de l'organisation à l'intérieur des caravanes, de la perception qu'ont les porteurs de leur travail, des possibilités de "promotion" par le commerce. Le recours aux enquêtes orales permettraient certainement d'avancer quelques hypothèses dans ce domaine.

La question du portage au début de l'ère coloniale confirme qu'il n'existait pas de volant de main d'oeuvre prête à s'engager dans cette activité, même rémunérée. La recrutement obligatoire de porteurs fut particulièrement important dans la région de Beyla, très mal reliée aux autres centres du Soudan ou de Guinée et productrice de caoutchouc. Les réquisitions de main d'oeuvre concernèrent tout d'abord le ravitaillement des postes puis le transport des produits acceptés en paiement de l'impôt; peu à peu l'administration collabora avec les maisons de commerce et se chargea de recruter des porteurs soit illégalement,[26] soit en créant 5 compagnies de porteurs en 1905.[27] Elle transforma un phénomène marginal en charge pesant sur les colonisés, perturbant l'organisation de la production argicole.

L'incapacité des sociétés paysannes à répondre à cette exigence ainsi que le salaire dérisoire offert—0,5 fr. par jour plus une ration— expliquent aisément les résistances aux recrutements, la désertion des porteurs. C'est dans ce cadre que l'essentiel du caoutchouc fut transporté puisque le chemin de fer ne relia Conakry à Kankan, son terminus, qu'en 1914 (terminus à Kouroussa en 1910). Il n'y a donc pas de continuité entre le groupe des porteurs étudiés ici et les réquisitions administratives. Les exigences des colonisateurs dépassaient largement la disponibilité locale en main d'oeuvre non paysanne et désorganisèrent gravement la production agricole. Les porteurs participant au commerce des noix de cola continuèrent leurs longs périples en s'adaptant aux nouvelles conditions politiques et économiques; ainsi ils modifièrent leurs trajets suivant les règlementations douanières, intégrèrent peu à peu le sel européen dans leurs cycles commerciaux et adoptèrent, surtout après la deuxième guerre mondiale, les camions, moyen de transport correspondant aux exigences de rapidité des colas. Ce dernier élément transforma fondamentalement les conditions de commerce des noix de cola en permettant d'accoître le tonnage transporté, l'offre suivant le demande accrue.[28]

NOTES

1. Kpelle, appellation locale, semble devoir être préférée à Gerze nom sous lequel ce peuple est connu; même chose pour Loma et non plus Toma.

2. Archives Nationales du Sénégal (ANS) 7G 50 rapports agricoles et commerciaux du poste de Nionsomoridougou (cercle de Beyla). Il existe des listes de ce genre pour d'autres cercles du Soudan.

3. Il subsiste cependant des notes manuscrites faites par l'administrateur Maupoil et portant sur la période 1892/1940; très en désordre, elles concernent en fait les années 1905/1914 pour les plus anciennes: ANS 1G 32, série moderne, versement 104.

4. Voir par exemple l'article très partisan (pro-français) de L. Peyrissac (1912); en fait en 1892 le région n'était pas connue et les limites territoriales très théoriques. La région de Beyla qui revenait à la France fut occupée postérieurement et le Libéria ne contrôla pas la zone qui lui était attribuée.

5. Voir ANS 7G 49/50 et Chevalier et Perrot (1911:156), "5° Pays des Tomas et des Guerzés"; il est signalé "qu'à Boola, et dans les environs, nous n'avons observé que quelques kolatiers autour de chaque village" p. 158.

6. Cf. 1G 32 série moderne, versement 104 op.cit. lettre du commandant du 4/11/1909 à un nouveau commerçant Tessier (Chevalier et Perrot, 1911: 372).

7. ANS 7G 50 rapport politique du 1er semestre 1897.

8. Samori n'était pas intervenu dans le commerce des produits non stratégiques mais avait facilité les échanges; il fut arrêté au Sud-Est de Beyla le 29/9/98.

9. La frontière restait fictive entre la Guinée et le Soudan.

10. En 1905 le statut de "région militaire" fut créé pour contrôler cette zone.

11. ANS 7G 50 statistiques commerciales annuelles de 1897.

12. Le travail porte ici sur le "commerce intérieur" car cela évite de comptabiliser deux fois les mêmes caravanes et qu'il y a des lacunes pour le commerce extérieur; néanmoins tout écart significatif de résultat sera évoqué et analysé.

13. Curtin (1975: 272) évoque des caravanes de 2000 personnes, scindées en groupes de 30 à 40, au moment de la traite des esclaves. Lovejoy (1971: 539) mentionn des caravanes Hausa de plus de 1000 personnes vers 1800/50.

14. ANS 7G 49 bulletins agricoles et commerciaux de 1894.

15. Person (1968: 113sq): les porteurs libres recoivent 10% de ce qu'ils portent et peuvent ainsi économiser pour démarrer un commerce seuls. Fonds Curtin Tape 13 (face 1-2) Commerce diakhanke par Bakou Kaba à Tamboura dans le Bundu (sur l'apprentissage du métier de commerçant).

16. Curtin oppose ceux-ci aux esclaves en transit sur les routes Est-Ouest.

17. Voir par. ex. Lipschutz (1973: 180 sq); Archives du Public Record Office, Kew: Colonial Office 267/405/18007 lettre du 23/10/1893; Foreign Office 27/3357/1897 lettre du 8/7/1897 au F.O. en réponse à une lettre du Baron de Courcel, ambassadeur de France à Londres (comprend une lettre de Cousturier, gouverneur de Guinée, au ministre des colonies); A.N.S.O.M. Guinée XIV Travail et main d'oeuvre/esclaves,d.3.

18. Ces enquêtes répondent au questionnaire du 10/12/1903 sur la captivité; par une circulaire du 17/9/1902 l'interdiction de la traite avait été réaffirmée pour la Guinée (cf annexion du Sud du Soudan—où se trouve Beyla—en 1900).

19. A.N.S.O.M. Guinée XIV d.3 (une enquête par cercle).

20. Fonds Curtin Le commerce du Bundu et de Diakha, Cassette 7 face 1.

21. Amselle (1977: 134) "l'âne est absolument inutilisable pendant la saison des pluies"; Person (1968: 113); "l'âne va jusqu'à la zone courtière pendant la saison sèche mais remonte en avril-novembre au Nord de la ligne Kankan-Bougouni"; Lovejoy évoque l'emploi d'ânes mais sans préciser l'aire d'utilisation (1980: 91, 92, 116) cf infra article de Duffill et Lovejoy "Merchants, porters and teamsters in 19th-century central Sudan"; font allusion à la forte mortalité des ânes dans le Sud.

22. Voici, à titre d'indication, la valeur mercuriale d'un âne à Nioro: 60/70 frs.

23. ANS 7G 34 liste des chefs de la région Sud du Soudan en 1897/99 donnant des renseignements sur leur itinéraire politique et professionel.

24. Il s'agit bien sûr d'estimations car les cours dex noix fluctuent beaucoup en fonction de la période de l'année, de l'état des transactions . . . aussi bien dans les régions productrices que dans les marchés du Nord.

25. Cf. infra art. cit. de Duffill et Lovejoy: mettent en valeur l'existence de nombreux porteurs volontaires.

26. "Il est absolument contraire aux règlements de procéder militairement ou administrativement à des réquisitions d'hommes, de chevaux, de vivres et de matériaux quelconques pour le compte de particuliers, à des prix arbitrairement fixés à 50% au-dessous de leur valeur. De pareils faits n'existaient pas jusqu'en présent en Guinée; ils sont contraires à tous les règlements adminisratifs." ANS, Q 50 Le commerce en A.O.F. 1896/1903: lettre du gouverneur Cousturier au gouverneur général du 29/6/1900, juste après l'annexion du Sud du Soudan par la Guinée.

27. Arrêté local de Guinée 7/11/1905; cf. Goerg (1981: 429-445): "l'intervention administrative dans les transports commerciaux."

28. Cf. 1G 32 disette dans le cercle de Beyla en 1909 7G 58 rapport sur la région forestière en 1903 (incrimine le portage). Lovejoy, (1980a), qui évoque le très fort accroissement du volume de noix échangées découlant des transformations des moyens de transport.

REFERENCES

AMSELLE, J. L. (1977) Les négoçiants de la savane. Paris: Anthropos.

BAILLAUD, E. (1902) Sur les routes du Soudan. Toulouse: Privat.

BLONDIAUX (1895-1896) Région sud du Soudan, A.N.S. 1G 171.

CHEVALIER, A. and E. PERROT, (1911) Les kolatiers et les noix de kola. Paris: Challamel.

COHEN, A. (1966) "Politics of the kola trade: some processes of tribal community formation among migrants in West African towns." Africa 36, 1: 1 8-36.

CURTIN, P. D. (1975) Economic Change in Precolonial Africa. Senegambia in the Era of the Slave Trade. Madison: University of Wisconsin Press.

d'OLLONE (1901) De la Côte d'Ivoire au Soudan et à la Guinée. Paris: Hachette.

GALLIENI, J. S. (1891) Deux campagnes au Soudan français. Paris: Hachette

GOERG, O. (1981) "Echanges, réseaux, marchés: l'impact colonial en Guinée (mi-XIX°-1913)." Thèse de 3ème cycle, Université de Paris.

HOPKINS A. G. (1973) An Economic History of West Africa. London: Longman.

LIPSCHUTZ, M. R. (1973) "Northeast Sierra Leone after 1884: responses to the Samorian invasions and British Colonialism." Ph.D. thesis, University of California, Los Angeles.

LOVEJOY P. E. (1980a) "Kola in the history of West Africa." Cahiers d'études africaines 20, 1/2: 97-134.

———(1980b) Caravans of Kola: The Hausa Kola Trade, 1700-1900. Zaria and Ibadan: Ahmadu Bello University Press and University Press.

————(1971) "Long-distance trade and Islam: the case of the nineteenth-century Hausa Kola trade." Journal of the Historical Soiciety of Nigeria 5, 4: 537-547.

MEILLASSOUX, C. [ed.] (1971) The Development of Indigenous Trade and Markets in West Africa. London: Oxford University Press.

————(1963) "Histoire et institutions du Kafo de Bamako d'après la tradition des Niaré." Cahiers d'études africaines, 4: 186-227.

PERINBAM, B. M. (1977) "The Dyulas in western Sudanese history: developers of resources," in B. Swartz and R. Dumett (eds.) West African Culture Dynamics: Archeological and Historical Perspectives. Paris: Mouton.

PERSON, Y. (1974) "The Atlantic coast and the southern savannahs, 1800-1880," in J.F.A. Ajayi and M. Crowder (eds.) History of West Africa, vol. 2. London: Longman.

————(1968) Samori, une révolution dyula. Dakar: IFAN.

————(1963) "Les ancêtres de Samori." Cahiers d'études africaines, 4, 1: 125-156.

PEYRISSAC, L. (1912) "La frontière franco-libérienne." Bulletin de la société de géographie commerciale de Bordeaux: 19-40.

POLLET, E. and G. WINTER (1971) La Société Soninké (Dyahunu, Mali). Bruxelles: Editions de l'Université de Bruxelles.

ROBERTS, R. (1980) "Long-distance trade and production: Sinsani in the nineteenth century." Journal of African History 21, 2: 169-188.

TRIMINGHAM, J. S. (1975) A History of Islam in West Africa. London: Oxford University Press.

5

CAMEL CARAVANS OF THE SAHARAN SALT TRADE
Traders and Transporters in the Nineteenth Century

E. ANN McDOUGALL

Though long a symbol of the exotic, the camel's significance in West African history can best be measured in more utilitarian terms: the milk and meat products it produced with a minimum intake of food and water; the mobility it gave to seek healthier environments or flee enemies in war; the strength it represented in combat with other herders or sedentary cultivators; and the transport it provided for a wide variety of goods and large numbers of people. In many ways it was the last attribute that had the most profound effect on the development of the West African interior, for it was the camel caravan that allowed man to exploit one of the desert's few resources—the salts that form on and just below the Saharan sands.

By the time European sailing ships made their appearance along the coast, camel caravans dominated transport in the southern Sahara and sahel. The battle between the caravel and the camel had relevance primarily for those concerned with the trans-Saharan trade in imports and exports; mastery over the internal movement of goods—salt, slaves, grain, and cloth—remained more or less unchallenged in the hands of camel breeding Saharans. In fact, as these enterprising merchants quickly discovered, camel transport could be profitably turned to feed Europeans on the coast as well as North Africans in Timbuktu.

Camel caravans integrated trade to the coast with the internal, desert-side economy (Ca da Mosto, 1937: 16-21; Fernandes, 1938: 78-83, 114-119, 136-145). By the nineteenth century, as the French pushed their commercial and military interests into the interior, Saharan *azalay* (''string of camels'') pursued a thriving commerce from the Upper Senegal to the Niger Bend. And camels, though able to thrive in the sahel only during the dry season, constituted the principal means by which goods in general were transported. For all intents and purposes then, much of the region's economy lay in the hands of the Saharans. With their salt and their camels, they not only influenced the volume, value, and seasonality of commerce in Sudanese markets, but reaped a large part of the profits (Curtin, 1975: 279-281; McDougall, 1980: 171-176). From the point of view of the French, the imposition of authority in the Sudan had to confront the powerful presence of an independent and resistant Saharan society. Consequently, French forays into desert politics, as well as French assaults on Saharan commercial interests, mark the history of the Upper Senegal-Niger after about 1890. The battles dragged on for almost two decades before resolution on either front was achieved. In the end, it was the railroad that won the real victory, not French military prowess or commercial acumen. Despite attempts to push Saharan salt off the market with sea salt and imported French imitators, it was the arrival of large quantities of cheap, rail-shipped salt after 1905 that began to undermine the Saharan's quasi-monopoly.[1] A gradual but nonetheless irreversible change was underway in the role of desert salts and consequently, in the role of the camel in the Sudanese economy.

In the nineteenth century, a Saharan caravan might follow any one of several routes to the Sudan depending on the source of salt. Coastal mines such as N'teret supplied some sea salt, and merchants obtained varying qualities of earth salt in southern Saharan *sbakh* (depressions) such as the one at Tishit. But by far the greatest proportion of desert salt traded in the south came from the two rock-salt mines Ijil and Tawdenni (see Map 5.1). Azalay from Tawdenni passed through Arawan toward Timbuktu and Kabara,[2] from where the salt was usually transported up or down the Niger by boat. A good proportion of Tawdenni salt, however, was sent from Arawan overland to Walata and even Tishit from where it went south as far as the Niger markets of Sinsani, Nyamina, and Bamako. The Ijil industry generated a comparable network. While it tied into some southern Mauritanian marketing systems, its principal artery was directed to the south and

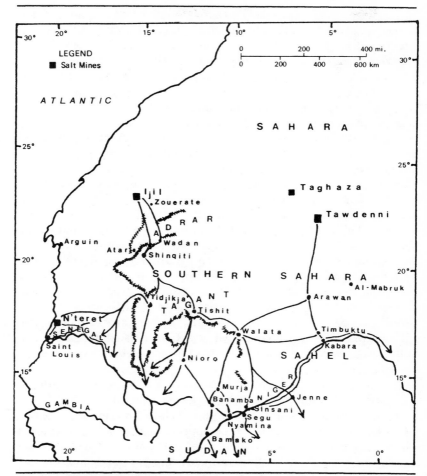

Map 5.1:   Principal Salt Caravan Routes, Nineteenth Century

east, toward Tishit. From Tishit (also the source of *amersal*)[3] routes radiated in all directions toward the sahel and Sudan (McDougall, 1980: 199-220, 232-249).

An Ijil caravan of the 1900s was usually large, several tribes and factions traveling together. Even when these slow-moving associations broke up into smaller groups (which they often did in the sahel), an average caravan might well number 200 to 300 camels. Units of under 100 operated in both the desert and sahel, but these were more likely to be "off season" travelers or those trading small amounts of salt in the context of transhumance (Meillassoux, 1963; Baillaud, 1902: 42; McDougall, 1980: 253-257). These variations in the size of an average caravan related to the problem of security. All accounts of nineteenth- and early twentieth-century travel warn of the dangers travelers faced from bandits.

In the nineteenth century, ratios of one man to four or five camels were common, depending on the nature of the terrain and, presumably, the cargo. When heavily loaded (up to 200 kilograms), badly fed camels managed between 16 and 25 kilometers a day; a fresh, lightly loaded animal averaged between 30 and 40 kilometers (Curtin, 1975: 280; Daniel, 1974). In contrast, alternative forms of transport in the sahel— donkeys and oxen—could carry 50 or 100 kilograms (respectively), travel about 30 kilometers a day, and required one man for every five animals. This situation gave camels a carrying capacity of more than double that of donkeys and 50 percent more than oxen. In areas of difficult terrain, such as that between the upper Senegal River valley and Segu, efficiency varied considerably as frequent loading and unloading necessitated one man for each animal. Hence routes where camels could be used were usually preferable[4] (Curtin, 1975: 280). As Soleillet noted in 1878, "transport of ten leagues in the Sudan is more difficult than 200 in the Sahara where one man leads five camels and where each camel carries at least the load of two oxen or four donkeys" (Soleillet, 1887: 179).

The transport advantage of the camel over other livestock resulted in a geographical anomaly whereby it was cheaper to transport goods a greater distance by camel than follow a shorter route by donkey or oxen. By the 1890s, imports of blue cloth *(guinée),* which used to come across the Sahara, were finding their way to the interior via the Senegal River, following an overland route from the port of Medina to the desert-side salt market of Nioro. This development generated an extensive trade in which traders *(juula)* carried the cloth from Medina and Nioro to Banamba (north of Bamako) where they exchanged it for Saharan salt. Although guinée cloth could have been traded directly for salt in Nioro, Baillaud discovered that it was cheaper to bring cloth and salt to Banamba before making the exchange. In Nioro one piece of guinée was 7.50 F and one bar of salt 17 F, but in Banamba cloth and salt sold for 10 F and 30 F, respectively. The proportional rise in the value of salt was substantially greater than that of guinée, hence, for the Saharans, there was a strong incentive to bring salt as far south as possible.[5] As Baillaud (1902: 43) explained, juula also gained: "The duulas [juulas], not using camels, are most interested that the Moors bring the salt as close as possible to the place of sale, that is, to the Niger bend and the river. They pay more to offset the transport cost of the Moors."[6] The impact of the camel's competitive edge was striking: in 1896 a breakdown of livestock carrying 12,500 tons of goods included 4600 donkeys, 1500 oxen, and 17,000 camels. Camels, therefore, were responsible for 74 percent of all freight transported (Curtin, 1975: 280). Undoubtedly, heavy burdens of desert salt made up a very large part of this volume.

SAHARAN SOCIETY AND THE SALT TRADE

In the nineteenth century three main social groupings, each associated with specific activities, characterized Saharan society. Warriors (*arab hassan*) were responsible for secular administration and warfare; men of letters (*zawaya* or marabouts) prayed, taught, and provided spiritual guidance; and tributaries (*aznaga* or *lahma*) produced the material life of society. They worked. In reality, zawaya families were often able to use the prestige earned by their saintliness to manipulate others, to gain the alliance of warriors, and, hence, to exercise political power. Fractions of zawaya were even known to carry arms and were little different than their hassani neighbors in terms of their activities. The relationship of tributaries to individual tribes or families was often ambiguous. Groups that had been weakened by some disaster (drought, disease, war) might seek the protection of a wealthier tribe, thereby becoming clients. Others, in contrast, were forced into this position by tribes with the military capability to extract tribute. Even among zawaya, those who sought spiritual guidance or mediation services from a particular Shaikh entered into relations of interdependence in which they paid for the advantages they gained with religious offerings and gifts (Miské, 1970: 93-104; Stewart, 1973: 54-65, Leriche, 1955; Hamidoun, 1952: 41-47). But as Charles Stewart (1973: 61-62) has pointed out, "the differences between spiritual and physical threats as a means to encourage gifts from a subordinate in nineteenth-century Mauritania appears to have been slight." The power of such subordinates lay in their ability to seek new alliances—to weaken the resources of one patron by moving into the sphere of influence of another who could provide for or protect them better. This "lateral mobility," writes Stewart (1973: 61-62), "could determine the balance of military power between opposing hassani groups; in zawiya units the movement of dependents meant a shift in labor and thus, in economic power.''

These complex relations were evident in the organization of both Ijil and Tawdenni transport. Of the many tribes involved in the Ijil trade, some like the Kunta, Id aw Ali, Tekna, and Awlad Nacer were completely independent and owned their own camels. Others stood in various tributary relationships to them, the Kunta-dominated Touabir, Ahl Tenegant, and Diebas being only a few cases in point (Poulet, 1904: 29-39; Marty, 1921b: 182-201). Because of the pivotal role of Tishit in the marketing network, its merchants were especially prominent. Nineteenth-century sources reported that "the Tichitts [were] particularly given to commerce" and carried on salt exchanges of a "special nature" throughout the sahel (Bouët-Willaumez, 1848: 36; McDougall, 1980: 251 n. 93). These were in fact clerics, the Awlad Bella and Shurfa of Tishit. The Awlad Bella, once a powerful warrior faction, assumed a clerical role after the Kunta and Awlad Nacer defeated them in the eighteenth century. Subsequently, they paid tribute both to the victors, whose exactions were often pressing, and to a new power in the region, the Mechdouf. Awlad Bella often joined the Mechdouf confederation in desert salt caravans, as well as traveling on their own in the sahel. The Tishit Shurfa comprised two groups, divided into four fractions, the largest of which was the Ahl Masna. Like their neighbors, they were part of the Kunta sphere of influence and by 1890 paid tribute to the Mechdouf (Marty, 1921a, III: 280-286; Poulet, 1904: 106-110). A mid-century account of these Tishit Moors suggests that most were actually sedentary wholesalers who preferred to let others look after their long-distance trading interests (Mage, 1868: 120).

While the transport of Tawdenni salt to Sahelian markets was in part provided by North African merchants in the context of trans-Saharan trade, by the 1850s the principal Saharan participants seem to have been the Tajakant, Awlad Daoud, and Kunta. The two Tajakant fractions, the Deilouba and Ousra, were clerics. They had large camel herds and participated regularly in the Tawdenni azalay. The Ousra apparently paid protection money to most of their neighbors that often included salt bars (Marty, 1921a, III: 88-91). The Awlad Daoud comprised several tribes of which the Awlad Boradda and the Tormoz were most active in the salt trade. The latter, though frequently victims of pillage and extortion by their more powerful relations, the Awlad Allouch, were considered "great warriors and camel raisers." The Boradda too were known for raising fine camels and were prey to exactions by several neighboring tribes, especially the Awlad Allouch. In the nineteenth century they were tributary to the Mechdouf as well. Awlad Boradda participation in the Tawdenni azalay usually consisted of several hundred camels, and many Awlad Boradda were known as specialized salt merchants (Marty, 1921a, III: 16, 43-51).

The third main group involved in the Tawdenni trade was the Kunta, or more specifically, the eastern Kunta tribes of the Azawad and Hodh as distinct from their "cousins," the Kunta al-Qibla (Kunta of the West) who were engaged in Ijil commerce. By the late eighteenth century Kunta political strategy, commercial interests, and religious leadership under Shaikh Sidi al-Mukhtar al-Kunti had brought the tribe to great prominence across the southwestern Sahara as propagators of the Qadiriyya brotherhood.[7] Involvement in the salt trade played no small role in this rise to power (Batran, 1971: 94-104; McDougall, 1980: 101-107). In fact, it has been argued in a recent study (Batran, 1971: 112) of the Kunta Azawad that,

> Kunta al-Qibla control of the salt mines of Ijil in the second half of the eighteenth century and the concomitant rise in wealth, prosperity and prestige vis-a-vis other Zwaya [Zawaya] of Mauritania were the main-spring of the success the Qadiriyya enjoyed in the Western Sahara.

Similarly, in the east, Kunta participation in the salt trade from Tawdenni constituted a "basic occupation" by the eighteenth century and was "a crucial factor in the germination and growth of their strength and popularity in the region" (Batran, 1971: 94-104). Sidi al-Mukhtar al-Kunti organized the Kunta commerce efficiently and profitably. He not only gave attention to the exchange of salt and other goods, but to the transport of these commodities. In addition to raising fine herds of goats, sheep and other livestock, the Kunta specialized in breeding camels. While certain types were best for riding, and others for food, most notable were those the Kunta raised for transport. Tradition recalls Sidi al-Mukhtar as "special" because he was able to use only his own camels in the azalay, a reflection of the importance attached to the control of animal labor in the salt industry (Batran, 1971: 261).

LABOR IN SAHARAN COMMERCE AND SOCIETY

Nineteenth-century caravans were often in the hands of pious leaders (shurfa), but not everyone in a caravan owned the camels they led or the salt they carried. As for the domestic chores, these were invariably undertaken by less-than-free workers—slaves or freed slaves called *haratine,* or religious students (*talamidh*). Indeed, a wide range of socioeconomic statuses characterized nineteenth-century caravans. René Caillié (1979: 256-257), who traveled in West Africa in the early nineteenth century, observed that:

> The cameleers do not follow one master. Each is the *maître de la conduite* of his own camels, however few he has. Some have fifteen, others six or ten, and still others three. I have even seen those with only two. These are the poorest. They join with the richer [merchants] driving their camels, receiving in payment food and water [by no means inconsequential] along the route.

The socioeconomic inequality represented in the composition of these great moving communities was no less striking on the level of tribal and factional participation. Subordinates included tributary groups, clients of other tribes, individuals and factions who were religious students of prominent clerics, and servile laborers of assorted status who were found among each of these groups. No particular form of labor recruitment was specific to any one aspect or any one network of trade; rather, labor recruitment and merchant investment were part of the broader structure that characterized Saharan society.

The predominant Kunta influence in the Tawdenni trade nurtured the recruitment of labor among religious students, which, in time, gave the term talamidh itself a much broader meaning. As Stewart (1973: 109, 112-113; on talamidh, 112-122) has shown, the Awlad Ibiri rose to a position of religious and political prominence in the nineteenth century under the guidance of Kunta disciple Shaikh Sidiyya al-Kabir because of their exploitation of talamidh labor:

> The principal elements of the Shaikh's economic power were revenue from religious offerings (*hadaya*), agricultural lands, [and] his group of talamidh. . . . [Here] the Shaikh's economic organization rested squarely on a foundation of the cadre of talamidh who sought out his protection and spiritual guidance. The world talamidh did not simply imply "students" . . . [it] also connoted a socio-economic group of in-

dividuals, families or fractions who were joined in their loyalty to [the] Shaikh.

Talamidh figure prominently in Stewart's discussion of the Awlad Ibiri's herding and salt trading organizations. The caravans themselves varied according to whether they were "small-scale domestic caravans" of under 100 animals traveling mainly in the sahelian regions, or "large-scale long-distance enterprises" of 300 or more camels. The former provided transport for the coastal salt coming from N'teret, while the latter comprised a segment of the Ijil network. This trade to the Adrar was a commercial innovation acredited specifically to Shaikh Sidiyya and his economic reforms (Stewart, 1973: 115-120).

Among the Kunta Azawad, to whom the origins of talamidh as a "socioeconomic supratribal body" can be traced, talamidh were instrumental in conducting business interests. Already in the late seventeenth and early eighteenth centuries, one Kunta family operating from Arawan used three talamidh to manage their affairs. One organized and conducted the azalay, a second supervised the mining and preparation of the salt blocks, and the third attended to the livestock and camels. It is said that the one who managed the mining sector amassed a considerable fortune through his own private trade, which suggests that talamidh may have been given some sort of payment in kind for their services (Batran, 1971: 94-104). By the early nineteenth century, the practice of using talamidh to operate Kunta salt caravans was common (Batran, 1971: 261).

In both the Ijil and Tawdenni systems, servile labor was widespread among tribes and fractions of every status. Servile labor referred to haratine (freed slaves with remaining ties of dependency) and 'abid (slaves). Haratine usually traveled with the main camp and furnished most of the shepherds for herding livestock. In time, some haratine became sufficiently independent to establish autonomous camps and possess their own herds; nevertheless, they remained attached to the main tribe whose name they continued to use. Haratine also worked the date-palm groves and cultivation areas in the Adrar and Tagant. While these communities were more or less autonomous, part of the food they produced belonged to their former masters, who arrived annually at the *guetna* (harvest) to collect their due.

Slaves tended to live within the confines of their master's camp. Warriors and zawaya possessed more slaves than anyone else, but even clients and haratine used slaves for domestic chores. Treatment varied according to status and the master. *Nanma* (slaves descended from the early Almoravid conquerers of the region) could easily be mistaken for members of the extended family; women often served as nannys and concubines, and no nanma could be sold. Inherited slaves *('abid tilad),* in contrast, had no special role and no rights; the same was true of the *teryha* (new acquisition). Children of slaves were still 'abid tilad, though those born of a free master and slave concubine were free. Generally speaking, it was considered a pious act to free a slave or to allow a slave to buy his or her freedom. While this did happen on occasion, freedom was more likely to come as payment for some special service, to evolve over time as a group of slaves gradually became wealthy enough to be self-sufficient, or to be granted on the death of a master (Marty, 1921b: 335; McDougall, 1980: 143-147; Hamidoun, 1952: 48-49).

In the salt trade, slaves were more visible than haratine. Haratine were primarily employed in the herding, mining, and agricultural sectors of the economy, although some slaves were also used. At Tawdenni, for example, haratine and 'abid both were employed by various tribes to dig and prepare salt. The Tajakant kept a few servile workers at the mine all year round to exploit salt and to care for the camels they pastured in the vicinity[8] (Rougier, 1929: 477). Some of these 'abid (and possibly haratine) also accompanied the azalay, just as they did elsewhere.

In the nineteenth century, the daily chores of caravan travel were almost invariably the work of slaves. These responsibilities included loading and unloading the cargo, pasturing the camels, seeking water and wood for cooking, and preparing the meals. In the Ijil trade women sometimes accompanied caravans on the Tishit-sahel part of the journey, those of servile status sharing the domestic chores and serving their mistresses[9] (Caillié, 1979: 269). Leopold Panet, in a less-than-pleasant experience in an Adrar caravan, found that slaves were usually forced to walk even under difficult circumstances. In this particular situation, water shortage had become acute and the slaves had been allowed to ride only so that their water rations could be reduced even further. Other experiences with the difficulties of desert travel confirm that when food or water supplies diminished, slaves were usually the first to suffer (Panet, 1968: 104-110; Riley, 1965: 263-267). Nevertheless, those involved in transporting salt may well have been better off than slaves engaged in agriculture or herding. They, at least, had the opportunity to trade on their own account (albeit on a small scale) and were well-placed to do special favors for their masters for which they might expect a reward. Marty (1921a), for example, mentioned that slaves were sometimes freed in return for having carried out "advantageous commercial transactions." Others, like the former slave of a Moorish salt merchant whom Mungo Park met, were freed on their master's death. Involvement in commerce gave certain advantages, and this particular slave had managed to become a successful salt trader in his own right (Park, 1969: 179).

The Tishit-based commerce in particular included a high proportion of slave laborers. A mid-century account of "Tishit Moors" suggests that most were actually sedentary wholesalers who preferred to let others look after their long-distance trading interests (Mage, 1868: 120). The Awlad Bella probably epitomized this sort of organization: Their slaves collected salt both from Ijil and the nearby amersal deposits, transported it to the sahel, and took responsibility for marketing it.[10] In line with observations Panet made in the Adrar, and elsewhere along the desert edge, an individual's scale of operations need not have been large. Among the Awlad Bella it could have involved as few as five slaves[11] (Panet, 1968: 76-78; Park, 1969: 106-107; Curtin, 1975: 283-284; Colin 1882-1883: 159-180).

Slaves were also a commodity of desert-side trade. The point of intersection between servile labor, the salt trade, and clerical power in the southwestern Sahara is a crucial one for any socioeconomic analysis, including an analysis of transport labor. Though every social group made use of slave labor, clerics probably employed the greatest number (Miské, 1970: 99; Hamés, 1977: 12, 17). Only they had the recognized right to control and exploit economic resources—to dig wells, mine salt, cultivate date-palm trees, and trade (Stewart, 1973: 60). Hence, not only was the zawaya need for labor greater, the zawaya access to labor was better. While hassani were dependent largely on raiding for slaves, clerics could trade for them, not only a more reliable form of supply but one which permitted control over the age and sex of the slaves they acquired. While many of the slaves flowing across the desert edge in the second half of the nineteenth century were destined for North African markets, a significant number were absorbed into the Saharan economy itself. Whether or not these then remained slaves or freed, became haratine, their source remained no less important—namely, the slave trade with the Sudan. And those engaged in this trade were none other than salt merchants. According to El-Wasit (Chenguiti, 1953: 115-116), a Mauritanian scholar writing in the early twentieth century:

> In the past, commerce flourished in Mauritania. The principal object was salt which one traded for slaves in the Sudan. The salt was transported in bars attached to the backs of camels. On arrival in the Sudan, the bars were deposited and cut according to the contour of the foot of the slave to be traded, the piece taken from the bar representing the price of the slave. It was said that a slave sold himself by the measure of his foot. But . . . today, a camel load [of salt] is exchanged for one slave of either sex. . . . It is said that some trade their children for salt. This salt was extracted from the [Kunta controlled] salines of Ijil. . . . The buyers come from the Hodh, Tishit, Reguibat and the Tagant . . . they transport the salt to the Sudan from which they return with slaves. One part of these slaves serve as payment for the debts contracted on departure, another part is sold to the Trarza [Moors] and some are kept to work as domestic servants.

Unfortunately, data are not sufficient to assess the proportion of slaves retained in the desert in the nineteenth century, or, most pertinent here, the number that contributed to the reproduction of the region's servile labor force, but it is clear that labor recruitment tended to reinforce traditional social relations and enhance the position of the zawaya. And in this, the organization of labor in the Saharan salt trade was part of the recruitment of labor in society as a whole. Consequently, increasing demands for labor in any sector of the economy were likely to draw on some form of dependent or servile labor—on clients, talamidh, haratine, or slaves.

CONTINUITY AND CHANGE IN CARAVAN TRANSPORT

Commercial expansion in the nineteenth century was related to the availability of credit from Moorish merchants, increased cultivation of grain and cotton by Sudanese farmers, and the steady, indeed expanding, supply of slaves from nineteenth-century *jihads* (McDougall, 1980: 226-258). This economic growth in turn placed new demands on Saharan labor. While sources and mechanisms of recruitment appear to have undergone few notable changes, the scale of employment and degree of specialization increased considerably. The slaves sent by sedentary merchants to distant markets had different responsibilities.

There were those who loaded cargo and those who cared for livestock, while only the oldest and most reliable were entrusted with the direction of the caravan and sale of the salt. When not actually engaged in trading, some slaves were free to seek extra work in the date-palm groves or aid women in preparing grains. They were able to accumulate some wealth and engage in petty trade on their travels. In the Adrar, servile workers could acquire skills in handling salt-laden camels (especially along the treacherous trails leading to and from the Ijil mine) which they could later use on their own account.[12] Panet met an Awlad Bou Sba merchant who had left his caravan in the hands of his "servants" while he proceeded to Shinqiti. In this instance, the loads were too heavy and a considerable amount of salt was unloaded and left to be collected later. Panet's discussion suggests that this situation was by no means unusual (Panet, 1968: 76, 87). Indeed, as merchants became sedentary, their servants or trusted slaves took over not only the actual work but more of the decision making and direction involved in the operation of the caravans themselves. A prime example of this type of growth was the Tishet-based Haidara family. The caravans of Moulay al-Mahdi Haidara and his brothers were family operations and were highly dependent on slave labor. Slave agents handled the transport and sale of salt in the desert and the sahel, and slaves were even settled at Banamba to farm and look after business all year round. The Haidara brothers exemplified the type of Moorish salt trader who seems to have become quite common in the Sudan by the 1890s. Binger (1892: 32) characterized these great merchants as those "whose slaves traded for them while they remained sedentary and lived a life of luxury" (cf. Marty, 1921a, IV: 75-5).

Increased specialization among some nomads also occurred. By the end of the century, the Awlad Bou Sba, the Tajakant, and the Laghlal were "almost exclusively" devoted to transport. The Awlad Bou Sba was a large confederation consisting of many warrior and clerical fractions. They operated between Cape Blanc and Marakesh, with some fractions plying the salt route between Ijil and Tishit. Awlad Bou Sba merchants, such as the one Panet met, comprised one of the largest components of Shinqiti's sedentary community around the turn of the century. As their warrior fractions brought respect for the tribe with military victories, the commercial activities of other groups acquired for it the additional reputation of being great traders (Binger, 1892: 32; Faidherbe, 1859: 135-136; Panet, 1968: 76). And in the Tawdenni trade, yet another fraction (Ahl Kabla) had long specialized as guides and escorts between Timbuktu and the mine (Adams, 1816: 133; on the Awlad Bou Sba: 135-136).

Similarly, the widely dispersed Tajakanat, also known as clerics and merchants, arrived in the vicinity of Arawan and Taodeni around 1850 to trade in salt. "At first," according to one report, "they did not participate at all in the extraction of salt. It was only after the miners [belonging to other tribes] refused to work for them that they put some of their own haratine and slaves to work." Soon after, they were joined in this "purely commercial enterprise" by Tekna, originally from the Oued Noun region. These Tajakanat caravans, together with their Tekna allies, travelled from Shinqiti to Arawan carrying Tawdenni and Ijil salt. In 1897 the Tajakanat not only traded "for Moors of the same origin" (that is, the same tribe) but on behalf of other fractions. And these activities appear to have expanded in scope. A few years later, the Tajakanat were described as "pastoralists, agriculturalists, and merchants . . . the great *convoyeurs* of the desert," with activities extending "great distances" to the east and south from Saquia al-Hamra[13] (Poulet, 1904: 138-139; Marty, 1921a, III: 88-91; Rougier, 1929: 477). The Laghlal, a similar group but of purely zawaya character, also traded in salt at least from the middle of the century. While their herders tended camels, sheep and goats, their merchants operated as far north as the Algerian frontier and as far south as Banamba and Segu. By the 1890s, they conducted as much commerce in the circle of Nioro as all the other Saharans together, and were described as forming "the greatest part of all caravans carrying salt to the Sudan"[14] (Faidherbe, 1859: 144). This trend was strengthened, indeed encouraged, by changes occurring in the broader pastoral organization of society. During the latter part of the century various factors (including drought and warfare) were pushing some tribes into the southern fringes of the desert where they concentrated on raising small livestock—goats, sheep, and even oxen where possible. They became clients and tributaries of those who remained in the desert—the "grand nomads" as Paul Marty (1921a, III: 16-17) described them in the early twentieth century. These were the camel raisers and hence, the only ones who could continue to engage in large-scale, long-distance trade.

Although the structure of these transport services between fractions and tribes is not entirely clear, there is evidence suggesting that contractual arrangements for both human and animal services became increasingly common. Again, the Kunta's organization of the Tawdenni trade proves enlightening. By the early nineteenth century, it is said that Sidi al-Mukhtar al-Kunti operated his personal affairs through hired agents ('ummal) and that they were permitted to carry on their own business at the same time, providing they produced accounts for inspection on demand. According to Batran (1971: 261-262), the activities of one of these agents (from the hassani tribe of Awlad Delim) took the following form:

> Al-Hajj 'Uthman [the agent] would leave al-Hilla at the head of between 500 to 1,000 camels. On his arrival at Tawdenni the Qa'id of the village loaded the camels with salt. Al-Hajj 'Uthman, it is said, used to appropriate several hundred of these camel loads for himself, selling them on credit to the Barabish and other salt dealers to be paid in gold in Timbuktu. He would then hire caravans to guide the azalay to an agent in Timbuktu. . . . Having thus dispatched the salt on its way to Timbuktu, he returned to al-Hilla where he was given camels and various other commodities (wool, hides, dates, etc.) to sell together with the salt on the market of Timbuktu.

Tradition makes the point that Sidi al-Mukhtar was "special" because he used 'ummal rather than the talamidh employed by other traders. But the form of payment—the right to several hundred loads of salt to trade on his own account—does not appear qualitatively different from the arrangements sometimes made with talamidh. What is striking here is the identity of the agent—a hassani of the Awlad Delim. Sidi al-Mukhtar was effectively using the practice of contractual labor, which had evolved within his tribe to accomplish what was ultimately a political as much as an economic goal, namely an alliance between powerful zawaya and hassani interests. With respect to the agent's activities, it is notable that he chose to hire caravaneers for Sidi al-Mukhtar's salt, but sell his own on credit. One could postulate that sales of this nature were a way of disposing of camels who had made several trips and whose value, therefore, was diminishing. But perhaps most importantly, it suggests that skilled caravaneers were few in number and high in price.

Caillié's (1979: 229-230) observations (ca. 1820) confirm that this was probably the case, though it seems he was speaking of a less skilled group than the Kunta salt traders employed. He commented on the scarcity of Tuareg transporters between Kabara and Timbuktu as "only the poorest among them . . . make their living this way; the others are too proud." In contrast, half a century later Lenz found several groups selling comparable services in Timbuktu and Arawan. In 1880, he was able to strike a bargain with some Toromoz salt traders over the rental of five camels with drivers. The agreed price of twenty bars of salt (worth some twenty mithcals of gold) was "relatively high," but not, in his opinion, excessive given that several competitors were demanding as much as seventy mithcals for the same service. The transporters par excellence, however, were the Berabish based in Arawan. Trans-Saharan caravans heading for Timbuktu were "encouraged" to sell their camels and buy new ones from the Berabish, or pay a very high tax—both in "exchange" for guaranteed security on the last leg of the journey. Camels thusly acquired were, of course, recycled into the transport business a few months later. At the time of Lenz's passage through Arawan, Tawdenni salt caravans were exempt from such exactions, possibly because the Berabish themselves were also engaged in the trade (Lenz, 1868-1867: 90-98, 142). If the practices of the Kunta agent discussed above were representative of Berabish involvement in the salt industry, then the tribe was able to expand its camel herds as well as its overall wealth through salt loads acquired on credit at the mine. Indeed what we know of Kunta and Berabish activities suggests that the provision of credit and transport were often related. The Kunta may have sold camels and salt to the Berabish on credit, but others undoubtedly made use of Berabish camels as well as personnel to transport their salt to Timbuktu. In addition, from at least the late eighteenth century, much of Tawdenni's salt was extracted on behalf of the "Qa'id"—the representative of a southern Moroccan family whose claim to proprietorship over the mine dated to the late sixteenth-century Moroccan invasion of Songhay. Apparently, several tribes were involved in transporting this salt, which would be given them "on credit," as far as Timbuktu. Sidi al-Mukhtar al-Kunti and his agents were among the more prominent of these customers. According to Batran (1971: 259), most Kunta business was transacted along these lines, which is equivalent to saying that the role of transporter, operating at Tawdenni, was an intrinsic element of their commercial organization. Nevertheless, indications are that the potential for expansion of contractual transport in the Tawdenni salt trade had barely been tapped by the latter part of the century.

Though the picture is by no means clear, the development of a Tawdenni "transport industry" around the turn of the century appears to have been shaped by the same conditions which affected the structure of pastoralism more generally. The distinction between groups was reduced to the issue of who did and who did not have their own camels. The Kunta, for example, remember that when the French arrived in the country (presumably the 1890s), their herds had recently been decimated. Consequently they had to rent camels from the Tuareg at a cost of half the salt transported. The Kunta were sufficiently wealthy to rebuild their herds and free themselves of the need to hire transport (Génévière, 1950: 1118). But few others were able to do likewise. During the early colonial period, only the Kunta, the Toromoz, the Berabish, and some Tuareg continued to send their own azalay to Tawdenni (Clauzel, 1960: 89-92). By 1910 the majority of tribes engaged in the salt trade hired camel transport. In 1915 this "contract de transport" usually cost three bars in four delivered to Timbuktu, hence, the transporters' pay fluctuated according to the price of salt in a given season.[15] The implications of the growing role played by these caravaneers in the Tawdenni commerce was painfully felt in 1910 when salt prices fell so low drivers refused to make the trip. In the words of that year's commercial report, Timbuktu was "threatened with famine [and] one envisaged the ruin of the Town."[16]

Contractual arrangements were also common in Mauritania. In 1850, Panet's (1968: 65-66) description of the organization of the salt trade between Shinqiti and Tishit showed an arrangement similar to the one found in the Tawdenni operation:

> Each year when the rains cease to flood the desert routes the Arabs [Saharans] of Tishit travel to Chinguetti and Wadan, and purchase large amounts of *guinée* and salt. . . . All affairs of importance when they involve credit, give place to a written contract which stipulates the merchandise sold, the period for which credit is extended, and the way in which payment will be made.

And Al-Wasit's account of the Ijil salt trade, in which salt was given on credit to transporters who repaid their debts with slaves, indicates that a comparable organization characterized trade to the sahel-Sudan. In the desert salt trade, where travel was difficult and costs high, the extension of credit and the provision of transport were two sides of the same coin. Sedentary merchants in Shinqiti, Tishit, and other communities either turned increasingly to the use of slave labor (like the Haidara), or they came to depend more and more on the services of camel breeders like the Tajakant, Laghlal, and Awlad Bou Sba. By the early twentieth century, even the Kunta clients who mined salt at

Ijil were able to establish themselves as part-time transporters using Kunta-owned camels. They carried salt over the difficult trail to Wadan for a payment of one bar in six (approximately one bar per load; Prudhomme, 1925: 216).

The development of specialized transport services provided new options to tribes and fractions with camels (or access to camels through client relationships) but also reinforced these traditional socioeconomic ties by favoring growth in the pastoral sector. And because these new options were inextricably bound up with trade, they also enhanced the already prominent position of the clerics. Although some warrior groups were becoming professional protectors for caravans (Poulet, 1904: 162), most continued to operate in their more traditional mode, which is to say offering merchants the choice of payment or pillage. By the end of the century, most tribes whether hassan or zawaya, in fact included warrior fractions. In the 1890s, for example, the Adrar Kunta actually had more warriors than any single warrior tribe and included an infamous "brigand organization" of haratine, the Soukabes, who were said to spread a "reign of terror everywhere they appeared." In 1897, though the Kunta considered themselves an "exclusively religious group," they were "above all warriors"[17] (Bou el Mogdad, 1952: 117-20; Bâ, 1932: 84; Marty, 1921b: 196). Investment in long distance trade required one's own protective force.

CONCLUSION

In the southern Sahara and sahel, as in many other areas of Africa, long-distance exchange was a means of realizing wealth from surplus production. Concomitantly, control of labor was critical both to the success of this exchange and to the ultimate translation of its wealth into power. In several cases in this collection, nineteenth- and early twentieth-century changes in trade were generating new forms of labor control and new kinds of workers who in turn altered existing balances of wealth and power. In these instances trade was based upon a variety of export commodities and involved considerable European capital in its organization. Such export-oriented specialization invariably depended upon the fluctuations of an external economic system for its existence—or, at least its existence in a particular form. The Saharan-sahelian salt trade was notably different. Labor was drawn from pre-existing social categories and organized according to relations which permeated society as a whole. Control remained in the hands of a "traditional" elite, and the expansion of this trade in the nineteenth century acted to consolidate the wealth and power of this group vis-à-vis others. More specifically, it allowed some zawaya to prosper at the expense of hassani groups as well as weaker clerical tribes. The explanation for this continuity may lie in the fact that the salt trade was based upon the exchange of internally produced and consumed commodities. External goods were for the most part incorporated into existing networks, thereby tending to reinforce rather than disrupt established relations of trade and production. Similarly, the commercial capital underlying the trade was generated within Saharan society; hence, it was extracted from traditional forms of labor. Commercial expansion was likely to entrench rather than uproot these forms.

Whereas the "labor of trade" in so many other areas seems to have provided an important channel for the penetration of wage labor, this particular trade spread the social and economic relations of Saharan society into the sahel. These forms of labor mobilization in turn, stood in direct opposition to the penetration of capitalist relations of production. The sale of human and animal labor by contract had certainly emerged in the Arawan-Timbuktu corridor by the middle of the century, although it took some time to penetrate the salt industry. These developments had the potential of creating groups or classes of Saharans dependent on selling their labor as transporters, but in reality, the very nature of camel transport precluded the realization of this potential. For even among the larger, more commercially oriented tribes like the Kunta or Laghlal, access to camels remained the critical variable, and access to camels continued to be carefully controlled by existing relations of production. To whatever extent one can argue that a transport industry had evolved by the turn of the century, it is clear that the reproduction of the means of transport—the camel—was still dependent on Saharan pastoralism and its attendant social structure. Significantly, the only evidence we have of transport camels being sold, as distinct from being rented, refers to Kunta agents in the early part of the century and the Berabish sales to trans-Saharan traders. In relation to the Kunta, apart from the possibility that this was a means employed occasionally to recoup some value from worn out animals, there is no indication that pack-camels were routinely sold. Quite the opposite, if practices of the early twentieth century are any indication. The Kunta, who were great herders and merchants of animal products during the colonial era, sold camels for butchery, for milk and riding, but they avoided selling transport camels (Généviève, 1950: 1113).

Berabish camel sales, in which the price was calculated to equal costs which would otherwise be extracted as protection "taxes," were little more than a complex system of taxation which regulated the flow of camels in Saharan trade. In fact, in its role as a mechanism by which camels could be shifted between the Saharan salt commerce and the trans-Saharan trade, it provided a point of intersection between regional and international transport investments.

As long as access to camels remained circumscribed by Saharan social relations, the labor involved in camel transport did not emerge as a marketable commodity. In fact, far from alienating labor, increasing market participation in the form of rental contracts seems to have tied the worker even more closely to traditional sources of control. The Berabish, for example, used a specialized group of haratine to tend the camels they bought and sold. And the twentieth-century "contracts de transport," like their nineteenth-century precedents, involved renting camels which came with a stipulated number of drivers. There was no role, yet, in this Saharan sphere for the independent or free laborer. The transport sector of the Moorish economy experienced considerable development in the late nineteenth century, which was not inconsequential for Saharan and sahelian growth. But it was, nevertheless, a development firmly rooted in a social structure still capable of supplying the animal and human labor it needed; in this respect it did not differ from the demands placed on Saharan relations of production by other sectors of the economy. Consequently, the long-distance salt trade did not reflect the complex changes in labor and labor relations that characterized nineteenth-century transport and exchange elsewhere in Africa.

NOTES

1. AM IQ 40 Rapports commerciaux du Soudan Francais, 1904–1917; AM IQ 44 Rapports commerciaux du Cercle de Bamako, 1903–1916.

2. According to information collected by 'Aziz Batran (1971: 262) about contemporary azalay, the journey takes nine days from Tawdenni to Arawan and six from Arawan to Timbuktu. Caravans traveling from November to January (the "great azalay") travel during the day, while the "small azalay" making the journey from April to May (in great heat) travel between early evening and sunrise, resting during the day.

3. A kind of earth salt or natron that forms on the surface of the earth and can easily be scraped up in pieces; usually used for animal feed.

4. ASAOF 16 46, Soleillet, 1879.

5. The proportional rise in the value of the guinée was 33 percent, and in salt 77 percent. Consequently, salt rose in value by some 44 percent more than guinée by being taken as far south as Banamba by camel.

6. The cost of replacing injured and aged camels also had to be covered. Cortier (1906: 329) estimated the life-span of a camel making semi-annual trips to Tawdenni at six to seven years. In 1950 depreciation of a camel was calculated at approximately 150 francs per bar, as a transport camel worth 6000 francs was able to make, on average, ten return trips. This gives a slightly shorter life-span than Cortier suggested (Génévière, 1950: 1121).

7. The Qadiriyya was a mystic Islamic brotherhood that took hold and subsequently spread through much of West Africa as a consequence of Kunta propagation in the eighteenth and nineteenth centuries.

8. ASAOF 16 254, Pichon, 1900.

9. Interviews Drame, Gakou, Muhammad, 1977/78. (Interviews in Banamba listed in McDougall, 1980.)

10. Interview Muhammad, 1977/78.

11. Interview Muhammad, 1977/78.

12. Interviews Diakite, Drame, Gakou, Muhammad, 1977/78.

13. ASAOF 16 224 Capt. Lartigues, Notice sur les maures, 1897.

14. AM ID 24 Adams, Introduction à la politique maure du Sahel, 1898; ASAOF 16 224, Lartigues, 1897.

15. It is interesting that Clauzel's much more recent work (1960) cites the same price, "up to three bars in four," though of course the real value has changed. His discussion of the tribes involved in the trade and the variations of this organization is excellent (1960: 89-92).

16. AM IQ 40, 1910-1915.

17. ASAOF 16 224, Lartigues, 1897.

ARCHIVAL SOURCES

National Archives, Républic of Mali, Kouluba (AM)

AM ID 11 Appendices sur le notice sur les Maures
AM ID 24 Adams, Introduction à la politique maure du Sahel, 1898
AM 2E 75 Renseignments sur les tribes maures du Sahel, 1898-9
AM IQ 37 Rapports agricoles et commerciaux, Soudan Français; 1907-1908
AM IQ 40 Rapports commerciaux du Soudan Français; 1904-1917
AM IQ 44 Rapports commerciaux du Cercle de Bamako; 1903-1916

National Archives, Republic of Senegal, Section A.O.F., Dakar (ASAOF)

ASOAF 1 46 Soleillet, Voyage de Saint Louis à Ségou-Sikoro, Avril 1878-Octobre 1879
ASAOF 1 224 Capt. Lartigues, Notice sur les maures, 1897
ASAOF 1 254 Lt. Pichon, Rapport sur Araouwan-Taoudenni, 1900
ASAOF 3Q 5-AF Letters concerning the activities of the Compagnie de Sel Aggloméré (pour l'exportation) de l'Afrique Occidentale Française, 15 Rue Pasquer, 1897-1899.

REFERENCES

ADAMS, R. (1816) The Narrative of Robert Adams, a Sailor, Who Was Wrecked on the Western Coast of Africa, in . . . 1810. London: Murray.

BA, A.M. (1932) "L'Emirat de l'Adrar mauritanien, 1872-1908." Bulletin de la société de Géographie et d'Archéologie de la Province d'Oran 53: 83-119, 263-298.

BAIER, S. and LOVEJOY, P. (1975) "The desert-side economy of the Central Sudan." International Journal of African Historical Studies 8: 551-581.

BAILLAUD, E. (1902) Sur les routes du Soudan. Toulouse: Imprimerie et Librairie Edouard Privat.

BATRAN, A. A. (1971) "Sidi al-Mukhtar al-Kunti and the recrudesence of Islam in the western Sahara and the middle Niger, ca 1750-1811." Ph.D. thesis, University of Birmingham.

BINGER, L. G. (1892) Du Niger au Golfe de Guinée par le Pays du Kong et de Mossi, 1887-89. vol. I. Paris: Hachette.

BOU EL MOGDAD (1952) "Rapport sur ma mission en Adrar en 1900 (Mission Blanchet et Dereins)." Revue d'Histoire des Colonies by G. M. Desiré-Vuillemin t.39: 103-126.

BOUET-WILLAUMEZ, L. E. (1848) Commerce et traite des Noirs aux côtes occidentales d'Afriques. Paris: Imprimerie Nationale.

CA DA MOSTO, A. da (1937) The Voyage of Cadamosto and Other Documents on Western Africa in the Second Half of the Fifteenth Century (G. R. Crone, trans., ed.). London: Hakluyt Society.

CAILLIÉ, R. (1979) Voyage à Tombouctou, vol. II. Paris: François Maspero.

CLAUZEL, J. (1960) L'exploitation des salines de Taoudenni. Alger: Institut de Recherches Sahariennes.

COLIN, M. (1882-1883) "Le commerce sur le Haut-Sénégal." Bulletin de la Société de Géographie Commerciale de Paris 5: 159-80.

CORTIER, M. (1906) "De Tombouctou à Taodeni." La Géographie 14: 317-41.

CURTIN, P. D. (1975) Economic Change in Precolonial Africa: Senegambia in the Era of the Slave Trade. Madison: University of Wisconsin Press.

DANIEL, G. (1974) Ma vie avec une caravane de sel: des salines d'Idjil à Tidjikja. (unpublished journal, Zouerate)

EL-WASIT (1953) by Ahmed Lamine ech Chenguiti. Etudes Mauritaniennes, no. 5. Saint-Louis, Sénégal: Centre IFAN-Mauritanie.

FAIDHERBE, M. (1859) "Sahara comprise autre l'Oued Noun et le Soudan." Nouvelles Annales des Voyages (August): 129-156.

FERNANDES, V. (1938) Description de la Côte d'Afrique de Ceuta au Sénégal (1506-1507) (P. de Cenival and Th. Monod trans. and ed.). Paris: Larose.

GÉNÉVIÈRE, J. (1950) "Les Kountas et leurs activities commerciales." Bulletin de l'Institut Fondamental d'Afrique Noire, sér. B, 12: 1111-27.

HAMÈS, C. (1977) "Status et rapports sociaux en Mauritanie précoloniale." Cahiers du Centre d'Etudes et de Recherches Marxistes 133.

HAMIDOUN, M. (1952) Précis sur la Mauritanie. Sénégal: Centre IFAN–Mauritanie, Saint Louis.

LENZ, O. (1886-1887) Timbuctou. Voyage au Maroc, au Sahara et au Soudan, vol. II. Paris: Hachette.

LERICHE, A. (1955) "Notes sur les classes sociales et sur quelques tribes de Mauritanie." Bulletin d'Institut Fondamental de l'Afrique Noire, sèr B, 17: 173-203.

MAGE, E. (1868) Voyage dans le Soudan Occidental, Sénégambie-Niger. Paris: L. Hachette.

MARTY, P. (1921a) Etudes sur l'Islam et les tribes du Soudan, vol III, Les tribes Maures du Sahel et du Hodh; vol. IV, La région de Kayes, le pays Bambara, le Sahel de Nioro. Paris: ed. Ernest Leroux.

———(1921b) Etudes sur l'Islam et les tribes maures: Les Brackna. Collection de la Revue du Monde Musulman. Paris.

McDOUGALL, E. A. (in press) "The view from Awdaghust: war, trade and social change in the Southwestern Sahara, eighth through fifteenth centuries." Journal of African History.

———(1980) "The Ijil salt industry: its role in the precolonial economy of the Western Sudan." Ph.D. thesis, University of Birmingham.

MEILLASSOUX, C. (1963) "Histoire et institutions du 'Kafo' de Bamako d'après la tradition des Niaré." Cahiers d'études Africaines 4: 186-227.

MISKÉ, A. B. (1970) Al Wasît. Tableau de la Mauritanie au début du XXe siècle. Paris: Librairie C. K. Lincksieck.

PANET, L. (1968) Première exploration du Sahara occidental: relation d'un voyage du Sénégal au Maroc, 1850. Paris: Le Livre Africain.

PARK, M. (1969) Mungo Park's travels in Africa. London: J. M. Dent & Sons.

POULET, G. (1904) Les Maures de l'Afrique Occidentale Française. Extraite de la Revue Coloniale, préface M. Binger. Paris: Libraire Maritime Coloniale.

PRUDHOMME, D. (1925) "La Sebkha d'Idjil (Mauritanie)." Bulletin du Comité d'études Historiques et Scientifiques d'Afrique Française Occidentale 8: 212-16.

RAFFENEL, A. (1856) Nouveau voyage dans le Pays des Nègres suivi d'études sur la colonie du Sénégal. Paris: Imprimerie et Librairie Centrales des Chemins de Fer.

RILEY, Cpt. (1965) Sufferings in Africa: Captain Riley's Narrative (G. H. Evans, ed.). New York: C. N. Potter.

ROUGIER, F. (1929) "Les salines de Taodeni." Bulletin du Comité d'études Historiques et Scientifiques d'Afrique Française Occidentale 12: 476-483.

SOLEILLET, P. (1887) Voyage à Ségou, 1878-1879. Paris: Challemel ainé.

STEWART, C. C. with STEWART, E. K. (1973) Islam and Social Order in Mauritania. Oxford: Clarendon.

6

LIGNAGE, ESCLAVAGE, CONTRAT, SALARIAT
L'évolution de l'organisation
du commerce à longue distance
chez les Kooroko (Mali)

JEAN-LOUP AMSELLE

LE WASOLON
À L'ÉPOQUE PRÉ-SAMORIENNE

Le Wasolon, pays d'origine des Kooroko, se définit par la présence de Fula cultivateurs et éleveurs sédentaires, parlant le maninka et possédant les pratiques de cette population. Dans le sillage de ces Fula vivaient des gens de caste forgerons (*numu*) et griots (*jeli*). En occupant le Wasolon, les Fula ont créé ou recreéh certain nombre de petites chefferies qu'on nomme *jamana* et qui sont l'équivalent des *kafo* qu'on trouve en pays banmana et maninka.

Le processus de création ou de recréation de ces chefferies est le suivant: un groupe de Fula occupe une portion de territoire, le chef s'installe dans un village et place ses "frères" ou ses "fils" dans d'autres localités. La descendance de ces "frères" et de ces "fils" forme une série de lignages entre lesquels se distribue le pouvoir. Bien que des règles de transmission strictes règlent la succession à la chefferie, celle-ci est également liée de façon directe à la guerre. Tout grand chef est un *kèlèmansa* (chef de guerre) et la détention du pouvoir est synonyme de celle du fusil. Ceci s'intègre dans le cadre de la traite des esclaves atlantique puis interne qui affecte l'Afrique à cette époque.

Au milieu du 19 ème siècle, avant la conquête du Wasolon par Samori, il existait une forte demande d'esclaves notamment dans le

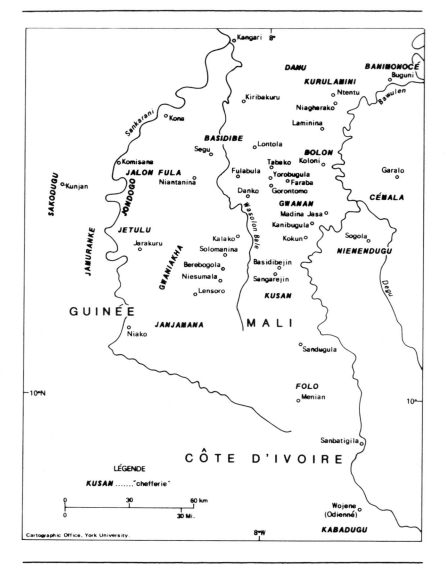

Map 6.1:   Le Wasolon avant Samori

Sahel. Ceci amène le développement des guerres intestines ou fratricides (*badenkèlè* ou *fadenkèlè*) et ceci d'autant plus que le Wasolon est une région au peuplement extrêmement dense. Pendant cette période, la guerre est assimilée au brigandage (*tègèrè* ou *nganan*), en conséquence les villages se fortifient et s'entourent d'enceintes (*jin*). Les captifs âgés sont vendus tandis que les hommes robustes et les belles femmes sont conservés par les guerriers et placés dans des hameaux de culture (*wurunde*) ou gardés à la maison.

Le Wasolon, comme du reste les régions environnantes, était donc composé de chefferies qui se battaient entre elles et qui étaient également le théâtre de conflits internes. Du fait même des conflits qui les animaient, elles donnaient prise aux Etats voisins qui pouvaient assurer leur autorité sur le pays (Segu, Kabadugu, etc.). Mais l'activité de ces chefferies ne se réduisait pas à la guerre; l'agriculture, l'élevage, la chasse et l'artisanant y occupaient également une place importante.

La pratique de l'agriculture par les Fula tient au fait qu'ils ont épousé des femmes maninka ou des captives banmana et qu'ils ont absorbé des groupes entiers d'agriculteurs sédentaires. Mais, en fait, la plus grande partie des travaux agricoles était effectuée par des esclaves, car ainsi que le dit un des nos informateurs: ''Autrefois les nobles et les griots (jeli) restaient à l'ombre.'' L'élevage est lui-même la conséquence de l'origine Fula de ces populations et il semble bien que la race Wasolon meren (ndama) qu'on trouve dans la région et qui a la propriété de résister à la mouche tsé-tsé, provienne du Futa Jalon. Au Wasolon, comme du reste en pays banmana et maninka, la chasse jouait et joue encore un rôle majeur tant au plan de l'organisation de la guerre qu'au niveau de l'alimentation et de la structure sociale (confréries de chasseurs). Pour ce qui concerne les activités artisanales, il faut noter que l'exploitation de l'or se faisait en de nombreux points de cette région. Les autres activités artisanales comprenaient le travail du cuir qui était exercé par les jeli ainsi que celui du bois, de l'argile (poterie) et du fer qui était pratiqué par les numu, groupe auquel était lié les Kooroko.

L'ORGANISATION DU COMMERCE AVANT SAMORI

C'est donc dans le cadre d'une économie centrée sur la guerre et l'esclavage qu'il faut replacer le commerce effectué au Wasolon pendant la période pré-samorienne. Bien que les informations divergent sur ce point, il semble que dès cette époque, c'est à dire vers 1850, certains Kooroko allaient acheter, avec l'or et la gomme que leur remettaient les chefs de guerre Fula, des fusils en Sierra Leone. De même, quelques uns emmenaient des esclaves jusque sur les marchés du Sahel pour les échanger contre des chevaux, des barres de sel gemme et des vêtements.

Toutefois la plupart des Kooroko répugnait à s'éloigner du Wasolon où ils bénéficiaient d'une protection relative de la part des Fula, en raison du pacte de *senankuya* qui les liait à eux. Cette situation est d'ailleurs celle décrite par Binger (1892, T1: 31). Les Kooroko

commencent par fabriquer de la poterie, des objets en bois ou en fer, de la vannerie, qu'ils vendent contre des cauries. . . . Lorsqu'ils ont un lot de quelques milliers de cauries, ils s'en vont sur les marchés à colas, achètent une petite charge de ce fruit, et vont à 300 ou 400 kms plus au Nord . . . l'échanger avec un modeste bénéfice contre du sel. Le sel à son tour est porté sur la tête jusqu'aux marchés à colas les plus éloignés, jusqu'à ce qu'ils aient gagné un certain nombre de captifs leur permettant de se livrer à un commerce plus lucratif et d'opérer sur une plus vaste échelle.

Les Kooroko, en contrepartie, se procuraient auprès des marchands Jula et Marka qui fréquentaient ce réservoir d'esclaves qu'était le Wasolon des fusils et des chevaux, c'est à dire des moyens d'extorsion destinés aux chefs Fula. Ils participaient donc directement au fonctionnement de l'économie prédatrice qui régnait à cette époque. L'or servait également à acheter des barres de sel gemme qui étaient apportées par les Marka à N'Tentu, Kona et Kankeri mais cette marchandise pouvait être également achetée avec des cauris que les Kooroko se procuraient en vendant les produits de leur artisanat.

Une fois achetées, les barres de sel étaient transportées sur la tête ou à dos d'âne à travers le Wasolon jusqu'à certains marchés à cola du Woorodugu (pays de la cola) comme Menian, Kalifilia et Kurukoro. Le voyage durait une huitaine de jours, il était effectué par les Kooroko adultes et leurs esclaves, les vieillards et les enfants restant au village. Les jeunes gens et les esclaves portaient des charges sur la tête tandis que les vieux surveillaient les ânes. Les femmes portaient des charges mais étaient surtout chargées de faire la cusisine. Un homme pouvait porter une barre et demi de sel alors qu'un âne pouvait se déplacer avec trois barres.

Arrivés sur l'un des marchés à cola, ils descendaient avec les chargements chez leurs logeurs (*ja-tigi*), des autochtones qui procédaient à l'écoulement des marchandises. A Kurukoro, la cola était apportée par deux catégories de commerçants: les Maoka (Mau) de la région de Tuba qui l'achetaient aux Jafuba (Dan) et les Konian qui se la procuraient chez les Gerze. Le lundi qui était jour de marché à Kurukoro, les vendeurs de sel et de cola exposaient des échantillons sur la place du marché qui se tenait en plein air sous les arbres à proximité du village. Les commerçants confiaient à un de leurs parents la garde de leurs échantillons de sel tandis qu'ils parcouraient le marché pour faire leur choix. Lorsqu'ils avaient trouvé un lot de cola qui leur convenait, ils en faisaient part à leur logeur qui allait trouver le logeur du commerçant de cola chez lui et entamait le marchandage. Quand celui-ci était achevé, le logeur demandait à son hôte s'il était satisfait des termes de la transaction, auquel cas le marché était conclu.

L'exposition des échantillons n'avait lieu que le jour du marché. Les autres jours, les transactions n'étaient effectuées que sous l'égide des logeurs qui se rendaient les uns chez les autres afin de s'informer des marchandises détenues par leurs hôtes respectifs. Cette organisation répondait au double souci des commerçants, d'effectuer des transactions dans de bonnes conditions en laissant aux logeurs le soin de marchander puisqu'eux seuls résidant sur place connaissaient les cours et de soustraire les marchandises aux convoitises des brigands en les entreposant dans des concessions. Une fois les transactions effectuées, les Kooroko faisaient un cadeau de sel à leur logeur et repartaient vers le Nord avec leurs chargements.

Dans le Nord, les Kooroko écoulaient leurs paniers de cola à N'Tentu, Kankeri et Kona. Les échanges sur ces marchés se faisaient exactement de la même façon que dans le Sud. Binger (1892, T1: 54) signale en effet qu'à N'Tentu: "le sel, les colas et les captifs se vendent dans les cases" et que "le surveillant du marché sert généralement de courtier pour ces opérations."

Ainsi, l'une des activités des commerçants Kooroko était constituée par la participation au commerce à longue distance, fruit lui-même de la division internationale du travail qui régnait en Afrique de l'Ouest à cette époque. Les Kooroko occupaient, en effet, une place non négligeable dans le grand système d'échanges qui consistait à transporter le sel gemme du Sahara vers la savane et la forêt, à diriger la cola produite dans la zone forestière vers la savane et le Sahel, à mettre sur le marché les esclaves et enfin à alimenter le Wasolon en armement, en chevaux et en biens de prestige. Toutefois, ce commerce entrepris sur des distances moyennes ne permettait que rarement aux Kooroko d'amasser de grosses fortunes. On cite néanmoins le cas de commerçants qui étaient parvenus à accumuler des quantités importantes d'or et de cauris et à posséder un grand nombre d'esclaves. Il devait s'agir de marchands étendant leurs activités jusqu'en Sierra Leone pour l'armement et au Sahel pour les chevaux et le sel.

Ainsi le grand père d'un de nos informateurs âgé d'une soixantaine d'années en 1969, Dugufana Jawara et qui résidait à N'Tentu possèdait quatre hameaux de culture dans lesquels étaient installés plusieurs centaines d'esclaves. En dehors des captifs qu'il utilisait pour la culture, ce commerçant avait également sept esclaves nommés *jula kuntigi* (chef commerçant) qu'il consacrait au commerce. En fait ces captifs devaient être également utilisés comme porteurs car à propos d'un Kooroko du même village, le commandant de cercle de Buguni note en 1894 que: "Faman Diawara frère du chef des forgerons de Tenentou... est... parti de Bougouni... avec 1/2 barre de sel, 7000 cauris et 4 captifs porteurs à Massigui, pays de Tla Koumadougou pour y acheter du grain."[1] Au début de sa carrière de commerçant, Dugufana Jawara se déplaçait lui-même, puis lorqu'il devint prospère, il demeura à N'Tentu et envoya le fils de son frère aîné, son fils classificatoire effectuer les transactions à sa place. La totalité des bénéfices résultant des opérations effectuées par le jula kuntigi et son "fils" revenaient à Dugufana Jawara, de telle sorte que la possession d'esclaves et de dépendants était à la fois la cause et la conséquence de son accumulation.

Néanmoins le cas de ce commerçant devait être assez rare car les Kooroko n'opéraient que sur de faibles distances et ne pouvaient donc qu'ajouter que peu de "valeur" aux marchandises dont ils faisaient le commerce. De même, leur marge de spéculation restait limitée et ils ne parvenaient sans doute que difficilement à réaliser ces gros "coups" caractéristiques du commerce traditionnel. A cette première cause de freinage venaient d'ailleurs s'en ajouter d'autres qui contribuaient à limiter considérablement l'ampleur de leur accumulation. En effet, bien que les Kooroko aient bénéficié d'une sécurité relative à l'intérieur du Wasolon grâce à la *senankuya* Fula-numu et à leur statut de forgeron, ce qui leur évitait notamment d'être tués ou réduits en captivité, ils n'en étaient pas moins soumis aux exactions des bandits Fula.

LES COMMERCANTS KOOROKO SOUS SAMORI

En 1882, Samori conquiert le Wasolon et incorpore une partie des Kooroko comme commerçants au sein de son armée qui peut être assimilée à un appareil d'état. Ces Kooroko étaient nommés *Kooroko kuntigi* (chef Kooroko) ou jula juntigi (chef commerçant) et possèdaient un statut très particulier, celui de commerçant-client ou dépendant. Ces Kooroko étaient soigneusement sélectionnés par l'Almami qui avant de les employer comme commerçants faisait procéder sur eux à une enquête minutieuse. Rien ne leur appartenait en propre: Ils étaient totalement dépendants de leur maître qui les emmenait avec lui dans ses déplacements et les utilisait au gré de ses besoins. Ces Kooroko étaient répartis en deux groupes: l'un était chargé de lui fournir l'armement, l'autre les chevaux.

L'ARMEMENT

Les Kooroko qui étaient chargés d'approvisionner l'armée et en chevaux devaient vraisemblablement faire partie de ces "caravanes officielles" dont parle Person (1968-1975, T2: 934) puisqu'ils étaient escortés au cours le leurs voyages par des "sofas" de l'Almani qui étaient censés contrôler leurs transactions. Les armes (fusils à pierre et fusils à tir rapide) et les munitions (balles, poudre) étaient achetées dans les comptoirs anglais de Sierra Leone (Freetown) et de Gambie (Bathurst), à Conakry et également dans ceux de Monrovia (Libéria). Les moyens de paiement utilisés pour l'achat de cet armement étaient surtout semble-t-il l'or, le bétail et les pièces d'argent.

LES CHEVAUX

De même que pour la fourniture d'armes, les Kooroko participaient aux "caravanes officielles" chargées d'assurer la remonte de l'armée samorienne. L'Almami ou ses lieutenants leur confiaient des esclaves qu'ils avaient pour mission d'acheminer jusqu'aux marchés du Nord où étaient achetés les chevaux. Lors de ces voyages, ils pouvaient être accompagnés par des "sofas" de Samori qui étaient chargés d'empêcher les révoltes d'esclaves et de protéger les caravanes contre des razzias éventuelles.

Sur les marchés à chevaux du pays soninké (Banamba, Tuba), sur celui de Kayes, sur ceux de la région de Segu (Fana, Barweli, San), du Baninko (Masigi) et de Bole qui étaient les plus fréquentés par les Kooroko, les esclaves constituaient pratiquement le seul moyen de paiement accepté pour l'achat de chevaux, les cauris par exemple ne pouvant jouer qu'un rôle d'appoint. Les prix variaient considérablement en fonction de l'état des deux marchandises (chevaux et esclaves) mais également d'autres facteurs tels que la valeur ajoutée par le transport, l'offre et la demande.

Si les chevaux achetés par les Kooroko pour le compte de l'Almami ne pouvaient être payés qu'avec des esclaves, cette dernière marchandise pouvait par contre servir à l'acquisition d'autres biens tels que la guinée, le sel gemme et des marchandises diverses. Parallèlement à ce qu'on pourrait appeler à la suite de Polanyi et al. (1956: 262) un commerce d'Etat (administered trade) effectué pour le compte de Samori, de nombreux Kooroko étaient engagés en tant que commerçants indépendants dans le lucratif commerce à longue distance axé sur l'approvisionnement de l'armée samorienne ainsi que de celle de Cèba, roi du Kènèdugu. Il n'est pas douteux que les guerres de la fin du 19 ème siècle (El Hadj Omar, Samori, Cèba etc.) ont entraîné un élargissement considérable du marché sous la forme d'un afflux trés important de captifs. Des régions entières étaient vidées de leurs habitants (Wasolon) tandis que dans les pays de destination se développaient les rapports de production esclavagistes (Meillassoux, 1975) Ces nouvelles conditions éminemment favorables à l'exercice du commerce profitèrent à plusieurs groupes de commerçants ouest-africains de cette période: Marka et Jula notamment, et conduisirent un nombre important de forgerons du Wasolon à se lancer dans la traite des esclaves et par là-même à devenir Kooroko. Ces Kooroko indépendants sortaient pour la première fois du Wasolon afin d'approvisionner les armées combattantes mais aussi pour exercer sur une plus grande échelle le commerce plus ancien de l'or, des colas, des bandes de coton et du sel gemme.

Le docteur Collomb[2] signale deur présence à Bamako dans les termes suivants: "les habitants du Wasolon apportent à Bamako, des captifs, de l'or, des kolas, des pagnes et des tissus blancs." Le relevé statistique des caravanes de passage à Bamako en 1886 indique que dans le sens nord-sud, ce sont surtout des chevaux et du sel gemme qui transitent par cette localité. Dans le sens sud-nord, il s'agit principalement de captifs, en fait essentiellement des captives et des colas. La proportion plus forte de captives (le double)[3] est sans doute due au fair qu'à l'issue des combats menés par les troupes de Samori, les hommes sont tués ou enrôlés dans l'armée. Les captifs ont la propriété d'être une marchandise qui se transporte toute seule et qui a de plus la faculté en transporter d'autres. Souvent les colas sont ainsi portées sur la tête par les esclaves. Mais les tableaux révèlent aussi que même lorsqu'une caravane comprend des captifs, les paniers de cola, par exemple peuvent être chargés sur des ânes ou des boeufs porteurs. Il s'agit sans dourte dans ce cas de préserver la santé des esclaves afin d'en tirer un meilleur prix sur les lieux de vente.

A Bamako, une partie des marchandises apportées par les Kooroko faisait l'objet de transactions. Ainsi les colas et les bandes de coton étaient échangées contre le sel gemme apporté par les Maures à dos de chameau ou sur des boeufs porteurs. Les Kooroko descendaient avec leurs marchandises chez les Drave, lignage important de la ville. Les Maures eux, logeaient et entreposaient leurs barres de sel chez les Ture, des notables, à qui ils laissaient le soin de les vendre si à l'approche de l'hivernage, ils avaient décidé de regagner leur pays alors que le sel n'avait pas été écoulé en totalité.

Les Kooroko qui ne comprenaient pas le hassaniya s'en remettaient à leurs logeurs pour effectuer les transactions. Ils se rendaient avec ces derniers chez les logeurs des Maures afin de leur montrer des échantillons. Dès lors, il existait pour les marchandises, deux possibilitiés d'écoulement. Ou bien les colas et les bandes de coton intéressaient les Maures et alors les logeurs respectifs des Maures et des Kooroko débattaient du prix et effectuaient la transaction, ou bien, ces marchandises n'intéressaient pas les marchands de sel et l'affaire ne pouvait être conclue. Les Kooroko étaient alors contraints de vendre leurs colas et leur bande de coton contre des cauris qui avaient cours à Bamako. Cependant, ils n'étaient pas arrivés au bout de leur peine car les Maures n'acceptaient pas non plus les cauris qui n'avaient pas cours dans leur propre pays. Les Kooroko confiaient donc ces cauris à leurs logeurs qui achetaient des marchandises prisées par les Maures. Il s'agissait surtout de cotonnades blanches ou teintes à l'indigo et de bukar (pagnes noirs). Une fois ces marchandises en leur possession, les logeurs des Kooroko pouvaient enfin se rendre chez les logeurs des Maures pour procéder à l'achat de sel gemme. Ces logeurs jouaient donc également le rôle de banquiers puisque l'Afrique de l'Ouest à cette époque était divisée en zones monétaires différentes (or, cauris, some, gwinzin etc.). Si les commerçants-clients de l'Almami eurent à pâtir de leur incorporation dans l'appareil d'Etat samorien, il n'est pas douteux par contre que les Kooroko indépendants trafiquant avec Samori réussirent à accumuler une grosse quantité d'or, d'ânes, de femmes et surtout d'esclaves.

LES DÉBUTS DE LA PÉRIODE COLONIALE

Au début de la période coloniale, c'est à dire au tournant du siècle, il est probable que les Kooroko poursuivirent pendant un certain temps la traite des esclaves, puisque certains d'entre eux n'ont acquis de captifs qu'après la capture de Samori (1898). Toutefois le commerce des captifs qui sera définitivement prohibé en 1905 ne constituait pas l'essentiel de leur commerce.

L'époque de début de la colonisation peut être considérée comme une période de transition pour ce qui concerne le commerce des Kooroko venus se réinstaller à la faveur de la pacification au Wasolon et dans les régions environnantes. Celui-ci possède, en effet, nombre de traits précoloniaux comme la périodicité, le mode de transport, l'organisation sociale et la nature des produits échangés et pourtant il a également acquis une série de caractéristiques nouvelles telles que l'allongement du rayon d'action et l'emploi accru de numéraire et de marchandises nouvelles (sel marin, étoffes importées, verroterie). Le commerce demeure à cette époque une activité de saison sèche en raison de la difficulté des déplacements pendant l'hivernage. Ce sont les moyens de transport précoloniaux qui sont toujours utilisés: le portage pour les pauvres, l'âne, le boeuf porteur et les captifs pour les riches. Les voyages continuent donc comme par le passé à être effectués au moment de la saison sèche, une ou deux fois par an au maximu, étant donné la lenteur des déplacements. La structure des échanges connait quant à elle, des changements sensibles, car s'il s'agit toujours pour les Kooroko de transporter et d'échanger des marchandises provenant de lieux éloignés: sel gemme, bétail, bande de coton et cola, certaines marchandises telles que les armes, les chevaux et les esclaves perdent de l'importance ou disparaissent complètement en raison de la cessation de l'état de guerre.

En outre interviennent des modifications qui tiennent elles-aussi, directement ou indirectement aux incidences de la colonisation. Pour la première fois de leur histoire, grâce à la "pacification" et à la sécurité qu'elle procure sur les routes commerciales, les Kooroko vont s'aventurer très au sud (Man, Danane, Daloa, Nzerekore etc.) à la recherche de la cola et plus au nord, dans le pays du sel (Kogodugu). Au Woorodugu, les Kooroko descendaient avec leurs marchandises chez des parents et des alliés qui constituaient avec ceux installés à Bamako, Wolosébugu et Buguni l'amorce des premiers réseaux marchands du groupe. Ces parents et ces alliés ou d'autres marchands soudanais (Jula-ba ou Marka) servaient de logeurs aux commerçants Kooroko ambulants et leur procuraient de la cola, en dehors de la période de récolte.

Parallèlement à ce commerce à longue distance axé sur l'échange des boeufs, du sel, de la bande de coton et de la cola, les Kooroko opéraient à l'échelon régional ou local. Certains se rendaient à Kankan et à Sigiri en Guinée où ils achetaient aux maisons de commerce européennes du sel marin qu'ils revenaient vendre au Wasolon.

D'autres étaient utilisés comme "acheteurs" ou "sous acheteurs" de mil, de beurre de karité ou d'arachide par ces mêmes maisons de traite. En effet, ces sociétes ne faisaient que collecter les produits dans quelques grands centres. Le ramassage à l'échelon du village et des centres secondaires était effectué par tout un réseau d'intermédiaires africains. Ces sociétés remettaient de l'argent à des ''acheteurs'' qui sillonnaient les differentes régions. Comme les véhicules ne pouvaient pas circuler sur les petits chemins, les ''acheteurs'' remettaient l'argent et des sacs vides à des ''sous acheteurs'' qui allaient faire les achats dans les petits villages et centralisaient le mil, le beurre de karité ou l'arachide au bourg. L'acheteur pesait alors les produits pour voir si les quantités apportées correspondaient aux sommes avancées.

Aujourd'hui, certains Kooroko qui ont commencé leur carrière comme acheteurs de maisons de traite ou de commerçants libanais et qui ont été ensuite chargés de la commercialisation de l'arachide par l'Etat malien ont repris du service, depuis la libéralisation de ce commerce en 1982, en opérant à leur propre compte ou pour des Libanais.[4]

LA PÉRIODE COLONIALE À BAMAKO

Ces activités régionales ou locales étaient toutefois insuffisantes pour retenir au Wasolon et dans les régions environnantes l'ensemble des Kooroko. Ceux-ci avides de profits vinrent se fixer en grand nombre à Bamako qui devint la capitale du Soudan et qui à la faveur de la construction du Dakar-Niger en vint à occuper le rôle de plaque tournante du commerce de la cola entre la Côte d'Ivoire et le Sénégal.

Sur l'axe nord-sud: Côte d'Ivoire-Bamako, le commerce de la cola conserve jusque vers 1935, les caractéristiques de la période précoloniale. Les voyages ont lieu une ou deux fois par an au maximum, les paniers qui à l'èpoque ne contiennent que 30 kgs de cola contre 55 actuellement sont transportés par les chefs de famille, leurs "frères," "fils," "épouses" et captifs ou sur des ânes. Mais il faut noter que les captifs perdent progressivement de leur importance. Sur l'axe Bamako-Sénégal, dès 1905 et jusqu'en 1920, les Kooroko chargent les paniers de cola sur le train jusqu'à Kayes et de là, sur des chalands et des pirogues qui descendent le fleuve Sénégal. Vers 1920, le Dakar-Niger met des wagons à la disposition des marchands qui les utilisent jusqu'à Kayes ou jusqu'au Sénégal mais ce n'est que vers 1935-1940 que sont installés les premiers réseaux d'apparentés couvrant les différentes étapes du circuit de distribution de la cola depuis la Côte d'Ivoire jusqu'au Sénégal. L'installation de ces réseaux est entre autres raisons liée à l'apparition de camions sur l'itinéraire Côte d'Ivoire-Bamako. L'existence de moyens de transport modernes tout au long du circuit de distribution modifie radicalement l'exercice du commerce de la cola. L'accroissement de la productivité qui en résulte a pour effet d'accroître les quantites mises sur le marché, de diminuer le prix de vente et donc d'augmenter les profits des marchands. La cola, de bien de prestige devient un produit de grande consommation.

Du fait des quantités accrues de cola mises sur le marché, il devient nécéssaire que l'information sur les cours soit transmise plus rapidement. L'utilisation de moyens de communication modernes—lettre, télégramme—permet de faire face à ces nouvelles conditions en même temps qu'elle nécessite la présence d'un réseau de correspondants tout au long du circuit de distribution.

Ces réseaux intégrés sont composés d'un chef de réseau *(jula-ba)*, de commerçants itinérants *(jula-den)* et logeurs -correspondants *(ja-tigi)*. Avant l'éclatement de la Fédération du Mali en 1960, les chefs de réseaux résidaient à Bamako, un de leurs logeurs-correspondants était installé en Côte d'Ivoire, le principal pays producteur, l'autre au Sénégal, gros pays consommateur tandis que les commerçants itinérants faisaient le va et vient entre les deux sections du réseau: Côte d'Ivoire-Bamako et Bamako-Sénégal.

Les chefs de réseaux bien que recrutant principalement dans leur patrilignage ("frères," "fils") sont également amenés du fait de la disparition del'esclavage à embaucher de jeunes commerçants dans le lignage de leurs femmes, sur la base du voisinage ou d'une commune appartenance à l'Islam.

Ces jeunes commerçants qui sont liés à leurs patrons par un contrat oral opèrent dans des conditions différentes de celles des membres du patrilignage. Après avoir travaillé un certain temps pour le jula-ba en étant simplement nourri, logé et vêtu, le jeune commerçant est fondé à demander à son "patron" une certaine somme lui permettant de se lancer dans le commerce à son propre compte, c'est à dire en fait pendant une certaine période, en association avec le jula-ba. L'absence de largesse des jula-ba a conduit, dans les années 50, un jeune commerçant à essayer de regrouper l'ensemble de ses confrères bamakois pour exercer une pression sur ceux-ci et obtenir des conditions de travail plus favorables.

Parallèlement à l'utilisation de parents, d'alliés et de clients travaillant sous »contrat«, les chefs de réseaux emploient également pour la manutention des paniers de cola, des manoeuvres salariés. Ces manoeuvres sont des migrants saisonniers, originaires de la région de Segu qui viennent chaque année à Bamako pendant la saison sèche et qui touchent une rémunération forfaitaire pour le travail de chaque panier. Il faut noter que cette organisation du commerce à longue distance n'est pas propre aux Kooroko et au commerce de la cola, elle concerne également d'autres groupes de marchands maliens (Jula-ba, Marka et Jawambe) et d'autres types de commerce, celui des grains et de l'arachide par exemple.[5]

CONCLUSION

Dans le cadre du commerce à longue distance effectué en Afrique de l'Ouest depuis la période précoloniale se sont développées un certain nombre d'activités reposant sur la parenté, l'esclavage, le contrat et le salariat. Dans une perspective marxiste (Amselle 1977: 207-216), il est d'usage de distinguer au sein du commerce, les activités productives que Marx nomme les "activités annexes du capital commercial" (triage, emballage, entreposage et surtout industrie des transports), des activités improductives (le fait d'acheter pour vendre). Cette distinction qui repose sur la théorie de la valeur-travail ne peut tenir que dans la mesure où on peut prouver qu'un autre système de commercialisation serait à même de remplir les mêmes fonctions dans de meilleures conditions. Or les différentes expériences d'étatisation du commerce menées en Afrique depuis l'indépendance montrent que l'efficacité des commerçants privés même si elle se double dans certains cas d'une exploitation des paysans, n'a jamais pu être sérieusement concurrencée par les différentes formes de commerce d'état, qu'il s'agisse de celui des biens primaires ou de celui des produits manufacturés. Par conséquent, il vaudrait mieux distinguer la puissance et l'acte et considérer que tant que la marchandise n'est pas parvenue au consommateur final, elle n'a qu'une valeur potentielle. Dans cette perspective, le véritable créateur de valeur serait le commerçant.

NOTES

1. Rapport politique du cercle de Bougouni, 1894, Archives Nationales, Koulouba.
2. Notice sur le cercle de Bamako, 1884-1885, Archives Nationales, Koulouba.
3. D'Avril à Novembre 1886, 407 hommes et 780 femmes.
4. Amselle, Baris, et Papazian (1982).
5. Ibid.

REFERENCES

AMSELLE, J. L. (1977) Les négociants de la savane. Paris: Anthropos.
———P. D. BARIS, et V. PAPAZIAN (1982) Evaluation de la filière arachide au Mali. Paris: Ministère des Relations Extérieures, Coopération et développement.
BAZIN, J. et E. TERRAY [eds.] (1982) Guerres de lignages et guerres d'états en Afrique. Paris: Editions des Archives Contemporaines.
BINGER, L. G. (1892) Du Niger au Golfe de Guinée par le pays de Kong et le Mosi (1887-1889), 2 tomes. Paris: Hachette.
GALLIENI, J. S. (1885) Voyage au Soudan Français (Haut-Niger et pays de Segou 1879-1881). Paris: Hachette.
MEILLASSOUX C. [ed.] (1975). L'esclavage en Afrique précoloniale. Paris: Maspero.
PERSON, Y. (1968-1975) Samori, une révolution dyula, 3 tomes. Dakar: IFAN.
POLANYI, K., C. ARENSBERG, and H. PEARSON [eds.] (1956) Trade and Markets in the Early Empires. Glencoe, IL: Free Press.

7

MERCHANTS, PORTERS, AND TEAMSTERS IN THE NINETEENTH-CENTURY CENTRAL SUDAN

M. B. DUFFILL
PAUL E. LOVEJOY

In the central Sudan long-distance trade (*fatauci*) was a highly specialized occupation that involved a large proportion of the population of the two states that dominated the region in the nineteenth century—the Sokoto Caliphate and Borno. Merchants fell on a continuum from the large–scale entrepreneur who needed the services of many different kinds of workers to petty traders who sometimes operated on their own account, but other times found themselves in the employment of more successful merchants. In terms of numbers, a majority of traders in most caravans (*ayari*) were drawn from the ranks of petty traders—those who traveled unaccompanied, carrying their own loads (*'yan gurumfa*), who drove their own pack animals, or who traveled with a "wife,"[1] a son, a junior brother or some other dependent member of the household. These small-scale traders, like all merchants, needed the services of caravan leaders (*madugai*), brokers (*dillalai*), and landlords (*fatomai*), but they did not require professional porters (*'yan alaro*)[2] or those who hired out pack animals and their own services as drivers (*'yan sifiri da bisashe*). Furthermore, these small traders did the greater part of the work of assembling goods and all the work of preparation and packing.

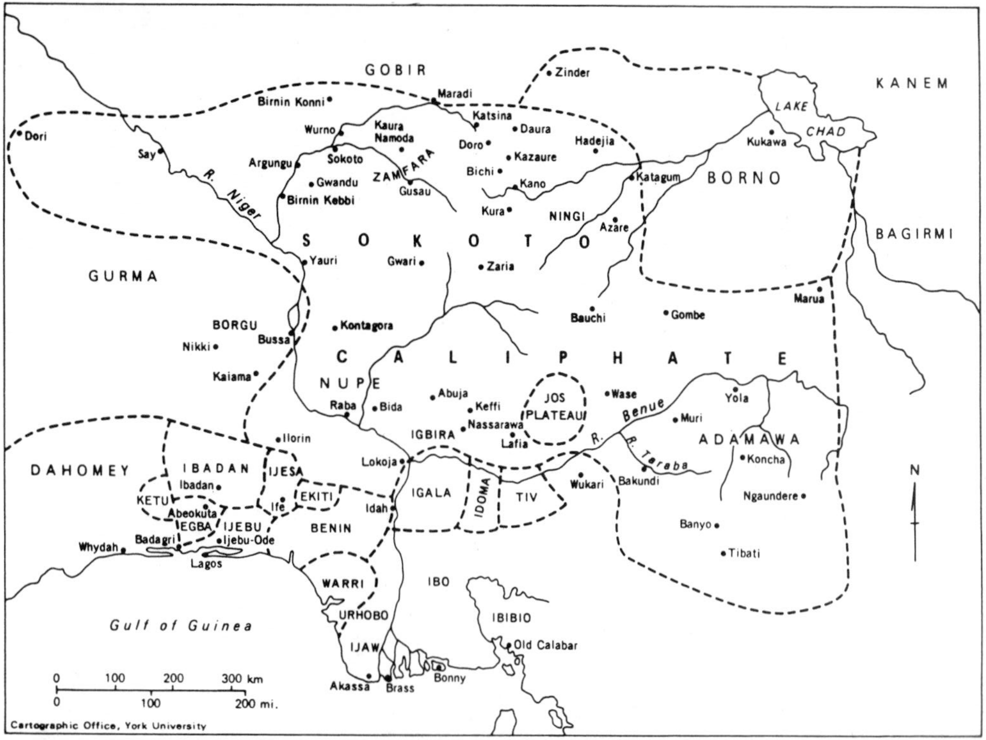

Map 7.1: Sokoto Caliphate

The relatively small number of wealthy merchants (*attajirai*) who operated from the major market centers were the ones who required professional porters (servile or free), teamsters, specialist assemblers, and packers of goods. The labor-intensive nature of the transport system upon which long-distance trade depended is brought out by the German traveler Passarge (1895: 479) on the basis of his experience in Adamawa and Mandara in the 1890s:

> The means of transport are very defective. Apart from the canoes on the large rivers no other vehicles are known. The wagon, indeed even the cart, remains unknown to the Africans. Camels are met with in Kuka [Kukawa] and Kano in the northern most part of the Sudan, pack horses rarely at any time, pack oxen . . . only in the North. In Adamawa only the donkey is used on a large scale; however the most important means of transport is man himself. Either the merchant travels with his slaves or he hires professional porters.

The majority of attajirai actively participated in long-distance trade themselves: that is, they traveled and worked hard at the business of buying and selling both at home and in distant markets. Very few operated on such a scale that they could be classed as sedentary merchants with sufficient capital and business acumen to spread their risks over several trading ventures at a single time. Those who could entrusted their goods to agents or partners, who traveled to and did business in distant markets, while they remained at home acting as bankers, brokers, importers, wholesalers, and distributors.[3] Undoubtedly many attajirai aspired to the role of sedentary merchant, but the risks associated with an attempt to enter the elite of this trading system were considerable. An aspiring merchant could easily be ruined by the dishonesty of agents or the importunity and rapaciousness of a ruling class, which could at will either give or withhold favor and protection, and besides there were disasters on trading journeys, the vagaries of markets and competition from other traders. The accumulation of sufficient capital and credit to transform business from single trading ventures to more complex transactions depended upon such factors as a willingness to take great risks, the making of a fortunate marriage, the securing of political patronage, dishonest dealing with clients and customers, as well as astute and energetic trading. Most long-distance traders, excepting only the greatest and most wealthy sedentary merchants, had virtually all their own liquid capital and often much borrowed capital invested in the ventures they personally undertook, and a disaster such as a market collapse could ruin them and their creditors (Duffill, 1984).

Participation in long distance trade was regarded as a sure way to acquire wealth and escape from the poverty and shame that were the lot of the vast majority of Hausa commoners (talakawa).[4] For this reason and notwithstanding the risks, long-distance trade exerted a strong influence on the imagination of many young men in the Sokoto Caliphate and Borno. In Hausa folklore, which reflects the prevailing ideological system, emphasis was placed upon trade, including long-distance trade, as the way to win fortune and gain prestige. The existence of such an element in the prevailing ideology was sure to have had some influence on the attitudes and probably upon the behavior of all those who voluntarily entered long-distance trade as porters and pack animal drivers (Sellnow, 1963: 410-432; Mischlich, 1943: 129-197).

As the career of Madugu Mohamman Mai Gashin Baki serves to show, young men became merchants in a small way, hoping that as a result of diligent trading and good fortune they would become wealthy and respected (Duffill, 1984). Mai Gashin Baki became a merchant as a young man and gradually built up his contacts with other merchants, acquiring knowledge of distant markets from southern Adamawa to Bagirmi and Borno. Eventually he became a caravan leader who headed expeditions 5000 strong. His success is representative in that most wealthy traders began in a modest way, but in this endeavour few succeeded and many fell by the wayside. As Passarge recognized during his travels in Adamawa in 1893-1894, "the Hausa is like a gypsy who is at home everywhere and nowhere and who roams throughout the whole Sudan as a porter, when he possesses nothing, and as a trader, when he has made some money" (Passarge, 1895: 31). Passarge's comment brings out the permeable nature of the interface between wage labor and entrepreneurship and also serves to confirm an emphasis in Hausa folklore on trade as a means to wealth and power. Though Mohamman enjoyed considerable good fortune and was a hard working trader and caravan leader, his career also shows how easy it was to fail. He was caught embezzling the funds of a caravan he was leading and faced the wrath of the caravan merchants. Mohamman was fortunate in that his involvement first with E. R.

Flegel and later with the Royal Niger Company gave him the opportunity to reverse his ill fortune, and he subsequently acquired some wealth as a broker in the important town of Bakundi (Duffill, 1984). This was the ambition of many long-distance traders, a comfortable income from investment in slaves and land and the opportunity to function as a broker and a wholesale purchaser and distributor of commodities.

Madugu Mai Gashin Baki was far from being the only merchant who operated on a large scale. Indeed every town in the Central Sudan had its merchant community with varying numbers of large merchants. A substantial list of these traders could be constructed for all the major towns of the caliphate and Borno. There were numerous commercial landlords (fatomai) who dominated the trade in natron, salt, livestock, and other goods. Some fatomai operated hostels that could accommodate as many as 150 merchants at a time. Usually these fatomai did not travel, but they often invested in trade and therefore required the employment of workers (Lovejoy, 1980; 1985).

LABOR OF THE CARAVAN:
THE CARAVAN LEADER AND HIS STAFF

Caravans required the leadership and direction of professionals and were generally led by experienced travelers, who were also traders on their own account (Lovejoy, 1980: 101-112). The caravan leader (*madugu*) was assisted by a staff consisting of a guide (*jagaba*), an assistant in charge of the caravan on the march (*uban dawaki*), caravan scribe (*malamin ayari*), and drummer (*mai gangan madugu*). Large caravans also had assistant caravan leaders in charge of sections of the caravan. This delegation of authority was necessary as the largest caravans (2000-5000 people with animals) were spread out over several miles of the route. The task of the leader, who usually took up the rear, was to see to it that the caravan reached its destination safely and expeditiously. It was a difficult job calling for leadership qualities of a high order. The caravan leader not only had to know the route and its dangers; he was also responsible for negotiating the price of passage and the price of entry into markets. He organized the defence of the caravan on the march or at halting places (*zango*) against the attacks of highway robbers (*'yam fashi*). He was also responsible for maintaining order within the caravan and settling disputes between members of the caravan. Though he could delegate some part of his responsibilities, for instance route finding and leading the line of march were the responsibilities of the guide, there was truth in the Hausa saying—"Jaji, shi ne sarki" (Jaji = madugu)—The caravan leader is a chief.

The madugu and his staff formed what might be termed a loosely organized business corporation or firm. The staff were in the regular employment of the leader and were sometimes members of his household. Their prosperity depended upon the leader's success and reputation. The leader in turn was dependant upon the efficiency and loyalty of his staff. Caravan leading was a demanding occupation and a risky one, but a madugu who was able to combine it with successful trading could become rich and influential. The caravan leader did not charge his clients a fee, though it was the practice for members of the caravan to give the leader a present before journeys and upon the safe completion of a journey. The caravan leader and his staff did not contribute to the tolls (*garama*) demanded by rulers through whose territory the caravan passed or whose markets the caravan's members desired to enter. This exemption amounted to a substantial subsidy to the caravan leader and his staff since, effectively, their share of the toll was paid by the rest of the caravan. Since it was the responsibility of the leader assisted by his staff to negotiate the amount of the toll with the local ruler or his representative and it was also their responsibility to apportion the contribution of each trader in the caravan, there was opportunity for deception and fraudulent dealing. A dishonest caravan leader could enrich himself and his staff at the expense of other members of the caravan, and it seems to have been a fairly frequent occurrence. However, such dishonesty depended upon collusion between the leader and his subordinates, especially the caravan scribe. Discovery or betrayal could result in disgrace, humiliation, and loss of professional reputation, as the career of Madugu Mohamman Mai Gashin Baki demonstrates (Lovejoy, 1980; Krieger, 1954: 289-324; Mischlich, 1942: 181-186).

When caravans halted for the night there was much work to be done by teamsters, porters, servants—free or slave—of the wealthy merchants, and the women who accompanied the traders. Indeed all members of the caravan, other than the wealthy merchants who took their ease reclining on undressed sheepskins, prepared the camp. Pack animals had to be unloaded, hobbled, fed, and watered, which occupied the attention of the teamsters. Merchants with sixty or more pack animals in a single caravan required approximately twenty teamsters, and an important merchant with that number of pack animals was accompanied by other servants, including women, plus any porters he required in addition to the pack animals.

After the animals had been unloaded and hobbled, the majority of the labor force prepared shelters for themselves and their masters, while some few attended to the needs of the animals and the remainder, especially the women, prepared food. Those engaged in the preparation of shelters unpacked equipment such as axes, sickles, and hoes, and made off into the bush to collect supple branches, canes, thatching grass, and fencing material. Since caravans often stopped in the same places on a given route, shelters were often in relatively good condition and only had to be repaired. While the teamsters, porters and others built grass huts (*bukkoki*) for themselves, the attajirai had superior shelters (*adadai*) constructed for their own use. These had a framework of branches over which were spread tanned ox-hides (*kilagai*), which were then tied down. Round the adadai and the bukkoki of those who had women with them, a fence or screen was constructed (Mischlich, 1942: 181-186; Monteil, 1894: 210-211).

LABOR AT MARKET CENTERS: BROKERS/LANDLORDS AND THEIR STAFF

Brokers and landlords needed assistance if they were to cater adequately to the needs of their clients and customers (Hill, 1971: 303-318; 1966: 349-366; Cohen, 1966; Lovejoy, 1980, 1985). Their *yara* ("boys" or servants) delivered messages, carried loads, and ran errands. Female servants, usually slave girls, prepared food, cleaned apartments, and performed other services for the guests. Grooms and ostlers tended the mounts and pack animals of the itinerant merchants and also cared for animals brought for sale, while guards and nightwatchmen protected the property of the clients. It is obvious that a landlord with a lodging house (*masauki*) needed a substantial staff, most of which was drawn from within the household, including and especially domestic slaves, who were often employed in agricultural production—either on farms or plantations—in the rainy season. Brokers, who usually specialized in particular commodities, did not require as many employees as landlords, though they did need the services of agents, who toured the country round the market center buying and selling on their behalf, especially when brokers became wholesale dealers or when they invested in manufacturing.

Most loads were prepared and loaded by household labor belonging to the trader or by teamsters and porters. Awkward loads including raw cotton and hides and skins required special preparation, packing, and loading. Kola nuts, though not an awkward load, needed careful packing and frequent inspection on the march to remove infested nuts. The preparation, packing and loading of goods for camel transport in the trans-Sahara trade also required the labor of specialists. When Krause (1882: 313) estimated the average costs of transporting goods from Tripoli to Kano in 1882, he reckoned packing of goods (materials and labor) as 14.7 percent of total transport costs. Loads leaving Kano or Kukawa by camel for the North also required careful preparation. Large tusks of ivory, for example, had to be cut up before they could be loaded onto camels (Flegel, 1883/1885: 134-135).

The tasks of caravan trading and market exchange clearly involved the labor of large numbers of people, and the nature of trade in the central Sudan invariably meant that most of these people operated on a small scale, even if some merchants were wealthy and employed workers to run their firms. The commercial vocabulary of the Hausa included a fair number of words describing the purchase of goods for resale and local trading by hawkers and pedlars. The purchase of goods for resale, including livestock, grain, cotton, and other goods, was connected with long-distance trade. Similarly local peddling tied in with long-distance trade if the commodities hawked were goods brought to a market center by long-distance traders. Stockholders played an important role in the assembly of goods for export, and peddlers were necessary for the distribution of imported goods. The existence of a pool of small merchants and others who could move into and out of trade on their own account facilitated the development of a labor market, which clearly functioned in the Sokoto Caliphate and Borno in the nineteenth century.

APPRENTICESHIP AND KINSHIP

The demand for labor was met in a variety of ways. Merchants attracted apprentices and assistants from among their sons and other junior kin and neighbors (Works, 1976: 63-79; Baier, 1980: 177-181).

These workers (*yara;* assistants, "boys") did not receive a wage but were treated as members of the household who received clothing, food, and shelter at the discretion of their *mai gida* (head of the house). All their needs were met. In return for their labor, they gained experience, contacts, and access to credit. Trusted slaves could—and often did— receive the same treatment as junior kin, even to the point of super- vising commercial operations and of serving as trustees to estates upon the death of a master whose surviving sons were minors. This household labor satisfied many of the needs of merchants, particular- ly with regards to agency, but many tasks were menial that could be undertaken by slaves and hired workers.

Traders who relied on their sons and other kin often began their careers as apprentices themselves (Alhaji Muhammad Lawan Barmo, 1970; Lovejoy, 1980: 91; Baier, 1980: 251-252). Profitable expeditions enabled these individuals to buy a slave or two, who then contributed to the business establishment of their master. These slaves—purchased early in the careers of successful merchants—were those most likely to become trusted agents (Works, 1976: 81). The household establish- ment of Madugu Isa na Garahu, an important kola merchant at the end of the nineteenth century, included thirty house slaves, thirty farm slaves, numerous kin, and other dependents. And he had slaves at his houses in Sokoto and Kalgo. He drew upon their labor in a variety of ways, taking many with him on trading expeditions (Muhammadu Isa Indole, 1970). Slaves were essential to the operations of most large merchants. By the time a merchant achieved a sufficient level of success to delegate responsibilities to junior kin and trusted slaves, he required more labor than his household could supply, especially since large-scale operations were more subject to the vagaries of the market than those of independent traders.

Besides their access to household labor, merchants had recourse to several other categories of labor; they could hire porters who were either freemen or slaves owned by other people; they could engage teamsters with their livestock; or they could force trade slaves on the march to carry loads. All three categories of labor were common; freemen, domestic slaves, and trade slaves supplemented household labor and appear to have offered competitive advantages that resulted in the purchase of additional slaves or the recruitment of extra free dependents.

PORTERS

The entrepreneur who required labor and pack animals beyond the resources of his own household was in a position in many markets to pick and choose among the strongest and healthiest men, women, and beasts who were readily available for hire. The Hausa merchants who employed these porters also used slaves and livestock to carry goods; invariably livestock died and could not always be replaced at a reasonable price, transport needs varied as goods were bought and sold, and trusted slaves could not be supplemented on the road. Hired labor was, therefore, essential to the operations of these merchants. It is clear from a legal opinion of Abdullahi, brother of Uthman dan Fodio and emir of Gwandu, that porters were being hired at least as early as the first part of the nineteenth century (Tukur, 1977: 369). The experience of the German officer, Kling, who traveled in the area between the caliphate and Asante in 1890, confirms that hiring continued throughout the century. Kling (1890b: 353) reported that "Hausas are the cheapest, most satisfactory and best porters of the western Sudan." Whether or not Kling exaggerated, his comments do establish that porterage was a professional activity that was widespread (Kling, 1890a: 145; Passarge, 1895: 31; Pigott, 1896).[6]

On the southern route to Lagos, which became well traveled from the 1880s on, porters were used whenever merchants needed them. Usually traders took donkeys as far as Agege, outside of Lagos, even through the mortality rate was high for donkeys that far south. As Alhaji Nagudu Abdullahi (1969) remembered it,

> if traders lost their donkeys on the trip to Lagos, they hired porters. A good porter could carry as much as a donkey. Before one was hired, they had to bargain over the price which would be paid. When the porter reached Kano, it was a big event; all the people would rush out to marvel at the tremendous loads they could carry. Most porters were Hausa; for example the Sarkin Zongo [in the early twentieth century] at Agege had been a porter.

Early colonial officials found that porters were easy to recruit, although not always at wages that were advantageous:

> Many thousands, probably twenty to thirty, of native carriers work caravans on their own account through the Hausa States and even to

Lagos. This service has been maintained for many years. The native, valuing his own day's work at a low figure and carrying only the richest products, such as potash [natron], or kola nuts, salt, cotton goods, and matches, remains months on the road [Girouard, 1907].

The estimate for the total number of porters must be treated with caution, but Governor Girouard, who made the estimate in the context of planning the construction of the Lagos-Kano railway, had undertaken a detailed study of transport needs.

In European travelers' accounts there are numerous descriptions of the bargaining that went on between caravan leaders and porters; indeed porters often recognized their own headman, who consulted his fellows during the bargaining process. Of these accounts that by Passarge is one of the most interesting because it reveals some of the customary features of portering work and the expectations of the porters. The German expedition of which Passarge (1895: 64-66) was a member had a number of Hausa porters from Lokoja whom the Germans considered undisciplined and difficult to manage on the march, the basic reason being that the German concept of good order conflicted with the norms of the porters. With Prussian thoroughness Von Uechtritz, the leader of the expedition, insisted on close order marching in file with a rest stop of ten minutes every hour. These orders did not suit the Hausa porters who were conditioned to another work regime. Normally, a group of porters would contract to deliver goods between Yola and Ngaundere, for example, in a specific time—seventeen days—but they would determine when and how they marched, either by day or night. They would decide the pace, the length of breaks and when they were taken. German attempts to alter this pattern of work inevitably led to disagreements, although the Germans went to some length to impose their work discipline: ·

Whoever stepped out or left the line or set down his load or lagged behind was driven on with a stick and if the offence was repeated the man concerned was punished by the withdrawal of the day's ration allowance, the most severe punishment for the negro, for the stomach comes before everything else. The Hausa only gradually and unwillingly accustomed themselves to the discipline of the march [Passarge, 1895: 65-66].

Although Passarge thought that the Germans were imposing discipline, in fact they were only altering an established routine. Passarge learned what one Hausa merchant arranged with porters for the same journey from Yola to Ngaundere. The merchant had paid the porters in advance and set their wages according to the weight and difficulty of the load. A porter carried a 50 to 57 kilogram load, for which he received 40,000 cowries (£1.00), or 2353 cowries (about £.05) per day, and a food ration of 200 cowries per day.

The Germans bargained with the porters over the ration allowance. The porters demanded 100 cowries per day; the Germans offered 30 cowries and after much haggling they agreed on 40 cowries with 10 cowries extra for the headman of the porters and for the interpreter (Passarge, 1895: 31-33). The variation between local practice and the arrangement with the Germans demonstrates that bargaining was a key element in the employment of porters. Porters had to maintain some degree of corporate identity in order to engage in these negotiations, and hence it is possible to say that the consciousness of porters as workers had become a factor in the organization and conduct of trade. Passarge recognized this crucial development in his observations of the porters in his caravan.

In 1891 Monteil (1894: 156, 178) also learned that porters shared a sense of identity as workers, although he was not as perceptive as Passarge. Monteil's party, which consisted of 10 donkeys, 4 oxen, and 50 porters, was traveling with a large Hausa caravan that was returning from Asante to Sokoto with kola nuts. On his way from Wagadugu to Dori, Monteil had trouble with his porters, and in Yaga, between Dori and Say, many of the porters deserted. One night 30 of the 50 porters left "sans que j'eusse les moyens de les faire joindre; les deux seuls chevaux, celui de Badaire et le mien, qui restaient, étaient incapables de se porter eux mêmes; nous avions dû pour cette raison faire bonne partie de la route à pied." The porters included 25 who had been recruited by capitaine Quiquandon and 10 recruited in Bobo-Dioulasso. Unfortunately, Monteil did not record whether the deserters and either of the two groups corresponded. "Quelles raisons les protèrent à s'enfuir? Je n'ai jamais pu me l'expliquer; mais, s'ils m'emportaient cinq fusils, ils m'enlevaient aussi le souce que j'ai signalé d'avoir à les nourrir." The firearms had been distributed among the porters in order to reduce the size of the loads; as it turned out this measure was naive. As was the case in Passarge's caravan, the porters were willing to take corporate action in their own interests. The reasons for their walkout are unknown, but at least momentarily they were conscious of themselves as workers.

The Sudan Interior Mission also found that the recruitment of carriers was difficult because porters acted in their own collective interest. Between Bida and Kano in 1895, Walter Gowans not only had trouble employing porters but also experienced "the continual danger of losing them" (Sudan Witness, 1963: 3). According to another missionary, Rowland Bingham,

> Carriers knew how to conduct a strike as effectively as any labour union at home [in Canada]. They would get about 20 miles from anywhere and then every man would put down his load and say, 'White man, we cannot go any farther unless you double our pay.' Because of these labour problems it sometimes took six weeks to go a six days' journey [Sudan Witness, 1963: 3].

Bingham and Gowans were probably naive in the way they treated carriers, since they saw in these workers potential converts to Christianity, but they quickly learned that porters were workers who knew how to bargain for higher wages. As had been the case with Monteil's carriers far to the northwest, the SIM carriers temporarily at least were behaving as conscious members of a working class. It must be stated, however, that this consciousness was probably temporary because portering was seldom a full-time occupation. When caravans disbanded, individuals went their separate ways, but while they were working for others they could not escape the inherent conflict that derived from relationships of employment based on wage labor. Employers, whether they were missionaries or Hausa traders, wanted to minimize wage payments and maximize the work load, while the priorities of the porters were centered on obtaining the highest wages possible for the least amount of work. Such a conflict of interest inevitably involved struggle.

Women were used as porters, although it is not clear how extensive their employment was. At Kulfu, the Nupe town between Zaria and the Niger River, Clapperton (1829: 137) observed "a great number of fine women [who] hire themselves to carry loads on their heads." They came from Borgu and were employed between Kulfu and the Bariba towns at least. In Adamawa, Passarge (1895: 255) met a large ivory caravan, carrying thirty tusks, between Garua and Ngaundere, which had both male and female porters. The owner of the caravan was from Zaria; most of his porters were women "who work more cheaply in Africa than men do." They carried loads of 50 kilograms.

Often professional portering seems to have been regarded as an occupation fit only for slaves or for those driven to take it up as a result of extreme poverty and ill-fortune. Portering was a dangerous occupation; journeys were long and often arduous, and caravans were frequently attacked and their personnel killed or enslaved. It was not unknown for traders who employed free porters to sell them into slavery at the end of a journey or in other ways to exploit or defraud them. The hazards associated with portering and its association with slavery or extreme poverty may well have served to limit the extent to which hired labor was available, particularly in good agricultural years or when craft activity was buoyant. If this was the case it may partly explain the use of trade slaves as porters and also the formation of specialised groups or companies of professional slave porters ('yan bojuwa). It may also explain the relatively high wages porters could earn.

Caliphate authorities do not appear to have regulated wages, but they took an interest in the labor of porters to the extent of defining their liability. A hired porter who accidentally damaged goods, according to Abdullahi dan Fodio, "is not liable to make good the loss. However, he will not be entitled to his wages" (Tukur, 1977: 369).

On the road from Kano to Sokoto in 1827 when he had trouble with his livestock, Clapperton (1829: 179) had to employ five men to carry the equivalent of a camel load of goods—at a cost of 2000 cowries for a day's work. This charge was high because of the situation; Clapperton was on the road and needed to keep moving, but surely this kind of problem faced merchants on a regular basis. A day's employment and a contract for a whole journey involved a different wage scale. Ogunremi (1982: 84-87) reports figures for the Yoruba/Nupe area that suggest that professional porters received wages considerably higher than that for day laborers. At midcentury, porters received 1200 cowries per day (1/2½), while laborers were paid 400 cowries per day (4½ᵈ). Porters carried loads of 65 to 70 pounds at twenty miles per day, for a cost of about 14.6d per ton/mile. By the 1890s, Robinson had to pay 1500 cowries per day between Lokoja and Kano, which at that time was worth 9d. From Keffi to Zaria—about 180 miles—

Robinson paid each porter 20,000 cowries, plus a food allowance of 300 cowries. In 1907, Girouard complained that head porterage had become a problem because "the remuneration invaraibly paid was and is high, much above the current rate of wages in the country, [and] increasing difficulty in obtaining head transport has been felt." By that time wages were approximately 2/-per ton/mile (Girouard, 1907; Ogunremi, 1982: 89-90).

Most of the labor force involved in the long-distance transportation of goods, whether free or slave (but excluding trade slaves), took up the occupation or were compelled to undertake it for readily understandable economic and social reasons. Some people needed to supplement household income during a season when there was comparatively little farm work to be done. Slaves who in the wet and harvest seasons worked the land engaged in transport for their owner or for others under *sufuri* or *murgu* arrangements, which provided the owner with the means of securing a return on his investment. The owner carried the costs of his slave's subsistence if the slave worked for him on a trading expedition, just as he did if he hired free labor or the labor of other men's slaves, but in sufuri and murgu arrangements, the costs of the slave's subsistence were transferred to the hirer.

Other people became porters or teamsters because of the opportunity presented by travel and such petty trade as they could arrange on journeys to distant markets to accumulate sufficient capital to be able to set up as independent traders. No great amount of capital was necessary to enable an individual to establish himself as a petty merchant, from which position he might succeed, given good fortune, in rising to the status of a more substantial trader, caravan leader or broker. Slaves (other than trade slaves) required to labor as porters and pack animal drivers also sought whatever opportunities they could to engage in petty trade on their own account. From the proceeds of such petty trade they might hope to accumulate and secrete the basis of a ransom (*fansar kai*) and have something left over to allow them to start a farm, engage in a craft or enter trade on a larger scale.

Professional portering was largely undertaken by slaves and members of the "lumpenproletariat" that existed in all the major Hausa towns and cities. According to Staudinger (1889: 141) porters were recruited from the poorest classes, a fact that was observable in their behavior and character. There are cases of freemen being sold into slavery to pay gambling debts; portering was suitable employment for such "riff-raff" (Duffill, 1984). Other social and political pressures contributed to the entry of free labor into employment in long distance trade. Travel to distant places offered a means of escape for criminals and those under severe forms of social and economic pressure, not to mention those under threat of political persecution. And slaves used the possibilities of travel as a means of escaping. One fugitive slave who fled from Bauchi in the 1880s was reenslaved in Keffi when his disguise as a Hausa merchant was disclosed. H. Johnston (1889: 109-110), who recorded this tale, accepted the claim of the slave that he tried to pass himself off as a merchant, but portering probably offered a more likely cover in similar cases. In any event, many "Hausa" porters did not in fact speak Hausa as their first language, but their acquisition of the language allowed them, albeit at a humble level, to participate in the Hausa commercial system. Long-distance trade was an important agent of acculturation and socialization.

Porters, whatever their background, rose above the ranks of the under- and unemployed, however temporary their employment. Although porters might become merchants or drift back into the "lumpenproletariat," they still came together as a recognizable and conscious group of workers. As Passarge (1895: 65) observed, "indeed they are not a special caste—since anyone can be a porter—but there are definite usages and customs regarding the regular conditions of hire between porter and master." Passarge specifically compared his porters with the Nyamwezi and Swahili porters of East Africa; in both the central Sudan and East Africa he thought that a "class" of porters had emerged as a result of the expansion of trade. Passarge's confusion over "caste" and "class" should not cloud the significance of his experience. He found that porters identified as workers and had to be dealt with on that basis.

Since portering as an occupation required little skill but plenty of strength and endurance, there was little scope for the emergence of specialized grades or categories of labor. However it is known that as a result of demand for high value goods, such as the first kola nuts of the season's harvest, entrepreneurs moved in to satisfy this demand and created a rapid transport service. In the process they brought into being a differentiated category of porters—'yan bojuwa—who specialized in the carriage of light high value loads. Adamu Bagwanje

(1969), for example, began his career in a team of 'yan bojuwa. Born in Gonja on a trading expedition, as his name indicates, Bagwanje traveled to Lagos as a young man at the turn of the century. Most merchants employed only two to four porters—as Bagwanje remembers—and went in groups of about thirty. They took textiles, sandals, and hides and skins south and brought kola and textiles back. The porters received one-third of the profits as wages (Bak'o Madigawa, 1969; Gambo Turawa, 1970). Nonetheless, there is no indication that 'yan bojuwa and other porters differed in the degree of their consciousness as a group. All porters recognized their status as workers, and that recognition—occupational in its basis—could, at least in theory, have become a foundation stone in a developing consciousness of class position and class antagonism. At best class consciousness was rudimentary in this economy and society and depended on social relations of production, distribution, and exchange that were never dominant. Occasional manifestations of collective action by porters and others cannot be interpreted as providing evidence for the existence of some "proto-working class." All that can be said in the present state of knowledge is that there was some potential for developments along these lines. The potential was in our view weak and in any case it was to be aborted by political developments—the colonial conquest—and subsequent technological and economic changes.

TEAMSTERS

Teamsters constituted a second category of workers in the structure of long-distance trade. There was always a large reservoir of donkeys and donkey drivers (if not of other pack animals—oxen, hinnies, and mules) in the countryside round the major towns and cities. Camels were also available for hire. Pack animal driving, though just as hazardous as load carrying, was not as physically demanding. The occupation—mainly a dry season one—tended to be taken up by those who had the resources to put together a team of pack animals or by those who had some experience and skill in pack animal driving. Generally one man could handle three donkeys or oxen or three to five camels. The owners of pack animals hired them out with the services of a driver, who might be the owner himself, a member of his household or hired labor, for both local and long-distance work. Some of the larger merchants and caravan leaders maintained their own teams and no doubt used members of their household, including slaves, as drivers, only hiring labor when they did not have sufficient household labor. Pack animals and their drivers do not seem to have been in short supply, particularly not in the major centers of trade such as Kano or Kukawa.

The role of hired camel transport in the trans-Saharan trade was noted by Clapperton (Denham and Clapperton, 1966: 709) in 1824: "The merchants of Ghadamis and Tuat never keep camels of their own, but hire them from this singular people [Tuareg], who carry their goods across the desert to Kashna [Katsina] at the rate of ten dollars a load, and likewise convey slaves at twenty-five dollars a head." Heinrich Barth (1857: I, 489), who used this service when he crossed the desert in 1849-1850, amassed a debt of 55,000 cowries "for the carriage of . . . merchandise from Tinteggan to Kano," and he owed an additional 18,000 cowries to a merchant who had rent him a mare and a bullock. A similar method of transport operated at the end of the century. Monteil (1894: 290) reported in 1891 that the Kel Ewey Tuareg "se chargent des transports pour un prix convenu a l'avance, et la plupart du temps les Arabes n'acompagnent pas les caravanes." Merchants also hired camels, together with their drivers, in the Bilma salt trade (Lovejoy, 1985; Baier, 1980: 62, 71).

The presence of camels in the savanna made it possible for the Tuareg to sell transport services to local merchants and to buy agricultural products on their own account which they then moved to market for sale. There is no way of telling the relative importance of the two roles. Tuareg camel owners probably filled both functions, sometimes speculating in produce and other times hiring their animals out to local merchants. Nonetheless, their position in the transport system of the caliphate is clear, as Baier (1976) has noted:

> Transport work during the dry season (called *sufuri* in Hausa) fitted nicely into the transhumance cycle of the nomads. Herders came south towards the savanna in December and January, grazing camels on southern pasture, and hiring them out for transport duties. When the rains began in May or June, they returned north.

Data are especially revealing during the boom in peanut exports after 1911, but camels were available for hire long before then (Baier, 1980: 130).

In the dry season those with a team for hire or seeking work as teamsters flocked into the towns and cities looking for employment in both long- and short-distance transport work. Such a labor market was not particularly conducive to the development of specialized animal transport business with the teamsters organised into effective guildlike organizations to regulate and improve returns to labor. However, it is known that the same development that took place in portering also took place in teamstering. The *'yan burabura* were a specialized class of teamsters who engaged in the rapid transportation of high value goods on lightly loaded donkeys.

Although it is not possible to estimate the total number of animals available for hire, figures gathered by the early colonial regime indicate that the number was considerable. In 1908 it was noted that "in the Northern Provinces, there is an increased tendency on the part of owners of pack animals to place them at the disposal of the Government for hire."[6] In 1907 over 3000 animals were so employed. The implication that livestock owners were being drawn into a newly created market for livestock should be dismissed, however. Certainly colonial demand for livestock was a new development, but livestock had long been available for hire.

Clapperton (1829: 76, 77, 88), on his second journey to the Sokoto Caliphate in 1827, entered into long negotiations with Madugu Abdullah, the head of a Hausa caravan returning from Asante to Kano. After protracted discussions, Clapperton arranged for the hire of fifteen oxen and donkeys to carry his goods. He signed an agreement with Abdullah that was written in Arabic "by which he was bound to carry my baggage and presents from Boussa to Kano; and for which I was to pay him, the day after my arrival in the latter place, two hundred thousand cowries." The negotiations probably took longer than usual because Clapperton was not able to put any money up front; he had to insist on paying in Kano. Nonetheless, Clapperton's deal is revealing. It is the earliest known example of such an agreement for the transport of goods, even though there are many details of the arrangement that are not clear. Clapperton chose to deal directly with the caravan leader; perhaps Abdullah owned the livestock but it is more likely that he acted as an agent for one or more merchants in his caravan. The terms of employment for the teamsters required to tend the livestock are not known. It is not even clear if they were employed for wages or were part of the personnel engaged by the merchants who supplied the animals.

Monteil (1895: 252-253) was more impressed than frustrated with the credit arrangements that were available in the caliphate. In Sokoto he was able to make arrangements for transport that would be payable in Kano.

Affluèrent immédiatement des gens, qui avec des bourriquots, qui avec des chevaux, pour me proposer leurs animaux *payables à Kano*. Moyennant des reconnaissances de la somme convenue pour l'animal, payable à Kano, je pus remonter en quelques jours une très belle caravane. Mes créanciers devaient faire la route avec moi ou me retrouver à Kano.

Unfortunately, Monteil did not provide details of such arrangements, so that it is not possible to analyse the methods of labor mobilization involved in hiring animals. Monteil either had to employ teamsters on his own, or they must have come with the animals and hence were the responsibility of the owners. A few days later, at Kaura Na Moda, he was able to "profite de la presence a Kaoura d'une caravane qui se rend a Kano, pour acheter, toujours contre du papier remboursable a Kano, les animaux qui me sont necessaires. Nous nous y arretons deux jours, pendant lesquels je suis en proie a une rechute du mal qui m'avait deja terasse a Zebba" (1895: 260). Animals could be purchased or hired on credit that could be collected in another town.

Clapperton's arrangement for fifteen oxen and donkeys between Bussa and Kano suggests a rate of 13,300 cowries per donkey or oxen for the trip; approximately fourteen cowries per kilometre. Later he rented an oxen to carry his goods from Kano to Sokoto for what appeared to be an excellent rate of 5000 cowries for the trip; less than seven cowries per kilometer, or half the cost of hiring livestock further south. Unfortunately for Clapperton (1829: 77, 88, 179) the ox was sick and did not get very far. Nonetheless, the rates are instructive of the kinds of decisions facing the traveler. On the road in the southern savanna region, Clapperton had to pay more than in Kano, where far more livestock were available. Clapperton not only had to compete with the needs of the caravan, which was returning from Asante heavily loaded with kola nuts, but he also had to contend with the fact that donkey and oxen prices were higher the further south one traveled. While Clapperton did not provide information on the cost of hiring men to tend the livestock, it is likely that these costs were included in the rent for the livestock.

In 1898 and 1899, British officers arranged for the transport oɪ goods to Gambaga by donkey as a means of eliminating the porterage system that was in use.[7] It was estimated that transport costs could be cut in half. In 1898 H. P. Northcott reported:

> The first caravan, consisting of 40 donkeys, leaves to-day for Kintampo, and each donkey is to carry two loads of those arranged for human transport. On these being delivered in good condition at Gambaga, the Hausa High-Priest [Sarkin Zango?] who is the contractor, will receive 10s. per load, but from the sum due will be subtracted the pecuniary equivalent of any loss or damage. The price compares very favourable [sic] with the cost of transporting a load from Kintampo to Gambaga under existing arrangements. The round trip occupies, on an average, 36 days, the pay and subsistence of a carrier amount to 1s. 6d. per diem, and it therefore costs £2 6s. per load. . . . It has only been with difficulty, and by a menace of drastic measures that I have been able to get the Imam to provide the donkeys for the use of the Hausa High-Priest, but I anticipate that all obstacles will disappear when payment is made for the first consignment.[8]

Although the trade to Gambaga was outside the caliphate, it was located along the main commercial axis that connected the Asante kola markets with the central Sudan, and hence transport arrangements along this route are an indication of the kinds of services that were available to Hausa merchants. In this case, the services of teamsters were associated with the hiring of livestock, which suggests that this was the usual arrangement. What was perhaps unusual was the role played by the "Hausa High-Priest," the Sarkin Zango.

TRADE SLAVES

The third category of labor for use in long-distance trade was trade slaves who carried loads as they themselves were being moved to market for sale (Krieger, 1954: 299). At times in certain places and on certain routes it may have been difficult for long distance traders to obtain professional porters or pack animals and their drivers. In such circumstances trade slaves were sometimes used as porters, although some merchants regularly used trade slaves as carriers. According to Clapperton (1829: 138), trade slaves are strictly guarded on a journey, and chained neck to neck; or else tied neck to neck in a long rope of raw hide, and carry loads on their heads consisting of their master's goods, or his household stuff; these loads generally from fifty to sixty pounds weight.

The fifty to sixty pound weight (23 to 27 kilogram) carried by these slaves was approximately half a normal load for a professional porter. Slaves that were intended for sale could be used to move light loads, but not at the expense of risking the health and hence the potential profits from these slaves. Trade slaves offered a merchant something like a ballast advantage. They were moving anyway and could carry goods at low, virtually marginal, cost, as long as they were able.

But trade slaves were not a reliable substitute for livestock or professional porters. As Passarge (1895: 261-262) observed

We came upon two Fulani accompanied by four slave women. One of them was an elderly and infirm woman who could hardly drag herself forward with a stick, the other three were bound by a rope round their necks and marched in train one behind the other. They also carried loads on their heads. This sad procession reminded us that we were in the land that is the principal supplier of slaves to the whole of the central Sudan. Earlier we have encountered such slave columns mainly in conjunction with cattle transport to Yola and Marua. They were not a pleasant sight. Old, feeble, emaciated skeletons, men in fetters laden with bales, feeble and wretched little children, who with bundles on their heads trotted along beside their unladen master, the pace of the march being too much for them unless they ran. Next the unlucky ones in iron fetters, sometimes five of them fastened to one fetter by the same foot.

The least valued slaves were those who came from Baia-land. Already weak and unable to take the unfamiliar Guinea corn food many of them died during transport. By comparison the Lakka slaves were much stronger and had more endurance. In the transport of their slaves the masters must be very watchful lest they run away or lest they furtively pick and eat the poisonous leaves of a certain bush in order to end their tormented existence. This bush is known as "gotska" in Hausa and is common in the bush. The Fulani use it as an oracle to ascertain the guilt of thieves.

Trade slaves, often recent captives, were seldom used to traveling great distances. They became lame and, unlike professional porters, were not motivated to work willingly. The prospects of escape and suicide limited their usefulness even more.

Eduard Vogel (1855: 251) observed similar problems with the employment of trade slaves as porters in the trans-Sahara trade in the 1850s.

> Two days after we had encamped in Gertruhn there arrived a caravan from Bornu with about 4-500 slaves. Then I saw for the first time what slavery and the slave trade is! The Tiboo forced their unlucky prisoners, mostly girls and boys under 12 years old, to carry loads of up to 25 pounds on their heads and in consequence nearly all had entirely lost their hair and the skin of the head was all rubbed off. By this means the drivers save on the number of camels employed and there were only some 35 camels accompanying the whole train. As far as Tedgerri all the slaves are fettered with an iron round the neck to which the right hand is bound with a leather thong. Adult men—of whom I only saw at most 15 brought in—remain in fetters until they reach Murzuq.

Fully loaded trade slaves, especially if shackled, slowed the pace of the average caravan. If trade slaves reached market in an exhausted or weakened condition observable to possible buyers, their value was lowered so that it was necessary for them to be rested, fed well, and perhaps given medical treatment before being put on the market. This extra care added to the slave trader's costs. Slave traders still found it expedient to use trade slaves as porters, particularly in the carriage of fairly light to medium loads of high value or in the carriage of foodstuffs and camping equipment, thereby relieving professional porters and pack animals of part of their loads and making it possible for them to carry larger quantities of trade goods.

The use of trade slaves as porters retarded the development of specialized professional transport services but did not prevent the emergence of 'yan bojuwa and 'yan burabura, who were able to offer a service for high value goods that was significantly better than that offered by the typical slow moving caravan with its usual complement of trade slaves. Trade slaves were relatively inefficient porters, and traders in slaves stood to gain more by getting their slaves to market in good condition than by giving them heavy loads to carry. Such profits as the traders could earn were likely to have been small when set against the profit margins on prime slaves.

LIMITATIONS ON THE
DEVELOPMENT OF WORKER CONSCIOUSNESS

A labor force recruited from slaves, the "lumpenproletariat," petty entrepreneurs, and their dependents was most unlikely to develop anything remotely resembling an effective corporate solidarity as an occupational guild, let alone any more advanced form of class solidarity. Those engaged in portering or teamstering on their own account wanted to improve their status, while the aspirations of slaves lay in the direction first of freedom (or at least of wardship)[9] and with it the opportunity to labor or trade for oneself. The strategies perceived by free commoners and slaves were predominantly individualistic, not collective.

It would, however, be quite wrong to conclude that hired porters and teamsters were incapable of collective action to improve their conditions, although there was generally a surplus of labor available for hire and as a result labor stood in a poor bargaining position vis-à-vis the traders and merchants. On the march, though, the trader and his goods were vulnerable, and dissatisfied porters and teamsters could give the traders and the caravan leader a lot of trouble if they modified working conditions.[10] Awareness of the trouble that dissatisfied porters and teamsters could cause gave merchants a further reason for making the maximum possible use of household labor. A merchant with a large proportion of loyal dependents in his train was in a better position to counter threats from dissatisfied porters and teamsters than one who relied on the labor market.

Porters and teamsters had to exercise some discretion in the way in which they brought pressure to bear on traveling merchants or the agents of sedentary merchants. In extreme cases they risked the possibility of a summary trial by the caravan leader for endangering the lives and property of members of the caravan. Alternatively they could find themselves being handed over to the authorities for trial when they reached their destination. Rather than face these prospects dissatisfied porters and teamsters were more likely to desert, though this in its turn risked enslavement. Occasional collective action by porters and teamsters to defend or advance their interests is really no more than one should expect given the nature of the labor market and prevailing economic and social conventions. What would be surprising in this context would be evidence for sustained collective action to improve conditions.

A major obstacle to the development of class solidarity among porters and teamsters lay in the existence in long-distance trade of loosely structured but powerful associations based upon ties of kinship, culture and common residence. Several well-assimilated communities of alien origin, such as the Agalawa, Tokarawa, and Kambarin Beriberi, came to occupy a major role in certain branches of long distance trade (Lovejoy, 1980: 75-100). Vertical solidarity within these trading associations cross-cut any potential for conflict between the interests of the merchants on the one hand and the interests of the porters and teamsters on the other when porters and teamsters were members of the same community as the merchants. Young men began their trading experience as humble load carriers or teamsters but with time they gained seniority and rank within the association. Because they acquired contacts and capital through inheritance, they could hope to achieve not only a respectable position in the community but wealth as well. Porters and teamsters from these communities had little or no interest in maximizing short-run returns to themselves as laborers while working for or with other members of the community. Their interest lay in the long-term prosperity of the trading association as a whole and in particular that of the *gidaje* (houses) of which they were members.

It is possible that effective occupational solidarity came to characterize the labor of the specialists in the rapid transport of high value goods, the 'yan bojuwa and 'yan burabura. When these specialists were able to monopolize rapid transit on certain routes and prevent competition, they were in a relatively strong position vis-à-vis merchants needing to hire their services. However, we need to know much more about the composition, organization and mode of operation of the 'yan bojuwa and 'yan burabura before we can say with any confidence that they had any of the characteristics of occupational guilds or embryonic trade unions.

An examination of the labor of long-distance trade in the central Sudan reveals that trade was labor intensive, as indeed were other sectors of the economy. There were few economies of scale in the organization of transport. Livestock could carry more than porters, but the number of teamsters per livestock only reduced the labor input by a third to a fifth, depending upon the type of livestock employed. While draft animals reduced the number of workers necessary to transport a given quantity of goods, the difference was relatively marginal when compared with the impact of the railways and lorries that have largely replaced porters and teamsters in the twentieth century. The limitations on transport capacity invariably meant that large numbers of people were involved in trade, especially since such staples as grain, salt, and metal goods, as well as luxuries, were exchanged. Many people participated in the market economy—as porters, teamsters, and merchants—but the market economy was imperfectly developed because of the transportation bottleneck.

The porters and teamsters of the central Sudan were highly motivated individuals who willingly undertook the long and dangerous journeys of caravan trading because they hoped to become independent, small-scale merchants on their own account. People considered commerce a means of improving social and economic status, even though the labor requirements of long-distance trade were such that new workers had to be recruited to replace those who successfully transformed their position in trade from that of porter or teamster to that of entrepreneur. Individuals might stop being workers, but the work still had to be done. Indeed the expansion of trade in the nineteenth century suggests that the number of workers actually increased, even though no *class* of workers evolved. The attitudes of most porters and teamsters seem to have been directed towards attaining self-employment, and with the possible exception of 'yan bojuwa and 'yan burabura collective action and group identity were confined to specific expeditions. The extent to which workers perceived themselves as workers was temporary and expedient.

The alternate means of mobilizing labor through slavery and through the household also undermined the ability of workers to identify as a collectivity. Slaves who hired themselves out under murgu arrangements occupied an ambiguous position in the class structure; they were slaves but worked for wages, less, of course, the amount paid to their masters. Household labor—both free and slave—did not rely on a wage system at all. Slave and free alike were treated as members of a family firm and were allotted food, shelter and clothing as needed. They were not independent workers alienated from the work place. The heads of commercial households could act arbitrarily, dismiss kin and other apprentices, and sell slaves, but the interests of the firm mitigated against such behavior. It was far better to encourage cooperative attitudes than risk the development of class antagonisms. Those masters who allowed slaves to work on their own account in return for a murgu payment risked the development of corporate interests among these slaves, but employment was usually seasonal and slaves returned to the bosom of the household during the rainy season. The step toward the creation of an independent work force was only partial and hesitant; the bonds of slavery prevented the evolution of a distinct class.

In the final analysis, free professional porters and teamsters, household laborers, and slaves who worked on their own constituted an amorphous group of workers. There was relative ease of movement between the three categories, as indeed there was between that of worker and merchant. Young men could leave their homes and join an expedition as a porter or teamster and still return home to engage in the business of the family firm. Slaves who worked for themselves behaved in a manner similar to free porters and teamsters, for they wanted to maximize their wages. And anybody could trade if he had some capital, as Resident Goldsmith of Sokoto complained in an early report on the difficulty of controlling the slave population of the capital district in 1906. Slaves could no longer be kept in place after the British conquest of 1903. They wandered about the countryside selling a piece of cloth or a goat and caused trouble when they had nothing to sell.[11] The advent of the British altered the conditions of employment; slavery was under attack, primarily because of pressure from the slaves themselves in a situation in which political authority was shakey, and a greatly expanded "lumpenproletariat" emerged as a result. The colonial era ushered in new class relationships, but there was already a mass of under- and unemployed individuals in the nineteenth century. Porters and teamsters—both slave and free—filled the pool of labor that had to supplement the labor of the household. The ease with which people slipped into or out of the ranks of the small merchants reveals the strain in this social formation. Whether slave or free, the desire was to escape wage employment, but while individuals might be successful in doing so, at least for a time, the reality of business was that not everyone could be one of the attajirai.

NOTES

1. Travelers' marriages *(auran matafi, auran zaure)* were common. According to Trimingham (1959: 168-169), "If a trader already has four wives but does not wish to take any one of them with him on his travels for fear of inciting jealousy or because

they are strictly *kulle* (scheduled), he will arrange a temporary marriage with a fifth. He informs a cleric that none of his wives can travel with him and he wishes to take a temporary wife. He arranges for the cleric to be in the *zaure* or entrance hut of his compound at the time he leaves it to commence his journey and is married for the period of the journey. The clerics connive at the practice for, they say, 'he has renounced his wives for that period', interpreting literally the ambiguous Qur'anic passage in sūrat an-Nisā, verse 28. On his return the divorce is automatic when, at the *zaure* he hands her the previously stipulated *mut'a* (consolatory gift), though it is always called *sadaki*."

2. *alaro* (1) A carrier or porter (= *dan/'yan alaro*), or (2) Carrying a load a distance for payment. The word is of Yoruba origin: *aláàru* = porter: derived from *aaru* = porter's work (Abraham, 1962: 3). The Hausa words *dan/'yan dako* were also used to refer to porters and carriers but in a somewhat restricted way. They referred to those who carried loads short distances for payment, for example, within an urban area. The words had a related or additional meaning, at least in Sokoto and Zaria, where they referred to young slave lads. It may be legitimate to conclude from this that at least in these two cities urban porterage was undertaken by young male slaves.

3. Partnership was certainly known in nineteenth-century trading activities in Hausaland. *Terayya, tarme, turewa, gamayya* (Katsina dialect) are all words meaning partnership. The word *gamade* (which Bargery equates to *gamayya*) has the more specific meaning of combining for purposes of trade. A partner was referred to as *abokin taraya* (and presumably a trading partner was called *abokin gamade/gamayya*). There is another word, *guri'a,* derived from Arabic, that Bargery equates to *gamade,* with the following meaning: an investment in something bought conjointly by two or more persons.

4. Several Hausa texts collected in the late nineteenth and early twentieth centuries emphasize trade as a means of gaining wealth and prestige. See the discussion by Sellnow (1963: 410-432). There is an important poem on the subject of "Poverty and Wealth" in which the connection between long-distance trading and wealth is firmly emphasized. Sellnow did not make use of this poem, which comes from a collection made by A. Mischlich (1943: 129-197). The English translations by S. Pilaszewicz (1974: 67-115) and I. Tahir (in Goody, 1982: 193-209), suffer from a lack of annotation and critical analysis.

5. Ferguson learned at Yendi that Hausa kola traders used "slaves, horses, donkeys and oxen" to carry loads; see George Ferguson to Governor, 18 August 1894, C.O. 879/41, #479.

6. Northern Nigeria Annual Report, 1907-1908, cited in Ogunremi (1980: 108).

7. Henry P. Northcott to Colonial Secretary, 28 May 1898, enclosed in Hodgson to Chamberlain, 20 July 1898, C.O. 879/54 #564. A. Morris to Colonial Secretary, Gambaga, 1 October 1899, enclosed in Hodgson to Chamberlain, 23 November 1899, C.O. 879/58 #585.

8. Northcott to Colonial Secretary, 28 May 1898.

9. In describing the status of a slave who has received the grant of freedom as a "ward" rather than a "client", we are departing somewhat from the usual description of this status position. In the text on slavery collected by Mischlich (1909) the relationship of the former master to his former slave is described by the use of the term *wakili,* steward, representative, guardian. To us it seems that this last term describes the relationship, and in English the usual object of a guardian's attention is described as a ward.

10. There are a number of Hausa proverbs that suggest that porters had little respect for those who hired them and were unconcerned about the safe arrival of the goods they were hired to carry; see (a) *Mai kaya ke tsoron fashi, dan alaaro sai an ba shi magana:* The owner of the load fears robbers (he acts cautiously for fear of losing his property); the carrier does not care (all you can do is warn him) (Merrick 1905: 64). (An alternative reading is possible—The owner of the load fears delay/breakage; for the carrier it is only talk.) (b) *'Yan alaro ba ka asara sai gammo.* Porter, you have nothing to lose but (your) headpad. From the collection of Major Edgar, National Archives, Kaduna. These proverbs can be interpreted in several ways, but one feature stands out clearly; the porters, *'yan alaro,* were a distinctly identifiable group of laborers who had no personal stake in the goods that they carried.

11. Goldsmith, Sokoto Province, Report for December 1906, SNP 7/8 1643/1907.

REFERENCES

Anon. (1963) Sudan Witness. Special Seventieth Year Issue, Sudan Interior Mission. Toronto: Sudan Interior Mission.

ABRAHAM, R. L. (1962) Dictionary of Modern Yoruba. Sevenoaks.

BAIER, S. (1980) An Economic History of Central Niger. Oxford: Oxford University Press.

————(1976) "Local transport in the economy of the Central Sudan, 1900-1930." Presented at the Seminar on the Economic History of the Central Savanna of West Africa, Kano.

BARTH, H. (1857-1859) Travels and Discoveries in North and Central Africa, 3 vols. New York: Harper and Row.

CLAPPERTON, H. (1829) Journal of a Second Expedition into the Interior of Africa, from the Bight of Benin to Soccatoo. London: John Murray.

COHEN, A. (1969) Custom and Politics in Urban Africa. London and Los Angeles: University of California Press.

DENHAM, D., H. CLAPPERTON, and W. OUDNEY (1966) Narrative of Travels and Discoveries in Northern and Central Africa in the Years 1822, 1823 and 1824 (E. W. Bovill, ed.). Cambridge: Cambridge University Press.

DUFFILL, M. B. [ed.] (1984) The Biography of Madugu Mai Gashin Baki. Los Angeles: Crossroads Press.

FLEGEL, E. R. (1885) Löse Blatter aus dem Tagebuche meiner Haussa-Freunde und Reisegefahrten, eingeleitet, mit Allgemeinen Schilderung des Volscharecters und der socialen Verhältnisse der Haussa's sowie mit Kurzer Lebensgeschichte des Mai gasin Baki versehen von E. R. Flegel. Hamburg: L. Friederichsen.

————(1883/1885) "Der Handel in Nigerbeit und seine voraussichtliche Zukunft." Mitteilungen der Afrikanisches Gesellschaft in Deutschland 4: 134-135.

GOODY, J. (1982) Cooking, Cuisine and Class. Cambridge: Cambridge University Press.

HILL, P. (1971) "Two types of West African house trade," pp. 308-318 in C. Meillassoux (ed.) The Development of Indigenous Trade and Markets in West Africa. London: Oxford University Press.

————(1966) "Landlords and brokers: a West African trading system." Cahiers d'études africaines 23: 349-66.

JOHNSTON, H.A.S. (1889) The History of a Slave. London: Kegan, Paul, Trench.

KLING, E. (1890a) "Bericht des Hauptmann Kling über seine letzte, von Lome über Kpandu, Salaga und Naparri nach Bismarckburg ausgeführte Reise." Mitteilungen aus den deutschen Schutzgebieten 3: 137-64.

————(1890b) "Über seine reise in das Hinterland von Togo." Verhandlungen der Gesellschaft für Erdkunde zu Berlin 17: 348-371.

KRAUSE, G. A. (1882) "Aufzeichnungen über die stadt Chat in der Sahara." Zeitschrift des Gesellschaft für Erdkunde zu Berlin: 266-337.

KRIEGER, K. (1954) "Kola-Karawanen. Ein Beitrag zur Geschichte des Hausahandels." Mitteilungen des Institut für Orientforschung: 289-324.

LOVEJOY, P. E. (1985) Salt of the Desert Sun. A History of Salt Production and Trade in the Central Sudan. Cambridge: Cambridge University Press.

————(1980) Caravans of Kola: The Hausa Kola Trade, 1700-1900. Zaria: Ahmadu Bello University Press.

MERRICK, G. (1905) Hausa Proverbs. London: Kegan, Paul, Trench, Trubner.

MISCHLICH, A. (1943) "Religiöse und Weltliche Gesänge der Mohammedaner aus dem Sudan." Studier zur Auslandskunde: Afrika 2, 3: 129-197.

————(1942) Über die Kulturen im Mittel-Sudan. Berlin: Dietrich Reimer.

————(1909) "Über Sitten und Gebrauche in Hausa." Mitteilungen des Seminar für Orientalische Sprachen 11: 215-274.

MONTEIL, P. L. (1894) De Saint-Louis à Tripoli par le Lac Tchad. Paris: Felix Alcan.

OGUNREMI, G. O. (1982) Counting the Camels. The Economics of Transport in Pre-Industrial Nigeria. New York: Nok.

————(1980) "The pre-colonial economy and transportation in northern Nigeria," in I. A. Akinjogbin and S. O. Osoba (eds.) Topics on Nigerian Economic and Social History. Ile-Ife, Nigeria: University of Ife Press.

PASSARGE, S. (1895) Adamaua. Bericht über die Expedition des Deutschen Kamerun-Komittes in den Jahren 1893/94. Berlin: Dietrich Reimer.

PILASZEWICZ, S. (1974) "The song of poverty and wealth: a Hausa poem on social problems." Africana Bulletin: 67-115.

SELLNOW, I. (1963) "Der Handel in der Hausa Literatur des ausgehenden 19 und beginnenden 20 Jahrhunderts." Mitteilungen des Institut für Orientforschung 9: 410-32.

STAUDINGER, P. (1889) Im Herzen der Haussaländer. Berlin: Landsberger.

TRIMINGHAM, J. S. (1959) Islam in West Africa. Oxford: Oxford University Press.

TUKUR, M. M. (1977) "Values and public affairs: the relevance of the Sokoto caliphal experience to the transformation of the Nigeria polity." Ph.D. dissertation, Ahmadu Bello University, Zaria.

VOGEL, E. (1855) "Reise von Tripoli bis zum Tsad-See." Petermanns Geographische Mittheilungen: 237-259.

WHITTING, C.E.J. (1967) Hausa and Fulani Proverbs. Lagos: Government Printer.

WORKS, J. (1976) Pilgrims in a Strange Land. New York: Columbia University Press.

ARCHIVAL SOURCES

George Ferguson to Governor, 18 August 1894, C.O. 879/41, #479.
E.P.C. Girouard to Secretary of State, Report on Transport Policy of Nigeria, 30 May
   1907, Zungeru. Nigerian National Archives, Kaduna.
Griffith to Knutsford, 28 December 1888, C.O. 96/197.
Hodgson to Chamberlain, 20 July 1898, C.O. 879/54, #564.
Hodgson to Chamberlain, 23 November 1899, C.O. 879/58, #585.
Low to Chamberlain, 1 May 1899, C.O. 96/339.
Pigott report, 20 October 1896, C.O. 879/45, #506.
Collection of Major Edgar, National Archives, Kaduna.

ORAL INFORMANTS (Lovejoy collection, Northern History Research Library, Ahmadu Bello University, Zaria, Nigeria)

Abdullahi, Nagudu. 25 October 1969, Kano.
Bagwanje, Adamu. 18 August and 10 September 1969, Kano.
Barmo, Muhammad Lawan. 5 January 1970 Katsina.
Indole, Muhammadu Isa. 18 January 1970, Kano.
Madigawa, Ba'ko. 1 December 1969, Kano.
Turawa, Gambo. 5 January 1970, Katsina.

8

THE LABOR OF VIOLENCE
Dar al-Kuti in the Nineteenth Century

DENNIS D. CORDELL

During the latter half of the nineteenth century in North Central Africa, the labor of long-distance commerce became increasingly differentiated from other work—small-scale agriculture, gathering and hunting, and local and regional trade. By the 1880s, long-distance exchange meant for the most part slave-raiding and trading, as well as commerce in guns, munitions, and ivory. Violence became an important element in the labor of long-distance trade, eventually disrupting earlier patterns of doing just about everything. Slave-raiders initially directed their efforts toward the acquisition of captives for export, but they also relocated people around their settlements. In and around these centers slaves worked in a variety of occupations. Although most were agricultural laborers, some joined the ranks of the raiders, and still others were craftspeople. Over time slave labor eclipsed kin-based patterns of work organization. Indeed by the end of the century the slave mode of production became primary in many regions of North Central Africa. The earlier domestic mode did not

Author's Note: I would like to thank Joel W. Gregory for his editorial and substantive comments on an earlier version of this chapter, and I wish to express appreciation to the Social Science Research Council for financial support.

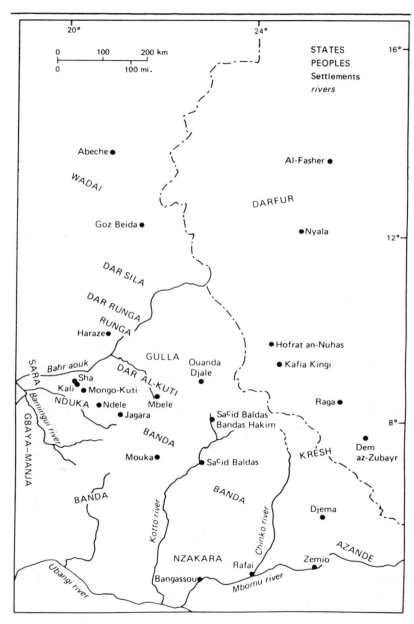

SOURCE: Cordell (1979).

Map 8.1: **Northern Equatorial Savannah (c. 1900)**

disappear, but it was closely articulated with and subordinated to servile labor.

Because North Central Africa is large, covering the southern Lake Chad and Ubangi river basins (see Map 8.1) this essay focuses on only part of it—the state of Dar al-Kuti. For most of the nineteenth century Dar al-Kuti was a farflung outpost of the northern Muslim state of Wadai, its territory confined to the lowlands south of the Aouk River that today mark the border between Chad and the Central African Republic (CAR). Small numbers of northern Muslims lived in the area where they traded with non-Muslim populations. Beginning in the 1880s, and particularly after 1890, however, Dar al-Kuti's hinterland grew dramatically southward and eastward eventually to include most of the eastern CAR savanna. Peaceful exchange gave way to slave-raiding as the state expanded under the leadership of Muhammad al-Sanusi, the most (in)famous dealer in captives in North Central Africa at the turn of the twentieth century.

This chapter charts this transformation, beginning with an overview of work associated with long-distance commerce early in the century; it then traces the implantation of Muslim communities in the south, and the subsequent rise of slave-raiding and trading as the major activities of long-distance trade. The expansion of commerce resulted in greater specialization in trade and production. Whereas labor had been relatively undifferentiated early in the nineteenth century, by the end of this period the organization of labor had become more complex. But even at this late date, the labor of trade was notably less specialized in North Central Africa than in other parts of the continent. Some slaves were used as porters, and a few merchants operated on a large enough scale that they required the services of clients, captives, and other workers. But most operated on far more modest levels. Dar al-Kuti remained on the frontier of more complex commercial networks.

THE LABOR OF EXCHANGE IN THE EARLY NINETEENTH CENTURY

Dar al-Kuti as such came into being in the 1830s with the southward movement of the Islamic frontier. The resources of the south attracted both Muslim immigrants and itinerant peddlers who traded with non-Muslim peoples such as the Banda, Sara, Nduka, Manza, and Gbaya. Most of these peoples lived in dispersed hamlets, working the land with kinspeople and a few clients; very few occupations were exclusively associated with long-distance trade. Communities consumed most of what they produced, and with the possible exception of peoples living along the Mbomu, Uele, and Ubangi rivers in the far south, there were probably not any societies or settlements whose inhabitants engaged primarily in production for exchange, commerce, or transport.

Nonetheless, long-distance exchange and tasks associated with it certainly existed. In North Central Africa both individuals and groups were more mobile than agriculturalists elsewhere. Perhaps because arable land of roughly uniform quality was readily available, and the population was not dense, migration was frequent. A very elastic kinship system also permitted individuals to move quite readily. Burnham has coined the term "permissive ecology" to describe the fluid character of Gbaya society (Burnham, 1979: 185-202); it may be applied to the other savanna peoples as well (Cordell 1983: 39-45). Trade occurred in this context of overall mobility; it was not a specialized activity.

Trade in mineral resources such as salt was a prime example. Most peoples burned plant leaves and washed the ashes to produce a bitter mixture of sodium chloride and potassium sulphate. Such work was not differentiated from domestic labor, and there is no evidence that salt was produced for exchange. By the late eighteenth century, however, mineral salt from the Sahara and Sahel had reached the borderlands of North Central Africa where it was highly valued (Chevalier, 1907: 221-222; Tisserant, 1953: 245; al-Tunisi, 1845: 317-318; 1851: 492). While the sources of this salt lay in Muslim hands, trade at the southern end of the network involved non-Muslims. Even so, there was relatively little specialization and little division of labor.

Although still closely articulated with domestic production, more specialized forms of labor grew out of trade in two other minerals—copper and iron. Copper ornaments from North Central Africa made their way to the Sahel as early as the 1790s when Browne (1799: 304) reported seeing large copper rings weighing twelve to fifteen pounds in Dar Fur; Burckhardt (1822: 442) wrote in 1817 of copper production south of Wadai, and Pallme (1844: 351n) saw large anklets in Kordofan two decades later. Most of this copper came from Hofrat al-Nuhas, mines in today's southwestern Sudan. By the early nineteenth century the mines were in Muslim hands, and although little is known about the labor force in the mines, most workers were probably non-Muslim slaves (Hayer, 1972: 4; Barth, 1853: 120). The transport and actual trading of copper to the Sahel were in the hands of Muslim traders—namely the Jallaba; Barth (1965: I, 521; II, 488) found copper from Hofrat al-Nuhas in Kano in the early 1850s, which attests to the opening of an east-west route as well.

Oral traditions suggest that non-Muslims from societies to the west also transported and traded copper from the southwestern Sudan. Among the Banda, for example, Kalck (1970: I, 262-263) collected testimonies thirty years ago recounting the itinerary from the mines; more recently, Banda informants claimed that Banda peoples traded and traveled east for copper anklets to include with bridewealth "a long time ago" (Abudullu Yiala Mende, Banda Ngao-Banda Marba-Kresh). The Manza did likewise (Chevalier, 1907: 115). Activities associated with the production, transport, and exchange of copper were certainly more differentiated from domestic labor than the production of local salt, but they were still influenced by the subsistence sphere. Dealing in copper was not a specialized occupation except in Hofrat al-Nuhas itself. The Banda, for example, confined their copper expeditions to the dry season when their labor was not needed for agriculture.

Still more specialized than work associated with salt production or with copper transport and exchange was ironworking. This work had little to do with the irregular distribution of iron deposits, since the laterite soil of North Central Africa is rich in ore; Chevalier (1907: 628-630) located four major deposits near Ndele, the capital of Dar al-Kuti, in the first decade of this century. In this case, it was indeed a question of specialization—in the extraction, smelting, and working of iron. By the early 1800s, Muslims of the desert-edge described many non-Muslim peoples as superior smiths; al-Tunisi (1845: 277-278) noted that craftsmen from Fertyt—a geographical and ethnic term Muslims used to refer to the non-Muslim peoples south of Dar Fur and Wadai—produced excellent knives, bracelets, armbands, and spearheads.

Evidence from much later in the nineteenth century suggests that there were many iron workers among the non-Muslim peoples of Dar al-Kuti. Whereas Banda Mbatta smiths only made tools and weapons for their own use, other smiths clearly produced ironware for exchange (Mittendumu Albert, Banda Mbatta-Banda Mbagga). At the turn of the century, for example, most Banda Dakwa villages in the Mbres region south of Dar al-Kuti had two or three forges used to manufacture knives and agricultural tools for exchange with their neighbors.[1]

The smiths of the nearby Banda Ngapu were renowned for their throwing knives, which circulated as far south as the Ubangi River. Whereas the knives served as weapons among the Ngapu themselves, they were rarer among the river peoples where they were valued as ornaments (Dybowski, 1893: 304-306). In general, the proliferation of knife styles and their wide distribution in North Central Africa suggest that this production for regional exchange was quite ancient (Cordell, 1973: 94-104). And the wide variety of ways in which societies have integrated their use reinforces this conclusion: some were weapons, others served as specialized currency for bridewealth payments, and still others came to be symbols of chiefly authority.

Al-Tunisi's awareness of the production and trade of iron goods in the south indicates that some items probably made their way further afield, at least by the 1830s if not earlier. And by the 1890s at least, northern Muslim traders dealt in iron goods. Following attacks on Muslim traders said to be involved in the slave trade, both Dybowski and Maistre, leaders of two early French expeditions, found numerous small iron pics and other iron implements in the merchants' baggage bound for Wadai (Prioul, 1981: 124; Dybowski, 1893: 273; Maistre, 1895: 137).

It is impossible to answer what is clearly a crucial question: To what degree did ironworkers produce goods destined mainly for long-distance trade? Among some groups smiths clearly produced goods with exchange in mind, but it does not appear that the commerce was ever sufficiently large to allow ironworkers to specialize completely in production for exchange; they continued to plant fields and to gather and hunt.

Sometimes, smiths constituted recognizable groups that were virtually autonomous, although the nature of the evidence makes it impossible to determine the links between these groups and other societies in North Central Africa. In the early twentieth century elders among the Dakwa, one such autonomous group, claimed that their ancesters had "always" been smiths,[2] which suggests that in their minds there was a close association between ethnicity and occupational specialization. In the organization of labor for trade and production, however, such ethnic consciousness marks an economy that was only marginally oriented toward production for exchange. In most cases, trade was local.

LABOR AND TRADE
IN DAR AL-KUTI, 1830-1870

Dar al-Kuti emerged as a discrete entity around 1830 when the sultan of Wadai laid claim to the region and sent a representative to reside south of the Aouk. The sultan's initiative testifies to the greater integration of North Central Africa into the Muslim economy of the Sahel. With this integration came increasing specialization of work associated with long-distance trade. This change manifested itself in three ways in the middle decades of the nineteenth century. First, new groups appeared in the region whose livelihood was partially or totally dependent on the market. Second, the older currents of long-distance exchange—the flow of products such as copper, salt, and iron, as well as ivory—were at times diverted into the growing streams of long-distance exchange. Third, long-distance trade brought demands for new products which in turn created new occupations and a need for new workers.

Muslim immigrants from Bagirmi in the northwest and Dar Runga directly north also began arriving in Dar al-Kuti in the first several decades of the nineteenth century. In Bagirmi, drought, conflict with Wadai, and the persecution of Muslim teachers in the 1810s and 1820s encouraged emigration; and while Dar al-Kuti was not close by, the Shari River afforded a natural route to the southeast. Some people came mainly to settle, taking Nduka wives and establishing permanent ties with local leaders. Temporary migrants included itinerant Muslim peddlers who came to trade in the October-March dry season when travel was easier, returning north before the rains. These traders exchanged northern imports for ivory and pepper (Yacoub Mahamat Dillang, Runga; Ngrekoudou Ouih Fran, Banda Toulou; Abakar Zacharia, Runga; Chapiseau, 1900: 124-125; Carbou, 1912: II, 223, al-Tunisi, 1845: 280-281, 467, 488); slaves were not a feature of the commerce at this time. Thus individuals who gained their living solely by long-distance exchange made their appearance for the first time. As time passed and the Muslim communities and their influence grew, a second temporary migrant appeared. This was the *faqih,* a teacher familiar with the rudiments of Islam who supplemented his income from petty commerce by selling Muslim charms and offering Qur'anic instruction.

The temporary sojourners stimulated the participation of the settled Muslims in commerce as landlord-brokers. The permanent residents' ties with local peoples assured the temporary migrants the security necessary for commerce, and provided needed information about the price, location, and availability of exports, as well as an assessment of the demand for imports (cf. Yacoub Mahamat Dillang; Assakin Mahamat Angula, Runga-Jallaba). They also housed the peddlers and stored their goods. To talk of a trading diaspora is to exaggerate the volume and intensity of exchange with the north—particularly before 1850—but the specialization of labor described above is characteristic of such networks (Cohen, 1971: 266-281).

The presence of Muslim migrants, both permanent and temporary, stimulated production for exchange. The Nduka, for example, began to gather pepper, which they already consumed and sold locally, for export north. But the ivory trade was perhaps the most important example of this transformation of "traditional" work: In the early 1870s, Nachtigal noted that Dar al-Kuti was famed for its abundant stocks of ivory (Nachtigal, 1971: 81-83). The Nduka claim that they have hunted elephants since time immemorial; while their claims may be exaggerated, it is clear that Nduka men did hunt elephants in the nineteenth century, dividing the meat in a prescribed fashion and presenting the local earth chief with the tusk that touched the ground first (Maarabbi Hasan; Abakar Tidjani; Yusuf Dingis). With the integration of Dar al-Kuti into the Muslim economy came a ready market. By Nachtigal's (1971: 202) time, the commerce was well organized and profitable:

> The foreign merchants who wish to deal in ivory sell their goods on credit to reliable natives, who then take them to the rich sources of ivory in the Bahr es-Salamat, Runga, and Kuti. In my time a centner of ivory, which in Egypt costs 150 dollars, could be bought in Kuti for beads or cotton strips to the value of ten dollars.

The Muslims also introduced new products, some of which came to be produced locally. The most important of these items was cotton cloth. Initially Bagirmi was an important center of cloth manufacture for the sahel and savanna east of Borno. Bagirmi cloth was popular among the peoples of Wadai and its southern vassal states, including Dar al-Kuti. When the Bagirmi migrated to their new homelands, they took cotton cultivation, spinning, and weaving with them. They also imported cloth from farther north, supplying prominent non-Muslims with cloth which was considered a prestige item (Nachtigal, 1967: II,

669; Chevalier, 1907: 219). While less is known about their activities in this sphere, the Runga also produced cloth and woven goods for trade (Khrouma Sale; Chevalier, 1907: 229).

The initial appearance of cloth probably only changed patterns of work insofar as some people began hunting elephants and producing pepper in order to buy it. By the 1860s and 1870s, however, the eastern Banda were growing cotton, spinning thread, and weaving cloth—for exchange as well as their own consumption. By the 1890s, the Manza and Akounga, among other peoples, were following their example (Prioul, 1981: 50-51).

The expansion of trade and the greater concentration on production for exchange increased the demands on transport; perhaps for the first time specialized tasks associated with commerce may be identified. By the 1870s, at least, considerable quantities of long-distance trade goods arrived in, or were exported from, Dar al-Kuti by headload or on pack animals. The traders themselves carried out most tasks associated with transport; the fragmentary evidence does not suggest the existence of many porters, animal suppliers, or guides who offered specialized services. (Nachtigal noted that transportation costs were high because sleeping sickness took a heavy toll among the animals.) Later in the century, greater specialization was necessary travel along the trade routes became less secure, and more porters, teamsters, and other workers were employed. Long-distance commerce between North Central Africa and the sahel became increasingly synonymous with the trade in slaves. Spiraling violence accompanied this transition and the flight of rural people created vast deserted areas; both made transport more difficult and required more organization.

THE TRANSITION TO SLAVE-RAIDING
AND THE SLAVE-TRADE:
DAR AL-KUTI, 1870-1890

The decades between 1870 and 1890 are a watershed in the history of Dar al-Kuti. The economy of the region became increasingly articulated with the Muslim economy of the sahel. As it did, the image of North Central Africa became more clearly defined. In contrast to the vague references to "kuti" by Barth in the 1850s, Nachtigal's account (1971: 59) twenty years later clearly reveals the growth of ties with the north. The demands of the larger Muslim economy very much determined the nature of Dar al-Kuti's participation in long-distance

exchange. Increasingly, northern slave-raiders saw the area as a reservoir of labor, a source of captives.

It is also apparent that the Muslim newcomers of earlier decades
tightened their control. Throughout the period, Kobur, a prominent
faqih-trader, presided in Dar al-Kuti. His commercial undertakings
offer some insight into the evolution of exchange. By prevailing stan-
dards he was successful, exchanging ivory, a few slaves, and lesser exports for the beads and cloth brought south by Muslim traders. As
a faqih, local Muslims and the foreign traders recognized and respected
him as a mediator (Cordell, 1985: Ch. 2). He was able to organize
his business on a significant scale and he was probably one of the first,
if not the first, merchant to require the labor of porters, teamsters,
and commercial assistants. He recruited these workers through slavery,
clientage, and kinship (see Cordell, 1979: 379-394).

Beyond this, the evidence does not suggest any major changes in
the labor associated with long-distance exchange in the 1870s, but
rather an intensification of already discernible trends. Immigration continued, although more commonly from Dar Runga than Bagirmi, and
the population became correspondingly more diverse. Foreign traders
became more numerous, including Muslims from Hausaland and Borno
and Jallaba from the Sudan (Yacoub Mahamat Dillang; Khrouma Sale;
Abakar Zacharia). Two of the major settlements in the region, Kali
and Sha, were inhabited by Runga, assimilated Runga-Nduka, and
foreign Muslim traders. These settlements had close ties with the third
principal village, Mongo-Kuti, the settlement of a prominent Nduka
earth chief who supplied ivory to the traders.

Little information is available on other activities stimulated by
greater contact with the north. However, Nachtigal's (1971: 82-83)
description of travel between Wadai and Dar Runga in 1873 offers
some insight into the organization of trading parties, modes of
transportation, and the stopping points along the way:

> It is possible indeed to take camels to Kuti from Abeshr in the dry
> season, but they promptly die there, and, cheap as they are in Wadai,
> still require too large an expenditure. Oxen and the ordinary donkeys,
> the prices of which do not exceed two to three, or at the most, four
> dollars in Wadai, certainly stand the test better, but they likewise usually
> die before one is ready to return after exchanging one's goods for ivory.
> One therefore has to count upon the loss of one's animals, to send
> somebody back to the north after the goods have been sold, in order

to bring back the required number of donkeys or oxen, and then immediately to set out on the return journey. The cause of the rapid mortality among these baggage animals is the virulent fly, *umm bujena.*

Nachtigal hoped to go to Dar al-Kuti, but had to limit his trip to Dar Runga. In preparation for that sojourn he bought a draught ox and a riding donkey; the sultan of Wadai had already supplied him with two other oxen (Nachtigal, 1971: 84). While traveling south and still in Wadaian territory, he and his companions stayed in *masjids,* inexpensive hostels maintained in many villages for itinerant Muslim scholars *(muhajirun)* by local Qur'anic students (Nachtigal, 1971: 92). Traveling south at the height of the rainy season in July and August, Nachtigal and his party turned back before reaching Dar Runga, further progress blocked by the swamps of the Salamat. His experience nonetheless suggests regular communication and a network of way stations between Abeche and the Salamat; beyond the Salamat such camps were less common.

If patterns of labor associated with long-distance trade within the region do not seem to have altered greatly by the 1870s, the intermittent appearance of slave-raiding parties from elsewhere was a harbinger of the violence that became the predominant influence on long-distance trade in the remainder of the century. During the 1870s, the greatest threat remained the infrequent incursions of raiders from Wadai (Nachtigal, 1971: 87). Several hundred kilometers to the southeast among the Banda, however, Sudanese slave traders known as the Khartoumers were already building armed camps (*zariba* [Arabic]) which served as headquarters for raiding parties. Closer to home, a group of raiders raiding on behalf of al-Zubayr, the governor of Dar Fur, ravaged major villages in Dar al-Kuti in 1876. In the same decade, Rabih, another Sudanese raider, pillaged Banda lands in the east and then invaded Dar al-Kuti and Dar Runga. In addition to these Muslim raiders, Ngono, a nearby Banda Ngao war leader with military and commercial ties to the Muslim slavers of the southwestern Sudan, attacked in 1874 and again in 1877 or 1878 (cf. Yacoub Mahamat Dillang; Yadri Sale; Yusuf Dingis; Yadjouma Pascal; Julien, 1925: 106-107, 113, 124-125; Chevalier, 1907: 131-132; Modat, 1912: 180, 272; Carbou, 1912: II, 129-130).

Greater changes arrived with Rabih b. Fadl-Allah, who first appeared on the Gounda River just east of Dar al-Kuti in 1878. Several years before, he had left the Sudan, having parted company with his colleague Sulayman, son of his former employer al-Zubayr (Dampierre, 1983: 36). He spent the next thirteen years in North Central Africa, a period critical for his later conquests of Bagirmi and Borno. Seeking commercial outlets and sources of arms and munitions, he pressured both Wadai and Bagirmi. He also built an army—in part through the purchase of captives, but mainly through extensive slave-raiding. When he arrived in the region he had only a few hundred men; in 1889, a year before he left Dar al-Kuti, he headed a force of 10,000 (Cordell, 1985; Ch. 3).

Rabih's presence dramatically expanded the scale of economic and military activity. Whereas the Wadaian slave-raiding expeditions were infrequent, Rabih's sustained search for slaves to incorporate in his forces, and weapons to arm them, brought continuous upheaval that made it difficult for people to return to earlier patterns of settlement and work after his departure. Not even Rabih's fellow Muslims were spared violence. He killed or took many Runga captive, and an intensive campaign in Dar Runga shortly before his final departure from the area is said to have stripped the region of its population.[3] During this period Wadai blockaded Dar al-Kuti economically, engaged the invader in one major but inconclusive battle, but never defeated him.

For long-distance commerce, then, Rabih's sojourn was a disaster. Either his forces or the threat of Wadaian attacks made travel very insecure. Moreover, his campaigns caused many people to abandon their villages. In 1891, shortly after Rabih's exodus, the Crampel expedition crossed a vast no man's land created by raiding south of Dar al-Kuti. Ten years later al-Hajj Abdo, al-Sanusi's advisor, told Chevalier that Rabih had "eaten the land . . . where he passed, he took all" (Chevalier, 1907: 226). Still later, Modat noted that among Muslims, a line of a popular cradle song went as follows: "Rabih came, the bullets fell" (Modat, 1912: 226).

The slave-raiding and slave-trading initiated by and encouraged by Rabih's campaigns signaled a major change in activities associated with long-distance commerce. The primary orientation of commerce shifted from hunting and trading ivory for cloth to hunting and trading people. Successful raiding required military superiority, derived from the possession of firearms. This, in turn, made it necessary to expand raiding constantly in order to supply the captives that the Muslim economy demanded for more weapons. The violence and upheaval accompanying the slave-gun cycle also produced larger population concentrations. People seeking security voluntarily settled around the headquarters of individuals such as Rabih; others were forcibly relocated. Still, had Rabih's need for soldiers and slaves to trade for arms been the only impetus for the commerce, such exchange as well as the violence associated with it would presumably have ended with his departure. As it was, three developments prevented the return to a more peaceful existence. First, the revolt in the Sudan against the Egyptian government and the rise of the Mahidiya between 1881 and 1898 blocked commercial routes in the eastern sahel and Nile valley, bringing a westward shift of the zariba system to North Central Africa. Second, rising demand for slaves in North Africa, and in Egypt in particular, led to increased trade on the major trans-Saharan route connecting the Mediterranean with Black Africa—that from Benghazi to Wadai (Cordell 1977: 21-36). Finally, and most important for events in the immediate area, Rabih left a client whose continuous presence, arms, and aspirations, would make of Dar al-Kuti a major slave-exporting state between 1890 and 1911.

THE NEW LABOR OF
LONG-DISTANCE TRADE: 1890-1911

Outsiders may have sown the seeds of slave-raiding and slave-trading in Dar al-Kuti, but they fell on fertile soil. Between 1890 and his assassination in 1911, Muhammad al-Sanusi routinized and "domesticated" the random raiding initiated by Rabih. The violence of enslavement in its various steps and phases became the most important "labor" associated with long-distance trade. Over much of the area, the violence disrupted the domestic mode of production, either eliminating it entirely by taking people into slavery, or forcing its articulation with an increasingly dominant slave mode of production.

The shift began with Rabih's departure in 1890, but it was not abrupt (see Cordell, 1985: chs. 3 and 4). Al-Sanusi's first years as "sultan" were spent searching for security. Placed in power by one of Wadai's most vociferous challengers and then abandoned, he had reason to fear retribution from the Muslim state to the north. And indeed it came in 1894 when a Wadaian cavalry attack destroyed his capital at Sha on the Aouk floodplain. The sultan, his Runga followers, and associated traders fled before the horsemen, and thus survived, but they did not return to the site. Finally, in 1896 he settled at Ndele where the lands of the Runga, Nduka, and Banda came together.

Ndele remained the sultan's capital until his death. A large rock outcropping (*kaga* [Banda]) with its own water sources lay at the center of the settlement, and there al-Sanusi built his compound. His sons, major military leaders, and their families and troops joined him. The major foreign slave dealers lived there as well. For the next fifteen years the population of Ndele grew, fed by captives taken in raiding or refugees seeking asylum. Now a periphery of the Sahelian periphery of the global economy, Dar al-Kuti furnished slaves and some ivory to the Islamic world.

Slave-raiding was not productive labor in the ordinary sense of the term—work that transforms unfinished goods or raw materials from one stage to another, and in so doing adds value to the final product. Slave-raiders did not "produce" slaves. Yet considerable resources of the state were invested in such activities to "produce" people— primarily for export and secondarily for settlement. In his overview of slavery in Africa in the nineteenth century, Lovejoy gets around the problem by adding quotation marks when referring to the recruitment of slaves into the armies of African states and their subsequent raiding for additional captives: "In the military slaves were not used for productive purposes, except in the sense that soldiers 'produced' slaves through wars and raids" (Lovejoy, 1983: 275). Writing of Borno at another point, Lovejoy notes that "organized slave-raiding reflected the dependence of the political economy on slavery. Slave-catching was a business" (Lovejoy, 1983: 70).

Inherently violent, this labor also undermined existing modes of production:

> In the 19th century ... there were states whose autonomy was ensured by the economic and demographic importance of the capitals, by the quasi-individual control of an important number of firearms, and by the formation at the center of a new mode of production whose extension was accompanied by the progressive destruction of the lineage mode of production. This new mode of production was based on the massive utilization of personal dependents and on the personal control of cultivable lands at the center [Jewsiewicki, 1981: 102].

Jewsiewicki does not consider in any detail the alterations in economic activity that created this new mode of production, but slave-raiding was clearly one of them. Within Dar al-Kuti some slaves were settled and engaged in true productive work. The labor of raiding is best analyzed as a means of reproducing the labor force. In all societies such reproduction occurs in two ways—through procreation or immigration. The domestic mode of production dominant in North Central Africa prior to the rise of Dar al-Kuti reproduced its labor mainly through procreation; societies invested a major portion of their resources in preparations and activities surrounding childbirth and childraising. In the successor societies where a slave mode of production prevailed, the state channeled its resources toward the reproduction of the labor force through forced immigration, which is to say slave-raiding. And just as some contemporary parts of the developed world import labor from the Third World when it is needed and deport it when there is no longer a demand for it, so Dar al-Kuti and other slave-raiding societies may have regarded export as a way of regulating the reproduction of the labor force as well as a means of acquiring vital imports.

In al-Sanusi's time raiding became a more regular activity than had been the case when Rabih sojourned in Dar al-Kuti. Rabih had a limited, albeit major objective—the building of an army to conquer lands elsewhere. His client transformed these ad hoc campaigns into an annual harvest of people.[4]

Raiding campaigns generally occurred during the dry part of the year, following the agricultural season; travel was also easier at this time. The scale of these operations was in keeping with their long duration. Ranging in size from 100 or 200 to as many as 1000 or 2000 men, raiding parties usually set out within a couple of months after the end of the rains and moved slowly toward the target area. While in the immediate hinterland of Ndele, the sultan's agricultural villages provided grain; beyond this zone, numerous small hunting and foraging parties scoured the countryside for game, shea butter nuts, and edible wild plants to supplement the food supplies carried by the expedition.

Once in the region to be raided, the marauders constructed one or more zaribas that served as headquarters for the operation. From there, smaller parties set out to raid the generally small and scattered non-Muslim settlements. Slaves taken in each encounter were then herded back to the zariba where they were held prisoner. After a sufficient number of captives had been acquired, they were tied together, and the expedition returned to Ndele (Yacoub Mahamat Dillang; Abakar Zacharia; Abdoulaye Oumbra; Konongar, 1971: 204-207; Dybowski, 1893: 268-69; Daigre, 1950: 47; Julien, 1929: 55; Modat, 1912: 233).

This procedure explains the large number of slaves taken in the few campaigns for which statistics are available.

Success depended on a combination of surprise, numbers, and the panic provoked by gunfire at close range. Unlike the raiding expeditions of sahelian states such as Wadai, Bagirmi, and Dar Fur, al-Sanusi's forces included no cavalry detachments. A large number of raiders usually made their way on foot to within striking distance of a village and set up camp for the night. The next morning they arose well before daybreak and set out after the dawn prayer. They attacked in the gray light of early morning with guns blazing. In most cases, villages were taken by surprise, and many people were killed or captured in the initial melee. Because others fled to hide in the bush nearby, raiding parties frequently camped in the abandoned villages for several days to hunt for refugees. The marauders also took this opportunity to strip the settlement of stored food and items of value, such as ivory, that had been put aside for trading with itinerant peddlers. The raiding party then returned to the central zariba (Abakar Zacharia; Julien, 1929: 55-56).

Slave-raiding, like other forms of violence, was dangerous. Al-Sanusi's forces triumphed in most encounters; however, they were not invincible, and they knew it. The frequent use of surprise tactics suggests that they feared defeat or unbearable casualties in a direct engagement. Another strategy also reflects this concern: The raiders sometimes approached a village slowly and quite openly, causing everyone to flee into the bush. They then withdrew. Thinking that the danger had passed, the villagers eventually returned. Shortly thereafter, however, the marauders abruptly reappeared, attacking and quickly subduing the population (Decorse, 1906: 174).

It is difficult to measure the effectiveness of these tactics. Certainly marauders on foot were more vulnerable than those on horseback. After the initial attack, their firearms were of little advantage since most of them were not rapid-firing weapons. On occasion, they sustained a fairly high number of casualties, occasionally even being routed (Julien, 1925: 143; 1929: 56; Gaud, 1911: 95-96; Chevalier, 1907: 280-228).[5]

The slave-raiders also employed terror to discourage opposition. How often or randomly such measures were used remains unknown, but in several instances the marauders bound all the males of a village and burned them to death in piles of grass, or severely mutilated and then slaughtered them (Chevalier, 1907: 283-284; Modat, 1912: 233).

Used primarily against villages that chose to resist rather than to sur-
render, such methods promoted the belief that the sultan's forces could
not be beaten. The slave-raiders did not attack each population each
year. For one thing, the violence and forced removal eliminated many
hamlets (Kumm, 1910: 187-188).

When the sultan's detachments arrived in the capital, slave-raiding
gave way to slave-trading. Many captives were already owed to the
Jallaba who supplied al-Sanusi with imports. But before the merchants
received their slaves, al-Sanusi and his major lieutenants divided the
prisoners among themselves. The owners then decided which captives
to sell and which to settle in and around Ndele (Maarabi Hasan;
Abakar Tidjani; Yadri Sale). The proportion sold and the proportion
settled varied from year to year, depending on whether the sultan and
his prominent followers were in greater need of labor or the imports
that the exchange of slaves provided. But despite the disposition of
slaves in any one year, there is no doubt that slave-raiding and slave-
trading were the predominant tasks associated with long-distance trade.
Because these activities produced the firearms, munitions, cloth, and
other supplies required to keep the sultan's operation afloat, they had
an impact on all other forms of labor.

NEW FORMS OF LABOR FOR
LONG-DISTANCE TRADE AND THE
TRANSFORMATION OF OTHER KINDS OF WORK

The rise of a predominantly slave mode of production in Dar al-
Kuti brought many changes. First and perhaps foremost was the appearance of striking inequalities in wealth and status. Slave-raiding
produced captives whose labor and sale enabled a new class to accumulate wealth. The slaves that were sold brought highly valued
imports into the hands of the Muslim ruling class—items such as those
Kumm (1910: 173) observed when he visited al-Sanusi in 1909:

> A number of magnificent Persian rugs covered the mud floor. We were
> installed in iron rocking chairs, and the rich wild smell of sandalwood
> and oriental scents filled the atmosphere.

Several kinds of beads, chechias, shoes and other ready-made apparel,
tea, sugar, soap, and salt also numbered among the major consumer
items imported into Ndele in the time of al-Sanusi (Julien, 1929: 674).

In addition, cloth of many varieties poured into the city (Cordell, 1985: Appendix 4).

The increased accumulation of wealth in the hands of a few fueled the demand for imports. Because of their major role in the purchase and export of slaves, the Jallàba remained the most important foreign merchant community. Yet in the first part of the century they were joined by increasing numbers of the other Muslims from the north. French victories over Bagirmi in 1897 and Rabih in 1900 opened the route from the Central Sudan to North Central Africa; by 1907, large numbers of Hausa and Bornoans were making their way east. Although these traders dabbled in the items mentioned above, they dealt mainly in sub-Saharan products and European goods imported through Nigeria and Cameroon. From Borno, Kanem, and Bagirmi, for example, they imported cattle, horses, sheep, onions, Arab-style leather footware (*markub* [Arabic]), *boubous,* and *burnus*; they also dealt in cloth that they dyed themselves, glassware, jewelry and other trinkets of tin, necklaces, and beads.[6]

As Ndele grew, the number of craftspersons also grew. Among them were many Bornoan and Hausa leatherworkers (Yadjouma Pascal; Yacoub Mahamat Dillang). The early career of Froumbala Boukar, a Bornoan who eventually settled in Ndele, illustrates this transformation. Born in Borno in 1881, and eventually so named because he spent many years at the town of Froumbala (today's Kembe) on the Mbomu River in southern Ubangi-Shari, Froumbala was thirteen when Rabih established his capital at Dikwa. Son of a farmer, he spent some years as a petty trader in his homeland before heading east in 1910 with a small group of Bornoan traders at the age of 29. Most of the party, including Froumbala, traveled on foot. They went first to Kusseri and on to Fort-Lamy (present-day Ndjaména) where Froumbala stayed with fellow Bornoans. From there his party went to Tchekna in Bagirmi and on to Fort-Archambault (present-day Sarh) in southeastern Chad. Still in the company of his countrymen, he headed south along the "route du Tchad," the French lifeline that joined the Ubangi River with central Chad. Stopping in Fort-Crampel (present-day Bandero), the major European post on the itinerary, he heard of commercial possibilities in Ndele. He departed soon afterward, arriving in al-Sanusi's capital in late 1910, a few weeks before the sultan was assassinated.

While Froumbala's trip from Borno to Dar al-Kuti was but the experience of one individual, it nonetheless sheds some light on the organization of long-distance trade. There was apparently no *khabir* as in the case of trans-Saharan caravans; Froumbala recalled that his party did not recognize a formal caravan leader, although "everyone listened to the merchants who were first in rank and age." Such an individual sometimes represented the party to outsiders, although Froumbala insisted that "he had no power, no power." As for size, parties were as large as twenty or thirty or forty merchants, although at other times three or four or five would risk setting out alone.

If Froumbala's experience was at all typical, the trade in crafts and European imports from the Central Sudan was of limited volume. When Froumbala left Borno he had a few pairs of shoes and a few skins that he carried on his head, and thirty Maria Theresa *thalers*. He sold some skins in Fort-Crampel, but waited until he arrived in Ndele to sell the footware; he used the thalers to buy other trade goods to take to Dar al-Kuti. Once in Ndele, Froumbala stayed with Bornoans—as indeed he had done all along the way. During the next month, he exchanged his goods for French francs, then headed north to Ati in Chad where he purchased cattle. He drove the animals south to Fort-Sibut in southern Ubangi-Shari, sold them for francs, and went west to Garoua in the Cameroon where he bought more cattle. Returning to Ubangi-Shari, he ultimately became a major trader in kola at Mobaye on the Mbomu. At one time or another he also dealt in ivory and rubber. Froumbala returned to Ndele in the 1930s where he became one of the most prominent merchants in the city.

Other occupations associated with long-distance trade expanded in the first decade of the century. For example, a regular commerce in cattle and donkeys developed between Ndele and small Muslim states to the north. Chevalier (1907: 155-156) reported that caravans from Wadai or Dar Sila arrived six or seven times each year.

While the preceding examples suggest that travel, transport, and commerce were loosely organized, merchant parties traveling east of Dar al-Kuti apparently conducted their business in a more formal fashion. Pierre Prins and Bonnel de Mezières, French travelers in eastern Ubangi-Shari in the first decade of the century, reported that parties of Muslim traders were led by caravan leaders carrying letters of introduction from Muslim rulers to the north. Prins's observation that caravan leaders usually dealt in more expensive goods suggests, in addition, that such individuals were wealthier than their fellow travelers (Prins, 1907: 138).[7]

Increased contact between Dar al-Kuti and points north, east, and west gave rise to new tasks associated with transport and the maintenance of the commercial infrastructure. Porterage, for example, was associated with long-distance exchange as early as the 1890s. In 1893 Brunache reported meeting fifteen travelers near the Gribingui River, twelve of whom were porters and probably slaves (Brunache, 1894: 199-201). Further north in Sara country, Maistre noted in the early 1890s that the Sara were clearly accustomed to supplying porters for visiting parties of Muslim merchants (Maistre, 1895: 118, 127, cited in Prioul, 1981: 133). And shortly after the turn of the century, the French resident Emile Julien (1929: 65-66) noted that al-Sanusi regularly requisitioned slaves belonging to his major lieutenants in Ndele in order to provide porters for commercial expeditions. This practice continued throughout the sultan's reign in Ndele. When Kumm (1910: 185) left Ndele for the Anglo-Egyptian Sudan in 1909, al-Sanusi provided him with slave porters. The German also reported that the sultan frequently sent caravans of 100 or 200 people loaded with ivory to the Sudan whence they returned with European cloth and other goods.

Long-distance trade required other services. The region was but an extension of the Muslim commercial zone farther north. Not only did villages provide porters for visiting merchants, but they also operated ferries across the major streams (Prioul, 1981: 126; Brunache, 1893: 201). East of Ndele the same was true (Kumm, 1910: 183-184).

The growth of long-distance exchange did not only create new occupations, it also redirected a part of agricultural labor. When French expeditions first appeared in Dar al-Kuti in the 1890s, the Europeans noted with some surprise that local peoples were accustomed to supplying foodstuffs to caravans (Prioul, 1981: 147). This was the case throughout central and eastern Ubangi-Shari as well. In the 1910s the Banda Tombaggo who lived southeast of Dar al-Kuti planted extensive plantations that produced surpluses for sale to Muslim traders. Other Banda groups did likewise.[8]

While some of these productive activities seem to have been spontaneous responses by local peoples to the opportunity to trade, al-Sanusi also set up agricultural settlements along major caravan routes. To the north, for example, his villages supplied passing caravans on the route to Dar Sila (Modat, 1912: 194). To the east slave villages supplied parties traveling between Dar al-Kuti and the Anglo-Egyptian Sudan; this was particularly important in the first decade of the century, for his raiding had provoked the almost complete depopulation of this vast region (Kumm, 1910: 177-178). Such villages also provided shelter. Approaching Ndele from Fort-Archambault to the west, Kumm (1910: 158) counted several dozen restcamps for traveling merchants and pilgrims.

The expansion of slave-raiding and the rise of a slave mode of production permanently altered all labor. For most of the nineteenth century, agricultural work had been the province of the domestic group. Slave-raiding allowed a more specialized disposition of such labor. Among villages transplanted en masse to Ndele as a result of violence, many kinspeople probably continued to work together, but al-Sanusi and the more prominent of his followers also set up large plantations worked by slave labor. Indeed on some occasions the transplanted village populations joined the sultan's captives in his fields. Outside the capital, al-Sanusi also founded agricultural villages where slaves and other clients lived and worked during the growing season (Cordell, 1985: Ch. 5). Hence domestic labor, to the extent that it survived at all, was ancillary to the slave mode of production.

As noted above, there were signs of greater specialization in work associated with long-distance commerce as well. And yet, slave-raiding, slave-trading, and slave labor remained the central set of activities that kept Dar al-Kuti together. Even when the French had conquered adjacent lands like Wadai, and had "liberated" labor, al-Sanusi resolutely held on to the system that had brought him fortune and power. This was not necessarily an act of [im]moral conviction. He had no choice, given Dar al-Kuti's dependence on the Muslim economy of the sahel. By 1902-1903 the labor of long-distance trade had undergone a transformation. Slave porters had appeared. The state managed the distribution of these porters because it controlled access to servile labor and sponsored the raiding and trading in slaves that produced it. But it is the brevity of slave porterage that is most apparent. Long-distance trade in North Central Africa, except for the export of slaves and the import of commodities exchanged for them, was relatively small scale. Trade required little labor beyond that of the merchants themselves. Whereas the sultan's slave porters represented a new development in the organization of trade at the end of the nineteenth century, the French conquest early in the twentieth prevented the emergence of a conscious class of porters. The colonial conquest replaced slavery with new forms of unfree labor.

NOTES

1. Bangui, Bibliothèque de l'Ecole national d'administration, Dossier: "Les Un-gourras"; Document: "Ngouras, 1906—correspondence départ (Livre de poste, district des M'Brès)," entry 218.

2. Ibid.

3. Archives nationales du Tchad (ANT), W53.9, "Documents et études historiques sur le Salamat réunis par Y. Merot: Rabih et Senoussi au Dar Rounga."

4. For a list of al-Sanusi's raids mentioned in the written and oral sources see Cordell (1985: Figure 4).

5. Archives nationales françaises, dépôt d'outre-mer (Aix-en-Provence), 4(3)D19, "Rapport du Colonel Mordrelle", 25 July 1910.

6. Archives nationales françaises, dépôt d'outre-mer (Aix-en-Provence), 4(3)D20, A.E.F., "Rapport d'ensemble sur la situation générale de l'Oubangui-Chari en 1913," Bangui, 18 July 1914; 4(3)D19, Estebe, "Rapport d'ensemble, 1912," Bangui, October, 1913.

7. Ibid., 2(D)21, "Rapport de M.A. Bonnel de Mezières", Paris, 31–December 1900.

8. Cabaille Documents, "Monographie de Yalinga," 14 (see Cordell, 1985: bibliography, for further details on this collection).

REFERENCES

The people of Dar al-Kuti supplied much of the information about the recent history of northern Ubangi-Shari. Microfilm copies of transcripts of interviews conducted in Dar al-Kuti in 1974 have been deposited with the Archives of Traditional Music, Indiana University; and the Memorial Library, University of Wisconsin-Madison. More detailed information will be found in the bibliography of Cordell (1985).

BARTH, H. (1965) Travels and Discoveries in North and Central Africa, 3 vols. London: Frank Cass.

———(1853) "Account of two expeditions in Central Africa by the Furanys." Journal of the Royal Geographical Society of London 23: 120-122.

BROWNE, W.G.B. (1799) Travels in Africa, Egypt, and Syria from the Year 1792 to 1798. London: T. Cadwell.

BRUNACHE, P. (1894) Le centre de l'Afrique—autour du Tchad. Paris: Ancienne Librarie Germer Ballière et Cie.

BURCKHARDT, J. L. (1822) Travels in Nubia. London: John Murray.

BURNHAM, P. (1979) "Permissive ecology and structural conservatism in Gbaya society," pp. 185-202 in P. Burnham and R. F. Allen (eds.) Social and Ecological Systems. New York: Academic Press.

CARBOU, H. (1912) La région du Tchad et du Ouadai, 2 vols. Paris: Leroux.

CHAPISEAU, F. (1900) Au pays de l'esclavage—Moeurs et coutumes de l'Afrique centrale, d'après les notes recueillies par Béhagle. Paris: Maisonneuve.

CHEVALIER, A. (1907) Mission Chari-Lac Tchad, 1902-1904: L'Afrique centrale fran-çaise, récit du voyage de la mission. Paris: Challamel.

COHEN, A. (1971) "Cultural strategies in the organization of trading diasporas," pp. 266-281 in C. Meillassoux (ed.) The Development of Indigenous Trade and Markets in West Africa. London: IAI and Oxford University Press.

CORDELL, D. D. (1985) Dar al-Kuti and the Last Years of the Trans-Saharan Slave Trade. Madison: University of Wisconsin Press.

———(1983) "The savannas of North-Central Africa," vol. I, pp. 30-74 in D. Birmingham and P. M. Martin (eds.) History of Central Africa. London: Longman.

———(1979) "Blood partnership in theory and practice: the expansion of Muslim power in Dar al-Kuti." Journal of African History 20, 3: 379-394.

———(1977) "Eastern Libya, Wadai, and the Sanusiya: a Tariqa and a trade route." Journal of African History 18,1: 21-36.

———(1973) "Throwing knives in equatorial Africa: a distribution Study." BaShiru 5, 1: 94-104.

DAIGRE, P. (1950) Oubangui-Chari, souvenirs et témoinages, 1890-1940. Paris: Maison provinciale des Pères du Saint-Esprit.

DAMPIERRE, E. de (1983) Des ennemies, des Arabes, des histoires. . . . Paris: Société d'ethnographie (Recherches oubanguiennes, no. 8).

DECORSE, G. J. (1906) Du Congo au Lac Tchad: La brousse telle qu'elle est, et les gens tels qu'ils sont (Mission Chari-Lac Tchad, 1902-1904). Paris: Asselin et Houzeau.

De VALLÉE (1925) "Le Baghirmi." Bulletin de la société des recherches congolaises 7 (2e, 3e, 4e trimestres): 3-76.

DYBOWSKI, J. (1893) La route du Tchad du Loango au Chari. Paris: Librairie de Paris, Firmin-Didot et Cie.

GAUD, F. (1911) Les Mandja (Congo-Français). Brussels: deWit.

GRECH (1924) "Essai sur le Dar Kouti au temps de Snoussi." Bulletin de la société des recherches congolaises 4: 19-54.

HAYER, J. E. (1972) "The copper of Hofrat en-Nahas." Presented at the seminar in African history, University of Wisconsin-Madison.

JEWSIEWICKI, B. (1981) "Lineage mode of production: social inequalities in equatorial Central Africa," pp. 92-113 in D. Crummey and C. C. Stewart (eds.) Modes of Production in Africa: The Precolonial Era. Beverly Hills: Sage.

JULIEN, E. (1925, 1927, 1928, 1929) "Mohammed-es-Senoussi et ses états." Bulletin de la société des recherches congolaises 7: 104-177; 8: 55-122; 9: 49-96; 10: 45-88.

KALCK, P. (1970) "Histoire de la République centrafricaine des origines à nos jours, 4 vols." Thèse de doctorat d'état, Université de Paris (Sorbonne).

KOGONGAR, G. J. (1971) "Introduction à la vie et à l'histoire des populations Sara du Tchad." Thèse de doctorat du 3e cycle, Université de Paris (Sorbonne).

KUMM, K. (1910) From Hausaland to Egypt, through the Sudan. London: Constable.

LANIER, H. (1925) "L'ancien royaume du Baguirmi." L'Afrique française: renseignements coloniaux 35, 10: 457-474.

LOVEJOY, P. E. (1983) Transformations in Slavery: A History of Slavery in Africa. London and New York: Cambridge University Press.

MAISTRE, C. L. (1895) A travers l'Afrique centrale du Congo au Niger, 1892-1893. Paris: Hachette.

MODAT, M. (1912) "Une tournée en pays Fertyt." L'Afrique française: renseignements coloniaux, 22, 5: 177-198; 22, 6: 218-237; 22, 7: 270-289.

MOHAMMADAOU, E. (1975) "Kalfu ou l'émirat peul de Baguirmi et les toorobbe Sokkoto." Afrika Zamani: revue d'histoire africaine/Review of African History 4: 67-114.

NACHTIGAL, G. (1971) Sahara and Sudan IV: Wadai and Darfur (G. B. Allan and H. J. Fisher, trans.). London: Christopher Hurst.

————(1967) Sahara und Sudan: Ergebnisse Sechjähriger Reisen in Africa, 3 vol. Graz: Akademische Druk-u. Verlagsanstalt.

PALLME, I. (1844) Travels in Kordofan. London: J. Madden.

PRINS, P. (1907) "L'Islam et les musulmans dans les sultanats du Haut-Oubangui." L'Afrique française: renseignements coloniaux 17, 6: 136-142; 17, 7: 163-173.

PRIOUL, C. (1981) Entre Oubangui et Chari vers 1890. Paris: Société d'ethnographie (Recherches oubanguiennes, no. 6).

TISSERANT, C. (1953) "L'Agriculture dans les savanes de l'Oubangui." Bulletin de l'Institut des études centraficaines (Brazzaville) 6, nouvelle série: 209-274.

AL-TUNISI, Muhammad b. Umar (Mohammed Ibn-Omar El-Tousy) (1851) Voyage au Ouaday (S. Perron, trans.). Paris: Duprat.

————(1845) Voyage au Darfour (S. Perron, trans.). Paris: Duprat.

9

WAGE LABOR IN KENYA
IN THE NINETEENTH CENTURY

ROBERT J. CUMMINGS

Charles New, in his travels of the late 1860s in East Africa, made the following observation in his diary (1971: 74):

> The day was drawing to a close, and we still had some distance to travel. There was no train, omnibus, cab, cart, truck or wheelbarrow, yet we had a good many things to carry. I was to learn how things were done in East Africa. A gun was fired, and in a few moments some of the villagers came down to us. These and our boatmen were *engaged* as porters. Soon each man, with a load upon his head, was upon the road.

How did this body of individuals come to be so readily available as porters for Charles New? By what process had the firing of a gun brought the "system" of caravan porterage to such an immediate response? These are among the questions that govern this chapter on wage labor in Akamba trade.

New's porters worked for wages. By the 1850s Akamba porters had come to provide essential services to the trade between the coast and the interior. By this time Swahili merchants, drawing upon the capital

Author's Note: I would like to thank E. J. McCready for her editorial comments on this chapter.

resources of India, dominated the commercial corridors. Thus, "it is fair to claim that without porters in the East African context, Asian merchants and Asian capital which basically financed the coastal economy would have been almost useless in the development of long distance trade relations during the period when such relationships evolved" (Cummings, 1975: 271). As such, an examination of hired transporters is a necessary corollary of studies dealing with, for instance, items of trade, entrepreneurs and theories of markets.

Prior to 1850 and the expansion of trade, the Akamba were chiefly engaged in agriculture and pastoralism, each of which was identified with specific regions. Generally, farmers were more involved in the labor of trade than were pastoralists. Farmers tended also to be hunters, supplying ivory and other goods for trade. Caravan leaders, guards, transport personnel, and cooks were also drawn from agricultural communities.

Pastoralism was limited to a particular environment and ecological situation and was characterized by a "more specific set of sociological requirements and a closer unity of institutional forms than most economic life modes" (Goldschmidt, 1965: 403). The time required to make the trade safari to and from distant territories discouraged the participation of pastoral lineages in either human porterage or the collecting agency of the trade since pastoralists were needed to tend livestock all year. Moreover, pastoralists thought that their labor, in a purely economic sense, should have a specific return that would sustain or increase their herds. Any labor other than for this purpose was perceived as irrational behavior (cf. Gupta, 1973: 66). The pastoral sector, as a result, was less suitable for the development of Akamba regional trade than was the agricultural sector. Notwithstanding, many pastoralists did play a major role in the development of this trade at the level of investment. Wealthy pastoralists were able to participate in trade in absentia by virtue of their store of wealth. According to Kavisu Lua of Thitani village:

Those people from large pastoral lineages with wealth who were not able to go to the coast because of their herds would send some people to take their goods to the coast and after they returned home, they were paid either goats or some pieces of cloths for their services. This was around the famine of Nyungui (c.1821-22).[1]

In the 1840s, another channel of economic redistribution was through the enlistment of certain leading men or their sons, or other kinsmen, into long-distance coastal-bound caravans. In order to join these caravans, an enlistment fee was required. These fees were used to obtain supplies and support labor. The remaining cost related to the caravans was secured via patronage. A necessary precondition for commercial expansion, patronage transcended both the agricultural and the pastoral sectors.

A system of hired porters developed in the context of the disparities of Akamba society. First, some Akamba lineages were able to accumulate cattle, other livestock and surplus food supplies. These lineages were able to extend their patronage to less fortunate lineages thus providing the necessary capital for trade. Second, periodic famine and other disasters created a reservoir of poor people who had to supplement their agricultural output as best they could. Some of these people became porters and thereby, temporarily at least, accepted the patronage of their more fortunate neighbors. With reference to the Mutulungo famine (c.1855), one informant explained: "While there was no forcing of people in those days to go to the coast by the council of elders, one was sent by the poverty at his home."[2] Still, not all porters were poor.

Free and enslaved Africans were thus induced to join caravans for various reasons. While the majority may have been forced to join because of periodic famine and drought, others enlisted for the adventure, knowledge, and prestige that accompanied the experience of travel. Moreover, porterage provided a valuable training in interculturalism. In fact, travel had great social prestige among many interior societies.

Successful regional trade required an effectively organized and dependable transport system. A system of *hired* transport—*kiloela*—created and supported by Akamba wealth and institutions, and headquartered in the Kitui-Mumoni area, developed in response to this demand.

Caravan leaders employed local connections and wage incentives to attract and maintain the production and labor personnel required by the expanding regional trade (Cummings, 1975: 147). The leadership skills and social contacts acquired by the caravan leaders in their roles as hunters and gatherers were redirected toward developing and sharpening the organizational skills needed to provide caravan support, to assure or guarantee a cadre of producers (hunters-collectors) and to obtain carrier labor in desired quantities.

In the 1820s, porters were selected in an orderly manner, with large numbers of recruits—generally only men—presenting themselves for hire. The leader of the caravan called upon the local priests to assist in raising interest. His subordinates sponsored feasts where it was made known that a leader intended to travel to a particular trading area within a specified period of time. Those interested in associating with him for the journey then informed him of their decision. Kaesa Muli of the Wamunya area of Machakos recalled the following story about his grandfather from Kutui:

> My grandfather was one of the leaders who used to select people to make up a caravan. He would first ask the people who came from the various *motui* (village-communities) at his request to attend his feast if they wanted to sell their bulls and make some profits; and if they did, then they would volunteer themselves to join him.[3]

The caravan leader then selected the required number of porters from among those interested. The sick, those known generally as lazy, and youths below the *anake* age-grade (14 years old) were usually prohibited from joining the caravan. This method of carrier recruitment remained basically the same through 1920, excluding the war period when participation was more or less forced.

The chosen men were later brought together as a group by the blowing of the *soo,* a horn traditionally used to call together Akamba warriors to raid cattle or to make war, but which was used after 1810 to muster caravans. The firing of the gun noted by Charles New was an adaptation of this tradition.

The group came together (a) to take their oath of unity, (b) to receive the blessings of their senior elders, and (c) to hear the predictions of, and receive the magical protective medicines from, the priest. Kitua Kithome claimed that:

> The seer would throw his nuts or stones onto the ground and the leaders were (officially blessed). Then the porters were given an oath to eat so that they would be united on the journey. They said: "if ever we meet danger on the way, should I fear let this oath be upon me" (and death was the sentence if the oath fell upon one who had so spoken).[4]

These oaths and medicines were a further adaptation of tradition; they arose out of cooperative ventures such as hunting but were now used for caravans that were dominated by those with trade capital.

The oath of unity was designed to promote caravan security. The German missionary, Reverend J. L. Krapf, benefitted from such vigilance in 1849, when he was joined by a group of about 100 Akamba who were returning home to Ukambani from the coast. In his entry for 26 July, recorded in the *Church Missionary Intelligencer* (1860: 303-306), Krapf wrote: "Today, the leaders of the Wakamba caravans made their people swear, that in case of an attack by the Gallas or Masai, they would not run away but would defend themselves." As a result, when the two groups (the Akamba and Krapf's party) were attacked by a group of robbers, the Akamba went into their defense "to the man":

> The Wakamba who were further behind threw down their loads at the sight of the enemy, allowing them to come and put them (the loads) on their shoulders, whereupon the Wakamba fired and shot three of the robbers dead; and we had one Mkamba wounded. When the enemy saw that the Wakamba made a stand and heard our firing they retreated to their hiding place, upon which time my scattered Wanika collected again, took courage, and joined the Wakamba, who had been exposed to the greatest danger. It was fortunate for me that the first attack had been on the Wakamba, for they defended their property, while my people cared neither for me nor for my baggage, but were anxious about their own lives alone.

Akamba caravan leaders thus benefitted from this adjustment of tradition; oaths bound porters and merchants together in a manner that safe-guarded the interests of the merchants.

The *kiloela* (porter-laborer) was responsible for driving livestock and carrying ivory and other goods to the coast where a form of "silent trade" took place. A 60 to 65 pound box or bag of cowrie shells or beads, a bolster of cloth, a circle of wire, a tusk of ivory, or perhaps some copper wire comprised a typical load. The porter was also responsible for scouting wild animals along the route and for keeping the livestock fed and calm during the journey. It is said that he was the only member of the trading party to see the faces of the coastal traders. The kiloela would remain behind with the livestock during the time that the coastal traders, such as the renowned Swahili ivory trader Mukuna Uku (cf. Jackson, 1972: 265), evaluated the commercial goods.

The kiloela had been able to join the business of trade as a wage-earner when the range of trade goods within Ukamba expanded to include salt, iron ore, pottery, gourds, wire, zinc, soda ash, foodstuffs, arrow-poison, and iron implements. He often received a small share of the trade goods as a wage; for instance, three sheets or panels of cloth. The "wage" could then be exchanged for personal needs, foodstuffs, livestock, or, in some cases, slaves.

One informant, Mumbua Kivonda of Kalama Location, was told by her grandfather how, near the "famine of Mutulungo (1855), slaves still were being captured in Ukamba. Such people were forced to carry trade goods somewhere to the coast."[5]

Wages represented a key motivational factor for joining a caravan. The wages were transformed into "power" for certain carriers, and social prestige developed from this new economic power base. The economic potential available to the young, enterprising porter, in fact, serves to illustrate how the distributive function enhanced social mobility in various interior societies. The influence of certain porters over their fellows and their experience and knowledge of the trade routes provided an opportunity to rise in the ranks, perhaps even to the position of caravan leader. An enterprising porter, able to exploit his wages and skills to establish his personal commercial relationships, could conceivably become wealthy enough to finance his own caravan.

Many slaves welcomed the opportunity to join a trade caravan for the same reason: the promise of social mobility. While many slaves took the opportunity to run off from the caravan once it was feasible, others used their wages to purchase their freedom.

Nevertheless, the potential for social mobility inherent in caravan participation was seldom translated into reality. Although the social and economic status of a person was not fixed and the structure was such that an Mkamba was encouraged to seek his fortune according to his ability, only a few men were able to realize the potential for amassing wealth offered by this system. Most kiloela were simply unable to overcome the various elements that controlled their socioeconomic status, such as the infrequency of caravans easily accessible to them, their total dependence upon the goodwill of their employers, and the recognized weakness of their social position—that is, abject poverty—to attract wages equal to other porters (Cummings, 1975: 165).

In theory, the distinction between porter and trader was clear. Porters were workers who, in purely economic terms, did not necessarily take the initiatives and risks involved in bringing together the resources of land, labor, and capital for the circulation of goods and services. These were the functions of the trader. Thus, the porter was "a carrier of property or things"; the trader "a carrier of profits." In practice the difference was not so obvious.

> When travelling to the coast members of the trade caravan not only carried their ivory and food with them, but they were taking some goats, cows and hens as well. They sold their goods to the *Asui* (coastal peoples) and were given cloths and other items in return. When they came back home and they sold some of their cloths, etc. to people who were unable to go to the coast, then, the porters became traders.[6]

Moreover, unless the porter received payments in usable goods, he sold his earnings on the market. Thus, temporarily at least, porters became merchants.

The Akamba distinguished between trade to the coast and trade elsewhere within Ukambani. Trade to the coast was referred to as *kukanisya* (to exchange with another), which implied impersonal economic intercourse: trade within Ukamba was called *kitandithya* (to acquire gain, wealth, or profits) and included a degree of social interaction as well as exhange. Trade with the coast involved a transformation in the commerce of the region; it resulted in a specialization that had been minimal in the internal trade. This transformation was clearly associated with the linkages with capitalism. At this time exchange within the regional trade network was favored as it offered items that were valuable in the eventual acquisition of wives and the purchase of local products. In short, trade offered an alternate method of acquiring status in Akamba society.

The once homogenous trading communities began to disintegrate in the 1860s. Dislocation occurred at both the local village level and the individual level. The leadership that was once dependent upon hunters and warriors no longer required their support. The local scene was changing as the rise of individualism offered a challenge to community independence. The individual Mkamba was now able to obtain capital or trade goods from exclusively non-*motui* sources. As Jackson (1972: 294-295) explained the change,

> Subsistence conditions were no longer as binding on the individual, no longer so constraining, and no longer so thwarting of individual aspirations. Under certain profitable conditions of patronage, an individual might have accumulated valuable goods that could have provided him a leverage on the local institutions and citizens of the village. In this respect, these citizens could—and did—act as counterposing centers of powers, standing in opposition to the corporate institutions of the villages. . . .

The rise of individualism in Ukamba was directly related to the coincident subordination of Akamba trade to the international market. The organizational hierarchy of export trade consisted of financiers who remained at the coast and Afro-Arab trading personnel resident in Ukambani. A new system of trade, dominated from the coast thus came to supplant the old order. The village communities, the large hunting parties, and even the great bands of porters that had characterized the early period, were superfluous to an export trade capable of sustaining itself with coastal or non-Akamba labor from elsewhere in the interior.

The takeover of interior long-distance trade by the Afro-Arabs established an alternate economy in Ukambani, as a cash-wage economy came to compete with the subsistence-oriented economy for labor. The latter economic structure, however, was able to meet the challenge at the local level since trade continued to play only a minor role in society. As a result, only a small cadre of Akamba were engaged to assist the Swahili encroachment. The Afro-Arab intrusion, then, did not significantly upset Akamba society, but it did offer stable employment to a minority of Akamba men during the two decades after 1860.

The essential role that had been played by the Akamba merchants in organizing and financing the caravans that brought together supplies of economic goods with the people who demanded them was steadily eroded. Coastal agents, employing a limited number of Akamba as intermediaries, penetrated the interior and attempted to usurp both the power and the prestige of their precursors, the Akamba merchants. The role of the Akamba trading community was thereby reduced from one of primacy—albeit on a regional scale—to one of subordination to the international system of trade.

The functions of the Akamba trading community changed considerably. For example, Akamba intermediaries were now dispatched to local village–communities to hire caravan laborers to transport local commodities to more centralized market centers within Ukamba. In addition, the Akamba *kyalo* (caravan) were employed to transport ivory from Mukaa to Kikumbulia and Kibwezi where Afro-Arab traders resided. Prior to Swahili residence in Ukambani, the Akamba agents had been responsible for transporting ivory and other goods as far as Duruma territory. There they had met the coastal caravans which took the tusks of ivory and the rhino horns into Mombasa (Cummings, 1975: 224).

Changes in the nature of Akamba commercial involvement were accompanied by a physical shift. The Akamba who participated in the new coastal-dominated trade formed a corps of petty merchants and middlemen now residing primarily in the Machakos-Ulu area. Kitui, by the 1860s, had lost its commercial predominance to Machakos due in part to the environmental conditions of Machakos and in part to the shifting migration patterns of elephants. Therefore, it was the trading Machakos Akamba, bolstered by their superior ecological situation, who now availed themselves to arriving Afro-Arab traders.

Transformations such as these forced the many Akamba who had come to depend upon trade for their livelihood to jockey for position in the new Swahili-controlled international trade. The famine of Mutulongo (1855) appears to have marked a break between the old order and the new. Thereafter individuals rose to prominence by attaching themselves, in various capacities, to Afro-Arab traders. The cooperative spirit that had characterized trade was thus undermined as the individualizing tendencies of the new system held sway.

The Akamba of Machakos, less experienced in caravan trade management[7] than their Kitui brethren, were apparently more willing to accept lower level positions under the direct control of the Swahili. Once they had gained the acceptance of their coastal employers, the Machakos Akamba tried to emulate the pre-1850 Akamba traders. They were not successful, however, in their efforts to recapture the spirit of that earlier period. Indeed, they achieved neither the level of cooperation and the security of a local economy nor the resourcefulness and expertise which had characterized their predecessors. The new Akamba wage-earners, having rejected the societal rules and ethics of their forerunners, were thus set apart from the earlier ivory porters "both in local legend and in actual history" by their "arbitrariness, their tendencies toward conserving of goods, and the harshness of their methods towards locals [other Akamba]. . . . They were a *comprader* group" (Jackson, 1972: 267).

The Akamba compraders' preoccupation with turning a profit was manifested in their general lack of concern for the health, not to mention the lives, of their porters. Many porters died as a result of thirst, malnutrition, and attacks by highwaymen. Inadequate planning and, according to Kiveta Mutwetumo, the "selfishness of their Akamba employers" were to blame.[8]

The transmutation of attitudes and behavior, the predominance of individualism and the status of the new *mundu mue* ("big men") were legitimized by the introduction of a new ideology, *umanthi*.[9] Umanthi emphasized personal initiative and encouraged material acquisition. The philosophy of umanthi played a key role in preparing the Akamba for their participation in the trade of the second half of the nineteenth century. Umanthi offered wage-earning caravan porters a practical orientation that helped them adapt to changes eminating from the coast. This is not to deny the impact of either natural phenomena such as famine, localized overpopulation, soil erosion and misuse, or intrafamilial conflict and wars with surrounding people. On the contrary, it seeks to identify the sociological motive that allowed the various sectors of Akamba society to cope effectively with their new situation. In short, beginning in the 1860s, umanthi helped individual members of the local trading communities to adapt to their role as wage-earning porters for the nascent coastal-financed trade system (Cummings, 1975: 221).

Continuity accompanied change since involvement in the Swahili-controlled trade was viewed by many as a means of social advancement and as a means of rising from porter to trader. In order to effect this transition, many Machakos Akamba misrepresented themselves to the coastal merchants who entered Ukambani from Mombasa (Lindblom, 1920: 249-250); these misrepresentations served to advance the growth of false Akamba "chiefs." At the local level these Akamba agents attempted to project an image of personal wealth by hiring workers in their own name, despite the fact that they had no real capital resources of their own and were being financed by others.

While they may, on occasion, have deceived their Swahili employers concerning their position in society, the Akamba agents were unable to enhance their local prestige to any great extent. They were often resented by the local population since they were perceived as men prepared to serve the economic interests of the Swahili traders at the expense of local interests. Increased exploitation of the Akamba under their employ was often the result of the agents' attendant frustration. They often inflicted harsh treatment, which served only to reduce further the social status of the agents in the eyes of the local populace.

As a result of their low status, many of these new Akamba trading–agents came to identify with their overlords and to internalize some of their values. Not only were these former porters more familiar than nontravellers with some of the ways of their Swahili backers, an example of the interculturation function of porterage, there was also a growing awareness on their part of how the Afro-Arab traders influenced the local scene and of their possible role in these changes. These Akamba intermediaries were well aware of the fact that since the Swahili had only limited access to local Akamba society, they played a vital role in maintaining the constant flows of ivory and other commodities required to meet the demands of the international export system.

The Akamba agents, however brief their tenure, were thus crucial to the development of wage-orientation in Ukambani. Workers were often recruited from the lower rungs of the social ladder: social outcasts, refugees, adventurous youths, and the rootless poor. The commitment of such men to the wage economy was indeed limited. Southall described a parallel situation: "the labor force of most plantations [in early colonial Kenya] is very unstable, with a high percentage of bachelors, so that . . . plantation existence may constitute only an interlude, though perhaps an oft-repeated one, in lives still firmly embedded in the fuller kinship system of rural tribal communities" (1961: 64). In spite of the differing contexts, in both cases the option of wage labor was seized as the best, if not the only, possible means of extricating oneself from an esphyxiating dependence on subsistence farming. In short, limited opportunity dictated an increased reliance on the sale of labor (cf. Fielder, 1968-1969).

The porter-laborers who enlisted with the comprader group were, in a sense, the first migrant workers of interior East Africa. Not only was their commitment to the wage economy limited, their interests were essentially local. They strove to maintain ties with kith and kin while working to raise their own socioeconomic position in society by participating in the small-scale transport system that characterized contemporary Akamba involvement in trade. Plying upon these needs, the comprader group of the 1860s and 1870s was able to develop a small, wage-oriented labor force in Akamba.

Many of the participants in the new Swahili-financed transport system were familiar with wage employment. When wages *(matuvi)* are defined as whatever "salarie"—local and coastal goods or cash— were acceptable to the caravan porters, many were in fact second generation "wage-earners." The major motivational factor in joining a caravan was, from the beginning, the wage. Wages offered the potential for amassing wealth. The promise of enhanced social mobility, represented by the wage, though realized by few, had long been the prime inducement in the transition from subsistence farming to porterage. In the new system of international trade, however, continuity was paired with innovation.

The coastal-dominated system of trade deviated from its Akamba-directed predecessor on several scores. For example, earlier porters joined Akamba caravans and journeyed to the coast, but these porters worked for Akamba merchants, not agents of the coastal Swahili. The nature of employment in the second generation was thus different. With non-Akamba hiring porters the gap between employer and employee was widened. As a result of this increased separation, wage labor assumed a new dimension, a new direction which was symbolized by the introduction of a cash wage.

During the time of the famines of Kiasa and Ngetele (c.1868-1872) there were "new leaders, unrecognized by our council of elders, who used the rupee *(ilovia)*, which they received from the *Asomba* (coastal peoples), to induce local people to make the safari from some *motui* to others along the major routes usually to where these Asomba were living."[10] The status of porters was therefore further reduced to one of wage–employment with the introduction of cash wages.

The porters resisted this reduction in status and thus the method of payment. Numerous Akamba trading stories speak of laborers either returning the rupees to their employer or throwing them away. Other stories tell of an increase in body ornaments with the rupees prominently displayed on both porters and their wives.[11] Finally, some tales speak of individuals who buried the new "money" upon returning home, vowing never again to work for the Akamba agents who had cheated their own people by paying them with the worthless coins provided by the Afro-Arab agents.

The introduction of cash wages brought into sharper focus the previously blurred distinction between trader and porter. Payment in kind had provided the porter with an opportunity to become, temporarily at least, a trader. Payment in cash reduced the status of the porter to that of a worker, compelling him to *buy* trade goods. This transition was most likely perceived by the porters as a reduction in remuneration. The refusal of porters to spend their wages, their insistence on discarding, returning, or even displaying the rupees as ornaments indicated a lack of worker discipline; they refused to act as workers who must spend their wages.

In the short run porters' protests were successful. As a result of such discontent, Swahili traders and their Akamba agents were forced to pay their hired labor with a more traditional medium of exchange. Coastal goods, such as cloth, beads, and cowries, exchangeable at the local level, proved a more acceptable means of payment and were thus "reintroduced" as wages. The wide-spread institution of cash wages would have to await European penetration into the area.

Human porterage continued in East Africa as the primary means of distributing trade goods into the precolonial and early colonial period. The experience of Charles New illustrates the efficiency and the high degree of organization which characterized the system during this period. The dimensions of the institution as it operated in the nineteenth century were indeed impressive.

The French traveler Guillain (1856: Vol. 3, 211) reported that the many Akamba carriers enlisted in caravans during the 1840s transported as much as four hundred *frasilas* of ivory weekly from the interior to the coast. By mid-nineteenth century, "between 2300 and 2600 *frasilas* (about 45 tons) of ivory per year" (Lamphear, 1970: 87) were being transported to Mombasa by various trading peoples of the interior, with the Akamba and Nyika in the forefront.

According to Muindi Tungu of Miaani village, Machakos, *Kikombe* (George C. Leith) was the first European to come to Ukambani. Leith visited Mbuani and Kuathi before settling at the Machakos station of the Imperial British East Africa Company. Leith was later followed by *Enzueni* (John Ainsworth) and *Mwanzi wa Maki* (C.R.W. Lane). These men, along with the missionaries then entering Ukambani, needed people to convey their goods. Most often they asked the elders of an area to provide them with porter-labor. Muindi recalled:

> During this time, the leading elders were required to produce their own sons first for such travel and then the council would assist in choosing the remainder. . . . I was chosen to be a porter by Mbuvi, together with

his son, Kivunzyu, and some others, to carry the goods of a certain Mzungu from Iiuni to Mbooni. We were not paid anything [cash wages emphasized by this time, c.1896] but we each received a piece of cloth for our service. I was able, however, to use the cloth in exchange for something else.[12]

Under Ainsworth, some Akamba were hired as carriers of mail between Machakos, Mombasa and Fort Smith. Others took jobs as laborers on the cart road then under construction south from Kibwezi to Tsavo.[13] As such, during this period the tradition of human porterage continued to flourish, even expand, alongside the new employment opportunities introduced by the Europeans. The Akamba continued to sell their labor as porters, interpreters, and guides, for there was a growing demand for the muscles, knowledge, and language skills of these people.

Caravan porters, as agents for distributing trade goods, represent a fundamental element in the study of East African economic history. Yet the system of human porterage provided much more than simply a means of transporting trade goods. The institution of human porterage facilitated both economic redistribution and interculturation. The tradition of porterage offered both free man and slave an opportunity for amassing wealth and for achieving social mobility. It provided its participants with a chance to test their manliness and their skills. It also furnished an opportunity to meet new people, and to both influence and be influenced by new ways. In fact, caravan porters appear to have influenced considerably the interior and coastal societies of East Africa throughout the nineteenth century. Through their function within the trade system, they affected the nature of economic interaction and induced profitable results within the wider system of trade. They also impinged upon social institutions along the caravan routes, as well as those of their own societies.

The most significant economic change in East Africa in the latter half of the nineteenth century was perhaps the often difficult transition from a subsistence economy, bolstered by periodic participation in a wage economy which offered payment in kind, to a cash-wage economy linked to the international system of capitalism. The comprader role, in fact, became the basis of a legacy which connected Akamba wage–earning labor in the nineteenth and twentieth centuries. Still, it was the caravan porters themselves—among the first "wage-earners" of East Africa—who most effectively served to link the subsistence and wage-oriented economies and also to bring the village markets together with the expanding and encroaching world economy through their distributive functions in the system of trade. Porterage was thus an *adaptive* process in East Africa, as porters learned to live in both the subsistence economy of their own societies and the wage economy of long-distance trade.

NOTES

1. Kavisu Lua, Akamba Historical Notes (AKAHN), interview no. 97, 3/15/73, Miwani Location, Kitui. (AKAHN—the complete set of oral data collected by this researcher in the form of tape recordings, field notes and textual translations.)

2. Kinyanzwii Kasiva, AKAHN, No. 17, 1/11/73, Masii Location, Machakos. See also Moango Muithya, AKAHN, no. 66, 2/22/73, Makueni Location, Machakos, who claimed birth during this period (1855 ± 10).

3. Kaesa Muli, AKAHN, no. 81, 3/7/73, Misinga Location, Machakos.

4. Kitua Kithome, AKAHN, no. 27, 2/24/73, Kilungu Location, Machakos.

5. Mumbua Kivonda, AKAHN, no. 3, 12/8/72, Kalama Location, Machakos.

6. Muindi Tungu, AKAHN, no. 8, 12/27/72, Kalama Location, Machakos.

7. These Machakos Akamba agents admittedly had limited experiences in this area, having played only a secondary role primarily to their kinsmen of Kitui. This is especially so in the case of magic, for the people of Kitui are considered even until today to have been more powerful "magicians" than their Machakos counterparts (see Cummings, 1976: 98-101).

8. Kiveta Mutwetumo, AKAHN, no. 1, 12/8/72, Kalama Location, Machakos.

9. *Umanthi* is the Akamba worldview or philosophical ideology that evolved before 1860. It stressed the concept of individual initiative (kwiyu-muya mundu mwene) for the progress of the larger local community.

10. Mutwetumo, AKAHN, no. 1; cf. Kimambo, 1970:85.

11. The Akamba were not impressed at all with the new money given for their labor and many were said to have buried it, thrown it away, or used it to enlarge their jewelry collections.

12. Tungu, AKAHN, no. 8.

13. Tungu, AKAHN, no. 8.

REFERENCES

CUMMINGS, R. J. (1976) "The early development of Akamba local trade history, c. 1780-1820." Kenya Historical Review 4, 1: 85-110.

———(1975) "Aspects of human porterage with special reference to the Akamba of Kenya: towards an economic history, 1820-1920." Ph.D. dissertation, UCLA.

FIELDER, R. J. (1968-1969) "Economic spheres in pre- and post-colonial Ila Society." Presented at the East African University Social Science Conference, Kampala.

GOLDSCHMIDT, W. (1965) "Theory and strategy in the study of cultural adaptability." American Anthropologist 64 (April).

GUILLIAN, C. (1856) Documents sur l'histoire, la geographie et le commerce de l'Afrique Orientale, 3 vols. Paris.

GUPTA, D. (1973). "A brief economic history of the Akamba, with particular reference to labour supplies." Journal of Research and Development 3, 1: 62-71.

JACKSON, K. A. (1972) "An ethnohistorical study of the oral tradition of the Akamba of Kenya." Ph.D. dissertation, UCLA.

KIMAMBO, I. N. (1970) "The economic history of the Kamba, 1850-1950," in B. A. Ogot (ed.) Hadith II. Nairobi: East African Publishing House.

KRAPF, J. L. (1860) Travels, Researches and Missionary Labours in East Africa. London: Frank Cass.

LINDBLOM, G. (1920) The Akamba in British East Africa. Uppsala: Archives D'Etudes Orientales.

NEW, C. (1971) Life, Wanderings, and Labours in Eastern Africa. London: Frank Cass. (Originally published in 1873)

SOUTHALL, A. W. (1961) Social Change in Modern Africa. London: Oxford University Press.

10

FROM PORTERS TO LABOR EXTRACTORS
The Chikunda and Kololo in
the Lake Malawi and Tchiri River Area

ALLEN ISAACMAN
ELIAS MANDALA

In the nineteenth century, the Chikunda and Kololo experienced exploitative and oppressive labor conditions. As porters, soldiers, and commercial agents, they suffered from the domination and indignities inherent in the appropriation of their labor. Yet, as the century progressed, they became employers, extracting the surplus labor of others. Their transformation from socially oppressed workers to labor extractors was not unique in the history of precolonial Africa. In a small, although not insignificant, number of cases other ex-laborers were able to accumulate wealth, power, and a privileged class position by controlling the labor of others. Because the Chikunda and Kololo both maintained their respective ethnic identities, this transition from worker to employer can easily be overlooked—suggesting that African labor history must somehow take account of the com-

Authors' Note: The authors would like to thank Dr. Kings Phiri for access to oral interviews and Barbara Isaacman for criticisms of an earlier draft of this chapter. The Graduate School of the University of Minnesota, the Office of International Programs at the University of Minnesota, and the University of Malawi Research and Publications Committee provided financial support for the project.

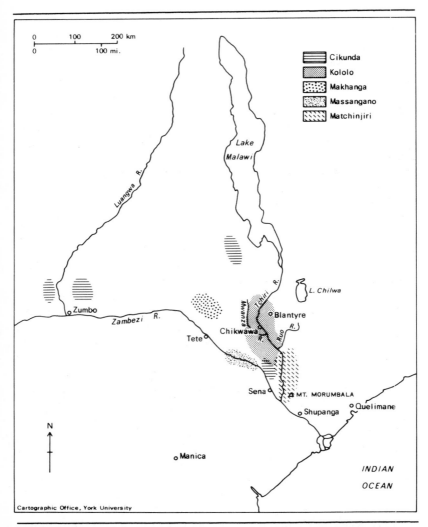

Map 10.1:   Lake Malawi and Tchiri River Area, Late Nineteenth Century

plex, varied, and often ambiguous relationship between ethnicity and class in the precolonial period.

Throughout the eighteenth century, the Chikunda were slaves of Portuguese and Asian estateholders *(prazeiros)* in Mozambique, particularly the Zambezi Valley, and one of their functions was to serve as "point-men" for the penetration of merchant capitalism into the societies of the interior. They traded for the prazeiros, and on caravan journeys they were porters, hunters, and occasionally raiders. Chikunda ethnicity developed in the context of this servile relationship between prazeiro and slave. In the nineteenth century, however, the efforts of the prazeiros to extract more from the Chikunda resulted in a number of rebellions and escapes that established some of the Chikunda as independent operators among the Chewa of the Zambezi Valley and among the Mang'anja of the Tchiri Valley. Under these circumstances, the Chikunda were able to transform their position from that of workers to that of employers.

The Kololo were initially corvee laborers in the service of the Sotho aristocracy that conquered the Lozi in the 1840s. They were pressed into the service of David Livingstone as porters and eventually found themselves at Tete, in the Zambezi Valley. By the 1860s these Kololo were no longer bound to the Lozi state but had become independent workers in the penetration of European interests up the Tchiri Valley to Lake Malawi. The Kololo used their access to firearms to conquer many of the small Mang'anja chieftaincies of the Valley, and they forced the subject population to work for them.

The paths of the Chikunda and Kololo crossed in the 1850s when a number of Kololo labored side by side with remnants of the ex-slave community in gold and coal mines around Tete and a decade later when they competed as merchants. By then the Chikunda had been in the Tchiri Valley and adjacent Chewa homelands as independent ivory hunters, merchants, and mercenaries for several decades.

The following study explores the history of each of these two groups in order to examine the kinds of transformations that were possible in South Central Africa in the late eighteenth and the nineteenth centuries. In both cases, emancipation consisted of a transition from servile laborer—slave or corvee—to free laborer. The Chikunda and Kololo went further, however, using their temporary status as free laborers to accumulate capital and ultimately control the labor of others.

What distinguished the Kololo from their Chikunda counterparts was their access to state power. Indeed, a comparison of the two cases demonstrates the critical role the state played in organizing labor in nineteenth-century Central Africa. The Chikunda were never able to impose their political hegemony over the Chewa and Mang'anja north of the Zambezi River in whose land they settled. Denied access to state power, they were unable to extract labor on a sufficient scale to mount large hunting and trading expeditions. In sharp contrast, the liberated Kololo conquered the Mang'anja and, in effect, reduced the subject population to a pool of servile laborers.

THE CHIKUNDA:
ORIGINS AND TRANSFORMATION

The Chikunda were originally slaves on the *prazos,* or Portuguese crown estates, located along the margins of the Zambezi River from the Indian Ocean to Tete (Isaacman, 1972; Newitt, 1973). The estate-holders (prazeiros) acquired their Chikunda retinues through commerce, conquest, raiding, and the forced enslavement of the peasants who lived on their lands (Miranda, A.N.T.T., Maço 604, ca. 1760; interviews: M. Domingos, L. Nhanticole, A. Pangacha, G. Tito). According to one eighteenth-century prazeiro "the largest part [of the Chikunda slaves] came to be captives during the times of famines, pestilence and locust, and because of their urgent needs they had no alternative but to offer themselves as slaves" (Miranda, A.N.T.T., Maço 604, ca. 1760). Strangers, orphans, social outcasts and those seeking legal sanctuary after committing serious crimes often exchanged their freedom for short-term security—a security rooted in a system of coerced labor extraction. A nineteenth-century traveler described the elaborate ritual known as breaking the *mitete* (reeds) by which many entered the slave regiments of the prazeiros:

> I will now explain what it is meant to break a Mitete. In the whole of Eastern Africa it is customary to give protection to any negro, freeman, or slave, who is fleeing from a persecutor, or from someone to whom he does not want to act as a slave for, from some powerful man, or again if he is in danger of dying of hunger. To get this protection all he needs to do is to break some utensil, or tear a cloth, however small, belonging to the person, from whom he desires help. This is done without a word being spoken. The new owner asks him why he is seeking refuge with him, whether he is a slave or free, and why he broke the Mitete. Then the old owner or persecutor can only get him back by paying a ransom which is usually double his value as a slave [Gamitto, 1960: Vol. 1, 145].

As part of the mitete ritual slaves received a guarantee that they would not be sold abroad. They often got wives, land that their spouses farmed, and the right to extract produce from peasants living on the estates. To an unattached individual, these benefits held an obvious attraction (Gamitto, 1859: 369-372; da Silva, A.H.U., Códice 1452, May 14, 1825; interviews: Dauce Gogodo, Chiponda Cavumbula, Gento Renço, and Alface Pangacha).

Although the exact number of slaves varied substantially from year to year, and the figures presented in Portuguese documents were probably inflated, contemporary accounts do suggest that the Chikunda constituted a substantial labor force. A leading prazeiro who did a survey in 1759 estimated the figure at more than 33,000 (Miranda, A.N.T.T., Maço 604, ca. 1760). Forty years later the Portuguese governor of the Zambezi calculated their numbers at about 22,000 (Truão, 1889: 8). While the size of the Chikunda population on any given estate ranged from under a hundred to several thousand, the Chikunda shared a common mode of organization throughout the Zambezi. On every prazo they were divided into a number of localized regiments *(butaka)* with fixed residence, each one of which was further subdivided into slave squads *(nsaka)* made up of ten to twelve male slaves and their families. Each regiment had a clearly defined chain of command. At the apex stood the slave chief *(mukazambo)* under whom were a varying number of subchiefs or squad leaders *(tsachikunda)*. Selected because of their professed loyalty and demonstrated service to the prazeiro, these slave leaders wielded absolute power among their subordinates and enjoyed a great deal of autonomy from the estateholders.

These slaves performed a number of critical political and economic roles. They defended the estates against external threats and served as the police and military arm of the estateholders, collecting tribute and annual taxes from the peasants, quashing rural protests, and generally helping to maintain the prazeiro's privileged, though precarious, class position. Other slaves worked on the estates as masons, blacksmiths, and domestic laborers (Isaacman, 1972; Newitt, 1973).

In their role as porters, traders and hunters, they provided an indispensable service for merchant capital that ultimately connected with Goa in India (Alpers, 1975). Each year, the prazeiros dispatched trading and hunting expeditions into the interior under the direction of specialized slave chiefs *(musambadzi)* selected from the ranks of the slave leaders. Chikunda caravans, sometimes with 200 or more slaves, carried imported and locally manufactured cloth, beads and alcohol as far north as the Lunda kingdom of Kazembe in Katanga and as far south as the Shona states of Manyika and the Muenemutapa of Zimbabwe (Alpers, 1975; Beach, 1979; Bhila, 1982; Isaacman, 1972; Newitt, 1973; Gamitto, 1859: 370). They purchased ivory, gold, copper, and slaves. The ivory and gold were exported to India or Portugal; the copper and slaves were largely traded in the interior, although by the end of the eighteenth century slaves became an increasingly important export overseas.

The slave caravans traveled to specific areas of the interior selected by the musambadzi—either fairs such as those at Manica and Luangwa or inland villages known to have supplies of ivory, gold, copper, or slaves. Once the trading party left the prazo, the musambadzi enjoyed complete responsibility for the caravan's success. He resolved all questions that affected the safety of the expedition, negotiated with chiefs to allow the caravan to pass through their territory, selected camp sites, and personally negotiated barter agreements. Indeed, the success of the venture depended on the commercial acumen of the musambadzi. As Gamitto (1960: vol. II, 27) observed in 1831,

> Bargaining over ivory usually lasts two or three days; it requires unbelievable patience to acquire an elephant's tusk, and it sometimes happens that when the sale is almost concluded the buyer or seller calls off the bargaining. And thus only natives are able to buy from natives because a European, however long he has been in the country, and however used he is to the habits and customs of these people, only rarely has the patience needed to reap any advantage.

In recognition of their critical role, the prazeiros customarily rewarded the successful caravan leaders with substantial gifts.

But if the success of the venture depended upon the commercial acumen of the masambadzi, it also depended on the brawn of the porters and the skill of the canoemen. Because the Zambezi Valley was a tsetse-infested zone, pack animals could not be used to transport goods into the interior (Barbosa, Ajuda 52-x-2 no. 3, "Analyse estatística," December 30, 1821). As a result, slaves had to carry such heavy commodities as ivory, hippo teeth, and copper great distances. The absence of roads made their task more difficult, as did the rapids and the swollen rivers which the caravans had to cross in the rainy season. Official Portuguese accounts noted the skill and daring of the canoemen who remained unintimidated by the large rocks jutting out of the Zambezi River north of Tete (Barbosa, Ajuda 52-x-2 no. 3, "Analise estatística," December 30, 1821; Botelho, 1835: 283).

In addition to natural barriers, slaves guarded the caravans against raids in the hostile chieftaincies that they traversed. Competitors, including other prazeiro-financed caravans and Yao and Bisa merchants who began to trade in the region during the second half of the eighteenth century, were another menace. One prazeiro lamented "that it was rare indeed when one of his musambadzi was not robbed or assassinated in the interior and the caravan returned safely" (Aboime, A.N.T.T., Maço 604, August 27, 1779). On several occasions trade to the Manyika fair was paralyzed for a year or more as a result of the sharp increase in the number of attacks on the Chikunda caravans (Isaacman, 1972: 84-85).

In addition to transporting bulky commodities and protecting the caravans, slave squads were periodically dispatched to hunt elephants when the caravans entered regions renowned for their large herds, such as the Luangwa Valley or the Dabanyi marshes. Armed with guns and axes as well as powerful hunting medicines, the Chikunda were reputed to be the most skilled elephant hunters of South-Central Africa. Elephant meat and other game were consumed by the caravan and traded with the local population for grain. If the caravan received permission from the local chief to hunt in his territory, the chief took the tusk closest to the ground, or an equivalent in cloth and other trade goods, and the hind quarter of the dead animal. If no prior agreement was reached, the caravan took both tusks back to the prazo (Mendonça, A.H.U., Cx. 3, December 3, 1751).

For the porters, the expeditions were long and arduous. Caravans were gone for upwards of a year and often traveled more than a thousand miles through rugged and hostile terrain with only short intervals for rest at hastily constructed bush villages, or *misasa* (Gamitto, 1859: 370). Sorghum and millet, normally the basis of their diet, were sometimes in short supply, so that the slaves had to rely on forest products that they hunted and gathered. Berries, honey, tubers, roots, game, and fish often supplemented their diet. Whenever possible, they exchanged forest products for sorghum or maize at interior markets or with the agriculturalists whose land they crossed. During periods of seasonal famine or more pronounced food shortages such opportunities disappeared altogether. During the first quarter of the nineteenth century, prolonged droughts and a deluge of locusts wrought havoc on the caravans, many of whose members died of hunger or deserted to avoid starvation (Castro, A.H.U., Cx. 38, April 27, 1799; Ferrão, A.H.U., Códice 1315, fol. 18, December 20, 1828). A Portuguese explorer recalled how he encountered remnants of a 300-man caravan, "many of whom had died from thirst and hunger and the remainder were so debilitated that they could not continue their journey" (Lacerda e Almeida, B.N.L., Pombalina no. 721, fol. 299, March 21, 1798).

The extent to which the estateowners *qua* merchant capitalists and their financial backers, located as far away as India and Brazil, relied on the labor of their Chikunda intermediaries is reflected in the handsome returns of the trading and hunting ventures. In the middle of the eighteenth century, for example, profits from the ivory trade were estimated at 500 percent (A.H.U., Cx. 3, Mendonça, December 3, 1751). Caravans were also a valuable investment because estateholders sometimes rented the services of experienced masambadzi and Chikunda porters and hunters if they lacked the need or the capital to mount their own expeditions (Anonymous, B.N.L., Fundo Geral, no. 826, May 21, 1762). Profits from the slave trade, with which Chikunda caravans became increasingly involved after the turn of the century, were even higher. Captives purchased in the interior were sold on the coast at between 650 and 1100 percent more than the purchase price (Isaacman, 1972: 89). By 1821, ivory and slaves brought almost entirely by the Chikunda caravans constituted more than 90 percent of the total value of exports from the Zambezi Valley (Barbosa, Ajuda 52-x-2 no. 3, "Analyse estatística," December 30, 1821).

Relations between Chikunda and the estateholders were ambiguous and often contradictory. As slaves, on the one hand, the Chikunda were subject to the arbitrary and capricious rule of their owners on whom they also depended for wives, cloth, guns, and at least some food. Commenting on the notorious excesses of the prazeiros, who were consumed by the notion that their slaves were "lazy" and "untrustworthy," one eighteenth-century traveller noted "few are those who act within the judicious limitations of propriety" (Lacerda e Almeida, 1936: 105). On the other hand, because they were well-armed, relatively autonomous, and strategically placed, the slaves posed a serious threat to any prazeiro who abused his authority or abdicated his power. Their common work experience, slave status, and permanent membership in a particular regiment combined to create a sense of collective identity that contributed to class-consciousness. Their shared experience seems to have blunted any tendencies toward interethnic conflict among the slaves, who came from more than a dozen different ethnic groups (Isaacman, 1972a: 448-449). As one leading estateholder complained in 1752, a "prazeiro cannot give a single negro of the slave regiment away without the others all mutinying" (Jesus, A.H.U., Cx. 3, April 13, 1752). By this date the Chikunda constituted a class-in-the-making prepared to act on its own behalf.

Indeed, the annals of Zambezian history are replete with examples of slave protests. Estateowners regularly complained of desertion, work stoppages, smuggling, thievery, and sabotage that they attributed to the "impudence" of the slaves (Perreira, A.H.U., Maço 38, August 27, 1753; Cirne, A.H.U., Códice 1468, June 29, 1831; Lacerda e Almeida, 1873: 65). During the eighteenth century desertion was the most common expression of slave dissatisfaction. The Chikunda's lack of any deep-rooted links to the land and their hunting and commercial forays into the interior facilitated flight. By 1753, the prazeiros faced such a grave situation that they mounted a full fledged military campaign against Mang'anja chiefs living in the Mount Morumbala region who were suspected of harboring runaway slaves (Perreira, A.H.U., Maço 38, August 27, 1753). Three years later prazeiros attacked a number of Chewa chieftaincies north of Tete in an effort to recapture other fugitives (Perreira, A.H.U., Cx. 5, December 1, 1756). Despite these punitive actions, the flight of dissident Chikunda continued to pose a serious problem for the rest of the century. In desperation, in 1803, the Portuguese government sent a formal delegation to Lundu, the senior Mang'anja chief, to secure an agreement not to provide sanctuary for the fugitives (Newitt, 1973: 202). The mission failed, however.

In the first decade of the nineteenth century, slave resistance became even more pronounced. In 1806, it was estimated that approximately half of the 20,000 slaves on the prazos had escaped (Truão, 1889: 8). This estimate may be exaggerated, especially in light of the continued unrest among the Chikunda over the next several decades, but certainly it is safe to say that resistance was on a larger scale than ever before and that flight continued to be a principal method of expressing discontent. Not all the runaways fled to the northern chieftaincies. Some sold their services to competing prazeiros who offered them a number of material inducements to settle on their estates (Diniz, A.H.U., Cx. 21, March 1790), while recent captives tried to make their way back to their natal societies.

More serious still, large groups of Chikunda rebelled en masse and then established free communities in the hinterland. These fortified settlements *(misitu)* were governed by the ex-slave chiefs (mukazambo). They presented a serious challenge to the prazeiros both because they offered sanctuary to other slaves and because they had the military capacity to threaten outlying estates. The misitu, like the maroon communities in the Americas, represented the most decisive protest the slaves could make against their subservient position. Because the Chikunda stayed together in large groups, these misitu are the clearest expression of the collective consciousness of the Chikunda. The effort to forge a new life free from the slave master is an excellent indication of the seriousness of class antagonisms (Newitt, 1974: 201-222). Chikunda discontent continued at a high level throughout the first half of the nineteenth century with the result that many estateholders were driven off their land (Isaacman, 1972: 116-117).

The pernicious desire of the prazeiros to profit from the Brazilian and Cuban demand for slaves explains this discontent. The prazeiros tried to sell members of their regiments, with predictable consequences. "The inability of the prazeiros to comprehend the ramifications of the slave trade," noted one official, "was the principal cause of the insurrections" (da Silva, A.H.U., Códice 1452, May 14, 1825). The rebellions came at a time of recurring droughts and famines related in part to the prazeiros' decision to export peasants from their estates. By the middle of the century, the number of functioning prazos had declined from 82 to 13. As Livingstone noted "the slave trade to Brazil was the primary and almost sole cause of the evil" that shattered the last vestiges of the prazo system (Livingstone, 1857: 340).

This disintegration left thousands of ex-slaves unattached. Many remained in the region to work as free laborers in the gold and coal mines north of Tete, where they subsequently encountered the Kololo, and others became porters, guides and elephant hunters for the diminished Portuguese and Afro-Asian merchant community (Livingstone, 1857: 635-640; Selous, 1893: 47). Other Chikunda became independent boatmen, traversing the Zambezi from Tete as far inland as Zumbo (Zambian National Archives, Feira Notebook; Deny, 1939). Still others became members of predatory bands which plundered peasants living on the decayed prazo estates (Cirne, A.H.U., Códice 1468, October 27, 1829). Ultimately, many of these predators were reenslaved by *mestizo* warlords who organized the conquest states of Massangano, Makhanga, and Matchinjiri that came to dominate the lower Zambezi in the second half of the nineteenth century (Isaacman, 1972; Newitt, 1973).

Many Chikunda escaped from this insecurity and turmoil by migrating outside the region. Like their ancestors, these fugitives found sanctuary among the decentralized Mang'anja and Chewa polities north of the Zambezi River. They came to form a Chikunda diaspora throughout this region. This diaspora took one of two forms: (1) un-attached individuals, sometimes with their families, settled among the Mang'anja and Chewa; (2) autonomous bands of between five and ten men, probably remnants of Chikunda butaka, established, with the approval of local land chiefs, temporary bush camps adjacent to the villages of the indigenous population. Over time, the immigrants either forged a more lasting bond with the local chiefs and were integrated into the larger population or migrated along the hunting and trading routes which extended northwest from Tete to the Luangwa Valley and Lake Malawi. The Chikunda who settled among the Chewa had a special name to distinguish them from those who wandered into and settled in the region between Zumbo and the Luangwa Valley far in the interior. According to one Chewa elder,

> The Chikunda came here from their original homelands which were along the Zambezi. What brought them here was the search for elephants, and they killed the elephants with guns which used iron stones for bullets. The most famous Chikunda in Chinsamba's area was Chilenga. We knew of him because he was given a wife by a local chief named Msekwe, he settled in Msekwe's village where his wife lived. Those Chikunda who did this were called *machona* (Joint interview: Mbalame Mwale, Belu Mailosi Phiri and Levi Phiri).

Freed from the grip of the prazeiros, the ex-slaves could operate as inland agents of merchant capitalism. Their hunting skills, knowledge of the inland regions, and the new ties to the local royalty enabled them to exploit the large elephant herds at a time when international prices for ivory were on the rise. Slaves, too, continued to be in great demand, and the Chikunda helped satisfy this market as well (Isaac-man and Rosenthal, 1984).

Whatever the form which the dispersal took, the Chikunda, unlike the Kololo, rarely attempted to conquer the indigenous population. As hunters, traders and porters they generally coexisted with the Chewa and Mang'anja and provided important economic and political services to the local aristocracy. Chewa traditions contrast the arrival of the ex-slaves with that of other immigrant groups who passed through their homelands. "They were not warlike, as were the Yao and Ngoni. They came here to kill elephants and then got tempted to stay forever" (Joint interview: Zephaniya Mwale and Chatsalira Banda). Other Chewa elders recalled how "the Achawa [Yao] and Aluya [Swahili] came here in large gangs to make war, while the Chikunda came in small groups. They just came here to kill elephants. The Aluya and Achawa were the ones who bought slaves" (Interview: Bishop Chapuka Mbewa). From the outset, the Chikunda came as stragglers or in small bands and depended on the hospitality of the land chiefs who allowed them to settle in their territory. For the Mang'anja and Chewa authorities the presence of the Chikunda offered a number of attractions that overcame their initial suspicions and fears and formed the basis for a more permanent alliance with these strangers.

The refugees performed an important service as elephant hunters. Armed with guns, axes, poisonous spears, traps, and special medicines, the Chikunda were far more effective than either the Mang'anja or Chewa (Joint interviews: Zephaniya Mwale and Chatsalira Banda; Ngwezu Chikho Phiri, Daniel Chinkhupiti Nthara and Kamachenjeza Mvula). Mang'anja hunting techniques were particularly crude (Mandala, 1983: 26-28). They relied exclusively on two types of traps—the *mbuna* holes dug in the ground with a grass covering or the *tchera* trap made of a sharp spear suspended from a pole with a trigger. Neither method yielded much ivory during the rainy season. Both Mang'anja and Chewa traditions recount the expertise of the Chikunda, who were not only excellent marksmen but daringly swung from the trees hacking away at the herds that passed below (Interview: Lukiya Chiwanga Phiri). After killing the elephants, the Chikunda presented the tusk closest to the ground and the hindquarter of the dead animal to the local chief as recognition of his position as owner of the land. They made a similar offering when they killed bush buck, buffalo, and other game. They smoked the remainder of the meat and occasionally invited other members of the local population to their camps for feasts.

> There was never a shortage of mouths when it came to eating meat. They [the Chikunda] lived on this meat while hunting in the bush. Then there were the people around who were always willing to be served. But the ivory belonged to the Chikunda alone and the chief with whom they lived [Lukiya Chiwanga Phiri].

In addition to their talents as hunters, the Chikunda were expert artisans. Mang'anja traditions recount their skills as metal workers (Joint interview: Aneala Baulo and Austin Nazing'omba). The immigrants forged hoes and guns which, in a region plagued by food shortages and warfare, were in great demand. Chewa chiefs also employed the Chikunda ivory workers to make bracelets that became new symbols of kingship and class privilege (Joint interview: Nalisemphere Phiri and Nathando Phiri).

Their formidable military skills were particularly useful to their host communities, which, as the century progressed, faced numerous attacks. By 1850, the region north of the Zambezi had become a zone of intense competition among Yao, Swahili, Ngoni, and Afro-Goan slavers. Without the presence of these ex-slaves the small Chewa and Mang'anja communities would have been relatively defenseless against the predators, and in some documented cases the Chikunda actually held off invaders. A group of ex-slaves residing in the Chewa village of Mamba defeated the Ngoni raiders of Msakamewa (Joint interview: Ngwezu Chikho Phiri, Daniel Chinkhupiti Nthara and Kamachenjeza Mvula), while other Chikunda played an instrumental role in driving off the Maseko Ngoni. According to one of the attackers,

we went to raid other Chewa in the west. We fought against peoples of Dzoole, Chinzu and Chinganyama. But we failed to break through the stockades of Chinganyama and Chinzu because of the Chikunda presence there. We always feared their guns [Interview: Lenose Chikuse Mwale].

Chewa elders also recalled how the Chikunda deterred the Ngoni from attacking Kanyenda's village, and those same Chikunda later drove off a combined Yao and Swahili raid. Although individual Chikunda musketeers were unable to prevent Yao slavers from terrorizing most of the Mang'anja country, they did help protect the Tengani chieftaincy against the initial Yao onslaught, played a decisive role in assisting Chibisa's community to resist the Afro-Goan warlords of Makhanga, and blunted the Gaza Ngoni advances (Cardenas, A.H.U., Códice 2-44-F D, fol. 84; Mandala, 1977: 192-196; Northrup, 1978: 19-24).

To induce the refugees to reside permanently in their villages, Chewa and Mang'anja chiefs offered the Chikunda land, hunting rights, and, most important, wives. "The chiefs wanted the Chikunda to stay," recalled an elder, "so they gave them daughters from the royal house"

(Joint interview: Zephaniya Mwale and Chatsalira Banda). This practice, which apparently was quite common (Joint interview: Yohane Banda, Tayesa Chinguwo and Lameck Banda), created a permanent bond between the royal family and the strangers and assured the Chikunda of a new network of kinship relations and domestic labor to work their fields and to bear children.

The opportunity for the ex-porters to acquire property and to satisfy entrepreneurial ambitions first developed during earlier involvement in the ivory and slave trade was also a powerful incentive to settle among the Chewa and Mang'anja. Free from the grip of the prazeiros, the ex-slaves could operate as autonomous inland agents of merchant capitalism. Their hunting skills, knowledge of the region and ties to the royal family, together with the presence of large elephant herds, made the potential profits enormous, as did the skyrocketing international prices for ivory and slaves and the demand for both commodities in the Zimbabwe interior (Isaacman and Rosenthal, 1984).

Ironically, transporting ivory posed the most immediate problem for the Chikunda. Their relatively small numbers made it impossible for them to carry the tusks to the coast or even to the adjacent inland markets. Their lack of political power prevented them from recruiting tributary or corvee labor, in contrast to the Kololo, to transport their wares. The indigenous population, fearful of traveling through unknown and dangerous regions, refused to serve as porters. "The land was dangerous in the past," recalled several Chewa elders. "Even the Chikunda who lived with us looked terrifying to us. We dared not move from home for fear of being killed. The land was full of kidnappers and other *vigebenga* [man hunters]" (Joint interveiw: Josiya Chitseka Phiri, Kazyolika Banda, Amon Chadza Banda and Eliyasi Banda). Others refused because they feared that they would be sold as slaves after fulfilling their duties as porters. "The Chewa did not accompany them because the Chikunda were armed and the Chewa feared that they might be sold as slaves if they followed them. The Chikunda found their own means of carrying the ivory" (Joint interview: Nathan Pelekamoyo Mbewe, Amazia Mawere and Keyala Maloni Mbewe).

As a result, the Chikunda, like their former prazeiro owners, came to rely upon slave labor. They purchased porters in the interior from Nsenga and Chewa villages (Interview: Mkota Mkhoma Zakaliya) and captured others during skirmishes with the Yao, Swahili and Ngoni. They obtained additional slaves from Chewa and Mang'anja chiefs as payment for their economic and military services or in exchange for guns and red cloth (Joint interview: Nathan Pelekamoyo Mbewe, Amazia Mawere, and Keyala Maloni Mbewe; Zephaniya Mwale and Chatsalira Banda; Mbalame Mwale, Belu Mailosi Phiri, and Levi Phiri).

Despite the diversity of sources that could be tapped to acquire slaves, increasing depopulation within the region and intensified competition for slaves prevented the Chikunda from securing servile laborers on a scale sufficient to organize large caravans. Chikunda slave-based trading parties rarely exceeded twenty and more often ranged from five to ten (Joint interview: Nathan Pelekamoyo Mbewe, Amazia Mawere, and Keyala Maloni Mbewe). In sharp contrast,

> The Yao and the Arabs came here in large numbers and everyone knew them. They travelled in large gangs. Occasionally the Chikunda and the Yao met in Mkanda's village and both groups did business at the same time.

Apart from the difficulty of acquiring porters, the Chikunda had to vie for ivory with the larger, and better capitalized Yao and Swahili caravans, which in the nineteenth century moved south from Lake Malawi and from coastal entrepots along the Indian Ocean (Joint interview: Zephaniya Mwale and Chatsalira Banda; Alpers, 1975). Indeed, by 1850, the region north of the Zambezi had become a zone of intense commercial rivalry among the Chikunda, the Yao, the Swahili, the Kololo, the adjacent *mestizo* warlords, and Bisa merchants and hunters coming from contemporary Zambia (Joint interviews: Nathan Pelekamoyo Mbewe, Amazia Mawere and Keyala Maloni Mbewe; Josiya Chiseka Phiri, Kazyolika Banda, Amon Chadza Banda and Eliyasi Kapantha Banda).

Given this intense competition, it is hardly surprising that the ex-slaves were not able to regain the dominant position in the ivory and slave trade they had held when they labored for the prazeiros. Nevertheless, their skills as hunters and merchants and their ability to acquire and control a minimum number of slave laborers made them an important source of ivory. In a few cases, most notably that of Chilenga, their hunting and commercial activities assumed quite substantial proportions.

> In this area, we had only one Chikunda family and it settled near the lake. That was the family of Chilenga. This Chilenga came from across the Dzalanyama mountains to the west, from Makhanga. He brought

muzzle-loading guns which we called *gogodela*. With these guns Chilenga hunted elephants in Malimba. Elephants were so plentiful in those days, but they gradually got exterminated by Chilenga and his followers until they fled to northern Nkhota-Kota. Chilenga himself became so powerful as a result of the wealth derived from the ivory that several Chewa chieftains—Msekwe and Myambo—took refuge in his *chemba* [stockade]. But the Yao from the Machinga tribe raided the surrounding villages for slaves but never raided the people of Msekwe and Myambo, as they were afraid of Chilenga [Interview: Lenose Chikuse Mwale].

Their liberation from the estateholders' ties to Indian merchant capital also enabled them to sell their ivory and slaves where they commanded the highest prices. Rather than continuing to send their caravans to the Zambezi towns of Tete or Sena, they dispatched trading parties to the coastal town of Quelimane where they often received 25 percent more for their ivory, thereby circumventing Portuguese and Indian middlemen (da Silva, A.H.U., Codíce 1462, fol. 42, July 15, 1860). In an even more adventuresome departure from past practice, Chikunda caravans went north to the Nkhota-Kota in the Lake Malawi area to exchange tusks with the Swahili of Jumbe who, although commercial rivals, were nevertheless anxious to acquire the ivory and wax the Chikunda brought (Joint interview: Zephaniya Mwale and Chatsalira Banda).

Although the Chikunda siphoned off some ivory northward into the Swahili commercial sphere, contemporary Portuguese accounts continued to acknowledge both their central role as elephant hunters and the dominance of ivory in the colonial economy of Mozambique (Almeida, A.H.U., Moçambique Pasta 21, August 19, 1863). Whereas in 1821 4538 arrobas of ivory were exported from Quelimane, the exports increased to 5259 arrobas in 1856, 6600 arrobas in 1863, and more than 7000 arrobas during the four-month period from December 1874 to March 1875.[1] Although the export statistics are fragmentary and the upward trend may not have been as pronounced as the figures suggest, official sources in 1863 are unequivocal that "ivory is the most important export commodity in the colony" (Almeida, A.H.U., Moçambique Pasta 21, August 19, 1863). This assessment was echoed twenty years later in an economic report written by the governor of Tete (Braga, B.O.M., 1886, /40, p. 492, July 1886). Nevertheless, by the 1880s the depletion of the elephant herds and intensified efforts by the newly installed British and Portuguese colonial regimes to restrict trade across the Zambezi-Tchiri frontier signaled the demise of the Chikunda as entrepreneurs (Selous, 1893: 47; Interview: Mkora Mkhoma Zakaliya).

THE KOLOLO

Unlike the Chikunda, the overwhelming majority of porters who came to be known as Kololo were never formally enslaved. Rather they were tributary laborers bound to the Sotho-Kololo aristocracy, which, under Sebitwane, had conquered Bulozi around 1840 (Mainga, 1973). Within a decade Sotho-Kololo hegemony was on the decline. Sekeletu, who in 1851 succeeded Sebitwane as monarch, faced a serious threat both internally from the subject population and from raiding Ndebele parties. To meet these challenges he turned to Swahili and European traders for guns, which he used to consolidate his position, thereby increasing domestic oppression.

One of Sekeletu's prospective allies was the influential Scottish missionary David Livingstone, who arrived at Linyanti, Sekeletu's capital, in 1855 on the final leg of his journey from Angola to Mozambique. Exhausted and with only meager resources, he convinced Sekeletu to provide porters and canoemen to carry his baggage and navigate the treacherous Zambezi River down to Tete. Of the 114 men given to Livingstone all but a handful were conscripted from the diverse ethnic groups—Barotse, Batoka, Basaleya, Basubia, and Mbundu—which had been forcibly incorporated into the Sotho-Kololo state (Wallis, 1956: I, 168; II, 388; Foskett, 1965: I, 220-221; II, 398). Toward the end of 1855 Livingstone and his entourage left Linyanti on their five-month journey to Tete.

The 114 men were organized into four ethnically based squads, each of which was under the direct supervision of a "headman" whom Sekeletu had appointed (Livingstone, 1858: 570-573). Throughout the journey, the headmen enforced the rules and prohibitions that Sekeletu had decreed before the caravans departed. They also transmitted Livingstone's orders and distributed food to their respective units. Contact among porters belonging to different units was minimal.

The journey was a real test of endurance. When the initial provisions which Sekeletu had offered ran out, Livingstone extracted tribute from vassals of the Sotho-Kololo ruler to feed the porters. Once outside Sekeletu's sphere of influence the porters adopted several strategies to obtain food. Some took to dancing and entertaining villagers along the route:

> The men got pretty well supplied individually, for they went into the villages and commenced dancing. The young women were especially pleased with the new steps they had to show, though I suspect many of them were invented for the occasion, and would say, "Dance for me, and I will grind corn for you" [Livingstone, 1858: 633].

They supplemented this food with forest products, but their lack of gunpowder and experience in hunting large game meant that they suffered periodic food shortages. Clothing was also scarce, although the more fortunate were able to sell their beads and other ornaments in order to obtain cotton cloth (Livingstone, 1858: 608). The majority reached Tete with almost nothing on their bodies:

> They were in a bad shape, poor fellows; for the rains we had encountered had made their skin-clothing drop off peacemeal, and they were looked upon with disgust by the well-fed and well-clothed Zambezians [Livingstone, 1858: 635].

There is no evidence, however, to suggest that the deprivations and the lack of compensation adversely affected Kololo relations with and attitudes toward Livingstone. No one deserted the party and many continued to respect the impoverished missionary after the trip. Apparently, they continued to see him as Sekeletu's emissary, and they provided their labor as part of their tributary obligations to Sekeletu.

Shortly after Livingstone's party arrived at Tete, Livingstone left for England. The porters remained behind as nominal guests of the governor of Tete who initially provided them with clothing, food, and lodging and offered them land to cultivate. Farming did not, however, prove attractive and most Kololo turned to wage labor. Some found employment as gold miners, coal diggers, and firewood hawkers for which they received a daily wage of two yards of unbleached American or British cloth (Livingstone, 1858: 680). It appears that some Chikunda also were engaged in similar wage occupations at Tete, so that it was at this time that the paths of the Chikunda and Kololo first crossed.

Those Kololo of Barotse and Basubia descent and perhaps others too who had substantial experience as boatmen before joining Livingstone's entourage became canoemen. Obtaining canoemen was always a problem for traders traveling from Tete to Quelimane. In addition to having a large number of resident merchants, Tete also served as the main port of call for ivory and slave dealers from the Zumbo area. Such traders would bring their ivory by Chikunda canoes to the Kebrabasa rapids from where they hired the Banyai to carry the goods down to Tete (Livingstone, 1865: 141-142). The Banyai would not, however, risk the journey to Quelimane. They were afraid of being sold as slaves at the coast (Foskett, 1965: I, 75-78). Those Africans who, like the Kololo, were willing to undertake the risky journey managed to extract substantial concessions from stranded merchants (Foskett, 1965: I, 111). The first Kololo contingent to be deployed as canoemen consisted of sixteen men who escorted Livingstone from Tete to Sena in May 1856. They returned as wage laborers transporting government goods in a canoe (Livingstone, 1858: 570-573, 696-698, 708). Because of the great demand, canoemen commanded relatively high wages, which they received before starting the journey from Tete toward the coast (Foskett, 1965: I, 75-78; Livingstone, 1858: 570-573; 696-698; 708).

Many Kololo found a new market for their labor after Livingstone returned to Tete in September 1858 as an agent of the British government in charge of an expedition to open Central Africa to British capital. Livingstone had sufficient funds to employ many of his former servants as wage laborers. There were about eighty Kololo at the time, because thirty had died in a smallpox epidemic and six had been murdered by Bonga, the ruler of Massangano. The six were the professional dancers who made a living by entertaining the residents of Tete and its neighborhood. Bonga suspected the entertainers to be witches sent by his rival Chisaka, the ruler of Makhanga (Livingstone, 1865: 43, 157, 248-249; Wallis, 1965: I, 42; II, 287). Of the survivors, some Kololo came to serve their old master as watchmen, guarding the expedition's warehouse at Tete. Others still became porters and crew members on the steam boats, the *MaRobert* (1858-1859) and its successor the *Pioneer* (1861-1864).

On the *MaRobert* the Kololo worked as unskilled laborers under the direction of European officers and African sailors, known as Krumen, brought from Sierra Leone. They performed menial labor as well as a number of arduous tasks of which the most significant was wood cutting. Because the furnace of the *MaRobert* consumed a great deal of timber, the steamer had to stop every other day in order to permit the Kololo to go into the bush and gather firewood. Often this task took the entire day and by the time the Kololo had returned they had little time to fish for their food (Livingstone, 1865: 90-96,

149-150, 352; Foskett, 1965: II, 391). Throughout their tenure of employment they always resented and remained contemptuous of the "puffing asthmatic," maintaining that a sailing boat "was vastly superior to a steamer because no wood had to be cut—and you had merely to sit still, and let the wind drive you" (Livingstone, 1865: 419). Besides cutting wood, the Kololo carried heavy loads from the Mamvera rapids to Lakes Chilwa and Malawi, and they kept the steamer in operation. Because the boat drew excessive amounts of water it regularly went aground on sandbars, and the Kololo had to free it. The ship also leaked so badly that the workers had to pump the engine room eight times a day. The laborers must have felt great relief when the ship sank to the bottom of the Zambezi on December 19, 1859 (Martelli, 1970: 162). Its replacement, the *Pioneer,* did not leak. But because of its larger size it required more firewood and grounded more frequently.

The porters who joined Livingstone on the expeditions to Lake Malawi, Lake Chilwa and the Tchiri river in 1858-1861 worked under very different conditions than they had on their previous expeditions. Sekeletu's headmen had lost their control over the porters during Livingstone's absence (Livingstone, 1865: 157). When the porters agreed to work once more for Livingstone it was not as corvee or tributary laborers but as independent workers attracted by the prospects of earning a wage. And because Livingstone rarely shared responsibility with his white officers, the workers fell under his direct command.

The Kololo had now made the full transition from corvee laborers to wage-earners, and this transition was reflected in a growing consciousness as workers. The Kololo found themselves in frequent disputes with the Krumen, who considered themselves superior because they were assigned better jobs than the menial labor that the Kololo had to perform. The Krumen would not eat "native" food nor carry heavy baggage (Livingstone, 1865: 84), and on several occasions European officers had to intervene between the two groups. The officers tended to side with the Krumen, and as a result the Kololo even attacked them as well (Foskett, 1965: I, 153, 219-221, 310-313; Wallis, 1956: I, 124-125, 174). The friction between the Kololo, Krumen, and white officers heightened Kololo solidarity.

The excessive demands of Livingstone also promoted Kololo consciousness. Livingstone wanted to achieve his objective of opening up Central Africa but he thought this could be done only by driving his subordinates unmercifully. At one point when the *MaRobert* would not pass through the Kebrabasa rapids, he forced his porters to use "a perilous and circuitous route, along which the crags were so hot" that they blistered the uncovered feet of the Kololo porters. The Kololo complained bitterly. When Livingstone refused to reverse his decision, they declared defiantly that "they always thought he had a heart, but now they believed he had none . . . and had given unmistakable signs of having gone mad" (Livingstone, 1865: 60). Despite such protests, the working conditions of the porters continued to deteriorate. Shortages of food were increasingly common and the contaminated flour and rotten meat that Livingstone provided were, according to one of his white companions, enough to "turn the stomach of anyone not living in the bush" (Foskett, 1965: I, 211). Moreover, Livingstone refused to allow the Kololo to hunt to supplement their diet and challenged their right to rest on Sundays or use that time to engage in their own private commercial ventures.

Tensions continued to mount. In 1860, nearly two-thirds of the Kololo refused to obey Livingstone when he ordered them to return to Bulozi and their subordinate status under Sekeletu. In 1861, during a particularly grueling journey to Lake Malawi, Livingstone tried to prevent the Kololo from hunting in the game-rich Linthipe region (Foskett, 1965: II, 314-317). Fifteen Kololo disobeyed. Furious, Livingstone dismissed the mutineers and abandoned them in the Tchiri Valley, thinking that they would either starve to death or be forced to return to Bulozi (Foskett, 1965: I, 314-317; Clendennen, nd, 1-2).

For the Kololo involved in the mutiny, the dismissal marked the end of their five-year career as wage earners. During this period wage employment broadened their conception of labor power, improved their material conditions, and helped them to develop a sense of group identity. Although the men had left Bulozi as members of different ethnic groups, they managed to overcome their backgrounds and adopt a common identity as Kololo or Magololo, thereby distinguishing themselves from both the Chikunda ex-slaves and the free peasants of Tete. By calling themselves Kololo the porters sought to emphasize their common experience as free aliens at Tete and their shared labor conditions under the Portuguese and the British.

As wage laborers the Kololo were able to improve their economic position considerably. Upon the completion of each journey the Kololo were paid in guns, powder, cloth, and other European articles. The porters sold some of the calico and kept the remainder, particularly trousers, which symbolized their claim to being Black Englishmen *(angerezi akuda)*. The firearms, which later became a critical asset in their struggle for mastery in the Lower Tchiri Valley, were initially used in hunting game and ivory. They sold their ivory at Tete and used the proceeds to obtain wives, to maintain a household, and occasionally to indulge themselves—which annoyed the more puritanical Livingstone:

> The Kololo have learned no good from the Portuguese . . . some of these men have only added to their own vices those of the Tete slaves; others . . . have got into the improvident slave custom of . . . spending their surplus earning in beer and *agua ardents* [Wallis, 1956: I, 163].

The Kololo viewed Tete as the land of opportunity in contrast with Bulozi, the land of bondage. More significantly, they came to challenge the Sotho-Kololo system of labor appropriation and Sekeletu's claim to the fruits of their labor:

> Our own men . . . had often discussed the rights of labour during their travels; and, having always been paid by us for their work, had acquired certain new ideas which rather jostled against this old law. They thought it unjust to be compelled to give up both tusks to the Chief . . . Sekeletu's law was wrong; they wish he would repeal it [Livingstone, 1865: 288].

In a clear expression of their autonomy and increasing class consciousness, nearly two-thirds of the Kololo refused to obey Livingstone in 1860 when he ordered them to return to Bulozi and their subordinate position under Sekeletu. They also internalized the idea that they had control over their own labor power and developed a relatively clear notion of what constituted appropriate conditions of employment. They insisted on receiving payment for each task they performed, and they demanded that their own time be recognized as being independent of their employer. Kirk found out how autonomous the workers could be in 1859 when he could not find a single Kololo to transport him in a canoe after the porters had received their wages for the journey to Lake Malawi (Foskett, 1965: I, 266). The porters preferred to utilize their time and labor to undertake private ventures or to arrange marriages. On long expeditions the Kololo porters, sailors, and wood cutters refused to work on Sundays except to hunt their own game and ivory. Indeed, the Kololo revolted against Livingstone precisely because he tried to alter their work schedule.

Livingstone's prognosis about the inevitable demise of the mutineers proved wrong. Armed with European weapons, the Kololo forged an autonomous political and economic empire imposing their hegemony over the politically decentralized and vulnerable Mang'anja population of the area.

Initially, Kololo domination of the Tchiri valley depended on their ability to curtail the cycle of violence set in motion by the slave raiding of the Yao, Swahili, and the Chikunda who were working for the Zambezian warlords (Mandala, 1983: 57-70). These raids had a devastating effect: "The whole country . . . is almost wholly destitute of inhabitants, though at present the river bank is lined with Misasa (i.e., camps) of fugitives from the other or eastern side where the Achawa (i.e., Yao) are ravaging. We had passed and were yet to pass many more [misasa]" (Bennet and Ylvisaker, 1971: 325). The Kololo defeated the slavers, to the great relief of the indigenous population. As one Mang'anja chief noted:

I have brave heart [sic] too, but what is the good of a brave heart: a brave heart alone is no good. Listen. The Mang'anja have brave hearts; the Ajawa came into their country; they go to fight the Ajawa, but directly they see them run away. Why? Not because they have not brave hearts; but because the Ajawa have stronger war medicine than they. Now you have a stronger war medicine than the Ajawa [Rowley, 1867: 149].

But the Kololo were not content merely to repel the attackers. Following the example of Livingstone and the Universities Mission to Central Africa (UMCA), the Kololo also took the offensive against the slavers, tracking down and ambushing caravans. The "liberated" men, women, and children, as well as the captured firearms and trade goods, were taken to the Kololo camp at Chikwawa. The most able of the freed slaves received arms and were integrated into the Kololo ranks as elephant hunters and soldiers. Others served as farm laborers working in the gardens of the Kololo. They were joined in the fields by the ex-female slaves whom the Kololo married. The incorporation of a number of unattached Mang'anja and Yao, who had been displaced by the famines in the middle of the century and by the wars of the Tchiri Highlands, swelled the ranks of the Kololo community. By May, 1862, the Kololo were reported as:

revelling in all the good things that part of the country could produce . . . monarchs of all they surveyed. They had goats by the score, fowl by the hundreds; they ate the finest corn and drank the best of *pombi*. They and their numerous wives were clothed and decorated without regard to cost. They had sprung at once from poverty to wealth, from a condition little removed from bondage to that of lords of creation [Rowley, 1867: 277].

Drought and the instability created by slave raids heightened the differentiations between clients and patrons and between slaves and masters. The Kololo settlement survived the disastrous 1862-1863 famine (Mandala, 1983: 57-70), weakened but nevertheless in better shape than the neighboring Mang'anja chieftaincies. Adequate supplies of grain and powder provided them with a modicum of security, which, in turn, attracted additional Mang'anja dependents. The famine also forced the UMCA missionaries, who had unsuccessfully competed with the Kololo for influence over the Mang'anja, to leave the country without their newly converted Yao protégés. Most of the abandoned converts had no alternative but to join the Kololo as slave warriors. The Kololo used this fighting force to subdue the remaining Mang'anja chieftaincies. By 1870 the Kololo had set up six small states in the Tchiri Valley.

The economic base of these states rested upon the extraction of tributary and slave labor. From the outset, Livingstone's ex-porters rejected the concept of free labor for which they had struggled when they had been wage earners. They suppressed all tendencies toward a wage labor system in favor of tributary relations premised upon their monopoly of political power. The chiefs deployed their subjects and slaves in their fields and as the basic work force in other branches of the economy—primarily ivory hunting and salt production—which they came to dominate. In short the Kololo reinstituted a system of exploitation that was more characteristic of their native Bulozi than the type of employment they had experienced under Livingstone. Wage labor had proved to be transitional. The Kololo had begun as corvee laborers; now they employed corvee and slave labor.

All the Kololo chiefs maintained large fields, known as *magala,* which were planted with food crops, cotton, and sesame (after 1880). Slaves and conscripted Mang'anja peasants worked the fields. Every Mang'anja headman was required to provide his respective Kololo ruler with male workers during the critical weeding and harvesting seasons, while slaves maintained the fields on a daily basis (Mandala, 1977: 108-109). To meet their growing labor requirements, the Kololo obtained additional slaves through raiding and by exchanging salt for captives with Ngoni and Yao warlords.

The Kololo aristocracy reorganized the production of salt, which previously had been undertaken by Mang'anja women in small kinship groups (Mandala, 1983: 24-25) but now became the work of slaves. Kololo chiefs Chiputula and Maseya started centralizing salt production soon after taking power. They employed their slaves to manufacture salt in the Dabanyi marshes and only permitted independent producers on the condition that they handed over part of the product. The two rulers maintained their hold on salt production until the late 1890s, when the introduction of foreign salt to the Ngoni and Yao areas undermined the market (Mandala, 1983: 86).

It was ivory, however, which constituted the staple of Kololo trade with the outside world. Before the Kololo came to power, elephant hunting had been the least developed sector of the Mang'anja economy. The acquisition of Yao slaves and the incorporation of Yao refugees, both of whom brought considerable experience in hunting and long distance trade (Joint interviews: Chipakuza and Sadriki Zimveka; Joseph Maseya and Clement Pemba), enabled the Kololo aristocracy to exploit the region's ivory resources.

They sent squads of Yao slaves to the Dabanyi marsh and the upper Mwanza Valley where the elephant herds resided (Mandala, 1983: 27-29, 87-90). Because of the proximity of elephants to the Kololo capitals, the expeditions enjoyed a relative advantage over their Chikunda competitors. Proximity to the hunting grounds also made it possible for the rulers to send porters to carry the meat to the capital, large quantities of which they distributed to their Mang'anja subjects. As the former Kololo chief Mlilima recalls:

> You speak of game? . . . no sir, this land was full of game. Meat was never a problem, never. The Magololo chiefs engaged their slaves in killing game. As I said earlier, the chief's capital was always full of meat, dried, fresh and so forth. Villagers came to eat the meat until they had their full. Women from all the neighboring villages were invited to take as much meat as they could carry [Interview: Mathias Chimtanda Mlilima].

While the production of ivory was a relatively uncomplicated business, its sale was not. Owing to the capacity of their Afro-Goan competitors to block the Tchiri and Zambezi waterways, Kololo caravans had to travel overland to the most distant markets at Angoche, Chisanga, Ibo, and Quelimane (Mandala, 1977: 122-127). Slaves were used to transport the ivory, and many of these carriers were ultimately sold with the ivory at the coastal markets (Interviews: Mathias Chimtanda Mlilima; Joseph Maseya).

The journeys were long and required considerable expertise on the part of the Yao caravan leaders and great endurance on the part of the carriers (Johnston, 1884: 532-533; O'Neill, 1885: 646-655; Rankin, 1885: 655-667). The round trips to the northern markets lasted up to six months. The porters suffered from shortages of food and drinking water. There were, however, several factors that tended to stifle any significant worker protest. Good conduct was the best guarantee against being sold at the coast (Interview: Mathias Chimtanda Mlilima), and the prevalence of lions and other marauding animals along the route acted as a powerful disincentive against desertion at night. The whole party huddled together around a blazing fire at night to keep off the animals. Lions often preyed upon caravans to carry off anyone found on the edge of the camp (Interviews: Mathias Chimtanda Mlilima).

In addition to protecting the party with their guns, slave leaders were responsible for negotiating with local officials, some of whom were well known plunderers and extortionists. The negotiations involved mostly the payment of "passage" and canoe fees and occasionally the remuneration of guides. Passage fees were made in ivory as well as alcohol, beads, brass rods, rifles, and powder, which were the items the caravans brought from the coast (Interview: Mathias Chimtanda Mlilima; Joseph Maseya; Mandala, 1977: 122). Given these difficulties in transporting the ivory to markets it is not surprising that the Kololo welcomed Scottish traders who arrived in the country in 1876, with the promise to buy the chief's elephant tusks.

The presence of the Scottish merchants increased Kololo dependence on the ivory trade. Chiefs like Mlilima and Mwita who previously had confined their hunting activities to the procurement of meat because of the difficulties involved in transporting ivory, also started collecting tusks. The ivory boom had far-reaching ramifications for Kololo society. To protect their privileged position the Kololo demanded that any subordinate who killed elephants in the Dabanyi marsh and the upper Mwanza Valley hand over the "ground" tusk (Mandala, 1977: 122). More significantly, the importance of ivory in the Kololo economy highlighted the contradiction inherent in the position of their Yao retainers. As hunters, they continued to enjoy greater material benefits in comparison to both the domestic and agricultural slaves and the Mang'anja peasantry. As slaves, however, they were never able to convert their economic privilege into political power and chieftainship. The Kololo had foreclosed this possibility when they decided to adopt a patrilineal descent system, despite the fact that the majority of the ex-porters had been raised in a matrilineal setting (Mandala, 1983: 104).

After some Yao hunters expressed their discontent by fleeing to the Tchiri Highlands (Joint interview: Chipakuza and Sadriki Zimveka), the Kololo aristocracy adopted several strategies to keep their workers under control. On the one hand, they tried to intimidate prominent Yao hunters suspected of disloyalty by accusing them of being witches and threatening to administer the *mwabvi* poison ordeal (Mandala, 1983: 2, 77-78). On the other, they coopted disaffected Yao leaders by giving them village offices (Mandala, 1983: 77) vacated by Mang'anja headmen who had failed to fulfill their corvee obligations.

The opening of the Tchiri Valley to "legitimate" trade provided Kololo rulers with an expanded opportunity to act as labor recruiters for merchant capitalism. As early as the 1860s the Kololo serviced international trade by renting canoes and paddlers to caravans crossing the Tchiri River. The aristocracy maintained its monopoly by prohibiting the Mang'anja from owning canoes (Interviews: Moses Ganamba; Herbert Maluwa). Later the rulers profited from the sale of Mang'anja labor as porters *(amtenga-tenga)*. The demand for porters increased dramatically after 1876 when Scottish missionaries, agents of the African Lakes Companies (ALC) and private traders and hunters settled in the region with the object of stimulating "legitimate" trade (Macmillan, 1970; McCraken, 1967). The Europeans required a substantial number of porters to carry their loads from Chikwana (Katunga's), where the ALC had a warehouse, to their settlement at Blantyre in the Tchiri Highlands and to Matope on the Tchiri River above the rapids. Matope was linked by a regular steamer service to the Scottish stations at Livingstonia and Karonga on the western shore of Lake Malawi.

All Europeans traveling to Blantyre and Lake Malawi and those going to the east coast turned to the Kololo for porters and paddlers. Aware of the dangers that an uncontrolled wage labor system could pose to their privileged position, Livingstone's ex-porters welcomed their new role as middlemen and prohibited all travelers from recruiting labor on their own. Chiefs Katunga and Kasisi institutionalized the arrangement by building guest houses at their respective capitals (Cotterill, 1968: 266; Macdonald, 1969: I, 68-69). Parties like those led by Mr. Young needed several hundred porters (Young, 1877: 51-53). Europeans spent their time comfortably in the guest houses while "messengers [were] sent to the neighboring villages to collect porters." Mang'anja headmen who failed to provide male workers were routinely deposed and replaced with new appointees. At the chief's court the porters were drawn up in a line in front of the guest house. "At a signal from the agent they dashed into the verandah, and amidst the wildest confusion struggled and fought for the lightest packages" (Rankin, 1893: 61). Then began the grueling 35-mile march up the rugged slopes with their sharp gradients to Blantyre (Buchanan, 1885: 35-38).

For their labor the porters received one and two fathoms of cloth (Cotterill, 1968: 269; Drumond, 1888: 23; Buchanan, 1885: 36), which they were forced to share with the Kololo chiefs. Indeed, it was a common practice for travelers to deposit the wages of the porters with the rulers before starting the journey. The arrangement was apparently designed to ensure that the porters carried the luggage to its destination without deserting on the route (Cotterill, 1968: 269). In reality the plan also gave the chiefs a chance to extort the wages. As one traveler commented after observing the reluctance of porters to work under the plan: "[I]t does not appear that they had any confidence in the chief's integrity of purpose . . . the men thought they were being 'done' " (Cotterill, 1968: 269). Even those Kololo rulers who did not require that wages be deposited with them expected "presents" from their subjects which sometimes amounted to the whole wage:

> I was very much struck with the kindness of one of my boys, to one of the chiefs, he came and asked me to give to the chief a prisant [sic] as he was his chief, as I would not do so he asked for his wages, I gave him them [sic] and he handed over to him. They were taken quite coolly, he did not even seem to recognize it [F. T. Morrison, Diaries, July 27, 1882].

Because of their interests in the *mtenga-tenga* system, the Kololo supported the wage demands of their laborers as a means of increasing their own share. When the Europeans refused to raise wages, the Kololo did not hesitate to withhold their laborers' services. In 1883 Chief Katunga prohibited his men from working for the African Lakes Company. When the company tried to substitute other workers—a strategy the Europeans tried repeatedly—the chief's son intimidated the recruits, who then fled. The result was a complete breakdown in communication between Blantyre and the outside world (Buchanan, 1885: 35-36; Macmillan, 1970: 187). Two decades later about 100,000 loads belonging to the ALC rotted at Katunga's camp because the Kololo refused to provide labor (PRO, FO2/470: From Sharpe and Manning, April-June, 1901).

Independent of the activities of their Kololo masters, the porters began to organize their own resistance, and thereby they helped shape the outcome of the growing discord between the Kololo and the British settlers. This resistance took two major forms. Although they were not permitted to sell their labor freely, Mang'anja porters did, as the Kololo before them, come to develop a clear notion of what constituted appropriate conditions of employment. They refused to transport over-sized packages. Loads weighing over fifty pounds were continually left at the chiefs' courts. So successful were Mang'anja porters in this respect, that fifty pounds became the standard weight for all loads passing through the Tchiri Valley in the 1880s and 1890s (Buchanan, 1885: 36).

Pilfering was a second expression of defiance. Porters frequently fled with European goods as they climbed the mountains to the Highlands. While some of the runaways apparently reported to the chiefs, it is clear that the majority of the thefts were perpetrated without Kololo knowledge. They represented, among other things, the porters' attempts to limit Kololo claims to a portion of their wages. The settlers failed to recognize that the porters were acting independently, and, whenever they were robbed, they demanded reparation from the Kololo. In 1883, for example, John Moir of the ALC, denied Kassi his right to a "ground" tusk as punishment for the thefts committed by his men (Morrison Diaries, Oct. 5, 1883; March 16, 1884). Kololo countercharges that the ALC hunters were operating in their territory without permission heightened the mutual distrust.

The tensions between the Kololo and the British settlers came to a head in 1884, following the murder of the Kololo ruler Chiputula by a former employee of the African Lakes Company. Chiputula's followers retaliated by killing the murderer, by sinking a company vessel, and by closing the Tchiri River to British traffic for nearly six months (Mandala, 1977: 135-152). The incident failed to spark a large-scale revolt because of the internal divisions among the six Kololo rulers and because the insurgent Kololo faction could not rally their Mang'anja subjects behind them. The Mang'anja interpreted the event as a conflict between competing exploiters—an assessment that was shortly proven right when, threatened with Portuguese imperialism, the British quickly mended fences with the Kololo's ruling class which, with a few exceptions, agreed to recognize England's colonial claims.

CONTINUITIES AND DISCONTINUITIES IN LABOR HISTORY

The Kololo, like the Chikunda before them, had transformed their position in the relations of production from worker to employer. Both had begun as servile workers, either slaves or tributary laborers, and subsequently acquired slaves and other dependents of their own. Because of this transition, it is easy to lose sight of labor and concentrate on the successful careers of individuals who were able to use ethnicity as a means of promoting the interests of a collective group of people. Both the Kololo and Chikunda emerged as distinct ethnic categories by bringing together people of diverse origins. Ethnicity was not given, but evolved in the context of specific historical circumstances and class relationships.

From the perspective of labor history, the Kololo and the Chikunda are interesting because of their dramatic transformation from bound to free laborers and ultimately to labor extractors. As slaves and corvee laborers respectively, the Chikunda and Kololo suffered all the indignities of socially oppressed workers. Once emancipated, they found employment as hunters, mercenaries, traders, porters, canoemen, and even miners. This transition marked a turning point in the history of both groups. Not only had they severed ties of servility, but the Kololo and more successful Chikunda entrepreneurs began to gain wealth, power, and a privileged class position by expropriating the labor of others. Work still had to be done, and it is instructive that slavery and tributary relations were still imposed as the means of extracting surplus labor.

Despite the continuity in the forms of labor extraction, wage labor was relatively new in the nineteenth century. The Chikunda had engaged in portering as slaves, not as wage earners. The Kololo began to take payment for their labor after they cut the ties of dependency with the Sotho-Kololo state, and their subjects in turn worked for wages, even though a portion of the wages had to be given as tribute to the Kololo. Wage labor in portering, river transport, and mining was a new phenomenon that was ultimately tied to the increasing penetration of merchant capitalism in Central Africa. Wage labor remained subordinate to the dominant relations of production, which continued to be based on tribute and slavery.

NOTE

1. Statistics compiled from A.H.U., Códice 1454, and Barbosa, Ajuda, 52-x-2 no. 3.

REFERENCES

ARCHIVAL SOURCES

Arquivo Histórico Ultramarino (A.H.U.), Moçambique, Cx. 3, Duarte Salte de Mendonça, December 3, 1751.

A.H.U., Moçambique, Cx. 3, Fr. Fernando Jesús, April 13, 1752.

A.H.U., Moçambique, Cx. 5, Pedro Jozé Perreira, December 1, 1756.

A.H.U., Moçambique, Cx. 21, Jozé Pedro da Diniz, March 1790.

A.H.U., Moçambique, Cx. 38, Mello Ribeiro do Castro, April 27, 1799.

A.H.U., Moçambique, Maço 38, "Proposta que se fez aos moradores de Senna para darem o seu votto p. escripto aos pontos seguintes," Pedro Jozé Perreira, August 27, 1753.

A.H.U., Códice 1315, Francisco Henrique Ferrão, December 20, 1828.

A.H.U., Códice 1452, João Bonifácio da Silva to Sebastião Xavier Botelho, May 14, 1825.

A.H.U., Códice 1462, Custódio José da Silva to José Maria Pereira Almeida, July 15, 1860.

A.H.U., Códice 1468, Manoel Joaquim Mendes de Vasconcellos e Cirne to Joaquim Maximo Figuerido, October 27, 1829.

A.H.U., Códice 2-44FD, Marco A. R. de Cardenas to Anselmo Gomes Xavier, June 25, 1849.

A.H.U., Moçambique, Pasta 21, João Taveres de Almeida to Ministro e Secretário dos Negócios da Marinha Ultramar, August 19, 1863.

Arquivo Nacional da Torre do Tombo (A.N.T.T.), Ministério do Reino, Maço 604, "Memôria sobre a Costa de África," António Pinto de Miranda ca. 1760.

A.N.T.T., Ministério do Reino, Maço 604, Diogo Guerreiro de Aboime, August 27, 1779.

Biblioteca Nacional de Lisboa (B.N.L.), Fundo Geral no. 826, Anonymous, May 21, 1762.

B.N.L., Collecão Pombalina, no. 271, fol. 299, Francisco José de Lacerda e Almeida to D. Rodrigues de Souza Coutinho, March 21, 1798.

Biblioteca Pública da Ajuda (Ajuda), 52-x-2 no. 3, "Analise estatística," José Francisco Alves Barbosa, December 30, 1821.

Boletim Oficial de Moçambique (B.O.M.), 1886 /40, p. 492, "Relatório Acêrca do Districto de Tete e Referido ao Anno de 1885," July 15, 1886.
Morrison, F.T. Diaries, 1882-7, University of Edinburgh Library (Gen. 1803-9).
PRO (Public Record Office) FO2/470: From Sharpe and Manning /58-143 (April-June, 1901).
Zambian National Archives, Feira Notebook, KSV4/1.

ORAL INTERVIEWS

Banda, Yohane; Chinguwo, Tayesa and Banda, Lameck. Chilowamatambe. August 29, 1973.
Baulo, Aneala and Nazing'omba, Austin. Chikwawa. January 16, 1980.
Cavumbula, Chiponda. Makhanga. October 16, 1968.
Chipakuza and Zimveka, Sadriki. Chikwawa. February 4, 1976.
Domingos, Mozesse. Sena. August 6, 1968.
Ganamba, Moses. Chikwawa. January 29, 1976.
Gogodo, Dauce. Caya. September 3, 1968.
Maluwa, Herbert. Chikwawa. January 29, 1976.
Maseya, J. and Pemba, C. Chikwawa. February 27, 1980.
Mbewa, Biskop Chapuka. Mchinji. September 24, 1973.
Mbewe, Nathan Pelekamoyo, Mawere, Amazia, and Mbewe, Keyala Maloni. Mkanda. September 24, 1973.
Mlilima, Mathias Chimtanda. Chikwawa. January 23, 1976; February 26, 1980.
Mwale, Lenose Chikuse. Chiwere. April 16, 1974.
Mwale, Mbalame, Phiri, Belu Mailosi and Phiri, Levi. Karonga. February 20, 1974.
Mwale, Zephaniya and Banda, Chatsalira. Dzoole. September 26, 1975.
Nhanticole, Lole. Chemba. August 26, 1968.
Pangacha, Alface. Cheringoma. September 4, 1968.
Phiri, Josiya Chitseka; Banda, Kazyolika; Banda, Amon Chadza; and Banda, Eliyasi Kapantha. Chimutu. April 15, 1974.
Phiri, Lukiya Chiwanga. Chulu. July 27, 1973.
Phiri, Nalisemphere and Phiri, Nathando. Chitseka. March 5, 1974.
Phiri, Ngwezu Chikho; Nthara, Daniel Chinkhupiti and Mvula, Kamachenjeza. Chikho. March 22, 1974.
Renço, Gente. Chemba. August 13, 1968.
Tito, Gimo. Sena. August 9, 1968.
Zakaliya, Mkota Nkhoma. Santhe. August 1, 1973.

PRINTED MATERIAL

ALPERS, E. (1975) Ivory and Slaves in East Central Africa. Berkeley: University of California Press.
BEACH, D. (1979) The Shona and Zimbabwe (900-1850). London: Heinemann.
BENNET, N. R. and M. LVISAKER [eds.] (1971) The Central African Journal of Lovell Procter, 1860-1864. Boston: Boston University Press.

BHILA, H. (1982) Trade and Politics in a Shona Kingdom. Essex: Longman.
BOTELHO, S. X. (1835) Memória Estatística sobre os Domínios Portuguezes na África Oriental. Lisbon: Imprensa Nacional.
BUCHANAN, J. (1885) The Shire Highlands (East Central Africa): as Colony and Mission. London: William Blackwell.
CHADWICK, O. (1959) Mackenzie's Grave. London: Hodder and Stoughton.
CLENDENNEN, G. (n.d.) [ed.] The Shire Journal of David Livingstone, 1861-1864. (unpublished)
COQUERY-VIDROVITCH, C. (1971) "De la traite des esclaves a l'exportation de l'huile de palme et des palmistes au Dahomey: XIXe Siècle," pp. 107-123 in C. Meillassoux (ed.) The Development of Indigenous Trade and Markets in West Africa. London: OUP.
COTTERILL, H. B. (1968) [ed.] Travels and Researches among the Lakes and Mountains of Eastern and Central Africa. London: Frank Cass.
DENY, S. R. (1939) "Some Zambesi Boat Songs." NADA 14: 35-44.
DRUMMOND, E. (1888). Tropical Africa. London: Hodder and Stoughton.
FOSKETT, R. (1965) [ed.] The Zambesi Journal of Dr. John Kirk, 1858-1863. Edinburgh and London: Oliver and Boyd.
GAMITTO, A.C.P. (1960) King Kazembe (Ian Cunnison; trans.). Lisbon: Junta de Investigações do Ultramar.
———(1859) "Escravatura na África Oriental." Archivo Pittoresco 2: 369-372, 397-400.
GRAY, R. and D. BIRMINGHAM (1970) [eds.] Pre-Colonial African Trade: Essays on Trade in Central and Eastern Africa Before 1900. London: Oxford University Press.
ISAACMAN, A. (1972). Mozambique: The Africanization of a European Institution: The Zambesi Prazos, 1750-1902. Madison: University of Wisconsin Press.
———(1972) "The origin, formation and early history of the Chikunda of South Central Africa." Journal of African History 13: 443-462.
———and T. ROSENTHAL (1984) "War, slaves and economy: the late nineteenth-century Chikunda expansion in South-Central Africa." Cultures et Development.
JOHNSON, W. P. (1884) "Seven years' travel in the region east of Lake Nyassa." Proceedings of the Royal Geographical Society (London) 6, 9: 512-536.
LACERDA E ALMEIDA, J. de (1936) Travessia da África. Lisbon: Imprensa Nacional.
———(1873) The Lands of King Kazembe: Lacerda's Journey to Cazembe in 1798 (R. Burton, trans.). London: John Murray.
LIVINGSTONE, D. (1865) Expedition to the Zambesi and its Tributaries. London: John Murray.
———(1858) Missionary Travels and Researches in South Africa. London: John Murray.
MACDONALD, D. (1969) Africana or the Heart of Heathen Africa. London: Dawson of Pall Mall.
MACMILLAN, E. W. (1970). "The origins and development of the African Lakes Company, 1878-1908." Ph.D. dissertation, University of Edinburgh.
MAINGA, M. (1973). Bulozi Under the Luyana Kings: Political Formation in Pre-Colonial Zambia. London: Longman Group.
MANDALA, E. C. (1983) "Capitalism, ecology and society: the Lower Tchiri (Shire) Valley of Malawi, 1860-1960." Ph.D. dissertation, University of Minnesota.

———(1978) "The nature and substance of Mang'anja and Kololo oral traditions." Society of Malawi Journal 31, 1: 1-14.

——— (1977) "The Kololo interlude in Southern Malawi, 1861-1895." M.A. thesis, University of Malawi.

MARTELLI, G. (1970) Livingstone's River: a History of the Zambezi Expedition, 1858-1864. London: Chatto and Windus.

MCKRACKEN, J. (1967) "Livingstonia mission and the evolution of Malawi, 1873-1939." Ph.D. dissertation, Cambridge University.

NEWITT, M. D. (1973) Portuguese Settlement on the Zambesi. New York: Africana Publishing Company.

NORTHRUP, N. (1978). "Southern Malawi, 1860-1891: a case study of frontier politics." Ph.D. dissertation, University of California, Los Angeles.

O'NEILL, H. E. (1885a). "Journal from Quelimane to Blantyre." Proceedings of the Royal Geographical Society (London) 7: 646-655.

———(1885b). "Eastern Africa, between the Zambesi and Rovuma Rivers." Proceedings of the Royal Geographical Society (London) 7: 430-455.

RANKIN, D. J. (1893) The Zambezi Basin and Nyasaland. London: William Blackwell and Son.

———(1885) "Journey from Blantyre to Quelimane." Proceedings of the Royal Geographical Society 7: 655-667.

ROWLEY, H. (1867) The Story of the Universities Mission to Central Africa. London: Saunders and Otley.

SELOUS, F. C. (1893) Travels and Adventure in Africa. London: Richard Bentley.

TRUÃO, A. N. de B. de V. B. (1889) Estatísticas da Capitania dos Rios de Sena no Anno de 1806. Lisbon: Imprensa Nacional.

WALLIS, J.P.R. (1956) [ed.] The Zambesi Expedition of David Livingstone, 1858-1863. London: Chatto and Windus.

YOUNG, E. D. (1877) Mission to Nyassa. London: John Murray.

11

PORTERS, TRADE, AND POWER
The Politics of Labor
in the Central Highlands
of Angola, 1850-1914

LINDA HEYWOOD

The economic integration of west central Africa with the world economy during the nineteenth century was in many ways related to the availability of porters who were able to link the interior markets to the coastal ports. In the case of the Benguela Highlands (central Angola) the emergence of a large scale porterage system coincided with the end of the export slave trade about 1850 and the growth of commodity exports, particularly in ivory, wax, rubber, and gum copal. Furthermore, the opportunities of porterage resulted in major social change, since many porters were able to transfer the gains from trade into the social sphere. The demise of porterage also had its social consequences. The imposition of the Portuguese colonial state (after 1890) and the subsequent construction of a road system and the building of the Benguela Railroad (1902-1928) ended the need for these porters. For a brief period, however, the organization of labor for transport purposes affected the structure of highland society.

The fact that the highlands were thickly populated and strategically placed between the producers of the major export commodities and the coast contributed to the prominence of the Ovimbundu—the inhabitants of the highlands—in the transport system of the area. The geography of the Benguela Highlands made human porterage the most feasible means of transport for bulky commodities. In the first case,

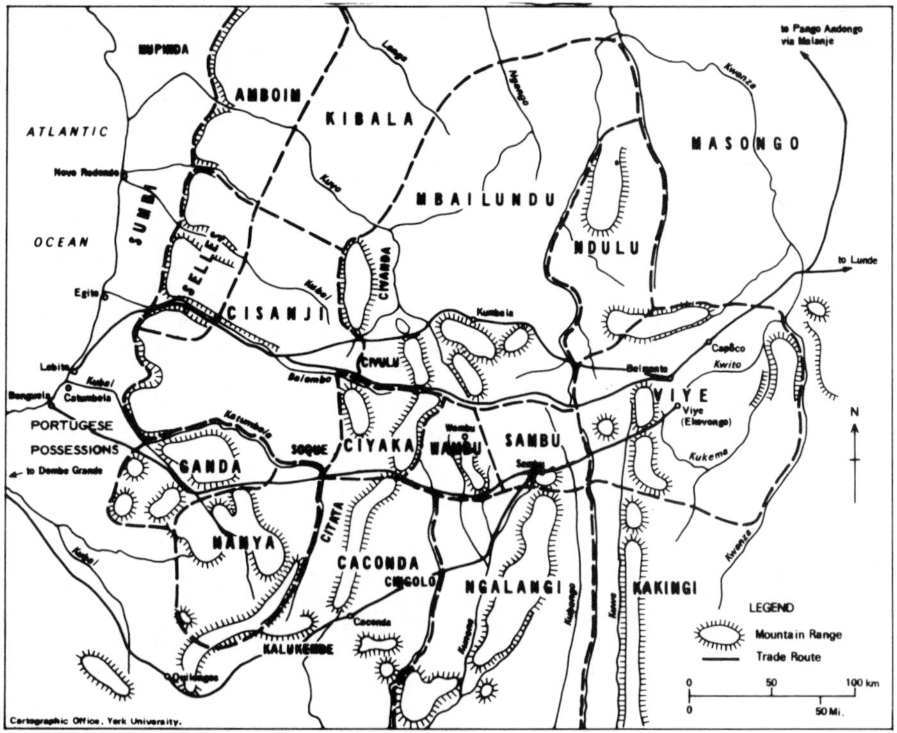

Map 11.1: Central Highlands (c. 1850)

the highlands lacked navigable rivers which might have allowed boats to be used for transporting goods. Farther north, the Kwanza and Zaire rivers provided some riverine transport for those regions, but they were only available for relatively limited stretches and left much of the producing region untouched (Heywood, 1984: 81-83). Animal transport, either as pack animals or to draw wagons, was also not feasible, as the disease environment prevented the breeding of draught animals, despite attempts on the part of Europeans to introduce livestock. The Boer ox wagon, which had proven successful elsewhere in southern Africa, was able to function somewhat, but even it proved commercially uncompetitive (Heywood, 1984: 84-85).

Before 1850 the Benguela highlands had long engaged in external trade, especially the slave trade which began in the late sixteenth century (Heywood, 1984: Ch. 3). However, the slave trade generated relatively few demands for transport, as the slaves could walk to the ports on their own. Some members of these caravans were clearly slave raiders, but porters were required to carry goods to those regions where slaves were bought (Heywood, 1984). It was not until bulky commodities began to be exported, however, that the need for porters greatly increased. The emergence of the Ovimbundu as renowned porters was primarily due to the nature of human porterage itself, and not to any special attributes. Humans, for instance, could travel under all conditions in the highlands, and thus porterage was faster than alternate means, such as the Boer ox wagon. Porters, who could carry as much as 35 kilograms each, could travel along any route in the highlands, while oxen had to pass through areas with sufficient grazing land and water supplies. In addition, wagons could only make the 550-kilometer trip in two months, travelling five hours a day (Malheiro, 1973: 97).[1] Porters could cover more than 19 kilometers per day and thus make the same trip in about 25 days, or less than half the time (Heywood, 1984: 86-87). Besides this, ox wagons were more susceptible to natural disasters than human carriers. For example, heavy rains might destroy the road and bridge system necessary for the wagons, but humans could bypass such impediments (Brásio, 1970: Vol. 3; 533, Lecomte to Rooney, 1 November, 1899). Moreover, the oxen were still vulnerable to disease, as the rinderpest epidemic of 1896, which virtually eliminated the use of oxen for some years, made clear.

Porters were, on the whole, a cheaper and less taxing form of transport than ox wagons, even when they functioned. In 1875 the Scottish explorer Cameron considered the porterage service of the Ovimbundu cheap when compared to what one paid on the east

coast of Africa (Cameron, 1875). There was virtually no investment, but the capital outlay for wagons was quite substantial.
For instance, in the 1890s the cost of hiring an ox wagon for a trip
from Benguela, the coastal port, to Viye, a major interior entre-
port, stood at $500.00 for a wagon load of 300 pounds (136.4
kilograms) a shipping rate of $0.37 per kilogram.[2] Porters, each car-
rying a load of 60 pounds, could be hired for a rate of $3.50 each,
a shipping rate of $0.12 per kilogram.[3] Thus, porters were the most
reliable, fastest, and cheapest form of transport for goods on the long-
distance trade routes that linked the heart of central Africa with the
Atlantic ports of the Angolan coast.

The Ovimbundu were known as capable porters even during the era
of the slave trade when they carried goods for Portuguese merchants
who visited the slave marts of the land beyond the highlands. They
had even reached Lunda (in modern Zaire) by 1800 (Vellut, 1972:
61-166). During the period of the slave trade, the organization of commerce was dominated by large, well-capitalized Portuguese merchants
(who had established a commercial base in Viye around 1770) and
members of the Ovimbundu nobility (Heywood, 1984: 60-65). The involvement of the Ovimbundu upper class was substantial, so much so
that a serious upheaval shook the capital of Viye in 1843 when the
Portuguese community was recalled to Luanda by their trading factors on the coast. Dom António Alemcastro Riambulla, the reigning
soba (ruler) of Viye, defended those of his subjects who looted the
Portuguese establishments and even killed and enslaved Portuguese
citizens by saying: "These bad treatments were a result of the lack
of trade goods *(fazenda)* which these lands have suffered after the slave
trade ended" (Graça, 1890: 397). This outburst of frustration punc-
tuated a period in the history of the highlands. It marked the end of
the period when participation in the slave trade required large investment and heralded a new era when other commodities gained predominance and porters would be needed on a massive scale.

Porters were largely slaves or dependents who were relatively
powerless in this organization and received little of the profits of
trading ventures. Their involvement in Ovimbundu long-distance trade
did not diminish, but in fact expanded significantly after the ending
of the external slave trade. Commercial contacts began to include the
coastal port of Benguela as well as the long-developed trade with Luanda, while more and more points in the interior fell into the orbit of
traders based in the highlands. Not only did the scope of trade widen,
but the domination of the trade passed progressively from the hands

of the Portuguese to that of the Ovimbundu, and moreover, the role of porters became more important and eventually porters even came to a dominant position in the conduct of trade.

During the period of the Atlantic slave trade, few commodities other than slaves were exported by Ovimbundu. However, conditions changed when the central highlands became the main route for the transport of other goods from central Africa to the Atlantic coast. The opening up of this new route was linked to the requirement for transporting the products which had replaced the slave trade. Ivory, wax, honey, and, later, rubber and gum copal had to be carried, unlike slaves who could walk and required only a light, armed escort (Heywood, 1984: 71). In addition, the Ovimbundu themselves began to export agricultural products such as maize and maize flour *(fuba)* to markets in the coastal cities of Benguela and Catumbella (Heywood, 1984: 171).

The expansion in trade brought about a restructuring of Ovimbundu society which was not evident in the period before the middle of the nineteenth century. Until then, the Ovimbundu states were characterized by strong central power exercised by the king *(soba* or *soma)* and various of his relatives. This power included the right of the state over the labor of subjects and the direct power of masters over their own slaves. The ruling class possessed, in addition, other rights which came to them through kinship and through voluntary citizenship (Heywood, 1984: 190-243). *Sobas* and their high-ranking relatives were supplemented on the local level by officials (*sekulu* or village heads) who had similar but less far-reaching rights. At the base of the society were the freeman and slaves who provided most of the labor for the dominant group (Heywood, 1984: 190-243).

The end of the external slave trade and the rise of commodity production gave individuals in Ovimbundu society the opportunity to enhance their social position and to increase their political standing. In the period immediately following the official end of the Atlantic slave trade, these opportunities were limited to the members of the dominant group who were able to exploit the labor of their dependents, clients, and slaves. In addition, these individuals were also in a most favored position to obtain credit from Portuguese factors on the coast. For example, in 1857 a Viye noble, later to become soba of Viye, established trading links with a local Portuguese company on the coast. In the course of their thirty-year relationship, credit was a feature of the transactions (Heywood, 1984: Ch. 8). Most caravans (maca) belonged to high-ranking Ovimbundu officials or to Portuguese traders.

The people who made up these caravans were usually kinsmen, slaves or pawns in the service of the head of the caravan (Magyar, 1857: 27-30). António Francisco da Silva Porto, a long time Portuguese resident in the Ovimbundu state of Viye, gave several examples of such chiefly caravans headed by sons, nephews or brothers of the *sobas*. The porters were slaves, clients or pawns (Silva Porto, 1884-1885: Vol. 11, n.f.). Portuguese caravans had a similar composition, as did the famous trading caravans of Lázló Magyar, a Hungarian adventurer who made his home in Viye from 1849-1857 (Kun, 1960-1964: 632, quoting Magyar; Magyar, 1857: 215, 216). Silva Porto maintained a sumptuous residence in Belmonte, near the capital of Viye, which was surrounded by villages of his slaves, from whom he drew the porters for his caravans (Silva Porto, 1884-1885: Vol. 11, n.f.). These caravans ranged far and wide over central Africa. Livingstone met several in Lozi country in the 1850s (Livingstone, 1963: 24; Livingstone, 1960, 232; Livingstone, 1957: 262), while in 1875 Cameron met others belonging to the Ovimbundu Soba. He also met another caravan of fifty or sixty persons headed by one of Silva Porto's slaves in Cokwe country (Cameron, 1875: September 13, 21; Cameron, 1877: 141, 191). Some of these porters were sufficiently well traveled to know Kiswahili, and they had even visited the Katanga (Shaba) kingdom of Garenganze.

Even during this period, some free men joined these caravans. When Magyar traveled to Lunda in 1850, he was accompanied by his wife (a daughter of the soba of Viye), his numerous slaves, 250 elephant hunters and free inhabitants of Viye who served as porters or traveled as independent traders (Kun, 1960-1964: 632; Magyar, 1857: 448). The distinction between porters and traders among members of such caravans was not particularly noticeable since both groups contributed labor for the transport of commodities. The organization of this labor was an elaborate affair, for mobilization of labor depended on the person organizing the caravan and the nature of the goods that had to be acquired. For instance, in the case of caravans being organized for ivory expeditions, recruiting was done openly among the free population. The prospective recruiters first paid a tax to the local village head (sekulu) in whose jurisdiction he wished to recruit. Such recruiting involved a contractual arrangement between the organizer of the caravan and the prospective porters who agreed verbally to the terms of payment and the conditions of work (Silva Porto, 1840-1887; Magyar, 1857: 446-450). The sekulu provided the initial contacts but, they had no control over the terms of these contracts. On many occasions, the sekulu or soba sent free men to act as porters, especially for in-transit caravans, and the men, after collecting their customary advance payment, carried the goods what they considered a fair distance. For example, Joaquim Rodrigues Graça, a Portuguese official on his way to Lunda in 1843, was unable to secure the intervention of the local soba in settling a dispute with 400 free porters who refused to go beyond a certain distance without receiving additional wages. Graça was forced to recruit a new set of porters (Graça, 1890: 382).

From the 1850s the recruitment of porters was arranged through a local magnate (*ocimbalo*) who agreed to supply porters for caravans. In such cases, the ocimbalo brought along his kinsmen and friends as workers, in addition to any slaves that he or the others might possess (Silva Porto, 1840-1887: II, 88-89, Magyar 1957: 446-450). Finally, free people simply joined a caravan or approached its leader as independent, small merchants carrying only a few goods of their own. Caravans that went from Mbailundu to the coast usually included small-scale operators transporting their own agricultural products for sale on the coast. Cameron (1877) encountered one such caravan during his descent from the highlands to Benguela in 1875. By the 1880s porters could be secured through any of these methods, but increasingly porters were hired or people carried their own products. In one month in 1885 alone a total of fourteen caravans entered the city of Catumbella, seven of which brought agricultural products (Silva Porto, 1840-1887: II, passim). Most of these came from Mbailundu, which was nearest to the coast; those that came from Viye, farther east, generally brought wax, ivory, or rubber (Silva Porto, 1840-1887: 5).

From the 1870s the types of porters and other people participating in the trade changed in response to the range of new products that were being exported, but the trade was still dominated by the Ovimbundu upper class and Portuguese traders. First of all the internal slave trade still required a huge outlay of capital which the ordinary freeman did not have. Ivory and wax could also only be obtained if one had trade goods. As early as mid-century caravans organized by members of the nobility were fitted out twice annually, comprising as many as 5000 men. Porters in these caravans had little scope for independent entrepreneurial activities as their stay at the coast was strictly controlled by the caravan head (Magyar, 1857: 27-30; Silva Porto, 1942: 96). On the other hand, the control that the upper classes maintained over the porters of caravans going into the interior was not subject to such strict control. As a result, porters could engage in a fair amount of entrepreneurial activity on their own account, and had no compulsion to report it, or their profits, to the caravan leaders. Wages were increasingly converted into commercial profit, as some porters carried trade goods in addition to their contracted loads. Cameron noted that their low pay was supplemented by raiding and pillage (Cameron, 1875: September 8, 13), the spoils of which were turned into trade goods, including slaves. Silva Porto, in a diary entry for 1885, noted that porters took various goods from one region and sold them elsewhere at a profit. The result of this petty trade could result in a fairly substantial gain over the course of a long trip. Thus the control that the upper classes maintained over laborers in the caravans was becoming more and more ineffective as the caravan trade came to dominate the lives of people who were formerly bound to the land as agricultural workers.

These shifts in the status of labor became increasingly noticeable during the period between 1870 and 1900 as Ovimbundu freemen came to dominate the trade between the producing areas of central Africa and the coast. The rise of rubber as the main export was in large measure responsible for this development. Even though at the beginning of this period some Ovimbundu porters had been able to acquire a few commodities, especially slaves and ivory, with the payments they received for their services as porters or from raiding while on a caravan, these activities could not be sustained. Indeed, by the 1880s when world demand for rubber increased, the Ovimbundu began to tap the wild rubber reserves that were found in the areas just west and south of the Benguela Highlands. The exchange of this rubber was on a small scale—a widely scattered population processed small amounts of rubber under the most rudimentary conditions. This situation favored the porters who could strike bargains with small groups of producers.[4] Rubber then joined slaves as the most important items of trade. The slave trade dominated the internal market, while rubber came to represent the main commodity in the trade between the Ovimbundu and the Portuguese traders on the coast.

Both the rubber and slave trade involved the majority of Ovimbundu men, though a large number of the female and youth population participated as well. In 1898, an exceptional year, a missionary noted that the demand for rubber and the desire for slaves "led to the greatest rush to the Gangelas [rubber producing areas] in the dry season that we have yet seen in the country. Every man with any energy left . . . was eager to go, while old men no longer able to travel were spurring on the younger men, boys and even girls."[5] In 1907, 200,000 porters were counted as they passed along the principal trade route from the rubber district (BRC, Relatório, 1908: 20). Population estimates for the region this route served suggest that there were about 500,000 people, of whom 140,000 were able-bodied males. Even allowing a large margin of error in the population estimates, it can be seen that a substantial proportion of the population did indeed engage in trade (Dinis, 1929: 158; Heywood, 1984: 287-290).[6] The facts that women mostly provided the resources and children participated as attendants further demonstrate the extent to which the trade dominated all aspects of Ovimbundu society.

The impact that this involvement had on society was felt by all social groups. In commenting on preparations that were made in one village for the trade, the missionary W. Currie observed, "the men were feeding themselves fat for the journey, the women were pounding meal for fathers, husbands, brothers. Animals were butchered and the meat retailed for beads [to sell in the interior] . . . the women barter away the beads from their hair and necks. These all went to increase the stock for trade."[7] In addition, he noted that "many young people were not willing to go when the day approached," and that several fled to the woods to escape. Others, however, were "tied to the loads and forced to go."[8] The coercive measures used to mobilize labor demonstrate that not everyone willingly engaged in trade. Family pressure had to be brought to bear on younger people because youths were less likely to benefit directly from the trade. Kinship is often seen as a means of achieving cooperative labor, but the Ovimbundu case also demonstrates that kinship as a mechanism of control was not effective and that measures such as physical threats were often resorted to.

Such participation in the rubber trade by the ordinary Ovimbundu perhaps had as many consequences for the individual as it had for the society. Some observers felt that the physical demands of the work did not have commensurate rewards. Such was the view of Currie, who wrote, "about 500 people have just left this district for the far interior, in about a year, worn by fatigue and privations of the journey they will turn their faces homewards."[9] The work was indeed exacting. Porters carried a load which might exceed thirty kilograms for a five-hour walk, when they had to stop, prepare a camp (which involved construction work), gather water and wood, before resting. All this was done on relatively limited rations (Johnson, 1969: 39).[10] Short journeys from the agricultural lands to the coast were even more demanding. People carried little or no supplies, and many ate nothing during the journey, obtaining their sustenance from drink (Johnson, 1969: 39; Cameron, 1877: 251).[11] Since the coast had a different environment, many found it unhealthy, in addition to the risks inherent to entering the wild, untamed life of the coastal cities. Some observers remarked that the return road was more like a graveyard, littered with the bodies of those who died on the way back home (Silva Porto, 1840-1887; Johnson, 1969: 35). Eyewitnesses never failed to mention that the bodies were of Ovimbundu traders since items of their trade were often left on the hastily dug graves.

The Ovimbundu expanded their trade inland to the area of the Ngangelas, the Luenas, the Lozi Kingdom, the Lunda Empire, and as far east as Luba and Garanganze. The most innovative aspect of this expansion was the extension of market demand for slaves and other commodities among people who had previously been only marginally involved in the regional network. In 1853, Livingstone met several caravans from Viye in the Lozi Kingdom buying and raiding for slaves. He cited an incident where they went among the Tonga

> who needed hoes, and having purchased some of the people near Sesheke [in Lozi country] they had induced those others living further east to sell both ivory and children. Even though they did not want to sell the children for mere clothing and beads, the iron hoes promised to decrease the normal labor of agriculture, since people were then using wooden hoes, and so they sold the children for the hoes [Livingstone, 1847: 525; 1960: 137, 178).

Cameron, writing some twenty years later, saw the process advance further as the Ovimbundu were then obtaining slaves from Katanga, where Msiri, in exchange for a payment, "allows some of his followers to accompany slave trading caravans on their raids, and on returning to his headquarters the slaves are divided between the traders and himself in proportion to the number of guns furnished by his people" (Cameron, 1877: 141). Only a small number of these slaves went to the coast as the external slave trade was over (Cameron, 1877: 141). The majority (especially women) were taken down to the Lozi to trade for ivory, while still others were traded with people to the south of the Ovimbundu, especially the Humbe, in exchange for livestock.[12]

By the late nineteenth century the trade had expanded into a complex pattern of local exchange along with the trade oriented to the coast. Cloth, beads, salt, and guns were sold to the Cokwe for ivory and wax, while slaves, ivory, and wax came from Luba. Viye traders then took these back to the highlands and traded them to the Mbailundu who carried those goods and agricultural produce to the coast. Viye traders in turn took slaves onto the Lozi, who sold them for cattle, which were sent to the coast through Portuguese traders (Cameron, 1877: 91).[13]

The quest for commodities and slaves, especially during the rubber boom, gave the Ovimbundu porters a widespread reputation of being slave raiders. In 1886 the missionary Arnot wrote in consternation that even though he had given his porters beads and cloth for purchasing goods and promised each one a tusk of ivory if they refrained from buying slaves, "I saw them, without exception, selling all they had— even stripping themselves and putting on sack cloth—to find the wherewithal to buy slaves" (NASA, Arnot Diary, 1888: 4-5).

The investment in slaves was crucial because slaves could be put to use as workers on their owners' behalf. This demand for slaves explains why their acquisition might offset the consequences of almost any other loss. Currie related the story of a man from near his mission station at Chisamba who, after having been chased away from two villages, managed to enter a third and "secured slaves and fought his way back through the natives who tried to prevent his path. True, he lost most of his goods, but he brought out slaves by whose help he has hopes of soon making up his loss."[14]

As a consequence porters gained the reputation of being competitive traders, as they combined porterage services with trading activities. During the period of the rubber boom their caravans, often comprising over 1000 people, entered the rubber producing areas and split up, so that porters bartered on a one to one basis with the individual producers right on the banks of rivers where the rubber was gathered and processed.[15] A similar arrangement worked in the wax trade as well, individual deals often being completed at the hive (Cameron, 1875, July 11, August 18; Serpa Pinto, 1881: 282). On the coast also Ovimbundu porters came to dominate the trade in the 1880s. The high level of competition for the goods—especially rubber—brought in by Ovimbundu caravans gave rise to the institution of *cambulação,* whereby large firms out bid each other by offering gifts of various sorts to the caravan leaders in the hope of persuading them to trade with this or that firm. If the caravan was small, the price paid to the African traders sometimes rose far above the normal market value, but the wholesalers knew that the possibility of inducing more caravans to sell their products with their firm was increased.[16] In any event, such trading techniques tended to expand the market to include even the lowest porter who exhibited more of a preference for transporting and marketing his own products than for working on behalf of someone else. Many observers noted that because of the high prices the Ovimbundu received, the profits were "quite an inducement to wish to trade . . . they are never contented to settle down for any length of time."[17]

During the rubber boom there was seldom an Ovimbundu male who did not participate in the trade, either as a porter or as a porter turned petty trader who hoped to make his fortune from rubber. The high prices which rubber fetched on the local market in contrast to all other local commodities at the height of the rubber craze guaranteed a ready return for anyone investing the time in procuring rubber. Because of the absence of proper methods of production and storage on the coast, anyone bringing in rubber was sure to receive a good bargain (Heywood, 1984: 103-110; Portugal em Africa 1, 1894: 192). This pattern continued until the end of the century. In 1899 the

> rubber trade increases, it appears because of the good price on the local markets . . . wax trade has decreased because the native only thinks of rubber as it is more profitable, skins because of the extinction of livestock owing to the rinderpest, ivory because of the extinction of the animal, not very numerous and pursued by hunters they have now almost all gone to the Belgian zones. The aguardente [local rum] trade actually decreases, but is easy for it to pick back up and even increase substantially (BO 5, 4 February 1899: 76-77).

Whereas caravans were organized either by the Ovimbundu upper class or Portuguese traders before the 1880s, thereafter the status of porters began to shift. Some who made the outward bound trip on behalf of a Portuguese trader, a member of the Ovimbundu dominant group or any group of foreigners, would invariably, on the return trip, transport a few kilograms of rubber bought with the cloth they received as wages. This rubber was then sold at the coast and more cloth purchased to start their own petty trading. The ease of access to commerce, both on the coast and in the interior, provided the opportunity for anyone to try his luck at trading. Even though the majority of these men remained porters, there were always a few who put to good use the strategies which made successful entrepreneurs. Annie Fay outlined these strategies as she saw them operating in 1889.

> The chief occupation of the men is trading, and in this they manifest a great deal of shrewdness. A man will start off with two pieces of cloth of 16 yards each . . . with which he buys a load of rubber of twenty pounds . . . after a rest, he trades this rubber for more cloth at the coast, and after one or two more trips in the interior, he has enough capital to buy a horn of ivory and a slave to carry it to the

coast. He then makes double profit by selling the slave. Or perhaps he may keep him for future use.[18]

For the rest, however, the thin line between petty trader and hired porter was easily crossed, depending upon whether or not an individual had access to some capital of his own. It would be foolhardy to argue, however, that porters were transformed as a class into traders. For the most part porters continued to be porters, even though some of them traded on their own account.

In any event the tendency of many Ovimbundu porters to become petty traders was a development that had serious consequences for the various groups who relied on porters—the Ovimbundu upper class and the Portuguese traders, including those in the highlands and on the coast. Whereas in the 1850s ordinary Ovimbundu normally went out on someone else's behalf, by the 1880s it was increasingly difficult to induce people to trade or carry for anyone but themselves. Silva Porto experienced this gradual development during the forty years that he resided in the highlands: "Bihanos [people of Viye] and Bailundus are trading independently and it is with difficulty that one can obtain porters in either country for the coast of Ganguelas" (Silva Porto, 1840-1887: XII, 62). The scarcity of porters was especially difficult for the new Portuguese traders, government officials and missionaries, one of whom commented in 1890 that "porters cannot be found, the chiefs monopolize all of them for their own business, the rest of the Africans trade independently, they are not prepared to be beasts of burden for whites" (Brásio, 1970: 4, 544). This change spared no one as there were even "successful African traders who cannot get carriers for their goods, so numbers of loads are stored up at Catumbela," on the coast.[19]

The most significant effect of this development was to weaken the links of dependency that bound the lower classes to the upper class. The ordinary porter was, in the words of a contemporary witness, able to "exchange his small remuneration that he had gained from porterage from the *sertanejo* [Portuguese interior trader] and then he ceases to be a porter, occupying the position of *pombeiro* [caravan leader], magnate in court or *seculo,* chief of a village."[20] In this period both members of the nobility and Portuguese traders found it difficult to use the coercive power of the state and the labor of kinsmen to acquire wealth and transport services (Heywood, 1984: 66-100). The nobility tried to slow the transition; sometimes a trader's goods were confiscated through accusations and legal proceedings *(mucanos).*

Despite the possibility of being fined unjustly, upward mobility was not unusual for porters. The steps outlined by Silva Porto concerning the pombeiro of an earlier period can be used to describe the gains which came the way of the lowly porters,

> When they are pombeiros . . . they gain many advantages, they leave the lower class for the nobility, they can have a great number of wives, ransom kinsmen and followers, and by paying the soba a sum in the value of one slave, they can obtain an honorary title [such as macota, sergeant or quinduras] being enabled to establish new villages, they become indebted to the sertanejos because, driven by ambition, they credit fazendas, remaining always in debt to those they serve [Silva Porto, 1942: 175].

Even though some Ovimbundu were ruined by the very nature of the trade, for others, however, the end result of this independent trading—if one were skillful and lucky, and there were surely many who were not—was the accumulation of durable and reproducing wealth, often in the form of slaves. Fay described the path such a career might take in a letter to her friends in 1889:

> If he has been successful in trading he has laid by four or five bales of cloth worth about $150 (U.S.). He may also have slaves whom he may send to trade for him that he may add to his wealth.[21]

Success at this level was relatively rare, for Fay went on to say that even though "there are a few men in Bie worth from $1,200 to $1,500 . . . the greater part of the people live from hand to mouth."[22]

Within a few decades the opportunities offered by trade and the consequent weakening of the lines of dependency within Ovimbundu society resulted in some marked changes in class relations. Members of the lower class were able to compete openly with the upper class in their ability to obtain the traditional symbols of wealth—conspicuous consumption, ownership of slaves or the support of other dependents, the ability to obtain political office and the like. Fay explained the precise manner in which some of this wealth obtained through trade was used:

> Occasionally, at feast days [a man] kills an ox, pig or sheep and has a great feast for his friends and relatives. But he is always careful to keep in reserve his fattened pig, the largest ox and the greatest part of his cloth for his funeral. The richer he is, the more ceremonies and

time spent over his body. A great deal of power is needed to fire off the guns which keep away the evil spirits. A great deal of cloth to wrap his body and food to entertain for a week.[23]

These developments threatened not only the power of the Ovimbundu dominant class but also the Portuguese resident in the state as well as traders on the coast. Silva Porto commented on the status of the new Ovimbundu traders: "when buying cloth they do not haggle, they buy everything, no matter what the price . . . and the luxury of being carried in a hammock, of having more than one wife . . . so that we [i.e. the Portuguese traders] are reduced to misery by the indigenous merchants" (Silva Porto, 1840-1887: II, 54). Later he noted that "Bailundos and Bienos are presently made merchants and consequently trade for themselves, so that they have no interest in sertanejos to whom they' owe this position . . . and among the Bihanos are some who were formerly our porters, and now we see them dressed [in European clothes] wearing hats with pants and being carried in hammocks like any European" (Silva Porto, 1885a: 18).

Commercial expansion also affected the position of women and other dependents in the economy. Women were called upon to produce not only subsistence but also for the growing market. Observers were particularly impressed with the increasing numbers of Ovimbundu caravans that brought locally grown and produced foodstuffs such as maize, ground maize, beans, tobacco, and the like for sale in Benguela as well as in the interior. Most of these goods were produced by women—some of whom were developing into a group of independent producers. In addition, some of the women, and children too, went on caravan trips; many sold their goods along the caravan route, while still others earned their cloth by selling their labor. Moreover, women and children often provided the labor needed by ambitious Ovimbundu porters who wanted to become independent traders. In one caravan bound for the interior in 1890, nine of its 97 members were pombeiros who carried no load, 50 were porters, and the remaining 36 were youths, many of them slaves who had to carry their masters' loads. Some were no older than nine or ten years (Johnson, 1969: 88). Often they provided other support services, such as searching for items to make relish when the caravan halted (Johnson, 1969: 88). Johnson, who observed the 1890 caravan, described the custom whereby men let their wives pound grain for the passing caravans. The women received a half a yard of calico each. This work relieved the man of his obligation to provide his wife with his traditional allotment of cloth. In effect, the status of women and other dependents did not change significantly, although the wife of a man who became rich in trade might well improve her lot.

If members of the upper class could not prevent the erosion of their power by the lower class, and if some lower class individuals were becoming independent traders, the Portuguese conquest of the highlands effectively transformed the nature of these changes in Ovimbundu society. This conquest began with an attack on Viye in 1890, and class tension sapped the ability of the Ovimbundu to resist. By the first decade of the twentieth century the Ovimbundu were conquered and the power of the Ovimbundu upper class all but eliminated. At this point, the Portuguese government tried to redirect Ovimbundu participation in trade and the economy as a whole to the new rulers.

The Portuguese conquest highlighted the fundamental problem that had plagued the former rulers—how best to exact surplus from the people. The Portuguese soon realized that the only way to gain was through the control of Ovimbundu labor, that is porters. The new economic prosperity which the rubber room had brought had resulted in a dramatic increase in the numbers of Portuguese traders in the highlands; now government officials, both military and civilian came too. This new Portuguese community soon realized that the success of government activities depended on the willingness of Africans to provide transport services. The competition for porters intensified at a time when the Ovimbundu no longer wanted or needed to do such service for others. This problem was of particular concern to the new Portuguese traders, many of whom were bent on making it rich quickly and returning to Portugal. A report of 1903 noted that many of the Portuguese were "skilled craftsmen who came to Africa to practice their profession and in a short time exchanged their tools for the key of aguardente (with more or less water) . . . rubber is their cry, a lot of rubber is traded: its profit is fabulous—such was their idea.[24] The government had to adopt measures to satisfy the appetites of these colonialists.

Portuguese officials and merchants tried to control Ovimbundu labor through force by obliging the conquered upper class to supply them with porters. Before long it was recognized that these leaders had lost the power to exact services from their people. In addition the competition for porters was intense. Merchants competed with each other and with the government and missionaries to obtain adequate numbers of porters for their goods, but still the demand was greater than the supply. Those Ovimbundu who were forced by their superiors to work for Portuguese officials often fled as soon as they were clear of the immediate area of Portuguese authority (Pimentel, 1903: 39-40).[25] Thus the complaints mounted, many arguing that porters were unavailable and when they were quite costly.

Under such conditions the colonial government had to intervene more directly in the control of the transport system and plan its transformation altogether. The first step was to bypass porters by building roads for ox wagons and by studying the feasibility of using some of the rivers for transport. Since building roads also depended on the control and availability of laborers in the short run, these measures were unsuccessful because the government had not yet established the state apparatus to enforce corvée labor. In addition, it was soon realized that ox-wagons, even when proper roads were available, were unable to compete with porters for speed and cost, a point that has already been noted. The fact that the climate and the geography of the highlands were more favorable to human labor made it even more important to control porters while at the same time continuing the efforts to find alternate means of transport.

Ox wagons still presented major problems without a proper road system. There were some merchants who experimented with the transport of rubber by ox wagon between 1911-1914, but the experiment was costly and proved a time consuming lesson. In 1914 a total of 70 wagons arrived in Huambo after a three-year trip from Humpata in the south to Lunda—thus bypassing the central highlands. During this journey the organizers lost 1500 oxen and 22 wagons. Bridges had to be built along the way. Only 2000 kilograms of rubber were transported, and the venture was deemed a total failure.[26]

Since the 1880s, the potential for profits from the control of transport had led several local Portuguese merchant houses, companies, and private speculators to apply formally to the government for a concession to build a railway from the coast to the highlands.[27] One group even sought a concession from the coast to Lozi country in modern Zambia. The group hoped to obtain the essential capital from an alcohol tax and duties on imported cloth and export products, especially rubber. They calculated that such a railway could bring in a monthly income of 130 *contos* of *reis*.[28] None of these projects were approved since the Portuguese government was not concerned with staking out its own claims.

In 1902 the government gave the British capitalist Robert Williams a concession to build the Benguela Railroad through the central highlands to the copper producing area of Shaba (Katanga) on the

Zambia-Zaire border, along the traditional route followed by traders (Katzenellbogen, 1973). Even though the railway authorities looked to the profits from the transport of copper as their main reason for building the rail line, they were aware that they could displace the porters. The period between 1902 and 1914 witnessed the most systematic attempts to eliminate porters as a means of transport as the railway was extended from the coast to Viye, 520 kilometers inland.

In 1906 the railway contractors concluded that no other intermediate region was as important for the railroad as the heart of the Ovimbundu domain.[29] They wanted to tap the labor as well as the extensive trading network that had developed in the nineteenth century. In this process they hoped to replace all traditional forms of transport in the area of the railroad, especially porterage, which they argued did not contribute to the formation of "civilized life" among the Ovimbundu (BRC, 1912a: 9). In addition, railway authorities argued that Ovimbundu labor could be redirected from porterage into the production of agricultural goods. This would in turn help relieve the ailing Portuguese local and national economy. The authorities encouraged government officials in the hope that the redirection of Ovimbundu labor to agriculture would bring about increased revenues by the surety of collection of taxes (BRC, 1912a: 9; 1912b: 7), which all depended on as the most important source of colonial revenues.

The prospects of diverting Ovimbundu labor was spelled out in a report of 1907 that noted, "in Bie a good number of natives would work on the railway in the dry season when it reaches that district, but probably a smaller proportion of the inhabitants than lower down, as in Bihe a number of natives trade on their own accounts."[30] The general view was that "the local native is a good carrier but has little inclination for manual labor . . . all cultivation is done by women."[31] It was genuinely believed that by the time the railway reached the highlands (1911), the men would have to find alternate means of employment—preferably in agriculture since "their profitable carrying business will be at an end. Ox teams will haul all freight to the sides. The railway [will haul] all through traffic and the rubber trading will be done on the ground where it is produced. The principal sources of revenue will be agriculture and stock rearing."[32]

The pressure on Ovimbundu trade and carrying services not only came from the railway but most directly from the colonial government. As early as 1895 the competition for porters had so inflated a porter's wages that the government instituted wage scales that established maximum wages for various stages of the journey from the coast to the last government post at Moxico, near the border with Zambia. In 1895 a porter making the 20 day trip from Viye to Moxico received between 6$500 reis and 9$000 reis return, or between 350 and 450 reis per day.[33] By 1910 the wage was set at 400 reis per day (BO 17, April 23, 1910: 208). Given the fact of inflation and the decreased opportunities to bargain for higher wages in 1910 as compared to 1895, a salary of 400 reis per day represented a real decrease in earnings. Working as porters on behalf of Portuguese traders did not significantly increase the real wages of a porter, since for a three month journey the porter received 120 yards of cloth worth 8000 reis, a smaller amount than what he might obtain on his own account.[34] Essentially the government's intervention led to a decrease in the wages received by porters.

Government measures to control Ovimbundu labor and thus to increase profits also took other forms. After 1902 caravans were required to receive travel permits at the various government posts along the route.[35] In 1906 the government introduced a hut tax which initially had to be paid in rubber or other local produce (BO 42, October 20, 1906; A Defesa de Angola December 12, 1907). When the railway officials began pushing Africans to grow so-called "poor products"—maize, beans, manioc, potatoes—as opposed to export products like ivory, wax, and rubber, official policy was quick to adapt to what seemed to be the only alternative for redirecting and controlling Ovimbundu labor. Regulations were soon adopted that required all African adults to cultivate these "poor products," and village authorities were required to distribute land and seeds (BO 46, November 14, 1906:1019; BO 43, October 24, 1914:941).

The prospects for selling their products at a competitive price induced many Ovimbundu to grow more of these crops to trade on their own. Railway statistics show that the export of maize from Benguela increased from 490 kilograms in 1909 to 1355 metric tons in 1913—most of this was produced by the Ovimbundu (BRC, 1915: 52). Exports of maize flour also grew from a low figure to a total of 2244 tons in 1914 (BRC, 1915: 52). The government, intent on pushing settler agriculture in the hopes that this would increase their control over Ovimbundu labor, acted to reverse this trend through several measures. The increase in agricultural production was followed by laws that were aimed at reducing independent Ovimbundu participation in the production and marketing of these and other crops. For example, laws already outlawed the use of slavery and other forms of dependent labor (such as pawns) by Africans intent on increasing production.[36] Another law made it illegal for African households to cultivate more than two hectares of land without special permission.[37] Thus Ovimbundu porters found that under colonial rule there were fewer opportunities for entrepreneurial ventures than were available previously.

Despite these restrictions, however, many Ovimbundu porters were able to combine agricultural, trading and porterage activities under the relatively lax system of controls that existed up to the First World War. A report of 1908 noted that for some parts of Huambo "all the people are occupied in rubber trade and also as porters . . . many of them . . . in the season when they do not have to transport merchandise . . . dedicate themselves to rearing all kinds of livestock."[38] Statistics also reveal that during this period a significant number of Ovimbundu still traded independently. The records for Viye show the extent to that both trade and porterage remained in Ovimbundu control. Registers of passports issued to caravans show that caravans under the direction of Ovimbundu greatly exceeded both the size and numbers of those under European direction. Europeans organized a dozen or so caravans with about 100 carriers per month, while Ovimbundu included anywhere from 10 to 40 caravans with as many as 1000 total carriers. Since the Ovimbundu traders were likely to evade government restrictions more than Europeans, it is clear that government intervention promoted European control of transport, even though Ovimbundu participation was still very significant.[39]

The caravans were also as varied as they were before the Portuguese conquest. Monthly reports for Mbailundu for 1908 showed that a total of 2407 Ovimbundu requested permission to trade. Of these the majority (1835) were men over 14 years of age. Women over 14 (673) and children (235) were still an important part of caravans.[40] Of the total, 1900 people went to the Gangeulas, 360 to Benguela and 147 to Catumbela.[41] Reports for the period also show that many caravans frequented the Lozi markets.[42] Competition for the products brought in by the Ovimbundu was still intense. In 1908 when there were only two wholesale merchant houses in Mbailundu, there were a total of 118 "shops to barter with the natives."[43] As was noted before railway authorities estimated that the number involved in porterage in that trade as late as 1908 amounted to nearly 200,000 (BRC, 1908: 20).

But gradual decline set in, as fewer and fewer caravans were making the trip to the coast. In 1908 a local Benguela newspaper noted the gradual disappearance of the caravans which "do not come down here with the frequency of happier times" (A voz de Angola, February 16, 1908: 2).

The disappearance of Ovimbundu caravans and with them the African porters aspiring to be merchants began the moment the railway line reached the highlands in 1911, although even then "most of the traffic is still carried by the natives on their backs."[44] In 1911 the railway reached Huambo (Wambu), the major town in the highlands, and railway statistics show that the bulk of the rubber—2221 tons—was transported by rail, whereas only 473 tons were brought to the coast by porters, generally from areas far removed from the railhead, from where it was still more convenient to carry rubber to Benguela and Catumbela (BRC, 1912: 8). The sudden collapse of rubber prices in 1913-1914 further influenced the decline of porterage (BO 4, January 24, 1914: 68). From a high of $275 per kilogram in 1909, the price of rubber fell to $7 per kilogram in 1914 and by 1918 it was only $42 per kilogram.[45]

The action of the railway authorities also contributed to the quick demise of porters and traders as professional groups among the Ovimbundu. Railway authorities were quick to see the advantages from the rubber bust. In 1912 the company had "reduced by 50% the tariff for rubber delivered for transport at the terminus [Huambo] station." They further noted that the reduction would only be 25 per cent in the case of consignments delivered "at an intermediate station."[46] With the rubber crisis of 1913-1914, the railroad announced plans to continue the ad valorem tariff for rubber "once the railway reached the Cassai [Kasai] river and the border of the principal rubber producing area."[47] The reasoning of the company was that "the producer would be better paid and therefore would devote more time to rubber production as there would be an abundance of native labor obtainable on account of the thousands of carriers which would be thrown idle with the advent of our line in this district."[48] The profits from rubber in 1913 constituted a total of 18 percent of the profits of the railway company.[49]

Railway authorities hoped that the crisis would help eliminate wagon transport also and thereby lessen the competition that they still faced from Boer wagons in the areas served by the railway. A report of 1914 noted that once the line reached Viye the company would introduce special rates that "will also influence the Boer wagons to carry freight from the terminus of the line to the interior. Even now these wagons which come down to Huambo will disappear altogether within the next few months."[50]

By the beginning of the World War I, the era of prosperity which had witnessed the rise of the Ovimbundu as porters and their dominance in trade had effectively ended. The new era was heralded by the shift from trading to agricultural activities. In a few years observers noted "the increasing amount of agricultural work which the men are carrying on since the passing of the trading days."[51] Others predicted an era of greater hardship for the Ovimbundu, especially as the government was more successful in instituting measures to extract surplus in the form of taxes. Woodside saw this trend clearly in 1914. He noted "heretofore it was not great hardship on the people as it was rather an easy matter for them to obtain the rubber and a couple kilos paid the tax."[52] The drop in rubber prices, together with the greed of merchants who openly cheated the African trader, meant that in 1914 many Africans needed four times the amount of rubber required just a few years earlier to pay the tax.[53] With the end of trade and porterage, the era of social mobility that might see a humble man rise to a minor official and village ruler in his lifetime was over. The colonial era that had dawned would show the Ovimbundu much harder days than they had known.

NOTES

1. Arquivo Histórico Ultramarino (hereafter AHU) Angola, 2ª Repartiçào, Caminho de Ferro de Benguela, "Tarifos."

2. National Archives of Zambia (hereafter NAZ), HM8 2/3/2. Diary of Walter Fisher, fol. 398-9, 26 March 1891.

3. Canadian Congregational Foreign Missionary Society Archives (herafter CCFMS) Victoria College of University of Toronto, Angola Mission, General Correspondence, file 13 (1888-89), Currie to F. E. Jeffry, 1889.

4. SGL: Res. 146-C-6, Silva Porto, "Apontamentos," vol. II (1887), in Luba; AHM Caixa 12, Doc. no. 20, "Missao Agricola at Regiào das ganguelas, Ambuelas e. Luchaze" por John Grossweiler, 1907: 25 and 53.

5. CCFMS, Angola Mission, General Correspondence, File no. 9, Report for 1898 by Walter Currie, p. 16.

6. O Jornal de Benguela, 23 August 1918, p. 3.

7. CCFMS, Angola Mission, General Correspondence, file no. 3, 1888-1889, Currie to Bro. Hill, Cisamba, Bie, August 17 1889, pp. 11-12.

8. Ibid., p. 13.

9. Ibid., p. 14.

10. NAZ, HM8/F12/3/1, Diary of Mrs. Fisher.

11. Ibid.

12. SGL, Mss. nos. 1-60, 1877, fol. 3 and 1878 fol. 1. Hermangildo de Brito Capello and Robert Ivens.

13. Ibid.

14. CCFMS, Angola Missionary Correspondence, File no. 9, Currie Report of 1898, p. 25.

15. AHM, Cx. no. 20, "Missão Agicola," pp. 36-37, 52-53. SGL, Res. 146-C-6, Silva Porto, "Apontamentos," vol. II, fols. 169-170; Johnson (1969: 107).

16. AHU aª Repartição, Maço 788, Prata 4 (1884), "Relatório do governador geral de Angola sobre a sua visita aos portos do sul ao ministerio e Secretaria de Estado dos Negocios do Marinha e Ultramar"; Heywood (1984: 103-110).

17. ABCFM, vol. 23 A, WCA Woman's Board of Missions 1886-1907, Doc. no. 140, Annie M. Fay, December 29, 1889.

18. ABCFM, vol. 23 A, Doc. no. 99, Fay to Friends, 6 June 1899.

19. NAZ, HM9/F13/1/1, Diary of Annie Fay, fol. 29, 1889.

20. AHU, Cr. "Ecplorações Cientificas, Silva Porto, Doc. 4, 1885, fol. 18ff.

21. ABCFM, vol. 23ª WCA Women's Conference, doc. 99, Fay to Friends, 6 June 1889.

22. Ibid.

23. Ibid.

24. AHU: Repartição Militar, Maço 968, Relatório of the Capitão-Mor, 1903.

25. Centro de Documentação e Investigação Historico (CDIH), Estante (Est.), 68, Cx. 1, Bailundo, doc. no. 17, Capitao Mor, Bailundo to Secretary, Governor of Benguels, 17 April 1930.

26. TANKS, Extracts from Africa Reports, 1915-Report of General Manager, 31 December 1914.

27. AHU, 1 Repartição, Angola, diversas, Maco 467; AHU 1ª Repartição, Angola, Diversas Maço 783; AHU, Diecção geral das Colonias, 2ª Repartição Angola, Assuntos Diversos, Maço 778.

28. Jornal das Colonias, 23/8/1902; A Provincia de Angola, 28 September 1934, p. 3.

29. TANKS, Benguela Railway, Letter from contractors J. Norton Griffiths, 24 February, 1960; ibid., File 39, Sir D. Fox and Partners, 1903-1932, letter from Company, 25 May 1905.

30. TANKS, BR 42, Resident Engineer's Report 14 March 1907.

31. Public Record Office (PRO), FO 367, Africa, Portugal (1907), /48 Portugal /7568-42585.

32. ABCFM, vol. 19, Doc. 177, Ennis to James Brown, 10 March 1910, p. 2.

33. CDIH, Est. 74, Cx. 1, Bie, Cap. Mor of Bie to Secretary of the Governor of Benguela, 2 December 1895.

34. TANKS, BR 42, Resident Engineer's Report, 14 March 1907.

35. CDIH, est. 74, Cx. 1, Bie, Capitão Mor of Bie to Secretary of governor of Benguela, April 2 1903.

36. CDIH, Cx. Huambo, oficio do govenador do Distrito de Benguela to the Administrador do concelho de Huambo, September 11, 1914; CCFMS, Angola Correspondence, File no. 33, John Tucker to Rev. Barton, November 3, 1913.

37. B.O. 35, September 2, 1911; PRO, Fo 367 (1910), Portuguese Files 6486, 26311, 27921.

38. CDIH, Est. 71, Cx. 1, Huambo, Report of 1908.

39. CDIH, Est. 74, Cx. 1, Bie Capitão Mor to Secretary of the Governor of Benguela, March 31, 1903; Ibid., Est. 78, Cx. 1, Bie, Capitão Mor to Secretary of the Governor of Benguela, April 2, 1903; Ibid., Est. 68, Carxa 1 (1894-1908), Doc. 32, Estatístico 1908; Ibid., Est. 68, Cx. 1, Huambo, no. 15, Relatórios Mensais, July 1909.

40. CDIH, Est. 68, Cx. 1, no. 15, Relatórios Mensais, July 1909.

41. Ibid.

42. AHM, Cx. 18, no. 8, Relatório do Capitão Mor do Cuito, 1912.
43. CDIH, Est. 103, Cx. 3, Bailundo, Report for 1908.
44. ABCFM, vol. 19, Doc. 262, Hollenbeck letter, July 1911.
45. TANKS, BR7, Report for 1913.
46. TANKS, BR7, Extracts from Africa Report 1915—Report of General Manager, 31 December 1914, p. 8.
47. Ibid.
48. Ibid.
49. Ibid., BR7, Report of 1913.
50. TANKS, BR7, Report of General Manager, 31 December 1914.
51. ABCFM, vol. 18, Doc. 166, "Report of Sachikela Station," June 1918, pp. 5-6.
52. Ibid., vol. 19, Doc. of 11 December, 1913, Woodside to Barton.
53. Ibid., CCFMS Angola Correspondence, File no. 39, Tucker to Dun, 26/1/1916.

REFERENCES

Newspapers:
A Voz de Angola
A Provincia de Angola
Defensa de Angola

Official publications:
Benguela Railway Company, Relatório e Contas, 1908-30; cited as (BRC)
Portugal em Africa, 1894-1910.
Boletim Official da Provincia de Angola, 1880-1930; cited as (BO)

Archival abbreviations:
ABCFM—American Board Conference of Foreign Missions, Boston University
AHM   —Arquivo Histórico Militar, Lisbon
AHU   —Arquivo Histórico Ultramarino, Lisbon
CCFMS—Canadian Congregational Foreign Missionary Society, Toronto, University of Toronto
CDIH   —Centro de Documentão e Investigação Histórico, Luanda
NASA —National Archives of South Africa
NAZ   —National Archive of Zambia, Lusaka
PRO   —Public Record Office, London
TANKS —Tanganyika Concessions Holdings (London)

ARNOT, F. (1888) Diary of Fred Arnot (National Archives of South Africa).
BRÁSIO, A. (1970) [ed.] Angola. Spiritana Monumenta Histórica. Pittsburgh: Duquesne University Press.
CAMERON, V. (1877). Across Africa. New York: Harper.
———(1875) Diary of Vernon Cameron (National Library of Scotland).
Caminho de Ferro de Benguela (1912a) Relatório dos Serviços de Caminho de Ferro de Benguela. Lisbôa: Caminho de Ferro de Benguela.
———(1912b) Relatório e Contas. Lisbôa: Caminho de Ferro de Benguela.
DINIS, J. de O. F. (1931) Relatórro de Serviços de Negócios Indigenas. Luanda: Imprensa Nacional.

GRACA, J. R. (1890) Descrição de viagem feita de Loanda com destino as Cabaceiras do Rio Sena." Annães do Conselho Ultramarino. Parte não oficial. 1 (1854-58). Reprinted as "Expediças as Muatauanvua." Boletim da Socidedade de Geográfia e de história de Lisboa, 9.

GRAY, R. and D. BIRMINGHAM (1970) [eds.] Pre-Colonial African Trade: Essays on Trade in Central and Eastern Africa before 1900. London: Oxford University Press.

HEYWOOD, L. (1983) "Production, trade and power: the political economy of central Angola 1850-1930." Ph.D. Dissertation, Columbia University.

JOHNSON, J. (1969) Reality Versus Romance in South Central Africa. London: Frank Cass.

KATZENELLENBOGEN, S. (1973) Railways and the Copper Mines of Katanga. Oxford: Clarendon Press.

KUN, N. de (1960-1964) "La vie et voyage de Ladislaus Magyar dans l'interieur du Congo en 1850-52." Bulletin des sèances de l'Academie royale des Sciences d'outremer, 6.

LIVINGSTONE, D. (1963) Livingstone's African Journal (I. Schapera, ed.), 2 vols. London: Chatto and Windus.

———(1960) Livingstone's Private Journals 1851-53 (I. Schapera, ed.). London: Chatto and Windus.

———(1857) Missionary Travels and Research in South Africa. London: John Murray.

MAGYAR, L. (1974) Reisen in Sud-Africa 1849-1857 (T. Hunfalry, trans.). Pest: Lauffer and Stolp.

MALHEIRO. M. (1972) Indice Histórico—Corografica de Angola. Luanda: IICA.

PIMENTEL, F. (1903) Invesitgação Commercial na Provincia de Angola 1902-3, Porto.

SERPA PINTO, A. A. da R. (1881) Como un atravéssai a Africa do Atlántico ao Mar Indico. Viagem de Benguella a Contra-Cost (1877-79). 2 vols. London: Bancroft.

SILVA PORTO, A. F. da (1840-1887) Apontamentos de um Portuense em Africa (Sociedade de Geografia de Lisbõa), vols. 1-13. (unpublished).

———(1942) Viagens e Apontamentos de um Portuense em Africa. Excerptos do 'Diario' de António Francisco da Silva Porto. José de Miranda and António Brochado, eds. Lisbon: Agencia Geral das Colonias.

———(1885a) "Novas Jornadas de Silva Porto no Sertões Africanos." Boletim da Sociedade de Geographia e da História de Lisbõa 5.

———(1885b) "Ultima Viagem." Boletim da Sociedade da Geographia e da História de Lisboa 5.

VELLUT, J. L. (1972). "Notes sur le Lunda et la frontière Luso-Africaine (1700-1900)." Etudes d'Histoire Africaine 3: 61-166.

12

THE STATE'S BAKONGO
BURDEN BEARERS

WILLIAM J. SAMARIN

       In taking possession of the heart of Africa in the last quarter of the nineteenth century, Belgians used Bangalas to carry their guns and Bakongos to bear their burdens. These were the first and most important Congolese—as opposed to expatriate—soldiers and porters of the initial period of colonization. They were critical for the Belgian enterprise, and for that reason their development was pursued consciously and vigorously. The intimacy of their involvement in the conquest of the Congo (now Zaire) River basin is portrayed iconographically in the innocent souvenirs recorded with the help of the new technology of photography: There in the picture is a group of porters at rest, some with their loads still on their heads (to show how carrying was done); to the side, in some kind of uniform, stands a man with self-conscious attention, rifle at shoulder.

Author's Note: Financial support for this chapter came from the University of Toronto (International Studies Programme and the Humanities and Social Sciences Research Programme), the American Philosophical Society, the Social Sciences Research Council (U.S.A.), and the Social Sciences and Humanities Research Council of Canada. I am grateful not only to these organizations but also to R. P. Abbé Michel Coune, head of the Abbaye St. André, for access to its library, and to R. P. Alexandre Gillès de Pélichy, Roger Liotard and Jean Liotard for access to the papers of Victor Liotard in Paris, and to Ann-Claude de Mazières for introducing me to the Liotard family, and to my colleague and friend, Peter R. Reich.

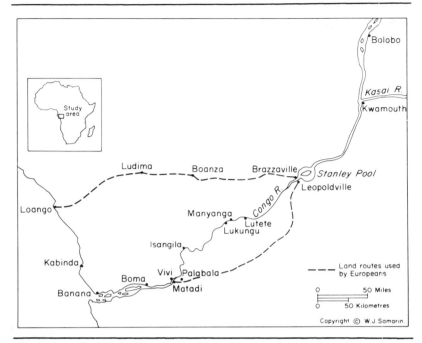

Map 12.1:   The Coast to Stanley Pool in the Nineteenth Century

This present study crops the soldier from the picture and enlarges that of the porters. Yet, as in a cinematic documentary, there will be flashbacks to the soldier, because we cannot fully understand why the Bakongos were porters without understanding why Bangalas were soldiers.

The names of these peoples, it should be understood from the outset, are labels of convenience. The Europeans participating in colonial events used the name Bangala as an ethnic one, but it applied in only a general way to the riverine populations between, say, the mouths of the Kwa and Mongalla Rivers on the Zaire (see Map 12.1). Some of them would have been what Europeans later came to identify as Bobangis, but many others—all possibly speaking closely related dialects—were included. Convenience does not, of course, fully explain the way Europeans perceived the indigenous populations. They were all more or less engaged in ad hoc ethnography; and like all ethnography it had its intellectual if not ideological presuppositions. In other words, the social, political, and economic structures that Europeans "saw" in Africa were based in part on what they observed in the field but also in part in what they brought with them as cultural (hence intellectual) baggage. Therefore the "tribes" they identified were to some degree or other of their own making. This topic is discussed in great detail with respect to the so-called Bondjo (Samarin, 1984d). It is to be expected that ethnicity (that is, the historical reality of a people) would in some cases be problematic. It is so with the Bangala, even though the Zairean historian, Mumbanza mwa Bawele, for example, argues (1971, 1974) for the existence of an authentic people—organized beyond low-level kin and clan units and self-conscious of their identity.

There is more justification for the use of Bakongo as an ethnic designation. (Since the first syllable of Bakongo is only a plural prefix, I prefer to use Kongo as the ethnic designation). That is to say, it has a much older history. In any case, regardless of the amount of integration of their societies in political units, such as that of the Kongo kingdom with which the Portuguese first came in contact, they spoke more-or-less closely related dialects, some of which, however, were not immediately mutually intelligible. This is not to say that nineteenth-century Europeans always recognized a vast Bakongo ethnolinguistic entity. Indeed, it is a fact of some significance that at the time when they were all talking about the so-called Bangalas, they were not equally categorical about Bakongos. The latter were generally referred to as the natives of the Lower Congo, or more explicitly Loangos, Kabindas, and other such ad hoc names.

The exploitation of the Kongo peoples had already had a history of almost four hundred years when King Leopold II of Belgium sent the Committee for the Study of the Upper Congo (replaced in 1883 by the International African Association) up the Congo River. They had been involved in trade, mining, and most of all in selling each other (and others) into slavery (Broadhead, 1971; Martin, 1970, 1972). The introduction of colonialism only altered the nature of interaction between Europeans and Kongos.

THE RECORD OF PORTERING

The Kongo peoples were indispensable for the establishment of Leopold's African empire (Liebrechts, n.d.: 201, published around 1900 or 1909). Transportation figures alone demonstrate the truth of this assertion. Calculate the number of kilograms of goods that had to be transported from the start of the cataracts to Stanley (now Malebo)

Pool, assigning 30 kilograms (65 pounds) per person, and one will have an idea of the number of human beings involved.[1] But this would only be the minimum, because every caravan required "support persons"—people to cook for the porters (many of whom must have been women) and others to carry the personal belongings of the porters (some of whom might have engaged in a little trade of their own); and children were frequently in these caravans, serving in different capacities. Figures for loads coming into and going out of the region give some idea of the number of human beings involved in portering, but they represent only the minimum volume of trade, being official figures of the Congo Free State. In early years, before the Belgian government had established its bureaucratic hold on the territory, much would have transpired, and much would have been transported, without the knowledge of its representatives.

European recruitment of local porters began between 1879 and 1883 (Van Schendel, 1932). These years represent the period of H. M. Stanley's first two trips up the Congo River, which includes the founding of the station at the Equator, so important for the subsequent recruitment of Bangalas into the work force. During this period he was concerned with establishing the claims of King Leopold in competition with the French. Speed in advancing into the interior was the most important factor. Nonetheless, he had 50 tons of shipment at Vivi, headed for Leopoldville, in 1880 (Stanley; 1885: 1, 159). When he arrived at Banana in December 1881, he had 600 tons of goods (Stanley, 1885: 468); not all of this went to Leopoldville, because some stayed at intermediate stations. Stanley himself provides little information about his recruiting of indigenous personnel: only that Kabindas were hired at the coast, that he had 206 workers at Vivi, that in March 1880 he had a work force of 110 not counting natives, and that his personnel needed 400 pounds of rice per day (Stanley, 1885: 31, 153, 196, 216, 221). Gisanura's estimate of Stanley's shipments to Leopoldville in 1883 is 54 tons or 1830 loads (Gisanura, 1971: 87).

Whatever we might make of Stanley's account of these first years, Liebrechts is explicit in saying that Stanley had in addition to 150 Zanzibaris the "renfort incertain" of some Kabindas to take over Stanley Pool and that early in 1883 a crew of 80 Zanzibaris had the heaviest responsibility of portering for the Pool (Liebrechts, n.d.: 22, 45). The absence of Kongo porters is confirmed by Wauters (1890a: 221), who reported that in 1883-1884 the International African Association found only "quelques rares auxiliaires" among the Lower Congo peoples. Yet 1200 porters had been used in 1883 (Congo Illustré, 1892: 19) and in 1882 through 1884 Leopoldville was being supplied every three to four weeks by goods from the coast with a crew of 40 porters (Guiral, n.d.: 237, published in 1889).

By 1884-1885 stations had been established as far as Stanley Falls for the consolidation of Belgian claims in the interior. Because of this penetration there was a greater importation of goods; and in this period Belgian agents assumed more responsibility for the execution of the King's plans. Captain Alphonse Van Gèle recruited 1500 porters on a single occasion in 1884, possibly at Lukungu (Lukunga or Lukungo) or Manyanga (MCC 1896: 210). The total number of loads taken to the Pool in 1885 was ten times what it had been two years earlier (CI, 1892: 19). The following year Coquilhat recruited 1000, including the 800 engaged in one day at Lutete (Coquilhat, 1886: 2, 34, 36-37).

In 1887 the volume reached 50,000 loads (CI, 1892: 19). By 1889, several thousand young men of 18-25 years of age were used every month as porters. They were recruited at Lukungu, Lutete, and Manyanga, where "toute la jeunesse . . . se fait porteurs" (Wauters, 1890a: 221). Lopasik's figure (1971: 66) of 18,000 for the year 1888 (if it applies to the whole year) is too low when compared to what went on in 1887. Lamotte (n.d.: 58, possibly published in 1894) said that on the left bank of the Congo alone and only during the latter eight months of the year, porters numbered 60,000. This was a busy year indeed, given the 1200 loads for the Emin Pasha expedition and the shipment of 6000 loads of the dismantled steamers "Ville de Bruxelles" and "Roi des Belges" (Wauters, 1890a: 222-223).

The construction of the railroad to Leopoldville, started in 1889, introduced another tremendous demand for porters, which continued until the first locomotive arrived at the terminus on March 16, 1898. When ships were unloading their cargos in 1892, it required 100,000 porters (Masui, 1894: 27) to transport the loads from a single steamer to the Pool (Belgique Coloniale, 1896: 231). For this year it was affirmed "without any exaggeration" that 40,000 men were engaged in transport. Where a dozen years earlier (i.e., 1880) one could not get even one porter now on a single day a person could see more than one thousand on march ("On initiating Negroes to European labor," CI, 1892: 19). It was also estimated that there were 4-5,000 identity cards for *kapitas* (i.e., caravan bosses) in circulation (1892: 179). There were not that many caravans at any given time, of course, but there were more than the "hundreds" of state caravans reported by Denis (1950:7). The word *kapita* is generally understood to be Portuguese in origin. Whatever its earliest meaning may have been, in the period under discussion the kapita's primary responsibility was to assure the arrival of each load at its destination in good condition. He probably also directed the personnel in other matters, and we can suppose that with the intensification of transportation his role assumed more importance. He was, however, not the sole representative of the European because soldiers frequently accompanied the caravans. In any case, the kapitas represented a special category of the Europeans' work force—men in an emergent "middle management" position. Kapitas were not necessarily Kongo men, although it can be assumed that those who spoke Kikongo were more useful to Europeans.

In 1896 P. de Deken (MCC, 1896: 210) reported that 90,000 loads were carried annually. This figure may be too high, given Lemaire's estimate (1895: 74) of 25,280 porters and ancillary personnel for 1893: 11,280 for the state, 9000 for the Belgian trading company, and 5000 for the missions and others. By the time the railroad was completed the number had grown to 100,000 per year (Aaron Sims, Annual Report, BMM, 1898: 443; Liebrechts, n.d.: 201). Lemaire (1894: 180) also estimated the total number of porters at 100,000, and he was only judging from the necessary labor required to transport the dismantled parts of the 43 steamers that were at that time plying the waters of the Upper Congo. The total, he says, equalled the size of the Belgian army! Contrary to what one might suppose, the railroad did not put an end to caravans. The caravan from Loango at least was still being used as late as 1908 (Deschamps, 1907: 14).

In the construction of the railroad the Kongos provided labor only for portering and other tasks requiring no special skills. Skilled manpower needs were satisfied by imported workers and, of course, by European management. The workers in Trouet's history of the construction (1898)—at which time he was its technical director—are identified as coming either from Senegal or the Gold Coast.

The examination of the use of porters has been restricted entirely to travel *toward* Stanley Pool, a bias that reflects the sources. Europeans described their achievements not merely in terms of their successes but also in terms of the hardships they endured and the obstacles they had to overcome. Getting their goods beyond the cataracts, over difficult terrain and in debilitating climate, was indeed a challenge that tested the best of men. But among all their difficulties—they made explicit—was the mobilization of manpower. Coquilhat was applauded after having described the way he recruited a thousand men in two weeks: "It wasn't without difficulty," he said. "Besides, one doesn't get anything without difficulty. . . . [These men] often made difficulties for me; it was the first time that they were working under the eye of a white" (1886: 2, 34).

What was there to tell about going to the coast, especially when for most narrators it meant returning to Europe? They were exhausted from a long tour of duty and usually seriously ill. Porters were just as necessary for transporting loads to Matadi from the Pool, but we have to go elsewhere for data to estimate the size of the labor force.

The volume of exports provides our downriver information, as investments provided data for the upriver journey. Exports rose from 4076 (presumably metric) tons in 1887 to 8722 in 1898 (Encylopédie du Congo Belge, 3: 385). The volume of rubber exports from the Pool rose from practically nil in 1883 to 30 tons in 1887; from that year to 1891 they went to 131 tons (Vansina, 1973: 427). In March of 1889 Europeans bought only 5 tons of ivory at the Pool, whereas 3 tons went to the coast by African caravans; the figure rose to 27 tons by 1895 (Gann and Duignan, 1979: 118, 123, citing Büchler, 1912).

The enormity of the cost in human effort, each man carrying about 30 kilograms on his head, is represented in the total quantity of exports over the twelve-year period: 2,730,533 man loads! And this, we must repeat, was only for the downriver traffic. This phaoronic figure does not, of course, represent individually named human beings. Some worked for longer periods of time, others for shorter. The figure is comparable in usage, nonetheless, to the long-established one of "manpower hours."

Kongo labor was used for portering because the Kongo lived in the very territory through which the Europeans had to travel. But location does not explain the whole story; it does not explain the fact that the Kongo people were virtually excluded from other forms of labor, particularly skilled work, but also specific projects like railway and telegraph construction. If there was no clear policy of exclusion, there certainly was one of preference for other groups of workers. Accounting for these differences must now be undertaken.

If Lemaire could say of 1893 that 245 "Bas-Congos" (that is, Lower Kongos) were serving in the district of Cataracts in positions formerly filled by foreign workers, he must have been referring to men who had already had experience working with Europeans, not "green recruits." Since emphasizing indigenous labor encouraged the investment of capital in the Congolese enterprise, Lemaire and others probably suppressed information about foreign recruitment, which played an important role for quite some time. For example, in 1894 the missionary George Cameron wrote: "At Sierra Leone we took on board about a hundred Africans coming to Congo to be soldiers or labourers in the service of the government. They belonged to five or six different tribes, speaking as many different languages" (MH, 1894: 360). Inventories of personnel reveal the importance of these coastal workers. For example, literate young men—foreigners—could be found at the coast for certain tasks, but launderers and tailors came from among the Lower Congo people (Donny, 1897: 37). One would have thought that since the railway went through their territory, the Kongos would have been involved in more than a trivial way in that project. It would appear that they were not. Indeed, most of the African workers were foreign. In 1894, the only year for which we have a figure, there were 419 Congolese at work among 3000 (that is, 14 percent), the total Black work force being 2000 in 1890 and 7000 in 1897 (Cornet, 1947: 248, 176; MH, 1898: 246).

Non-Kongo workers also predominated in other projects. The Boma-Kwamouth telegraph line was built during 1895-1898 "especially by the Bangalas" (Musée, 1903: 122). They took part as well in the mounting of 40 steamers at Leopoldville—they in addition to other Upper Congo people, but without Lower Congo ones (Lemaire, 1894: 177). In a later publication (1895: 56), but possibly for the year 1894, he quotes Liebrechts as saying although "Manyangas"—that is Kongos—as well as Bangalas were involved in remounting the boats (Lemaire, 1895: 56). In 1894 "Bangalas, Kassais [and] Weles are drivers, mechanics, fitters, on the boats, on the routes of the State, [and] in the workshops on the railway" (P. de Deken, MCC, 1896: 212). Besides Kongos, liberated slaves from the Kasai River and people from as far away as the Wele River were trained workmen. These "Weles" were probably Yakoma-speaking people (Samarin 1982a, 1982b).

This difference in (if not discrimination against) the employment of Kongo peoples must be explained. Since some of the work required travel up the Congo River beyond the Pool, the Kongo people may have feared encountering others whose bad reputations they feared, or, unlike the upper populations, they were unaccustomed to traveling about on the Congo. Without further information such considerations are only speculative.

Portering was hardly an employment with enduring inducements. The journey was long, over hilly terrain protected by little shade. By foot one covered 368 to 400 kilometers from Matadi to Leopoldville in fifteen to twenty days (Denis, 1950: 7; Bailey, 1894: 137).[2] In

1890 there were five barges *(allèges)* with eight teams of men (Lemaire, 1895: 51, 52) incessantly occupied with transport between these ports. The loading of goods in the earliest years had been done by Zanzibaris; in other words, Kongos were not trusted or were not available for this work. Guinness's description (1890: 57) of the northern route, for example, characterizes it as unfortunate because it was "very difficult, rocky ground in a gorge naturally poor and barren, and not very populous." Before the completion of the Belgian railroad, the Loango journey took "at least 35 days" (Dias-Briand, 1982: 59). Although longer, the Loango route had fewer streams than the Matadi route, along which one could be delayed for long periods of time when these were swollen after rains. At one point, the route rose 250 meters/820 feet in 20 kilometers/12.4 miles (Deschamps, 1911: 19; also see Foà, 1900: 274; Masui, 1894: 29; and Vandrunen, 1900: 250). These routes had been used by caravans for a long time, probably centuries (MacGaffey, 1977; Martin, 1970: 144).

Portering was a task that tested the mettle of the strongest of men (de Deken, 1902: 72-73), many of whom died on the path, leaving by 1898 "thousands of skeletons" along the way (de Mandat-Grancey, 1900: 176). (See also Michaux, 1907: 68-69.) Not all of these were men either—as we generally understand the term: They were in large numbers young adolescents (de Deken, 1902: 72-73) and by 1892 even children of 7 to 9, carrying loads of 10 kilograms (Lopasik, 1971: 71). Coquilhat's account, cited above, may have been intentionally untruthful or in the earliest years more mature men may have been available.

PAYMENT OF PORTERS

Since carriers entered service in different ways, it is not easy to characterize the way they were remunerated—if at all. But an attempt must be made, because they took part, willingly or not, in the emergence of a laboring "class" in central Africa. It is clear from the records that free individuals were recruited for portering, but it is also clear that slaves were common. Although many voluntarily sought employment, force was also used on the Kongos. M. Juhlin-Dannfeldt, a Swedish army officer who had served twice as a District Commissioner for the Congo Free State between 1883-1891, noted in 1891 (as quoted in Lagergren, 1970: 110) that

recruitment of labour to these caravans was carried out by special expeditions consisting of a white officer and a number of soldiers. The chiefs of the various villages were required to place a certain number of carriers at the disposal of the caravans, and, if the carriers were not available at the time appointed, the soldiers took a number of prisoners, usually women and children, in the refractory village. These were kept, often under harsh and humiliating conditions, until they were exchanged for the men who could be used as carriers.

Other Europeans did not, of course, have the authority to impress people into service. They had their own agents—labor brokers we might call them—who, undoubtedly working for their own profit as well, went about the country in search of porters (CI, 1892: 178; Masui, 1894: 26). These were therefore independent entrepreneurs and must not be confused with the kapitas, who were employees of the Europeans. Payment in money for portering was an innovation, introduced by Europeans, but the use of slaves was not; Europeans exploited a system that had existed for centuries.

Nonetheless the Kongo responded to European needs for labor, although they usually wanted to be paid in kind. They may have seen temporary employment in their own territory as a means to build up capital for enriching themselves in trade—an activity they understood and valued (Wauters, 1890b: 176). As late as May 16, 1894, Thomas Adams of the Livingstone Inland Mission wrote: "Up here [at Leopoldville] we cannot buy food or hire boys for money [;] it must be articles of real value such as clothing etc." (ABHS, 82). In 1885 the mission employed 32 or 33 "Loangos" at Leopoldville, at the Equator station and also on the mission's steamboat, the "Henry Reed," all of whom had to go south to Palabala (Mpalabala) to be paid their monthly salary of ten lengths of cloth (Aaron Sims to J. Clark, Leopoldville, March 11, 1885, AHBS). Cloth was also used in the early days (around 1882) as payment for Kongo porters (P. de Deken, 1902: 72), because it was a currency that could be used in trade.

According to Liotard (ANPM, Journal, writing on August 28, 1891), the State paid 36 francs to a Portuguese entrepreneur, who made a profit of fifteen francs for each recruit. It is not clear how much each carrier received. As late as 1888 or 1889, Probert—missionary of the Livingstone Inland Mission—wrote (1889: 135), "Carriers take cloth or handkerchiefs. They also get beads or knives to purchase food while traveling [to the Pool]." The statement suggests that these workers were "tipped" rather than remunerated in a systematic way. Lari workers were paid just one mitako (brass-rod currency) per day (Vansina, 1973: 303). Whatever this was worth (and Vansina provides a comparison of the various currencies), this was just enough to buy food for one day (Coquery-Vidrovitch, 1969: 462). In 1891 one mitako bought only three eggs at Wangata, which was on the Upper Congo where prices were somewhat higher (MRAC, Lemaire, March 18, 1891). In 1885 Coquilhat (1888: 353) recruited nine "young guards" for a period of ten months at 45 mitako (11.50 francs) per month, in addition to their rations and clothing. (In this case we see not so much the monetary inflation of the Upper Congo but the value that was placed on Bangala military labor.) According to W. H. Bentley (MH 1887: 440), at about two pounds per year the Bangalas were "far cheaper than any other labour available." He was obviously comparing the hiring of natives to foreign workers, since he mentions the Kroo in this context. Laborers did not actually get all the pay that French and Belgian officials wrote about. Clerc (1911: 300-301), who was at Bangui (on the Ubangi River) in 1910, had the following to say of the porters that military personnel were entitled to (eighteen for a captain, twelve to fourteen for a sergeant-major, eight to ten for a sergeant) and who were "relayed" every two days.

> Ils doivent accomplir 25 à 30 kilomètres chaque jour moyennant 1 fr. 10 par ètape. . . . Souvent leur salaire ne leur est pas donné en mains, de suite, mais simplement défalqué de l'impôt dû par leur village. Il n'obéissent donc que sous la menace et la contrainte à des réquisitions que les postes opèrent dans un rayon étendu.

The Casimir Maistre expedition to the Upper Ubangi (i.e., from Bangui northward into what is now Chad) paid soldiers who were recruited on the west coast of Africa 35 francs per month (Comité de l'Afrique Française, 1892); rations consisted of one coffee-spoonful of *bayaka* beads every five days—and these cost only 75 centimes the kilogram (Chapiseau, 1900: 192). With this ration the men were able to obtain provisions, the help of natives to carry their own loads, and even "the favors of women." Four years later, 100 percent inflation apparently having set in, canoemen on the Ubangi were paid two spoonful of beads (or two copper bars of 60 grams [2 ounces]) every five days (Bruel, ASOM, October 10, 1896). But for the year 1897, and in connection with the Marchand expedition to the Nile, a canoeman received the value of twenty centimes (i.e., one-fifth of a franc) in two coffee-spoonful of beads for each day's work: one for work and one for food (Dyé, 1899: 446), although Bobichon, the administrator in Bangui, paid only one spoonful per day (Baratier, n.d.: 24).

SLAVES AS PORTERS

Slaves and former slaves were also a source of porters. For example, when S. de Brazza left Franceville in June 1880 on his mission of exploration, he noted that his "men" were former slaves (Brunschwig, 1966: 17). Those called Kabindas, always referred to as liberated, figure most frequently. For example, nineteen of them were part of the garrison of Leopoldville in 1882 and in 1884 two of them were part of Coquilhat's force in the Upper Congo (Coquilhat, 1888: 55, 228). That was before the French put a stop to the emigration of workers from their territory. Therefore, when we read of liberated slaves nine and ten years later, we can assume that they were "Kabindas."

The French obtained some of their men from one with the Portuguese name of Carvalho, who is described as a "former merchant of slaves" and as an "agent *libérateur*" (with quotation marks and italics in the original source). In 1892 he was even operating in the Kasai River area, where he got a premium of 100 francs for each "liberated" slave (Cureau, ANPM). In the previous year he had furnished the Casimir Dybowski expedition with 33 men, whose provenience and ethnicity are not mentioned (Dolisie, ANPM). Many other instances of the use by Europeans of slaves or "liberated" slaves can be cited.

The Tio (Teke), who were the upcountry traders the Kongo had to deal with depended on slave porters. At the Pool, the Tio were devoted exclusively to long-distance trade: upriver with the Bobangis and downriver with the Kongos. Caravans came to them from downriver peoples or they sent their own, always respecting ethnic territorial rights (Vansina, 1973). The Tio do not seem to have gone to the coast itself. Because of Tio demand for slave labor, there was an active slave market at the Pool. Slaves were still being bought at the Pool in 1883, according to T.J. Cromber, an English missionary, who observed that there was "a sprinkling of Bakongo from Congo, Zombo, Makuta, etc.—chiefly slaves brought up and sold to . . . Nga-Liema, for ivory" (MH 1883: 79). Ngaliema was a Tio notable.

Europeans came to learn that the Tio, while hiring out some of their slaves to work, did not themselves deign to "work" at all, other than engage in trade. For the period we are examining, it would have been as impossible for a Tio trader to hire out a son or nephew as it would have been for Jacob Meyer (1792-1868), whose Rothschildian fortune made possible the creation of the railway system in France, to have hired out his son to work along with the urban proletariat in the gangs constructing the railroad! This is why there was no exploitable labor force at the Pool when the Europeans began to establish themselves there. The Tio also refused to work for missionaries at the Pool and were reluctant to have their youths taught by them. The Tio did not "work" because they did not have to. By contrast people further in the interior worked more willingly. At Bopoto, far up the Congo, east of the Bangala area, also in 1894, for example, "There is a great demand for workmen and workboys in these parts, and high wages tempt the elder boys to leave their towns, and to go to work at factories [trading centers] or on steamers" (F.R. Oram, MH, 1894: 220). Reticence to let their sons become mission pupils could be expected of people who had had little contact with Europeans, but the problem was more than the usual one of culture contact. Missionaries in this period engaged school children in various kinds of work (that others would have been hired to do) to pay for their schooling. The aversion to manual labor consequently reinforced other attitudes among the Tio toward the European presence.

Only those Tio located away from the Pool were willing to work for wages. In 1880, for example, de Brazza was able to use Tio porters (Brunschwig, 1966: 253), but they came from the high plains, whose economy was not based on trade as was that of the Tio of the Pool. But even this exception must be treated with caution, because ethnic designations by Europeans were often confused. For example, Vansina (1973: 303, citing a report made by Pradier in 1886, as reported in Coquery-Vidrovitch, 1969) states that currency could not hire labor in the Tio economy, but that the Kongo Lari worked for one mitako per day. It is therefore important for the study of labor recruitment to identify these Kongo Lari. Coquery-Vidrovitch did not call them Kongo Lari but Lali (1969: 462,276), and she identified them with the Teke, not the Kongo. Fehderau on the other hand (1962) identifies the Lari (also known as Ladi, Laadi, Lali, and Bwende) as one of the Kongo groups. Moreover, Coquery-Vidrovitch (1969: 97, citing Sautter in Brunschwig, 1966: 174) states that the Lali, a "Teke group," located on the Niari River about a twenty-day journey from the Teke at the Pool, were "commercial intermediaries" between the Loango coast and the interior.[3] In any case there seems to have been some kind of Lalis working on the Catholic mission's steamboat *Léon XIII* in December 1892 (Sallaz, 1893: 73). It is reasonable to suppose that they were "common laborers"— deck hands, choppers of wood, and the like.

ETHNIC STEREOTYPES

The last possible explanation for the way Kongos seem to have been restricted to portering is that of European attitudes. If we could find prejudice against them—a form of selective racism—this would have explanatory power. But whereas coastal Blacks are described as a rapacious, thieving, lying, lazy, and besotted population, the people in the region of Mount Bidi, between Vivi and Leopoldville (the very Kongos who served as porters) were seen as strong, industrious, and eager to work (Coquilhat, 1886: 2,35). Nonetheless, it is the Bangalas who came to have the best reputation:

> [the Bangalas] are, by unanimous consent, the finest people on the river—athletic, intelligent, manly, energetic, and fearlous [sic] to a degree. They rather delight in exhibiting their superabundant energy. By many they are regarded as equal to the much-lauded Zanzibaris as personal servants. They are employed at every station of the State from Boma to Stanley Falls (George Stapleton, MH, 1892: 226-227.

The same year in which that statement was made there appeared an article in the *Congo Illustré* devoted to the Bangala "nation" (1892: 169-170); it was equally well-disposed. Chapaux considered the Bangalas (1894: 530) the only people on the Congo River with useful skills, to be compared with the Tio and Bobangi who appeared to be engaged in nothing but trade.

An explanation of racial stereotyping as a factor in hiring practices must incorporate both comparative ethnology and colonial history— both conceived processually and dynamically. Whereas Europeans came to Africa with ideas about Africans already formed, these took specific shape according to the various circumstances that characterized the European-Black contacts. When Stanley arrived at the West Coast on his first journey, he distinguished, favorably or unfavorably, the peoples with whom he had to deal. When personal "knowledge" is shared and adopted by others, it becomes social truth, powerful enough to influence subsequent events. Stanley condemned the people on the lower Ubangi River as "pirates," and as a result he may have created the myth of the terrible "Bondjos," who, although elusive and changing in ethnic identity, plagued Europeans as far as Bangui (Samarin, 1984d).

Accidental factors in European-Black relations played a part in the general admiration of the Bangalas at the expense of the Kongos.

However it may have begun, it was reinforced by each succeeding decision on the part of Europeans in choosing who served them and what they were employed at. The exclusion (in proportional, not exclusive, terms) of the Kongos from general and diversified employment was cumulative in force. Moreover, this type of discrimination occurred in other parts of Africa, as, for example, among the Yakoma-speaking peoples of the Upper Ubangi River, who, like the Bangalas, came early into the best of European employment (Samarin, 1984b).

EXTERNAL POLITICS

Not only were the Kongos at the mercy of the increasing exploitation of the Congo basin, as manifested in the development of trade, they were also pawns in the competition between Belgians and French. The French forbade the "Loangos" from taking employment in foreign territory (Bentley, MH, 1887: 439), although there is no evidence that this restraint had much effect.[4] Indeed the French had little impact on the development of a labor market, at least until 1889. For one thing, many people going to French posts used Belgian transportation facilities. For another, it was de Brazza's plan to beat the Belgians to the Upper Congo by going directly east on the rivers, avoiding the costly and time-consuming journey to Stanley Pool.

In 1889 the Belgian government, at the highest level in Belgium itself, assumed full control of labor recruitment in the Congo Free State. Edict No. 90 (Boma, June 26, 1889) required those who hired Blacks in the state's territory to obtain a license. This law was meant to consolidate the power of the Free State, raise revenue for the state, and reserve manpower for the railway project. Albert Dolisie, the administrator in French Brazzaville, viewed this Belgian action with alarm (August 6, 1889, ANP). He saw as one consequence foreign recruitment of Bakongos in the French Congo. The only way, he wrote, to keep the Kongos "for our own use" was to "call" (by which he meant "restrict") them to the Loango route. In other words, he was suggesting the creation of a French land-route different from and in competition with that of the Free State's. It was eventually inaugurated, but the French did not handle the matter as categorically as the Belgians. Recruitment seems to have been left to private parties. In some cases in 1893, government loads were transported from Matadi to Brazzaville on French territory but using the Nieuwe Afrikaansche Handels Venootschap (New African Trading Company; Dolisie, ANPM), even though early in 1893 the Société d'Etudes et d'Exploitation du Congo français (SEECF) was established for the explicit purpose of moving loads into the interior from Loango (de Mazières, 1982: 71).

By turning to the Kongos for porters the French added to the numbers, already nearly unbelievable, of carriers these people were providing. Although Kongos were used in some of the expeditions into the Ubangi basin (Samarin, 1928a, ms.), for example, they were assigned lowly tasks (except, of course, for those from the coast who were literate). Indeed, much of the indigenous manpower in the French possession of the Upper Ubangi appears to have been recruited in the Congo Free State. For example, in his expedition on 1894 Casimir Maistre had thirty liberated slaves from the Upper Kasai (Maistre, 1895: 40; Samarin, 1928a, ms.) Indeed official decrees did not always have the effect they were meant to have; the recruitment of labor was determined as often by immediate circumstances as by governmental policy, and slaves—liberated or otherwise—continued to figure significantly among the workers of the Europeans.

WORKER CONSCIOUSNESS

In the light of the foregoing history we can assume that the Kongos would have seen themselves as exploited and oppressed, especially in comparison to other indigenous peoples. Indeed the great Kongo strike of 1887—one of several collective actions on the part of porters against their exploitation—demonstrates that such consciousness in fact existed. The strike is extensively described by Lieutenant Franqui, one of those responsible for recruitment at that time (and quoted in Wauters, 1890a: 222ff). He does not call it a strike; that would have been inappropriate where the pervading metaphor was conquest. He explains that there was "a momentary halt" in recruitment at the beginning of 1887 because of a few "intestine wars" and especially the unhappiness of the natives who feared competition following the establishment of several trading posts at Leopoldville. The event is mentioned by Lamotte (n.d.: 58) but without explanation. It is ironic that in the propagandist literature, such as the *Congo Illustré*, it was reported (CI, 1892: 179)—with obvious allusion to labor trouble in Belgium and for the purpose of assuring capitalist investors—that the porters were not civilized enough to strike! Moreover, this was about two years after the first organized march of workers on May Day that took place in Vienna. In connection with these 1887 conflicts, Ngaliema, the wealthy Tio trader at Stanley Pool, appears to have organized his own ivory caravans to the coast, although the rulers at

Manyanga tried to stop them and even robbed them (Vansina, 1973: 428; citing Dupont, 1889: 213, 263). If this connection is accepted, then the work stoppage of the Kongos was directed against European and African merchants alike. Although Belgians interpreted the Kongo resistance to recruitment in terms that were favorable to European investment, it is not yet clear how we are to interpret it today. More information is needed to explain the grievances of the porters as laborers and to delineate the incipient consciousness of themselves as workers, and other such matters.

There must have been other interruptions in the transport of goods from the coast, about which we have still much to learn. In early March 1885, for example, the missionary Aaron Sims reported from Leopoldville that native transport had ceased "for a month or two while they, the natives are engaged in trade with the coast" (ABHS). Normally, however, the period of trade from the Pool to the coast took place in the dry season during the months from April to September, not in early March (Vansina, 1973: 257-258). In August of that same year Vittu de Kerraoul had difficulty getting porters between Franceville and Diélé, not only because of interethnic strife but also because of dissatisfaction over pay (letter cited in Coquery-Vidrovitch, 1969: 291). Finally in 1892, there were further caravan troubles, perhaps indicating another strike (de Mazières, 1982: 71).

What then did the writer mean in the *Congo Illustré* (1892: 107), in an article devoted to "Initiating Negroes to European Work," when he said: "Generally, the laborer regenerated by work, considers himself as a kind of aristocrat in his tribe"? The answer is revealing; he was not writing of the Lower Congo peoples—who were porters—but the Bangalas—who were soldiers. By 1892 all those who held privileged positions in European service considered themselves better—and better off—than others. They were not restricted to carrying loads, like slaves. Besides, they were equipped with the symbols of authority: clothing and arms. Europeans recognized the power of such symbols. This was the period, one must remember, when civil and military service in Europe was expressed in an explicit language of dress, when in Vienna, for example, even the *Dienstmann* ("public porter" but all-round neighborhood servant), had his own pitiful uniform. The member of the Belgian Force Publique was generally better dressed and had better perquisites. He was, moreover, one member of a large new social unit, visible in its solidarity on frequent occasions, not to speak of the ritual ones at the military camp. And his confreres uniformed for other kinds of work also accepted the symbolism of this new social structure.

LABOR AND LANGUAGE

Language was both effector and effect in the novel and sustained interactions between Europeans and Africans during the years of exploration, trade, and colonization. This relationship is why a sociolinguistic perspective in African history is revealing. It reveals a strong correlation between the nature of work among different populations and the place of these peoples in the new colonial state, and it is revealed in the histories of the origins of Sango, Lingala, and Kituba (pidginized Kongo)—"new languages," all more or less pidginized, of the Congo and Ubangi basins; all now very important to the Central African Republic, the Republic of Zaire, and the Popular Republic of the Congo (Samarin, 1971, 1980a, 1980b, 1982a, 1982b, 1984b). The analysis of labor-mobilization reveals the historical process of linguistic development as no purely linguistic study has been able to do. It can be shown, furthermore, that Fehderau (1962, 1966) is wrong when he concludes that pidginized Kongo was a trade language at the end of the nineteenth century, on the grounds that interethnic trade leads to such a language. A reading of the primary sources demonstrates that there is no evidence for this assumption.

The earliest reference to an explicitly simple form of Kongo, the antecedent of contemporary Kituba, is that by the widow of W. Holman Bentley. She (1907: 285) used the terms "State Congo" and "dog-Congo." This pejorative designation for the pidgin has been misunderstood by Gann and Duignan, who claim (1975: 135) that because missionaries "at times referred to the official tongue of the Congo as 'the State jargon,'" they were hostile, as British citizens, to the Free State. At that time the Kongo language was hardly "official"! Moreover, the study of missionary literature reveals clearly that the Protestants lagged behind other Europeans, even Catholic missionaries, in the use of the emerging lingua francas (Kituba and Lingala) because they valued the ethnic (so-called tribal) languages as authentic carriers of culture and appreciated their richness in grammar and vocabulary. It was their appreciation for the indigenous African languages, not a presumed antipathy toward those who were not British, that explains the linguistic policies of these missionaries.

Instead, it can be concluded that there was a close relationship between labor and language. The Belgian edict of 1889 regulated the recruitment of labor and helped promote a pidginized Kongo. The new form of Kongo (Kituba) that emerged out of the Babel of tongues that characterized the building of the colonial edifice was a product of the connection between language history and labor history. The present argument is not *sufficient* for the linguistic demonstration; that will come only from a thorough analysis of the earliest linguistic data. But this is nonetheless a *necessary* argument. In the present state of knowledge, therefore, it is more credible to claim that Kituba arose in the context of the interaction between Kongo speakers and foreigners when the former were employed by the hundreds of thousands as, above all, porters than it is to say that it arose out of earlier trade between Europeans and Blacks or between various Congolese peoples.

Kituba seems to have arisen precisely where the most intense recruitment of labor by Europeans took place. It is related most closely to the central Kongo dialects and languages, closest indeed to the form at Manyanga (Fehderau, 1966: 76). The southern caravan route was especially important in the era before French and Belgian colonization, but that was not where Kituba seems to have developed. And although the Vili north of the Congo River were very much involved in the coastal trade earlier than the period discussed here, their language had even less effect, according to Fehderau, on vehicular Kongo. Whatever jargon may have developed in the nineteenth century, it was subsequently influenced more by Manyanga than by other dialects. From this perspective, vehicular Kongo is not and never was primarily a "trade language." It served as the language of labor.

The relationship between labor and language has not yet become the focus of examination in the same way that the languages of politics, law, and religion have. These varieties (to which one attributes the name "language") concern the sociolinguist, who seeks to identify the linguistic nature of all varieties of a given language and explain their function or role in the relevant social group. Some such languages emerge simply by semantic developments, or by the creation of new words, or by borrowing words from other languages (all three processes being illustrated in certain argots), or even by adopting an entirely different language. It is reasonable to suppose, for example, that in a large industry management and labor would use different "languages" for the same domains of experience. But languages do not merely indicate different social groups; they also serve as symbolic or real boundaries between them. European languages represented power and authority. This fact can be illustrated in the history of the construction of the Belgian railroad to the Pool. Trouet explicitly states (1893: 93) that all the [African] bosses, clerks, and craftsmen—who were the only ones in rapport with Europeans and spoke either French or English—transmitted orders to the workers in "the national idiom." In the context, this would mean the various native languages of the foreign workers and not one of the vehicular languages (emergent

Kituba or Bangala). As language separated management from labor, so it must have separated the two kinds of labor described in this chapter. In its earliest years pidginized Kongo was the language of the porters and pidginized Kibangi (Bangala/Lingala) the language of the military and of skilled labor (sharing this function with Swahili, brought by personnel from the east coast, until indigenous labor was developed). Linked as they were to both ethnic and labor differences, these new languages must have contributed to a consciousness of distinct classes of workers in the minds of both foreigners and natives.

The study of different varieties of language ("codes" in a generic sense) contributes to the explanation of social change. Language can also be seen as a means of influencing behavior. Fabian (1982), for example, goes beyond the purely linguistic description of the use of French in Shaba Swahili (Zaire) to attempt to account for this mixing of languages by workers as a positive affirmation of their own identity. And my own work on African lingua francas reveals how these new languages emerged in new social relationships established by the indigenous peoples with the foreign non-European workers. For this area of study we have, of course, practically no linguistic data whatsoever; our argument has to proceed with different kinds of non-linguistic data. From this perspective, vehicular Kongo is not and never was primarily a "trade language." It served as the language of labor.

NOTES

1. It is not yet clear how and when this arbitrary and standardized load was established. In African caravans load sizes varied. But even in those for Europeans we cannot be sure what actually was carried. Since caravan bosses had the real supervision of these caravans there must certainly have been great variation in what was imposed on a carrier; what he could get away with must have been more constrained—unless he was able to recruit his own assistant.

2. The intermediate distances are the following: Vivi-Isangila (93 kilometers/58 miles), Manyanga-Leopoldville (152 kilometers/95 miles). The distance between Isangila and Manyanga (128 kilometers/80 miles) could be covered by water.

3. Vansina (1973: 11, 124, fn31; 143, fn10; 146, fn21; 304) confuses the identification by using different spellings: Lari (Kongo); Lali, who call themselves Fumu; Kongo-Laari; Lari, "e.i. formerly the Fumu." The Loango inhabitants have also had a curious onomastic history. Although they are today recognized as Vili (e.g. Martin, 1970), in the nineteenth century they were almost always referred to as "Loangos". Martin herself uses this name in the form Maloango—with the plural prefix (ma) that is appropriate for bananas and leaves and not for people! Moreover, she also uses the name for the chief (or king) of that area.

4. Bentley's observations need confirmation from other sources, especially his claim that in the beginning of the Baptist missionary work "we had Kroo boys [from West

Africa], then Loangos were induced by us for the first time to leave their homes. Other people on the river profited by this to engage Loangos, and they became to a large extent the work people of the river." Since the people at Loango had been in contact with Europeans for centuries, it is inconceivable that the English-speaking missionaries were the first to have induced them to work in other areas. Bentley's claim cannot be applied to all Europeans. However, he may only have been comparing the Baptist hiring practice with that of the Livingstone Inland Mission, which was established at the Pool at the same time.

REFERENCES

Periodicals

BM. The Baptist Missionary Magazine. Published by the American Baptist Missionary Union. Boston: Missionary Rooms. (succeeded by Missions)

CI. Le Congo Illustré: voyages et travaux des belges dans l'Etat Indépendant du Congo. Publié sous la direction de A.-J. Wauters, Bruxelles, 1892-1895.

MCC. Les Missions en Chine et au Congo. Bruxelles: Les Missions de Scheut.

MH. The Missionary Herald. London: Baptist Missionary Society.

Archives

AHBS. American Baptist Historical Society, Rochester, New York. Foreign Missions microfilms, Reels 82,86.

ANP. Archives Nationales, Section Outre-Mer, Paris, France, File Gabon-Congo (GC).

Dolisie, A[lbert], Administrateur de Brazzaville, to Lieutenant Gouverneur, Commissaire Général. Brazzaville, August 6, 1889, GCXIV, Di.

———[presumed], Administrateur de Brazzaville, to Commissaire du Gouvernement. Extract of letter, August 14, 1891. GCIV, D14.

ANPM, Archives Nationales, Section Outre-Mer, Paris, France, Microfilms of Victor Liotard Papers, 213Mi. Cureau, Adolphe, to Victor Liotard. Brazzaville, October 28, 1892. 213Mi.1, Dossier 1.1. Dolisie, Albert, to Victor Liotard, February 23, 1893. 213Mi.1, Dossier 1.1 Liotard, Victor, Journal ("notes recopiées par la suite par un autre"). 213Mi.2, 2.

ASOM. Académie des Sciences d'Outre-Mer, Paris. Lettres de G[eorges] Bruel à sa proche famille durant son premier séjour. Dossiers Bl (1895-1896), B2 (1897-1898).

MRAC. Musée Royal de l'Afrique Centrale, Section d'Histoire, Tervuren, Belgium. Papiers [Charles] Lemaire.

Published Works

BAILEY, H. (1894) Travel and adventures in the Congo Free State and its big game shooting. London: Chapman and Hall.

BARATIER, (General) (n.d.) Vers le Nil: souvenirs de la Mission Marchand de Brazzaville à Fort Desai. Paris: Arthème Fayard & Cie. (date of publication is probably 1897)

BENTLEY, (Mrs.) H. M. (1907) W. Holman Bentley: the life and labours of a Congo missionary. London: Religious Tract Society.

BOONE, O. (1973) "Carte ethnique de la République de Zaire: quart sud-ouest." Annales, Série in 8°, Sciences Humaines, No. 78. Tervuren: Musée Royal de l'Afrique Centrale.

BROADHEAD, S. H. (1971) "Trade and politics on the Congo coast: 1770-1870."
Ph.D. dissertation, Boston University. (University Microfilm no. 71-16, 387)

BRUNSCHWIG, H. et al. (1966) "Brazza explorateur: l'Ogooué 1875-1879."
Documents pour servir à l'histoire de l'Afrique Equatoriale Française. Paris, La
Haye: Mouton et Cie.

BÜCHLER, M. (1912) Der Kongostaat Leopolds II. Zurich.

CHAPAUX, A. (1984) Le Congo: historique, diplomatique, physique, politique
économique, humanitaire et colonial. Bruxelles: Charles Rozez.

CHAPISEAU, F. (1900) Au pays de l'esclavage: moeurs et coutumes de l'Afrique
centrale, d'après des notes recueillies par Ferdinand de Béhagle. Paris: J.
Maisonneuve.

CLERC, [?] (1911) "Du Congo au Tchad: observations et documents recueillis par
M[onsieur] Clerc en 1910, extraits par M[onsieur] Zaborowski." Bulletins et
Mémoires de la Société d'Anthropologie de Paris, 6e série, 2, 3/4: 297-303.

Comité de l'Afrique Française (1892) "Mission Maistre. Etat de renseignements du
personnel noir emmené par la mission." Brazzaville, April 15, 1892. (ANX, Archives Nationales, Section Outre-Mer, Aix-en-Provence, France, file 2010)

COQUERY-VIDROVITCH, C. (1969) Brazza et la prise de possession du Congo. Paris,
La Haye: Mouton et Cie.

COQUILHAT, C. (1888) Sur le Haut-Congo. Paris: J. Lebègue et Cie.

———(1886) Conférences sur le Congo. Fascicule 1: January 20 and 27, 1886; Fascicule
2: February 17 and 24, March 10 and 17, 1886. Bruxelles: Société belge des In-
génieurs et les Industriels; Librairie Universelle de Ve[uve] J. Rozez.

CORNET, R. J. (1947) La bataille du rail: la construction du chemin de fer de Matadi
au Stanley-Pool. Bruxelles: Editions L. Cuypers.

DE DEKEN, (R. P.)C. (1902) Deux ans au Congo. Anvers: Clément Thibaut.

DE MANDAT-GRANCY, (Baron) E. (1900) Au Congo (1898): impressions d'un
touriste. Paris: Plon-Nourrit et Cie.

DE MAZIERES, A. C. (1982) La marche au Nil de Victor Liotard. Aix-en-Provence:
Université de Provence (Institut d'Histoire des Pays d'Outre-Mer).

DENIS, J. (1950) "De 1879 à 1908, 1514 Belges ont offert leur vie pour le Congo:
découverte et pénétration." Grand Lacs/Namur 65, 12 (New Series, 134): 5-11.

DESCHAMPS, (E.) (1911) De Bordeaux au Tchad par Brazzaville. Paris: Société Française d'Imprimerie et de Librairie.

DIAS-BRIAND, M.-C. (1982) "Les archives de Joseph Briand, médecin à Bangui
1898-1900." Mémoire de maitrise, Université de Provence, France.

DONNY, A. (1897) [ed.] L'Art militaire au Congo (Rédigé sous la direction du colonel Donny, par le capitaine commandant Avaert et al.). Bruxelles: G. Muquardt.

DUPONT, E. (1889) Lettres sur le Congo: récit d'un voyage scientifique entre l'em-
bouchure du fleuve et le confluent du Kassai. Paris: Reinwald.

DYÉ, A. H. (1889), "Les pagayeurs du Haut-Oubangui." Bulletin du Comité de
l'Afrique Française 9, 12: 444-447.

Encyclopédie du Congo Belge (1951, 1953) Vols. 1-3. Bruxelles: Editions Bieleveld.

FABIAN, J. (1982) "Scratching the surface: observations on the poetics of lexical
borrowing in Shaba Swahili." Anthropological Linguistics 24: 14-50.

FEHDERAU, H. W. (1966) "The origin and development of Kituba (lingua franca
Kikongo)." Ph.D. dissertation, Cornell University.

———(1962) Descriptive Grammar of the Kituba Language: A Dialectal Survey
(preliminary checking edition). Leopoldville: American Mennonite Brethren Board
of Missions.

FOÀ, E. (1900) La traversée de l'Afrique du Zambèze au Congo français: de l'Océan indien à l'Océan atlantique). Paris: Plon-Nourrit et Cie.

GANN, L. H. and P. DUIGNAN (1979) The Rulers of Belgian Africa, 1884-1914. Princeton, N.J.: Princeton University Press.

GISANURA, F. (1971). "La contribution des Zanzibarites à la création et au développement de l'Etat Indépendant du Congo." Présenté en vue de l'obtention du grade de Licencié en Philosophie et Lettres, Groupe Histoire, Université de Kinshasa.

GUINNESS, (Mrs.) H. G. [F. E. Fitzgerald] (1890) The New World of Central Africa, with a History of the First Christian Mission on the Congo. London: Hodder and Stoughton.

GUIRAL, L. (n.d.). Le Congo français, du Gabon à Brazzaville. Paris: Plon-Nourrit et Cie.

JEANNEST, C. (1883) Quatres années au Congo. Paris: G. Charpentier et Cie.

LAGERGREN, D. (1970) Mission and State in the Congo: A Study of the Relations between Protestant Missions and the Congo Independent State Authorities, with Special Reference to the Equator District, 1885-1903. (Studia missionalia Upsaliensis, 13). Lund: Gleerup.

LAMOTTE, E. (n.d.) Chez les Congolais. Bruxelles: De Callewaert Frères.

LEMAIRE, C. F. (1895a) Au Congo: comment les noirs travaillent. Bruxelles: Bulens.

———(1895b) La région de l'Equateur. (Trois conférences économiques. Société d'Etudes Coloniales, 1894). Bruxelles: A. Lesigne. (Also entitled Districts des Cataractes et de l'Equateur.)

———(1894) Congo et Belgique: À propos de l'Exposition d'Anvers. Bruxelles: Imprimerie Scientifique Charles Bulens.

LIEBRECHTS, C. (n.d.) Souvenirs d'Afrique: Congo Léopoldville, Bolobo, Equateur (1883-1889). Bruxelles: Lebègue.

LOPASIK, A. (1971) "Commissaire général Dragutin Lerman 1863-1918: a contribution to the history of Central Africa." Annales, Série in 8°, Sciences historiques, 4. Tervuren: Musée Royal de l'Afrique Centrale.

MacGAFFEY, W. (1977) "Economic and social dimensions of Kongo slavery," pp. 235-255 in S. Miers and I. Kopytoff (eds.) Slavery in Africa. Madison: University of Wisconsin Press.

MAISTRE, C. (1895) A travers l'Afrique centrale du Congo au Niger, 1892-1893. Paris: Hachette et Cie.

MARTIN, P. (1972) The external trade of the Loango coast, 1576-1879. London: Oxford University Press.

———(1970) "The trade of Loango in the seventeenth and eighteenth centuries," pp. 139-161 in R. Gray and D. Birmingham (eds.) Pre-colonial African trade. London: Oxford University Press.

MASUI, J.-B. (1894) D'Anvers à Banzyville: lettres illustrées du Lieutenant Masui. Bruxelles: Ch[arles] Bulens.

MICHAUX, (Commandant) [O.] (1907) Au Congo: carnet de campagne; éspisodes et impressions de 1889 à 1897. Bruxelles: Falk Fils.

MILLE, P. (1899) Au Congo belge, avec des notes et des documents récents relatifs au Congo français. Paris: Armand Colin et Cie.

MUMBANZA, J. E. (1971) "Les Bangala et la première décennie du poste de Nouvelle Anvers (1884-1894)." Mémoire de licence, Université de Lovanium.

MUMBANZA MWA BAWELE and NYABAKOMBI ENSOBATO (1974) "Les Bangala du fleuve sont-ils apparentés aux Mongo." Zaire-Afrique 90: 625-632.

Musée du Congo (1903-1905) "L'Etat Indépendant du Congo. Documents sur le pays et ses habitants." Annales (Ethnographie et Anthropologie) 4, 1-6.

PELET, P. (1899) Atlas des colonies françaises, Carte 12, 1: 3,000,000. (Paris: Armand Colin?)

PROBERT, H. (1889). Life and scenes in Congo. Philadelphia: American Baptist Publication Society.

SALLAZ, (R.P.) (1893). "Dix jours sur l'Oubanghi à bord du 'Léon XIII' (Lettre du R.P. Sallaz au R. P. Grizard)". Annales Apostoliques, 8(30): 68-75.

SAMARIN, W. J. (1984a) "La communication par les eaux et les mots oubanguiens," pp. 170-239 in J. L. Miège (ed.) Recherches centrafricaines: problèmes et perspectives de la recherche historique (Etudes et documents, No. 18). Aix-en-Provence: Université de Provence (Institut d'Histoire des Pays d'Outre-Mer).

————(1984b) "Communication by Ubangian water and word." Sprache und Geschichte in Afrika [University of Köln] 6.

————(1984c) "The linguistic world of field colonialism." Language in Society 13.

————(1984d) "Bondjo ethnicity and colonial imagination." Canadian Journal of African Studies 18: 345-365.

————(1984e) "Socioprogrammed linguistics: Commentary of 'The language bioprogram hypotehsis' by Derek Bickerton." Behavioral and Brain Sciences 7: 206-207.

————(1982a) "Colonization and pidginization on the Ubangi River." Journal of African Languages and Linguistics 4: 1-42.

————(1982b) "Goals, roles, and language skills in colonizing central equatorial Africa." Anthropological Linguistics 24: 410-422.

————(1980a) Colonization and Central African Linguae Francae: A Research Report. (unpublished)

————(1980b) "Standardization and instrumentalization of creole languages," pp. 213-236 in A. Valdman and A. Highfield (eds.) Theoretical Orientations in Creole Studies. New York: Academic Press.

————(1971) "Salient and substantive pidginization," pp. 117-140 in D. Hymes (ed.) Pidginization and creolization of languages. Cambridge: Cambridge University Press.

————(ms.) "Congo cohorts and copula sharing in Pidgin Sango."

STANLEY, H. M. (1885, 1970) The Congo and the Founding of its Free State: A Story of Work and Exploration, 2 vols. New York: Harper and Brothers; Detroit: Negro History Press.

TRIVIER, E. (1891) Mon voyage au continent noir. Paris: Firmin-Didot et Cie.; Bordeaux: G. Gounouilhou.

TROUET, L. (1898) Le chemin de fer du Congo. Bruxelles: J. Goemaere; Falk Fils. (Extract from the 4th fascicule of the Annales des Travaux Publics de Belgique, August 1898).

VANDRUNEN, J. (1900) Heures africaines: Algérie, Sahara, Congo, Iles de l'Atlantique. Bruxelles: Georges Balat.

VAN SCHENDEL, T. (1932) Au Congo avec Stanley en 1897: croquis anecdotiques. Bruxelles: Albert Dewit.

VANSINA, J. (1973) The Tio Kingdom of the Middle Congo 1880-1892. London: Oxford University Press for the International African Institute.

VINCENT, F. (1895) Actual Africa, or The Coming Continent: A Tour of Exploration. New York: D. Appleton.

WAUTERS, A.-J. (1890a) Stanley au secours d'Emin-Pacha. Bruxelles: Institut National de Géographie.

————(1890b) Stanley's Emin Pasha Expedition. Philadelphia: J. B. Lippincott.

Index

About the Contributors

JEAN–LOUP AMSELLE, an anthropologist at the Ecole des Hautes Etudes en Sciences Sociales in Paris, has published *Les négociants de la savane* (1977), *Les migrations Africaines* (1976), and *Evaluation de la Filiere Arachide au Mali* (1962) (with P. D. Baris and V. Papazian).

CATHERINE COQUERY-VIDROVITCH, Professor, Université Paris 7, and Director of the Laboratoire "Tiers-Monde, Afrique" of the Centre national de la recherche scientifique, has published several books on the colonization of Equatorial Africa and the Congo. Her latest book is *Afrique noire: permanences et ruptures* (1985).

DENNIS D. CORDELL, Associate Professor of History, Southern Methodist University, has published numerous articles. His *The Final Years of the Trans-Saharan Slave Trade: The Rise and Fall of Dar al-Kuti* appeared in 1985. He is also co-editor (with Joel Gregory) of *African Historical Demography: A Multidisciplinary Bibliography* (1984).

ROBERT J. CUMMINGS is a Director of Graduate Studies, African Studies and Research Program, Howard University, and President of the African Studies Association (U.S.A.). His research on the Kamba of Kenya has resulted in the publication of several articles.

M. B. DUFFILL, formerly of Ahmadu Bello University in Nigeria, has translated and published a number of Hausa poems and has annotated E. R. Flegel's biography of the Hausa caravan leader, Madugu Mohamman Mai Gashin Baki.

ODILE GOERG, Agrégée of the Université Paris and associate of the "Tiers-Monde," Université Paris 7, is a specialist on the history of Guinée. Her thesis on the history of commerce in Guinée at the end of the nineteenth century is in press.

PETER C.W. GUTKIND is Professor of Anthropology, McGill University, and author of many articles and books, including *Townsmen in the Making* (with A. W. Southall, 1956); *The Royal Capital of Buganda: A Study of Internal Conflict and External Ambiguity* (1963); *Anthropologists in the Field* (edited with D. G. Jongmans, 1967); *Urban Anthropology: Perspectives on "Third World" Urbanisation and Urbanism* (1974). He has also co-edited two books in this Sage series. He is Past President of the African Studies Association (U.S.A.) and has taught in Jamaica, the United States, and Nigeria, as well as in Canada.

LINDA HEYWOOD is Assistant Professor of History, Howard University. She completed her Ph.D. thesis on the Ovimbundu at Columbia University in 1984.

ALLEN ISAACMAN is Professor of History, University of Minnesota, and author of *Mozambique: The Africanization of a European Institution; The Zambesi Prazos, 1750-1902* (1972), which received the Melville J. Herskovitz award; and *The Tradition of Resistance in Mozambique: Anti-Colonial Struggle in the Zambesi Valley, 1810-1921* (1976).

PAUL E. LOVEJOY is Professor and Chairman of History, York University, and author of *Caravans of Kola: The Hausa Kola Trade, 1700-1900* (1981); *Transformations in Slavery: A History of Slavery in Africa* (1983); *Salt of the Desert Sun: A History of Salt Production and Trade in the Central Sudan* (1985). He is the editor of *The Ideology of Slavery in Africa* (in this Sage series, 1981).

ELIAS MANDALA completed his Ph.D. at the University of Minnesota in 1984 and is now Assistant Professor of History, University of Rochester. He has published several articles on the history of Malawi.

PATRICK MANNING, Associate Professor of History, Northeastern University, is the author of *Slavery, Colonialism and Economic Growth in Dahomey, 1640-1960* (1982) and more than seventeen scholarly articles.

E. ANN McDOUGALL, has taught at Duke University and has been a postdoctoral fellow at Dalhousie University and York University. She has published a number of articles on western Saharan history.

WILLIAM J. SAMARIN, Professor of Linguistics and Anthropology, University of Toronto, has conducted extensive research on the pidginization of African languages, especially in Central Africa. He has published many books and articles, including *The Gbeya Language: Grammar, Texts, and Vocabularies* (1966); *A Grammar of Sango* (1967); *Field Linguistics: A Guide to Linguistic Field Work* (1967); *Sango, Langue de l'Afrique Centrale* (1970); *Tongues of Men and Angels: The Religious Language of Pentecostalism* (1972). He is the editor of *Language in Religious Practice* (1976).